Youth Fantasies

YOUTH FANTASIES: THE PERVERSE LANDSCAPE OF THE MEDIA

jan jagodzinski

YOUTH FANTASIES
© jan jagodzinski, 2004

First published 2004 by
PALGRAVE MACMILLAN™
175 Fifth Avenue, New York, N.Y. 10010 and
Houndmills, Basingstoke, Hampshire, England RG21 6XS
Companies and representatives throughout the world

PALGRAVE MACMILLAN is the global academic imprint of the Palgrave Macmillan division of St. Martin's Press, LLC and of Palgrave Macmillan Ltd. Macmillan® is a registered trademark in the United States, United Kingdom and other countries. Palgrave is a registered trademark in the European Union and other countries.

ISBN 1–4039–6164–6 hardback
ISBN 1–4039–6165–4 paperback

Library of Congress Cataloging-in-Publication Data
Jagodzinski, Jan, 1953–
        Youth fantasies : the perverse landscape of the media / Jan Jagodzinski.
            p. cm.
        Includes bibliographical references and index.
        ISBN 1–4039–6164–6—ISBN 1–4039–6165–4 (pbk.)
        1. Mass media and youth. I. Title.

P94.5.Y72J34 2004
302.23′0832—dc22   2003067262

A catalogue record for this book is available from the British Library.

Design by Newgen Imaging Systems (P) Ltd., Chennai, India.

First edition: August 2004
10 9 8 7 6 5 4 3 2 1

Printed in the United States of America.

This book is dedicated to
my wife
Brigitte Hipfl
whose presence is always dabei

CONTENTS

ACKNOWLEDGMENT

I would like to thank Amanda Johnson for her belief and support in making this project possible. It seems that every time we sat together to discuss the book's parameters, my enthusiasm and desire for its completion were enlivened. I very much appreciate her encouragement to see it through.

Introduction: A Road Map
of What's to Come

There is something ironic about adults attempting to write a book on youth fantasies, whatever "adult" might mean today. It is impossible to "attain" our kids; to somehow turn back time and become a high school student once again like the figure of Josie Geller (Drew Barrymore) in Raja Gosnell's comedy *Never Been Kissed* (1999). Josie "Grossie," who is now 25, goes back to her old high school as an undercover journalist to do a story, and ends up facing her own repressed traumas with disastrous results. To "attain" our children; that is, to hold them captive for our own misguided ends turns them into monsters of our own creation—mommy's boy who is not permitted to grow up; daddy's boy who doesn't grow up being quite like him. Or mommy's girl who grows up being frighteningly just like her mom and daddy's girl who is always trying to please him. Youth has its own differentiations and struggles for recognition. It is a complex phenomenon, and for us to pretend that we have somehow "captured" it all is the worst kind of arrogance. There are many teens and young people whose knowledge is infinitely more detailed than our own, whose passionate attachments to their iconic musical stars infinitely more committed than ours. It is precisely because we cannot "attain" our children; a theme encountered once every so often throughout this book, that such a book has to be written. Parents have always scratched their head when it comes to youth, and the thesis of this book is nothing but another head-scratching. If it weren't for such head-scratching, the commitment and responsibility adults have to youth would be surely lost.

Our head-scratching comes from a particular perspective, that of Lacanian psychoanalysis, especially as it is developed by the spirited writings of Slavoj Žižek and other post-Lacanians. There is yet another irony to be stated here as well. Most of this book was written in Klagenfurt, Austria approximately an hour away by car from Žižek's home turf Ljubljana, Slovenia. However, he is seldom there, and when he came to Klagenfurt in 1992 to do a series of lectures with his circle of friends (Renata Salecl, Miran Božovič, Alenka Zupančič) few came to listen, less than a handful of people showed up, including us (Brigitte and myself). In the following week when Slavoj came, no one showed up in the afternoon except for myself. That has certainly changed! He now has a substantial following and a far-reaching global reputation. At that time we were smitten by the Slovenian circle's insightful interpretations (on the *Crying Game*, as can be recalled). No doubt the intellectual titillation came from the blend of serious philosophy intertwined with popular culture, a postmodern trope that has become standard fare.[1] Serious journalism has collapsed with the entertainment industry; hard-core scientific discoveries need to be popularized to sell. And, Žižek is, after all, very entertaining. However, we continue to stay smitten; not because Lacanian psychoanalysis is somehow able to offer a definitive account of youth culture, but rather we find that it helps edify some of the changes of the psyche that are taking place in the youth culture of postmodernism. As Žižek says somewhere, psychoanalysis can teach us something about the circulation of jouissance and its relationship to the Law, capitalized here following his lead to indicate the symbolic system of the big Other (language, social institutions as well as regimes of authority). In this book we have tried to invert Žižek's work. Žižek's brilliance as a philosopher of Lacan is to use popular culture, movies, and mostly dated classical music to illustrate Lacanian concepts. We have tried to stage the reverse: to use predominately Žižek's insights on Lacan to understand the fantasy structures of youth in the media of video games and the Internet. Music is examined in our accompanying book *Musical Fantasies of Youth Cultures*, while a book on television will follow.[2] In these books we accept blame for our particular misreadings of his insights, but make no apologies for the attempt of an application.

The best Žižek joke we have ever heard was: "Why is Žižek's writing like Mexican food?" Answer: "Because it is all the same but wrapped differently!" It may be that the same joke can be said of us. Often the same concepts emerge, but they do so with different examples and inflections. We could rationalize this and tell our readers that this was intentional, so that the concept can be understood better, but the truth of the matter (truth?) is that the repetition emerged when it did, when we developed the examples that we did. This repetition has surely something to do with the way we are driven— to reproduce (clone) ourselves or perish in these postmodern times; as if it is necessary to say something X-times before it sticks, like a commercial. This is the way we are assaulted by the contemporary media landscape: pithy, short impulse bursts as sound bites, and visual cuts. To sustain longer narratives that are not giving you constant "hits" is progressively more and more difficult to sustain as time in postmodernity is constantly being evacuated to speed things up.

It is our contention that youth fantasies can best be understood within the context of de-Oedipalization or post-Oedipalization, as the "loss" of trust in authority that is currently underway. It is marked by the change from a culture of desire to a culture dominated by the drive (*Trieb*), a Western culture that is deeply embedded by neoliberal values and politics that support global designer capitalism. These conditions have engendered a hypernarcissistic subject. We argue that this hyper-narcissism is conditioned by a new relationship to the mirror: a split-mirror as we name it, where an alter ego is created and projected. This emerging "schizo" self should not be compared with a Kleinian paranoid-schizoid position, which was radicalized by Deleuze and Guattari's own developments as schizoid and paranoid desire. Klein argued that the infant splits its internal representations of others and of aspects of itself into good (gratifying) and bad (frustrating) so as to create order out of the primal psychic chaos. The principal affect of the paranoid-schizoid position is a persecutory anxiety, the fear of being annihilated by destructive forces from either within or without. By introjecting the caring qualities of a "good-enough" mother, the infant builds the emotional stability of a "depressive" position. The split-mirror in our case, recast in Kleinian terms or radicalized by Deleuze and Guattari's terms, presents simultaneously both the paranoid-schizoid and the depressive positions at once through a radicalization of an alter ego. This "split" is externalized and inflected differently through the various media forms we discuss, but it is especially evident in the transgressive musical forms of "noise" that we discuss in the companion book. In our examination of fantasies especially circulating in the music scene this "schizo" self emerges as mask wearing, persona changing, and a.k.a. alter egos of rap. One aspect that we reserve for the second book is the development of the postmodern fan, who we identify as the fan(addict). Such a hyper-fan has a strong identification with a group or "figure," which we name as the ONE. The concept of the ONE is theorized in view of the difficulty that Alan Badiou's paradoxical neo-Platonism poses for rethinking postmodern identifications while preserving a Lacanian notion of the split subject. He disperses the ONE into its multiples, as pure difference and multiplicity, yet preserves its singularity by theorizing a "consistent multiple" as a composition of ONES (Hallward 2003, 61–66). We attempt to illustrate this concept through our notion of the fan(addict) as fully developed in chapter 14 in *Musical Fantasies of Youth Cultures.*

Postmodern media are defined predominately by a "culture of the *Trieb*," where jouissance is promoted as a demand by the superego. Fantasies that are structured by desire are more difficult to maintain. The expectation of instant gratification and addictive satisfaction predominate, as does a general cynicism. The generalized neurotic symptoms of hysteria and obsession in the media are "answered" by a generalized emergence of perversion. This *père-version* of the media landscape is a direct response to the "loss" of authority. Obsessive behavior is readily apparent in video games while hysterical behavior is more prevalent in the music industry as we develop it in our companion book through the emergence of various gurl/girl/grrrl cultures.

Our attempt has been to understand youth fantasies psychically as they present themselves in various media: video games and Internet in this book, music and television in the ones to follow. We have been interested in what is the meaning of youths' psychic investment in these various media forms. To grasp what their appeal might be, not in terms of an ethnographic study (or one of its many variations), but in terms of their relationship to desire and drive as it relates to transgression "to and beyond the Law." Desire always escapes language; it is precisely what is the excess of language, therefore, our analysis has been better served by grappling with what is the "unsaid."

What "youth" is today forms another point of contention. Postmodernity has opened up the space of adolescence that now extends and stretches from the teen years all the way through to the late twenties, and then some. Various types of odd-looking half-beards have emerged for men, and a rainbow of hair colors for women to indicate and define a space of postadolescence with adulthood being more difficult to define. Intergenerational media has become common fare. Where one stops and the other begins has been blurred. To demarcate this new space we employ a variety of neologisms to capture the blurring of postadolescence with adulthood such as bois, boyz, boys and girlie, gurlz, grrrls. Although we discuss youth fantasies, such fantasias cannot possibly be understood without examining a broader sociological perspective. Our main thesis tries to grasp the process of post-Oedipalization during this age of designer capitalism, otherwise known as postmodernism. We try not to lose sight that the bottom line is the political economy, which structures the horizons of the fantasies that are permitted in a global capitalist world. However, we concentrate mostly on youth fantasies that circulate amongst privileged youth. We are quite aware that our analysis does not apply to "all" youth, especially to those who are not "wired," meaning that they are not privileged to go on-line and download music, attend openings of movies, buy CDs, and have access to computer video games. Despite this, youth cannot escape the broader media influences regardless if they are underprivileged or not. Besides the usual access to television and radio, more and more schools have become wired. But our demographics tend toward the middle to upper classes. By and large our study confines itself to the last decade of the twenty-first century, from the 1990s until the contemporary present.

Designer capitalism colonizes "youth" in the sense that it turns "play" into money and profit. Youth, who were once a threat to reason through their nonsensical escapades, have been harnessed, but *not* entirely. Research and Design, rather than being strictly confined to serious scientific-minded experimentation during monopoly capitalism at the turn of the twentieth century, has been supplemented by the "free expression" of creativity. Game rooms to relax as young people "try" out new ideas, loosen up before they begin creatively programming or recording have been incorporated by both the video game and music industries. Creativity, which has always required gestation time—slacker time—has been recognized as a potential space for exploitation. The dividing li(n)e between work and play begins to disappear with flexible electronic capitalism. Its colonization is always presented in an oblique way as "part" of the job—an expectation to "jerk of" creatively, but stay productive.

At one time, what was considered moral and Good, it should be not forgotten, was equated with profitability—the legacy of a Protestant ethic wedded to capital. Evil was defined as a contrary, as its opposite—immoral, the place where the Good itself was canceled as its absence. Young children working for global capital for cheap wages is not considered immoral by many multinational executives. The justification for such labor is perceived as a cultural expectation in many parts of the world. In this and in our companion book, *Musical Fantasies of Youth Cultures*, the question of an "ethics of the Real" emerges,[3] over and over again, as we move over the terrain of various mediascapes, which addresses young peoples' conscious and unconscious complaint concerning society and its Law. The fantasies they develop are a form of "protection" from the Real of their drives, a way of coping with addiction, pain, and depression given the dramatic changes in familial structures and the superego's demand to get ahead. We introduce the "death drive" as both a metaphor for the transformation of the self, as well as a suicidal act in the name of an ethical Cause; something beyond capitalist profit, aimed at the impossible dream of continued democracy. Such an "act" appears nonsensical, always "beyond" the sense-making machine of the Good. It is paradoxically amoral in this regard, and has the potential of redefining the established axiology, establishing a new metaethics. We raise this question of the death drive in various contexts throughout this series of planned books: gangsta rap, school shootings like Columbine, and especially *Buffy, the Vampire Slayer* as developed in our television book.

Our understanding of the "death drive" is theorized more in keeping with Boothby's (1991) formulations, as a tension between the Imaginary and the Real psychic registers, although we recognize that there is a tension here between Žižek's (1993, 178–179) dismissal of Boothby's particular articulation. We feel that Boothby's second book, *Freud as Philosopher* (2001), has addressed Lacan's fundamental insight that the Symbolic Order "stands for death" in the way that language mortifies the body through the signifier, subordinates it and the imago to its "foreign automatism," and thereby produces a surplus of desire. We fail to comprehend why both of these views are incompatible since the same mechanism—the death drive—becomes ultimately a "life force" as the mortification of the ego is shattered. Isn't that precisely the question of radical Evil? The problematization of a place where life and death as defined by a particular axiology becomes suspended?

We are adamant about our argument that designer capitalism supports a poststructuralist subject of discourse. In our opinion, a cultural studies approach that fails to account the affects of an "ethics of the Real" falls into its own commodification. In our discussion of post-Oedipalization, we try to show that postmodernism is an inverted gaze that supports a poststucturalist hyper-performative subject of the surface "look." There is the danger of reducing subjectivity only to the signifier, denying singularity and uniqueness and avoiding the question of a "complaint" raised at the level of unconscious desire.

Throughout the book we have signaled Anzieu's (1989) notion of the skin-ego, when and where we felt it was a useful supplement to understand youth fantasies. Some theorists of transexuality like Prosser (1998) have argued that Lacan placed too much structural emphasis on the linguistic signifier and not enough on the body. We don't see the Lacanian paradigm as a major break with Anzieu's skin-ego hypothesis, but feel that Anzieu can be usefully incorporated in the Imaginary psychic register without somehow, outright dismissing Lacan on the grounds of his earlier structuralism. This is often the ploy of feminist theoreticians who supplant Deleuzian constructs for Lacanian ones, dismissing Lacan as being phallogocentric. We feel that there is a useful overlap between Lacan and Deleuze, and we incorporate Deleuze when it is helpful to understand youth fantasies. Tim Dean (2000) for example, has played such a ruse concerning the question of sexuality.

Stylistically we have utilized the third person plural "we." Rhetorically, this can be a problem. Theorists like Hayden White (1978) have alerted academics long ago about this seemingly innocuous third person neutral pronoun, especially in the writing of history. It assumes a collective ideological mask since all history is written from a particular viewpoint. The use of the third person "we" in our case, is not meant to be neither sinister nor devilish. With the best of intentions, it was meant to cover two authors—Brigitte and myself. Life, however, always has a way of derailing the best of intentions. Due to time and teaching circumstances this study ended up being unintentionally one-sided. One author, not two, became responsible for its final form. Brigitte Hipfl, my research partner, felt she was unable to find the time and commitment due to her own university pressures to see the book through in the time frame planned. The "we" preserves the intent, support, and spirit of her encouragement to see that the project was completed. This book is dedicated to her.

We have not dealt exclusively with film in any direct way; however, chapters are often peppered with films as examples to make our case. This is only to be expected given that a discussion on youth and media cannot avoid such a rich area.[4] We should also mention that the Web has been invaluable for our research, especially when it came to reading the lyrics of numerous music groups and playing the demo video games that are on-line. It seems such a study would have been impossible without access to the Net. As a final note, the reader will come across a number of German words that found their way into the text because of the context of the writing—Klagenfurt, Austria. These have not been translated nor, in some cases, put in italic; many of which are fairly obvious, and the one's that are not so readily obvious only require the minimum energy of a dictionary search.

SOME PRELIMINARY DEFINITIONS OF TERMS

For readers who are not familiar with the Lacanian paradigm, we attempt to provide some necessary understanding of terms throughout the book, especially in the first part where we develop our thesis and introduce Lacan's understanding of fantasy and jouissance. Our thesis clearly demonstrates the way all "reality" is itself structured by fantasy; fact and fiction support and intertwine with one another. Because postmodernity makes such a confusing mess when describing "reality," we have gone with the convention of writing "reality" as RL, meaning "real life" that many writers of cyberspace have chosen to do. For now, here are some brief remarks concerning some of the most common terms we use.

The term "jouissance" appears countless times throughout this book. Because of its ubiquity and importance it will not be given the usual italic. We suspect that eventually this term will find its way into the English dictionary. It remains untranslatable. Žižek has always used the term "enjoyment" as a substitute, but Lacanian-trained theorists such as Bruce Fink (1997) are not entirely happy with such a translation. For Fink, jouissance is more or less interchangeable with Freud's term "satisfaction." It implies an immediate discharge of tension. It is related to the demands, injunctions, desires, and values that the Other makes on the subject; and hence jouissance is always intersubjective, relational, and social with regard to the way the subject submits to, defies, loves, and hates the Other. This means it functions in a realm that is beyond "pure and simple" pleasure, for there is an impingement to the subject's "reality." Fink equates the colloquial expressions "to get off" and to get a "kick" as a more accurate sense of jouissance. It is the source of "satisfaction" that someone gets from "being cruel, inflicting punishment, embarrassing someone, living out a fantasy (regardless of its consequences for others), receiving a great deal of attention (a 'narcissistic' pleasure), lecturing, writing, painting, making music, dancing, singing, and so on" (225–226, footnote 15).

In our understanding, jouissance refers to libidinal bodily pleasure or *unconscious desire* that harbors within it the paradox of pain–pleasure. To use a Chinese food analogy here, the famous sweet/sour dish belongs to a taste all on its own. Adding too much sweetness (plum sauce) makes one regret for having swallowed the syrupy stuff, like a child who has eaten too much candy; too many Szechwan peppers and we want to spit the vile stuff out of our mouths. Here we have the indeterminate space of their exchange, which is eroticized on the surface of the tongue. Lacan used the term "extimate space" to capture this topological paradox between opposite terms. We have referred to Andieu's concept of the skin-ego, when possible, as a site of extimate space as well. Jouissance belongs to this liminal extimate space where the "twist" in a Möbius strip appears. The superego's consumer imperative demands us to "have your jouissance and eat it too," a bulimic Symbolic Order that has us bingeing on sweetness and throwing up our sour bile. Excess and addiction characterizes the designer capitalist superego. *Jouir* means "to come," as in climax or orgasm, while *jouir de* means "to get off on," "to take advantage of," and "to benefit from." Postmodernity is a culture of the excesses of jouissance with its "plague of fantasies" (Žižek 1997a). There is a catch though. This jouissance of life is what we introduce as *zoë* in our companion book. Most famously identifiable as Lacan's *objet a*, (see later) which can be a source of transformative change.

Drive or *Trieb* plays a central role throughout these books as well. Although we titled our book "Youth Fantasies," in many ways it is an ironic misnomer since these fantasies often turn into nightmares supported by the drives. Those readers who are followers of Deleuze will not be happy with the way we have maintained a Lacanian understanding of the drives, and have not followed the trajectory of the drive as a machinic *positive* mechanism. Rather, we have continued with Lacan's notion of *lack* because we feel it helps us theorize the "death drive" in a more profound way; plus it offers us a way to explore its ethics, which we do so especially in our concluding chapters. Although there is some reconciliation with Deleuzian paradigm—his idea of the simulacrum and an interpretation of anti-Oedipalization as a one-response to post-Oedipalization, our thesis remains predominantly Lacanian.

Objet a is yet another of those terms that is indispensable to reading this book. Since it too is untranslatable we leave it in its original French spelling, set in italic to make it visible. We develop this concept in the initial chapters more fully with examples. It is Lacan's crowning achievement. Without this concept and the Lacanian Real, we would fall into the poststructuralism of discourse theory. Rather than the performative subject, as theorized most notably by Foucault, we maintain that the Lacanian split-subject ($) provides us with more conceptual ground to understand the postmodern transition. We continue to be suspicious of the poststructuralist subject position because of its easily appropriation by designer capitalism (Hennessy 1993, 2000). By working with Lacan's split-subject we expect criticism that there is not enough attention paid to identity politics, or to the empirical voice that discourse analysis handles so well. However, we have avoided any heavy-handed discussion of identity politics in our theorizing, which, no doubt will annoy a number of readers. Rather, we have tried to overcome its divisiveness and poststructuralist understanding of "difference" by relocating difference at the level of the psychic Real. The psyche is foremost felt at the bodily affective level of the unconscious. In contrast, identity politics is lived at the conscious level of the Imaginary register, as a skin-ego that is structured by the discourse of visible color (amongst the litany of many other master signifiers). The affective bodily Real is a realm *before* the mirror stage of identification, *before* the visibility of color takes on force. We have tried to argue, now and again, that it is the relationship of jouissance to the Law that can unite youth to a particular Cause regardless of the master signifiers that write their bodies: sex/gender, color, race, age, ethnicity. This suggests an ethics of the Real at the bodily unconscious level that can transcend the color barrier that is so divisive. This is in keeping with the spirituality of religion in its fundamental sense as a rebinding or *religare*. Identity politics where only the Symbolic Order and the Imaginary define difference as so many possible categorizations and varieties is a repetition of designer capitalism's territorialization. Moving back into the space of *touch* of the skin before it knows its color is where we are staging this relocation. We see a difference between "touch" of the skin and its color. Touch belongs to the affective body of the Real, whereas color belongs to the psychic Imaginary. This does not mean we are insensitive to the identity politics that is already at play; it does mean that we are searching for a way around this. We do not deny that an identity politics is continuously at work in the Symbolic Order; however, we think that the segregations identity politics make are part of the problem rather than the solution to challenge consumer capitalism. Designer capitalism has already colonized the visibility of identity politics as yet another brand to wear, perverted it like the "colors of Bennetton." In terms of an ego-skin, the master signifiers that protect an identity are unwilling to be shed and opened up to face its own "death drive." Culture is fugitive and is constantly renegotiated, which is why the invisible dimension of the Real needs to be theorized as Žižek and others have tried.

The homology *site/sight/cite* is our shorthand for Lacan's three psychic interwoven registers—respectively, the Real, Imaginary, and the Symbolic. We explain more fully this homology when it first appears in the body of the text. The Symbolic Order appears capitalized throughout the body of the book to convey the notion that it is authority (institutional, discursive, and individual) that is being addressed, and that it is this big Other which all of us have internalized in our own conflicted ways.

Real remains a rather esoteric term for now,[5] we use it to refer to the affective body states that happen below the level of consciousness, as well as the impossibility of knowing the unconscious fully. We can only catch glimpses of its operation. The Real is characterized by non-sense, trauma, and a realm beyond both the Imaginary and Symbolic psychic registers. We develop it more fully in the first few chapters. It is capitalized to distinguish it from any confusion with the lower-case "real" and RL, terms that have a precarious existence in the theoretizations of postmodernity. To use a pun: the Real is part of the real, but remains invisible, a by-product of any frame we attempt to understand RL ("real life").

THE RESEARCHER AS NO-MAD; OR NO-MADIC RESEARCH

Lacanian psychoanalysis recognizes an impossible gap between the speaking conscious subject and the subject of discursive speech; between the uniqueness of the individual and the spoken, heard, and seen language of enunciation (be it alphabetical, character-based, visual, musical, and so on). The one subject cannot "attain" the other. Lacan and Derrida both share this impossibility. Desire, however, is the excess of language, and properly belongs to the unconscious. It is "invisible." Cultural studies is dominated by what we would identify as an "endothegmatic"[6] array of research procedures that take the enunciated voice as its primary data. "Voice" is forwarded as "authentic," "honest," "integral and sincere," avoiding the defense mechanisms of the ego that are at play, the unconscious disavowals, and repressions that take place. Discourse theory, which fairs much better by recognizing the constructivist nature of reality, is also left with the subject of conscious representation, and not the subject of the unconscious. A further censoring occurs by "informants" themselves when they feel that they are being "misrepresented" or "threatened" by the findings of the research, and ask the researcher to edit their descriptions. With the increase of societal litigation and the increased demand put on researchers to "protect" their informants, it has become progressively more difficult to "say" anything within the context of the research without some feeling of paranoia. As Žižek quips somewhere regarding the political situation in America: political correctness and human rights protection reaches a rather absurd point where only the radical Right dares to speak the "truth," politically they have nothing to lose. Politicians in power, in contrast, are afraid to offend. Those who tell it "the way it is" are the controversial extremists like Jean-Marie Le Penn in France and Jörg Haider in Austria who are perfectly aware of the racism that exists in their respective countries, and use it for their own political gains.

Perhaps we have been discouraged to avoid direct informant input in our study by the way designer capitalism uses endothegmatic sciences to "extract" the jouissance of youth and market it back to them. Through surveys, tracking trends, asking what youth want, following the "leaders" of peer groups, capitalist marketing practices take the voice of youth and manipulate it for its own ends. We are not suggesting, however, that the empiricism of voices from youthful fans or interested viewers are to be dismissed, but we wonder about the ethics of endothegmatic work that always remains troubled by such appropriations. Balibar (1991) has made it quite explicit in the way the Western research has cornered the idea of the Other for its own post-racist ends. By studying other cultures as self-contained entities is precisely the way exoticism occurs. The benevolence of an interest in the "foreign" becomes an excuse for claiming a friendship that is already one-sided, the weight stacked on the side of the researcher who approaches the Other with open arms to learn their "culture." Anthropology has been plagued by such questions that James Clifford (1988) raised quite some time ago. There is also participatory endothegmatic research that claims emic status because the researcher is already part of the subculture that is being studied. S/he[7] claims to have a deep and profound understanding of it because of this special status as a group member; but this also brings with it a particular myopic blindness. By being too close, critical distance is often difficult to maintain; mutual fantasies are acknowledged rather than questioned. All research is caught by such considerations, including ours. It is our own defensive position against those who immediately accuse such research of being devoid of "empiricism," which is often too narrowly defined. We consider our research empirical as well despite the lack of direct informant input. The voices we "hear" are indirect and read anamorphically.

This book is written from what might be deemed a "no-madic position." This does not mean some sort of neutral position in our attempt to grasp youths' passionate attachments with media. Jameson (1991) pointed out quite some time ago how difficult it is to locate oneself in the geographical space of postmodernity so that some sort of general picture might emerge. The "no-madic" position is our attempt to read the unconscious transferences of desire in media texts. Transference is the central means by which a person's unconscious desires and conflicts manifest themselves in analysis. In Seminar VIII, *Transference* Lacan developed his notion of the "agalma," by reading Plato's *Symposium,* a pre-discursive understanding of what was to become *objet a.*[8] Transference provides clues as to the fundamental conflicts between the ego and its internalized Others. Through their music, for example, youth address these internalized Others, as do the narrative structures of video games, television series, and films. All of us continually try to repeat in each psychic register (Real, Imaginary, and Symbolic) the original experience of being loved or recognized that forms the core around which our ego is constructed. As youth encounter actual or potential authority figures that represent their externalized Symbolic Order (individuals, institutions, discourses, and so on), they become their internalized Other. In this way they encounter their own internalized Symbolic Other and its master signifiers, which constitute their Ego Ideal. Such an encounter raises issues of recognition. Similarly, encounters at the Imaginary psychic order entail ego-to-ego relationships, which involve the dynamics of identification: of love, rivalry, and aggression.

Finally, transference also includes the subject's drives and fundamental fantasy. The psychotic figure of Gollum/Sméagol (in Tolkein's *Trilogy of the Rings*) provides a perfect example of what we mean here. Gollum is the name given for Sméagol's unconscious drive, his Real self that wants to possess the Ring. Gollum's *fundamental* fantasy is obviously his "Precious," the Ring that he wants to repossess. This is what defines his entire life. It is his *sinthome*. It paradoxically defines both his "life and death drive," which the hideousness of his body reveals to be the conflict within himself. It has slowly eaten him up, transformed him into another being.[9] By wearing the Ring he will (again) experience his most "precious" unconscious jouissance. Sméagol is his voice of conscience that battles with his fundamental fantasy so as not to be taken in by the Ring's evil, its power to make him feel invincible. By repossessing the Ring he hopes to recover his lost jouissance and make him feel omniscient again. When Gollum overpowers Sméagol it is a victory of the death drive. As Sméagol, he still respects Frodo Baggins on the Symbolic level as an authority figure—Frodo after all, is the Master who possesses the Ring; as well as on an Imaginary level—they share food and the journey together, Frodo recognizes Sméagol and not Gollum. But as Gollum, his libidinal and aggressive drives come together as a death threat directed at Frodo whose life is now in danger. Frodo now simply becomes for him a piece of shit, someone to despise and hate, to be used up and discarded, only a means for attaining his own jouissance—his "Precious." It does not take us far afield to recognize the same lures, the "agalmic" objects that can overpower us as innocently presented for our consumptive desires through the media.

Freud, Lacan, and Žižek's oeuvre are filled with literary and artistic examples of attempting to understand the way authority, fantasy, desire, and the drives are set in motion through these three psychic registers. This series of books purport to do the same with youth fantasies as they circulate in media texts of video games, Internet, music, and selectively in television. In an analytic situation, Lacan maintained that the analyst keeps the unconscious elements at play on all three registers so that they are not repressed or avoided. The contradictions and conflicts between the psychic registers are continually exposed and raised through "*bien dire*" (as the "good or right saying or word"), but a solution is never provided by the analyst. That is the no-madic place to be occupied. The discourse of the analyst, as Lacan develops it in his

S XVII, *L'envers*,[10] attempts to grasp the unconscious or Real self through the feelings and passionate attachments the analysand brings to the encounter. More specifically, the analyst was to avoid speaking from a position of an Imaginary other, as a friend or a rival, or from a position of the Symbolic Order, as an authority figure. Lacan argued that the analyst should take the place of the analysand's *objet a*. To find the "cause" of desire and work with it. The analyst was to attempt to understand the analysand's symptom from a position of his or her unconscious desire; to figure out what it is that structures the analysand's particular behavior from the position of seeming "nonsense," by paying attention to expressions of anger, hate, and the passionate attachments to particular objects, people, and ideas. By occupying the position of *objet a* of the analysand's drives and fundamental fantasy, the idea was to constantly forward and keep in play unconscious desire as a focal point. Eventually the analysand might have a breakthrough and recognize the place of this unconscious desire within the existence of his or her own being, and then take responsibility for it: "To 'enjoy' your symptom!" as Žižek (1992) ironically put it. Change can occur by renouncing certain forms of libido or aggression; or sublimating the drives in a more socially acceptable way. To occupy the position of *objet a*, we would describe as being "nomadic."

While there are no "live" subjects as commonly understood in our journey throughout these books, the intent is much the same as described earlier. The attempt is to try and understand the unconscious desires that operate in youth fantasies within the media, to find the core of their desires and gratifications that may be at odds with their conscious ones. This is done by examining autobiographies, musical lyrics, video games, and narrative structures of television series, and so on.[11] As Lacan (1977a) claims, the unconscious is not a "buried" phenomenon in some Gothic basement. Although it is indeed a censored "chapter of my history that is marked by a blank or occupied by a falsehood," it does reveal itself through bodily symptoms, "in archival documents" such as childhood memories, in the "semantics" of the language used that are the "stock of words and acceptions (*sic*) of my own particular vocabulary, my style of life and my character," as well as "in traditions, too, and even in legends, which, in a heroicized (*sic*) form, bear my history; and lastly, in the traces that are inevitably preserved by the distortions necessitated by the linking of the adulterated chapters . . . whose meaning will be re-established by exegesis" (50). What Lacan means here by the gaps in memory, exposition, and logic is that they become partially filled out through interpretative exegesis; all these manifestations of the unconscious occur in some degree throughout the youth fantasies as they presented themselves in the media that we analyzed. To occupy such a place of *objet a* so as to "read" unconscious desire is what we mean by "no-madic" research, to grasp "the sublime object of ideology" in Žižek's (1989) terms.

We identify such research as a form of no-madism in reference to, but also a modification and re-signification of the same term(s) Deleuze and Guattari (1987) developed and popularized in *A Thousand Plateaus*—nomadism and nomadology—as a "smooth space" that is deterritorialized or undergoing deterritorialization. Their discussion was raised within the context of state antagonism to a "war-machine." The war-machine's attachment to a territory is only for its temporary occupation, but not as a homeland. Nomads are, however, reluctant to leave unless they are driven away by force. With talk of weapons and tools, Deleuze and Guattari's conceptualizations describe quite accurately the nomadism that characterizes video game environments where avatars roam from one "world" to the next, usually armed, in some sort of rhizomatic (potentially) endless pattern. Al Qaeda is a nomadic war-machine with its own system of operations which rely on speed and fluidity, their cyberspace operations equally difficult to trace down. As an organization, they have become a "conceptual" or "virtual" object that resists the state and avoids capture.

This is not entirely the kind of nomadism we are referring to, although there are affinities. The no-mad space of *objet a* that is being occupied is a "suspension"; in the language of physics it is a "strange attractor" in that smooth space—an oasis as a black hole. What are the gravitational forces of desire that are being pulled into that space? What is the "cause" of its singularity? Attempting to occupy such a space is to avoid two dangers of postmodern designer capitalism—the first is on the level of the Imaginary register, while the second is on the level of Symbolic. (1) To avoid becoming branded or infected in any one of a myriad of ways into a form of cultism, metaphorically caught by the gravitational force of ONE means that continuous temporal movement has been stopped. This is a strange attractor with a fixed-point like the pendulum.[12] To do so would mean to occupy one level of the Imaginary psychic register, thereby losing the attempt to grasp the context of the broader social symptoms. Perhaps this is why there are so many "environments" analyzed in our writing, bearing an affinity with Deleuze and Guattari's "plateaus." (2) To avoid such Imaginary fan (addiction)[13] by setting up a form of protection so as not to lose sight of a commitment and responsibility directed to a broader democratic Cause that continues to question the restrictions and inequalities of global capitalism. We try not to fall into representatives of authority, at the same time we do not want to shirk responsibility from "telling it like it is" by unraveling youth as a fantasmatic object of postmodernity. How successful we have been in our no-madic analysis will be up to the reader to decide, once reading this series of explorations, whether the books "ring" true in its exposition of the unconscious investments youth have made in the media we have explored.

A BRIEF ROAD-MAP AS TO WHAT'S TO COME

The following chapters all stand on their own merits, however, we occasionally refer back to previous chapters as a shorthand to flag certain developments, as well as ahead to the companion books on music and television. This book is organized in a number of sections that attempt to cover the "landscape of media perversion." In part I, "The Non-Divide Between Fantasy and Reality: Setting Up Our Study," we begin by introducing our basic thesis concerning youth and presenting Lacan's contention that reality and fantasy are intimately related; that fantasy is the support of reality. Although it is tempting to utilize the spelling "phantasy" to distinguish this psychoanalytic notion from the usual misunderstandings of "fantasy" as simply referring to the imagination, we have decided to stay with this usage because of its widespread use in the psychoanalytic literature (this also applies to the use of such derivatives as "phatasmatic").

We then proceed with part II, "De-Oedipalization: Postmodern Drive Culture," by providing a historical backdrop to two further chapters where we establish the contemporary "loss" of authority and the "trust" in the Symbolic Order with the rise of the superego of designer capitalism's demand for "enjoyment." Chapter 3 has aspects of a sociological review showing the particular social symptoms that have arisen as a result of this demand: postemotionalism, fundamentalism, and cynicism.

We follow this with our analysis of video games and the Internet in part III, "Cyberspace as Obsessive Interpassivity." There are seven chapters that explore violence, video games, hypertext, and the myths of interactivity. We use Pfaller's (2002) term and Žižek's (2000a) development of it, the interpassive subject to show how obsessive behavior basically structures video games. Chapter 3 examines the rise of female action figures within the gaming world. The question of cyberfeminism is raised in the context of the larger issue of postfeminism.[14]

We end with a speculative conclusion: "Are the Kids Alright?"

I

THE NON-DIVIDE BETWEEN FANTASY AND REALITY: SETTING UP OUR STUDY

1

A Historical Andenken: Youthful Appropriations

Youth Demographics: The Difficulty of Boundaries

"Youth" as a dominant signifier of postmodernity is under constant semiosis. Its signification is constantly being redefined by newer technologies, like facial injections of Botox (botulinum toxin), for instance, taken every six months to take wrinkles away. The practice has become so common in Hollywood that directors have begun to complain that some actors who are chronic users are not able to express the full range of emotions because of their facial swelling which makes them appear to look younger. This "surface aesthetic" of everyday life seems all pervasive. Youth researchers operating with modernist tenants of scientific validity struggle to stop its slippage of meaning so as to work with clear, more precise, and bounded definitions for statistical and ethnographic purposes.

Age categorizations and generational cohorts have proven to be the most rhetorically successful and most effective *marketing* approach to sociological and anthropological research. The Internet is saturated with sites that have taken Strauss and Howe's four volumes (1991, 1993, 1997, 2000) of demographic generational predictions and categorizations to be the authoritative and influential account of the "way things are," in the United States at least. In their last book, *Millennials Rising* (2000), they also claim—outside Islam, Africa, and southern Asia—that an "echo" generation is unfolding in China, German, and Japan. In the postwar delay in Western Europe the first "echo" generation is only five years away. Despite the unstable shifts when defining cohort boundaries (e.g., in their first book, *Generations* (1991), they locate Gen Xers as those born between 1965 and 1976 and Millennials between 1977 and 1994. In *Millennials Rising*, they have now changed these dates to 1961–1981 and 1982–2002 respectively) their rhetoric remains persuasive. As patriots and marketers themselves (as well as academics in history and economics), Strauss and Howe have cornered the "generation" market. Currently, they run a strategic consulting firm, Life Course Associates, and two websites boldly offering advice to businesses about consumer trends which in some cases, have not yet materialized, but will emerge based on their own cyclical model of history of crisis every third generation, roughly every 80 years. Although the tragic event of 9/11 didn't quite live up to the parameters as to when the next crisis was expected to occur (ca. 2050) as developed in their last book, *Millennials Rising*, it was readily seized as the ordained event to present the necessary challenge for the newest generation to prove itself "heroic," like the GI generation did 75 years ago.

Euphemisms and categorizations such as the "GI generation," the "silent generation," "baby boomers," and "baby busters," together with numerical or alphabetical categorizations such as the Thirteenth Generation, "lost" generation, or Gen-X, and most recent, Gen-Y (a.k.a., N-Generation (N = Net), Millennials, Echo Generation), provide a somewhat homogeneous characterization of the experiences and mind-sets that each category has internalized and lives through as they pass through the life cycles of approximately 75–100 years. For marketing purposes, generational futurology is most definitely appealing in the way its probability statistics and charts can translate into profitability. Statistical demography has always been used as a tool for shaping sociopolitical policies. The Y generation is the latest updated attempt to identify a layer of American youth who are said to have the most consumer power per capita than that of any previous generation so defined. As the demographic mantra goes they are, by and large, the children of the postwar "boom" generation as well as the X generation that followed. Born after 1976 this cohort of teens and early twenties make up a bubble estimated between 75 and 80 million, three times the size of Gen-X and larger than the 72 million baby boomers. Our study, by and large, examines this particular cohort since its presence is overwhelmingly felt in the various media that we examine: video games, Internet, cinema, television, and music in *Musical Fantasies of Youth Cultures*.

These are all instances of categorizations based on biological, sociological, and developmental ages, typically thought as infants, children, preteens, teens, adolescence, young adults, adults, middle-ages, and seniors. In Strauss and Howe's model, the intricate sociohistorical and political interweavings are discussed primarily between Boomers, Xers, and Yers (Millennials), as the GI generation (born, 1901–1924) and the "silent" generation (born, 1925–1942) slowly lose their influence and recede in political power. It should not be surprising why capitalist marketing and Christian concerns are the two most predominant discourses on the Internet attempting to shape and define this new Y generation. It is refreshing to read, once in a while, an Internet posting by a "screamager" who pushes back the label once awareness of just how s/he is being "scoped" and positioned by market forces is found out, and the jokes that circulate to characterize their "over-protectiveness" by a sector of well-off Boomers and Gen-Xers. Question: "How many teenagers does it take to screw in a light bulb? Answer: None, their parents do it for them."

While this approach to youth culture has been useful and insightful, our approach, as shall be developed throughout this book, differs significantly in its attempt to grasp "youth" as symptomatic of a consumerist culture of the spectacle where the aestheticization of the body is intimately tied to globalized cartel capitalism of the marketplace and trade agreements, the libidinal economy of the newer digitalized media (television, film, music video (DVD), Internet, video games), and what we shall argue as the changed familial dynamic where the nuclear family as governed by the Oedipal myth is slowly decentering, into post-Oedipal forms (see part II). Rather than working with strict intergenerational demographic cohorts our supposition is that "youth" is a historically constructed object of contested discursive representation that varies from culture to culture, and from one historical period to the next. When a child turned nine in the Middle Ages, for instance, the boy and girl became an "adult," and were immediately subject to a moral code as defined by Church law, each gender being restricted differently with regard to sexual promiscuity. Childhood was decidedly shaped by religious discourses. Neil Postman (1983) provides a succinct and fascinating account of the sexual practices between adults and children before this "moral age" took effect, such as adults fondling a child's genitals, family members all sleeping together in a single bed, practices that would be considered pedophilic by today's standards.

There seems to be no purely biologically developmental grounds for a distinct identifiable category called "youth." The complexity of its definition is formed by a combination of sociological, economic, and cultural factors that play on the sex/gender of the body differentially. In some indigenous cultures of Papua-New Guinea and Melanesia the ritualistic homoerotic practice of fellatio performed by young men on their elders is a sign of passage into adulthood (Bleibtreu-Ehrenberg 1990). Swallowing their semen is a way to embody the spirit of strength to become a strong and fearless warrior. In these cultures, boys in particular are "shocked" intensely, and almost instantly into manhood, as they are taken from their mothers and made to undergo often painful and frightening initiate rites where blood is sure to flow. The ritual exorcism of a boy's "femininity" so that this "part" of him dies as he is "reborn" a virile "man," is marked by a sacrifice—a castration, whereby the skin-ego, both figuratively and physically, is cut to compensate for the missing invincible paternal metaphor as he enters the "brotherhood." It is to mark a sign of respect, to cover up and to mask the authority of the father as big Other who is, in effect, impotent, but whose potency must, nevertheless, be believed. The violence of the ritual is a reminder of loyalty and belonging to the male tribe and to submit to its Law where betrayal is subject to severe punishment.[1]

Age differences, rank, and status as well as ritual regulated the homoerotic practices of boys with their elders in Greece. These several dramatic examples demonstrate the *incommensurability* that exists between traditional, premodernist and a modernist culture where childhood as a protective time, according to Ariès (1962), was eventually adopted by the rising rich upper middle class. Ariès, of course, has been taken to task for his views. His demographics pertain only to the *haute* bourgeoisie and royalty, yet his historiographical data, largely artistic representations of childhood, cannot be denied. It points to a social value that emerged during that time as a fantasy space that filled hopes, fears, dreams, anxieties, and aspirations of a rising class. It was this nascent form of a youth fantasy that has come to its limit in postmodernity.

Youth and or/childhood as an event *in-itself*, as an object of desire is beyond the reach of representation. In effect, from a Lacanian psychoanalytic perspective "it does not exist," but remains a void around which images and discursive master signifiers circulate to frame a particular fantasy of its representation. It is *objet a*, the cause of desire. Historiographers like Ariès or DeMause (1974), who attempt its reconstruction can only be "failed" translators relying on the quotidian artifacts and texts they find. In the integrity of their translation, the "strangeness" of the past will always be lost. But this is not to say that the effort should not be made even if the past cannot be recovered. It is precisely from the present that understanding past differences enables change to take place. The past alters the future in the way it is confronted and interpreted. Childhood and youth have existed in every historical period, but as an object of fantasy youthful bodies were shaped by the social Imaginary at a time that itself was never completely "stable," but fraught with cognitive dissonance, competing ideologies, and conflict. A sociopolitical agenda is implicitly or explicitly at work in all such rhetorical constructions and reconstructions of youth/and or childhood given that every text from a psychoanalytic viewpoint says more and less than it intends. Its inconsistencies and slippages mask the anxieties, fears, and forbidden desires of those who produce them. "Youth" in postmodernity has become a conflicted fantasy object, a source of hope as well as anxiety by adults who wish to stay young, yet find themselves competing with young people, as the very Thing that they deny about themselves.

DESIGNER CAPITALIST EXPLOITATION

From the rhetoric of the capitalist right, the Industrial Revolution in Britain did not create child factory labor. It was an inherited problem from the feudal system where children of the poor already had to work the fields. Their labor power was already available. For an apologist of capitalism like Ayn Rand (1966), whose ethics was based on self-interest and a metaphysics of objective reality, the accumulation of capital actually *increased* the productivity of adults, a position she took late in her career—at the age of 61. According to Rand, this eventually enabled children *not* to work in the factories. Working in factories and in the cotton fields had only been a transitional and temporal phenomenon. Rand points to the lowering of the infant mortality rate and the rise of the population during the Industrial Revolution to score her point. At last, she says, the poor could feed themselves in their own self-interests for the first time. Yet, nothing is said regarding the highest recorded infant mortality rates in Britain, which occurred in the first half of the twentieth century! (Rose 1985). This paradox seemed to be beyond her.

Rand, like many capitalists today, are unable to recognize that the working classes stand out as a major contradiction—as the exception—to the ideology of a free-market system and social utopianism with the Romantic transcendental view of the child as its greatest achievement. The only freedom a worker has is to sell his or her own labor power to the market. But this is a spurious freedom. It is a "choice without a choice"; in this "free act" the worker becomes enslaved to capital; freedom is lost and a new commodity emerges—labor power. The only "true" choice is death itself. Removed from the means of production a worker's labor enables a surplus to be extracted, negating the equivalent exchange of value (wages) between labor and capital, which then supports capitalist's claims to nonexploitation (i.e., worker's free will) and social benefits (i.e., improved health and welfare). These dynamics remain internal to the logic of capitalism itself (Žižek 1989, 22–23). From a Marxist viewpoint, of course, capitalism was yet another form of exploitation that did have its "progressive" moment as the middle class pulled itself away from Church and royalty, developing various forms of a democratic nation-state. But its progress stagnated into monopoly capitalism and imperialism when it claimed its ideology *pour-tous*. It was not until 1833 that child labor laws were enacted in Britain as a pretense to hinder the capitalist exploitation of children in woolen factories. Its passage had more to do with the fear of working-class resistance of unruly and potential undesirable activities that were made possible by an independent income (Rose 1985). Such legislation required compulsory schooling and the cleanliness of the workplace. Fourteen years later the Ten Hour Act was passed (1847), limiting the number of hours worked by 13–18-year-olds to ten hours a day. Yet, it was not until 1867 that such laws were extended to cover small factories and workshops. Legislation is one matter, enforcement quite another.

Child labor laws are far from being universal and are often difficult to enforce. Cheap labor by children continues to be lucrative in many parts of the world as countries in South Asia as well as in India attempt to modernize by opening their borders to multinational corporations where the search for cheap labor and profit dollars relentlessly goes on. The same rhetoric of Rand's "objectivist philosophy" continues to apply. Children's labor is a transitionary phase as the country's wealth increases. Opening the country to the interests of trade and cartel capitalism will make the country rich and improve the lot of children. African countries like Ivory Coast, Ghana, and Nigeria, which rank as the world's first, second, and fourth largest cocoa producers, are known for child trafficking as slave labor to work the cocoa plantations. Egyptian children employed in the cotton-farming cooperatives work long hours, routinely face beating at the hands of foremen, and are poorly protected against pesticides and heat. In effect, childhood as the West had once constructed it, does not exist in many countries even though child labor laws have been legislated. Clearly the construction of "youth" is tied to the needs of a country's economy. The poorer the country, the greater the need to supplement the family's income through child labor. Western social workers tend to blame parents for such neglect in a direct misguided comparison with a sentimentalized view of childhood as being innocent and natural, rather than recognizing the economic source of poverty and the resulting cognitive deficits that result from malnutrition.

THE FANTASY OF DEVELOPMENTAL PSYCHOLOGY

Since the last half of the nineteenth century, childhood, public education, and economics have been intimately linked with one another. As Foucault (1979) had so well shown, the institution of public education was meant to "discipline" the body to read and write, and cultivate a character of self-control and contemplation through a utility-based curriculum focused on skills and obedience. Disciplining young people's social and moral values and behaviors meant disciplining the emotions through puritanical religious, scientific, and rational discourses. Children of the working poor, it should be noted, continued to labor in the mills and mines. Disciplining the body rigidly, where no questions are raised through the institution of schooling, was precisely the most effective way of instilling the Law of the Superego, of the social order. To install the Law requires it to remain nonsensical, not to be questioned and obeyed by the imperative: "This is the way things are." Being ignorant of the Law is no excuse for transgressing it. Its authority has to be internalized. To discipline the body through well-defined practices means to frame the mind. From this perspective, belief is not some interior contemplative phenomenon; rather it is radically exteriorized and embodied in the practical and effective procedures of everyday life. Belief then supports the fantasy that regulates reality.

It is a commonplace saying that the so-called classical school curriculum developed at the turn of the century contributed to the child's *mental* discipline. Through "faculty psychology" the mind was to be treated like a muscle, exercised through memorization and recitation of biblical passages, for instance. Comprehension was of secondary importance and consideration. Modernity accorded "divine powers to children" as the Child Study movement got underway way in both the United States and Britain. Children's phylogenetic artistic development was said to repeat the ontogeny of the human race because children's art was more "innocent," "pure," "free," and devoid of the rigidity of industrialization. It was compared with "primitive" African art that was such an inspiration to various modernist artistic movements at the turn of the century like Die Brücke, Cubism, Symbolists, and even Surrealism for its formalist simplicity and universality.

The Romantic fantasy of the "pure" child becomes a paradoxical object of both future projections (fullness, without lack) as well as disavowal of a nation's imperialism and racism. On the one hand the child's "innocence" and energy as *zoé* fills the West's lack. The child was perceived as "the father of man" and the "route to knowledge" (quoted in Burman 1994, 10). This curious and strange reversal identifies precisely the dream of complete creative fulfillment of a nation's potential, as well as oneself: progress in all its manifestations. On the other hand, disciplining was a way to disavow all that the nation was afraid would prevent such a realization: feeble-mindedness, the "primitive Other," and especially "sexuality" that became contained and controlled through a confessional model by the discourses of science—"scientia sexualis" as Foucault (1980) described them. Disciplining the child through a pedagogical discourse, in effect, meant disciplining the nation and oneself—inversely. The child becomes the "father of man" because as a fantasy object it exists outside the Symbolic Order in future anterior, in the time of *as if*—an empty (innocent, pure) signifier for the potential of what yet might become. The "route to knowledge" shapes the dream of the imaginary child's development, so that a secular economic, emancipatory, as well as an eschatological telos might be realized depending on what grand narrative was being promoted: capitalist, Marxist, and Christian respectfully, where the infant Jesus becomes the redeemer of the world. The child as "the father of man" seems to "classically" present Lacan's contention that the phallus is the privileged signifier in the Real since the trope of this fantasy has oriented modernity (see Žižek 1992, 124–148). The phallic transcendental object, namely the child, takes the place of what both the nation and the subject lack, namely the magical energy (*zoë*) of youth to remain progressive and forever young.[2]

For the middle classes, compulsory schooling in Britain seemed to repeat the same repetitive routine of the factory, with an equal amount of strict rules and regimentation. Authority of the phallic signifier was assured in this way. Elementary schooling provided sufficient knowledge to meet industrial demands of *lassez-faire* capitalism. From the very first elementary classrooms of the 1870s in Britain, school funding depended on the pupil achievement ("Payment by Results"). In the 1880s, both England and France eventually instituted compulsory education. Being poor, a "pauper," and criminal were considered genetic traits of character that a strict moral education could help rectify through the inculcating good habits (Hunter 1988). It is no surprise, therefore, that "adolescence" as a category only emerged at the turn of the twentieth century in both Britain and United States with the advent monopoly capitalism which required a labor force that had to stay in school longer (Friedenberg 1959; Acland 1995, 27). The first junior high schools (intermediate school) were established in Columbus, Ohio (1909) and in both Berkeley and Los Angeles in 1910 (Pinar et al. 1995, 93). Nor is it any further surprise why high schools and vocational education came into existence during the same time. A skilled labor force, past what a public elementary grade school could offer during the previous half of the nineteenth century, was needed as capitalism based on electricity and Fordist principles began to industrialize with research and design playing an ever increasing role in the efficiency of production. This instrumental and vocational model of education again required the continued measurement of skills as evaluated by psychologists. Taylorist behavioral principles of insuring the production of skilled work were applied both on the assembly line and at school to insure efficiency and control.

It has taken a long time for a segment of critical scholars to recognize *how developmental psychological theories that purport to chart the "normative" development of children through adolescence into adulthood are but the socio-historical structures of a capitalist logic made legitimate through the institution of public schooling that socializes a captive mandated audience.* Developmental psychology was a key discourse in the construction of the fantasy of a transcendent youth. As a technological discourse of the self, developmental psychology effectively pathologized those individuals and groups who failed to meet its fantasmatic ideal. Susan Buck-Morss's seminal essay, written in 1975 and followed shortly by Edward Sullivan in 1977, set the stage for questioning just how the stress on cognition as reason and rationality in schools, as manifested by Jean Piaget's stage of concrete operations, assigns the highest value to an Enlightenment philosophy of abstract scientific rationality of capitalist logic. Objectivity, logic, and abstract thinking, autonomy as self-governance and independence as self-direction became the highest values of achievement. Feminists further stressed that these were masculinist assumptions generalized on an androcentric model of what it meant to act rationally. Connected and contextualized knowledge as well as care became devalued. The biologically based theory of "genetic epistemology" as Piaget developed it, was essentially the inherent structuralism of advanced scientism of the time. It seems only a small managerial elite were capable of its achievement as Abraham Maslow, the founding "father" of humanistic psychology and self-actualization was to claim through his notion of "eupsychian management" (1965). According to Maslow, only 2 percent of the population could self-actualize. It seems that either too many barriers got in the way, or only 2 percent of the population were given the privilege and the chance to do so. Not coincidentally, it turned out that these 2 percent were by and large businessmen and scientists.

Lawrence Kohlberg's (1963) hierarchy of moral rational development based on Piagetian tenants was equally exposed for its masculine bias by co-colleague Carol Gilligan (1982), and for its morality based on individual rights and freedoms enshrined in the Western legal system based on property rights. Stage six, based on respect for universal principle and the demands of individual conscience, could only be reached by a select few, and only by those with an individual autonomy of conscience, an anathema to many non-Western cultures whose value system would be ranked low on Kohlberg's six-point scale. Similarly, "progressive education," which reached its peak in the post–World War II period, was a child-centered approach attending to a child's needs and interests. Under the rhetoric of individualism, democracy, and free play, however, a far different outcome emerged. As a number of critical scholars have effectively shown (Walkerdine 1990; Burman 1994), its self-actualizing discourse enabled a much more subtle technology of disciplinary obedience to develop by having children conform to the rules that appeared to arise out of their own deliberations and choices. The teacher became a governor, intervening only when it seemed that the independent-thinking children had made the "wrong" free choices. More deceptively, perhaps the fantasy of the self-governing innocent child actually policed the fear of encroachment of working-class values that were at odds with this "norm." Developmental psychology, as Burman (1994) shows, is used as a universal standard to "globalize childhood" despite cultural differences, a form of cultural imperialism in the name of transcendent progress.

This brief review concerning the constructions of childhood/youth certainly point to the limitations of what appears, at first glance, to be a natural biological process and its categorizations into succinct intergenerational cohorts of the dominant demographic paradigm. "Normative development" establishes an empty signifier that casts many as "deviant," "at-risk," and "deficient" in order to preserve and unconsciously maintain an ideology of white middle-class privilege. Effects of racism, classism, and sexism vanish from consideration. Critical researchers working within a poststructuralist paradigm of discourse analysis (e.g., usually Foucaultians like Norman Fairclough (1989, 1992)), make evident the way any hegemonic construction abjects and ignores differences between cultures, sexual preferences, gender, ethnicity, class, and other dominant variables that might be identifiable to be able to assert and maintain its dominance. Stuart Hall (see Slack 1996 for review) cleverly identified such an approach to be an "articulation" as to the way social identity may be formed through a complex fusion of traits. But knowing this does not solve the way such knowledge is disavowed, nor the way the fantasmatic objects continue to structure fantasies of Western development as spearheaded by the United States today with its New World Order. The sublime fantasy of the innocent child who was invested with an idealized embodiment of transcendent modernity has begun to decenter after a century. The wish for what the West never had in the first place has come to its own limit. Postmodernism is a time of facing the reality of that wish fulfillment—which, to the dismay of many, has become a horror—the consumerist demand to Enjoy!

THE FUTURE IS "NOW": THE RETURN OF REPRESSED YOUTH

When we come to the *post*-adolescent "youth" cultures that define our own postmodern culture of global capitalism with its liberalization of trade, and its characterization as a goods and service economy—a consumer society, the record on child labor laws has become equally suspect as those "othered" "have-not" countries where familial poverty drives children to work. McDonalds' restaurant, Woolworths, Tesco, Safeway, Burger King, Odeon Cinemas, Heritage Hotels, Fourbuoys, and Thorpe Park amusement park have all been successfully prosecuted in England for violating child labor laws. A McDonalds' franchise holder in Camberley, England was charged a record £12,400 penalty following an investigation that found school pupils working up to 16 hours a day in what was described as a "fast-food sweatshop." On school days, 15- and 16-year-olds were beginning shifts straight after class and then working through sometimes until 0200 hours the following morning. On Saturdays, a 15-year-old girl was starting work before 0800 and working through until 0120 the next day. The McSpotlight Web site has archival transcripts of libel trails of its past abuses and a debating room where workers can exchange horror stories about working under its protective Golden Arches. In the state of Maine, Wal-Mart retailing giant was found guilty in 1,463 cases for using child labor, incurring $205, 605 worth of fines. Wal-Mart also has factory sweat shops in Honduras where young women aged 14–17 labor 9 hours a day, often putting in three hours of forced overtime, ironing shirts and sewing clothing for the market. News stories such as these are not exceptional. The Internet is full of them should one take the time to search since they receive little attention in daily newspapers. More and more youth are working part-time at so-called McJobs to support themselves as postsecondary education becomes a necessity to eventually find employment, be it only on a semipermanent or contract basis, accommodating to the logic of post-Fordist capitalism (Harvey 1989).

When it comes to the question of youth, globalized capital seems to be blurring any smug romantic claim by the West of still having a protected time of "childhood." The pressure of educational institutions (secondary and postsecondary alike) to become more "pragmatic" and accountable to industry's needs is no longer in dispute. Universities have turned more and more to chasing external research dollars, fund raising, tuition hiking, and in some cases, the doing away with tenure track positions. Corporate universities that apply an updated curriculum to the new media (computer and information technologies) make no pretense that the "education" they offer is for anything other than the job market. Then there are "universities" which multinational companies have established specifically to *train* their own employees. No pretense to lofty ideals here either. McDonalds, Microsoft, Sony . . . all have such institutions with specific marketing curriculums.

The "loss" of childhood is further marked by the disappearance of identifiable sartorial distinctions between adults and youth. Even gothic and skater clothes have an adult appeal. Does wearing such clothes mean that a 50-year-old "Goth" is resisting the social order in the same way a gothic teen is? The answer remains ambiguous. Such a phenomenon offers new challenges for understanding identity formations. The same applies to leisure pursuits such as computer games, eating habits (fast food), and tastes in films, which seems to have become, by and large, intergenerational as well. Although a rating system exists for video games and movies, censorship enforcement is practically nonexistent. The "old" 1954 Comic Code Authority (CCA) of self-regulated conduct prohibited the drawing of exaggerated physical qualities of women (mainly breasts), as well as scenes of brutal torture, excessive and unnecessary gunplay, physical agony, gory and gruesome crimes, rape and seduction. Scenes dealing with the walking dead, vampires, and vampirism, ghouls, cannibalism, and werewolves were also prohibited. The expectation was always having Good triumph over Evil. All this has been done away with. Marvel has now its own rating system, which reflects the classifications approved by most movie rating boards: All Ages, Marvel PG, Marvel PG Plus, Parental Advisory/Explicit Content.

The lowering of the age of consent for drinking, driving, sex (in some states), and the false perception of the rise in youth crimes has led to more and more trails taking place in adult court. There has been legislative pressure to have the Young Offenders Act amended in both the United States and Canada, children are allowed to legislate against their parents, and now there is a newly established journal, *Youth Justice* (2002) to address these concerns. These indicate behaviors privileged only to responsible and mature citizens. The population of youth who are considered "at risk" is growing, teenage pregnancy is claimed to be on the increase, sexual activity begins at an earlier age, and increased drug abuse are further indicators of the dramatic changes that have taken place. These are symptoms of a "moral panic" that we address more fully in the second part of our book. They present several indicators of the way "normal" developmental transitions as established by the economic trajectory of capitalism identified by such terms as child, teenager, adolescence, postadolescence, and adult have been twisted into new configurations in both directions. The paradox is that children are given more "mature privileges" and responsibilities while teenagers and the 20-something cohort are, not able to take on adult responsibilities for economic reasons, while adults desire to be young. From this perspective development is not somehow "progressive," rather from a psychoanalytic view, birth, growth, and death cycles take on different meanings, shaped as they are by the hypercomplex play between designer capitalism and the web of competing desires.

The issue of the "rights of children" (both pro and con), the rise of "adult" comic books, the falling age of models in the advertisement industry, more nudity and exposed skin in every facet of public entertainment, and the growing openness to gay, lesbian, and transgendered representation are yet further indications of intergenerational confusion and moral panic. Sexuality, once the preserve of adults, can no longer be contained. The threat of AIDS has changed all that. Church authorities have been hard at work promoting abstinence as the sole solution to this anxiety. Any sense of "shame," as a residual holdover from the Puritanism of the Protestant ethic, is waning. Such a reading would constitute yet another aspect of the "return of the repressed." Capitalist ideology, as hypothesized by Max Weber and well documented by Beder (2000), was based on an asceticism of hard work and rational conduct, which manifests itself in the development of a strong moral character, who is then able to work for the greater glory of God that much better. In contemporary society, porn Internet sites are by far the most popular of all what is available on the www. (In the United States, the only time that the volume of porn Internet users actually dropped was during the 9/11 terrorist attack!) As for the work ethic, the tendency has been to blur the distinction between work and leisure and make leisure as profitable as possible.

When it comes to youth, the major shift from printing technologies to digitalized media technologies has caused the greatest concernment of all. Typographic print cultures that eventually replaced the Medieval chirographic (script) cultures introduced a form of literacy that eventually standardized spelling (Webster) and grammar, and produced a self-reflective individuality (Montaigne, Rembrandt) based on reason and scientific empiricism, and thereby essentially establishing a division between adult and children

based on ability to read and write. One could be 40-years-old and still be a
"child" in this sense. Since the invention of the printing press it took approximately a hundred-and-fifty years to shift from a mixed oral/script culture
to one where knowledge could be "objectified" in the form that was contained in a book and represented by a discipline (as developed by the French
Encyclopedists). Electric cultures at the turn of the twentieth century (cinema, electricity, telephone, and telegraph) have been supplemented and sup-
planted by our own electronic telematic informational culture based on
digitalization, computerization, and communication at a distance. In our
electronic age the objectively constructed visual illusion of typographical cultures remain both preserved and written-over (palimpsest) through digital
photography, television, video, cinema, and holography, much like oral and
script cultures were both preserved and over-written by typographic cultures,
never totally disappearing. These developments should not be interpreted as
yet another form of "technological determinism" that is shaping reality, rather
it is the fantasy formations that accompany the new electronic culture, which
is of particular interest for our study, which we deal expensively in part III
of our study on cyberspace. Designer capitalism based on the electronic revolution has also blurred the developmental distinctions between adults and
youth in the way the knowledge barrier has been inverted as information.
Adults are now in competition with young people in the electronic industries. The rhetoric of creativity, flexibility, computer savvy is placed on youthful
energy. It is the adults who have to catch up.

Given this decentering, should it be any wonder why the fantasmatic child
is once more being courted to restore faith in the authority of the consumerist capitalist system? Such fantasmatic recuperation is especially evident
in Strauss and Howe's thesis as developed in *Millennials Rising*. The
Net Generation is being courted as the next upcoming "heroic" generation
of the "fourth turning," capable of solving the next "secular crisis" that the
United States will find itself in post-9/11 climate. Strauss and Howe's
"journey into the future" means that there is a selective extrapolation of what
can be traced in the present to provide future possibilities. The "future" in
its kernel is already here, so to speak. The Net Generation is said to place a
high value on science and technology compared to the Boomers and Xers
because they have grown up in the computer age with all its advances. They
will provide technological and biotech solutions for the twenty-first century
and place America on top in both scientific research and practical application,
after the "scare" it experienced from Japan in the 1980s and early 1990s, and
now from the growing markets of The European Union. There are few
"slackers" amongst them, unlike Gen-X. This "echo" generation is said to be
more obedient of authority, more mature, and especially smart. "Smart"
refers to their more "pragmatic" approach to life. Because of the Internet they
now have access to information; anyone with a search engine can become an
"instant" expert, artist, or shopper. The result is that this Net Gen has
become even more "autonomous" in their decision making than ever before.
The most valued traits are said to be individuality and uniqueness. Crafting

a personalized image that communicates individuality, even as it paradoxically confirms membership in a group or groups, is what it's all about.

In chapters 2 and 3 we introduce our hypothesis concerning postmodern youth culture and the fantasies that structure it. We shall not follow Strauss and Howe's trajectory, although our examples throughout the study are, by and large, confined to the 1990s decade, the more recent developments in music in our companion books, the Internet, video games, and television. We attempt to provide an understanding as to why Lacanian psychoanalysis offers a unique way to grasp youth fantasies, and hopefully provide enough examples to grasp its conceptualizations.

2

OUR HYPOTHESIS: YOUTH FANTASIES
LACANIAN STYLE

Not yet *another* book on youth! We hope not. Our title, "Youth Fantasies," plays on a *double entendre*: the ambiguous meaning that "youth" has in our postmodernist consumerist culture. On the one hand, modernity defines youth through the discourses of developmental progress. From such a perspective, it seems unproblematic to suggest a developmental stage where maturity has not yet been achieved. Marked by exuberance that is rich in potential, "youth" has to still undergo a transformation to form a patina of historical traces in order to claim the rights of passage into a qualitatively different way of being. On the other hand, postmodern culture is itself defined by a deconstructive and decentering impulse to question this biological and sociological given through a myriad of technologies of the body that rage against the aging process. Through numerous forms of cosmetic surgery, hormonal treatment, and antiage gene manipulation, the search for a posthuman body is decidedly shaped by a fantasy that tries to cheat nature and death by reawakening the myth of a "fountain of youth" so as to remain "forever young."

This is humorously captured in Robert Zemeckis' film, *Death Becomes Her* (1992). A mysterious "elixir of pure libido" (*zoë*) that assures immortality, exotically stored and virtually priceless (well, almost!), is offered to two aging and highly competitive actresses—Madeline Ashton (Meryl Steep) and Helen Sharp (Goldie Hawn) by an unscrupulous vixen, Lisle Von Rhoman (Isabella Rossellini). As the two perpetually duel to replace the other as the wife of a prominent Hollywood plastic surgeon, Dr. Ernest Menville (Bruce Willis), death turns into a hoped-for blessing as their competitive narcissism holds no boundaries and no finite resting place. The fantasy of immortality and changeless beauty is brutally exposed as they literally "fall to pieces" toward the (non)ending of the film, as each searches desperately to restore her body that remains literally scattered "all over the place." In this regard, Michael Jackson must surely be the closest "living" enactment of such a fantasy with his fanaticism to protect himself from germs by cocooning himself into a controlled environment and wearing a bandana over his mouth (for a period of time) whenever he was in public. His probable pedophilic tendencies, his enthusiasm for Disneyland, and his castrato-like voice, pop lyrics, and constant surgical makeovers make the 42-year-old look and sound like a 12-year-old from a distance; never growing up, caught by his own self-imposed Peter Pan fantasy.[1] As a performer he was never a child, and as a child he never grew up. The figure of Jackson is where the two discourses of youth—one developmental and biological, and the other its complete denial—seem to cancel each other out in the production of a posthuman body that appears "monstrous" and uncontainable within its signification. In one sense, Michael Jackson has rhetorically constructed himself as a "figure" in Lyotard's (1991) sense of the term. His body is "nonsensical" in the way it disrupts discursive signification of the meaning of "youth," and at the same time he opens up the discourse of youth to a radical heterogeneity, to a "singularity," which is then unrepresentable. Perhaps this is best illustrated by his *Thriller* album (1982) and its hit song, unconsciously confirming and adumbrating his future "monstrosity" given that it stands out so starkly against the rest of his albums that celebrate narcissistic and romantic love.

The term "youth" has effectively overshadowed, if not entirely replaced the previous master signifier, "childhood," as the dominant zone of contention and concern that shapes postmodernity's social imagination. There is both a historical and psychoanalytic explanation as to why this is so. From a Lacanian psychoanalytic point of view, our thesis maintains that the *symptoms of today's postmodern "youth" expose the "truth" of the modernist fantasy of the "innocent" or "divine" child that continues to residually structure beliefs concerning the institution of education and the nuclear family. The attempt to restore faith in "authority" is its corollary. This "truth," we argue, helps to explain the source of mourning over the "death" of childhood and the trauma of "moral panic" that follows it. This is most clearly articulated by those who demonize the media* carte blanche *as the cause of violence and decay of our youth, and not just one of its many symptoms as this modernist fantasy begins to decenter itself.*

By "truth" we mean the exposure of a structuring fantasy where the horror of repressed desire is finally confronted, and the ensuing shock felt as the perception of reality begins to change and unravel. In order for an object to maintain its status as a structuring object of desire, it must continue to function in the capacity as a "sublime object of ideology" (Žižek, 1989); that is to say, such an object must be continually misrecognized as structuring the myth that makes sense of "reality" as it is discursively and imaginatively constructed. It must appear "sublime" in the sense that it escapes comprehension, and is then endowed with a fetishistic and magical (fantasmatic) investment. We argue that "youth," as both a noun and as an adjectival "effect," *is* such a sublime object in postmodernity. In effect, youth is a fetishistic object that has an immaterial existence. It can only exist in the unconscious (the Lacanian Real),[2] where, being endowed with magical qualities, it remains indestructible and immutable, a transcendental signifier that is beyond both language and the imagination.

In Lacan's early lexicon (S VII, *Ethics*), it is this fantasmatic object as Thing (*das Ding*)[3] which holds a culture's belief system together. Lacan termed this transcendental signifier that is without signification and hence nonsensical, as the phallus (paternal metaphor, Name-of-the-Father). The term is certainly not unproblematic nor free of its critics, in particular, feminists such as Luce Irigaray.[4] It refers to a transcendental realm that then supports symbolic authority; that is, unproblematized "reality" as such. It guarantees that the subject is without lack, seemingly whole. Consequently, we can interpret, for instance, the secularization of God's authority during the advent of Enlightenment, eventually paradigmatically manifesting itself as the Kantian transcendental subject constituted by a network of a priori categories of the mind, as the framework for "objective scientific knowledge." In Lacan's terms, this would be yet another appearance of the phallic transcendental signifier of paternal authority. Further to our primary thesis is a corollary, which we explore throughout the book: *that postmodernity is a radical time of decentering of authority with the subsequent attempts to restore its centralization. This process of de-Oedipalization or post-Oedipalization identifies the distinct change that youth are experiencing today.* We explore this fully in part II, "De-Oedipalization: Postmodern Drive Culture."

THE CHILD AS SPECTRAL OBJECT

In Lacan's later writing the fantasy object was designated as *objet a*, which could to be applied equally to an individual, nation, or a culture's fantasies. Any object what-so-ever could be elevated to the status of *objet a* as long as it is understood that *objet a* refers to an object's spectral or magical effects. This is the aspect of an object that remains unconscious and cannot be assimilated consciously into the Symbolic Order. It is *not* the actual material object that is fantasmatic, but its elevated status. The actual object functions only as a "lure" or an aesthetic surface appearance, which can be identified by a signifier and its signification. It completes or makes the fantasy possible. Put another way, *the* object as a lure is identified by both an *Imaginary* psychic register coupled with a symbolic linguistic order, a "sign" as such. The *objet a* is not the object *of* desire, rather it is the "object *in* desire" (Lacan 1977b, 28, emphasis added). It is its "other" existence in the psychic register of the unconscious Real that makes it fantasmatic, which is beyond both imagination and cognition; that is, its *effect* in the Real psychic register of the unconscious where it plays a logical paradoxical role as *both* lacking *and* being full. When we say that the child of modernity is a "divine" fantasmatic object of desire, we are not referring to any particular child, rather it is the fantasy that surrounds child/childhood, which acts as one of its centering myths for the West. The fantasmatic child as a transcendental signifier for bourgeois progress and modernization is removed from history and society. The biological "norms" that "track" a child's progressive development as specified by the discourses of developmental psychology since the early twentieth century, helped shape and create an "object" of the child that "does not exist." The various developmental stages of progressive growth that were empirically "discovered," turned out to be the same progressive stages of Western thought itself, as if phylogeny actually did recapitulate ontogeny. As *objet a*, the fantasy child exists outside the system of capitalist exploitation, devoid of the symbolic descriptors such as class, color, race, gender; thereby enabling precisely its reverse form to be instituted: namely, a masculinist, racist, white upper-class norm that abjects all those who failed to reach its "impossible" norm—all those who were feeble-minded.

Such a fetishistic misrecognition of the child by adults must appear in reverse form if the "innocence" of the child is to be maintained. Ideological mystification cannot function and reproduce itself without this fantasm. This is not to say that the fantasmatic child of modernity somehow masked ideology, was somehow "hiding" it; rather, by being overlooked and misrecognized, the fantasy of the child enabled modernity to continue to claim its grand narrative of progress at the expense of its abjected Other. The child in modernism appealed to a symbol of the West's ideal or better self. "The fundamental level of ideology, however, is not of an illusion masking the real state of things but that of an (unconscious) fantasy securing our social reality itself" (Žižek 1989, 33). In postmodernity, "youth" as a *contested object* has replaced the child of modernity as the fantasmatic object of desire. *The postmodern trend of staying forever young is equivalent to the fantasy of the modern child never growing up.* An interlude, a hesitancy, a vibration prevails in Western culture as the clash of "culture wars" continues to unfold before the system dissipates into perhaps a new geopolitical global centering, preserving the illusion of being forever young—like global designer capitalism that must continually keep renewing itself in its expansions and mergers. We theorize how such a hesitant, doubt-laden postmodernity presents an anamorphic projection of the sublime objects that fasten modernity, a chance to see modernity's "truth" otherwise. As Lyotard (1992c) put it,

> You can see that when it [postmodernity] is understood in this way, the "post" of "postmodern" does not signify a movement of repetition but a procedure in "ana"-: a procedure of analysis, anamnesis, anagogy and anamorphosis which elaborates an "initial forgetting." (93)

The relationship between modernity and postmodernity has been widely discussed; indeed postmodernity is often defined as a conversation with modernity, and hence successively following modernity in chronological order. This is, by far, the most common reading. To theorize postmodernism as preceding, rather than succeeding modernism, seems anachronistic, but that is precisely what a psychoanalytic reading would suggest. Lyotard (1992c) makes such a claim when he writes:

> A work can become modern only if it is first postmodern. Thus understood, postmodernism is not modernism at its end, but in a nascent state, and this state is recurrent. (22)

The postmodern in our thinking of youth fantasies is not a period that follows modernism; rather it is embedded in modernism itself at those places where the limits of modernism have been reached—youth "development" being one of them. The kernel of modernity's eventual deconstruction was already posited in its founding concepts as they came to paradigmatic fruition. It is precisely at the heterogeneous borders of modernity's limits where such deconstruction in the form of play and resistance is taking place. These are the interstitial, in-between places—Merleau-Ponty's (1968) chiasma—which mark the "dissipation of a system" (Prigogine 1997); they are the auto-poetic moments, the instances when the system seems to change into something else. In Vattimo's (1988) terms, a *Windung* rather than an *Überwindung* takes place. Postmodernism does not have an identity other than a "happening" in the spaces of difference, which mark the limits of modernity. It displaces and interferes with modernity, but this intervention comes from the inside of modernity itself. Only a modern subject can create the postmodern one. Its invention (in-*venire*) means to create, to forge, without truth or reality, the "new." We shall see that postmodern youth fantasies that have been invented in music and the media of music video, film, computer games, and television fill out the interstitial space of postadolescence, stretching it into a new space for creativity, exploration, and contestation. The need is for new signifiers—boyz, bois, girlz, gurlz, grrrls—to signal this change.

REVISITING THE FUTURE: THE "LOSS" OF THE INNOCENT CHILD

Postmodernity is a historical moment of the dissolution of fantasmatic objects that held the fantasy of what is generally called modernity together. The Western dream of progress, guided by a particular trajectory as to what is considered "normal," measured developmentally in biological terms, reaches its apex with the "full human potential" movement of humanist psychology by such well-known figures as Abraham Maslow, Carl Rogers, and Rollo May. In the postmodern context this has continued by way of the "cyborgianization" of the baby through the Institute for Human Development and the Better Baby Press. Based on Western developmental milestones in motor control through neurological research, the idea is to develop children who embody the ideals of flexibility and robust motor programming so that they can be effective information managers in the cognitive domain. As adults they will be able to manage and move with and for transnational capital flow, while others will be left behind (Croissant 1998, 292).[5]

Pursuing a neo-Darwinist theory of evolutionary progress into its abnormal or mystical ends, The Esalen Institute in Big Sur, California, under the leadership of its founder Michael Murphy, has integrated Eastern philosophies to claim the possibility of an inner transcendent consciousness. To what extent are such New Age religious developments yet another guise of the fantasmatic child represented as a transcendent vision of the potential of eternal creative youth? In the final analysis, the dream of Western Enlightenment was also an eschatological Christian trajectory of the infant Jesus perceived as the "light of the world." It is perhaps a short distance from here to suggest that the Divine Child of Buddhism, as an archetype of achieving spiritual androgyny, leads to Zen's transcendental Empty Circle of life-force energy variously called ki in Japan, chi in China, prana in India, the Stoic's pneuma in Greece, *élan vital* in the philosophy of vitalism, and even "The Force" in *Star Wars*! Lacanian and Freudian philosophy do not escape the same vexing limits to human knowledge. There are affinities between Lacan's Real and the cosmological first principle of Tao. Eros, Thanatos, jouissance, *Triebe*, *objet a*, and *zoë* are all energy-related terms that are beyond the bounds of knowledge as *connaissance*. Knowledge of the Real as *savoir* was Lacan's claim that psychoanalysis could achieve "scientific" status. He tried to formalize such knowledge through his mathemes, formulas of the human psyche that lie somewhere between pure mathematics and structures garnered from fictive literature and the clinic.

Although there is never complete agreement as to when precisely modernity began, we can certainly point to the fantasy space of bourgeois childhood as one of the key cites/sights/sites of its enactment, as part of the grand narrative of progress. Bourgeois humanist assumptions regarding the nature and development of the child with its misrecognized exclusions and hierarchies of race, gender, and class has led up to its postmodern disillusion where youth has reached a state of *stasis* as well as implosion. Postadolescence is an inversion of progress, its cancelation as a self-assured trajectory. As any number of authors in the recent past have claimed, there has been a "disappearance" or "death" of childhood in the West (Postman 1983; Winn 1984; Meyrowitz 1985; Sanders 1995; Steinberg and Kincheloe 1997; Buckingham 2000). This "disappearance" or "death" of childhood is the traumatic realization that something has been "lost," which Western culture thought it at one time possessed. Such a memory of loss, for Freud, was not considered redemptive in its recovery, but constitutive of a desire that passes into a recollection of such an object whose status remains in doubt. While the originality of the experience remains uncertain, the object continues to be striven for. A melancholia may persist or a process of mourning may begin. This "loss" of the idealized fantasy of childhood brings up a psychoanalytic concept of time that is quite different from everyday history. For something to have been "lost," it has to have been lost *twice* before the realization happens that indeed something had been "lost." One may lose a dear friend or parent and be traumatized by it, disavowing its impact on the self. A lingering pathological melancholia may set in. Freud used the term *Nachträglichkeit*, translated as "deferred action" by James Stratchey in *The Standard Edition of the Complete Works of Sigmund Freud* (SE) to identify a revisitation of such a trauma, as a loss of memory. Laplanche (1998) has suggested the term is better understood as "afterwardness" to grasp how the significance of a past event (of an individual or a nation) may change, or subsequently emerge only when it is re-lived through the occurrence of later events and experiences. "Afterwardness" captures the sense of the future anterior (what will have been) where an event in the present is already informed by its future past when it is revisited. As to just when that moment happens is not predictable. Every trauma is in fact two traumas. A loss is only realized in the future when the originary loss is confronted yet again. As Laplanche put it,

> I want to account for this problem of the different directions, to and fro, by arguing that, right at the start, there is something that goes in the direction of the past to the future, from the other to the individual in question, that is in *the direction from adult to the baby*, which I call the implantation of the enigmatic message. This message is then retranslated, following a temporal direction which is, in an alternating fashion, by turns retrogressive and progressive (according to my general model of translation-detranslation-retranslation). (265, emphasis added)

Postmodernism is this *second trauma*, an "afterwardness" experience of the originary modernist "loss" of the fantasy object of the transcendent child. Such a trauma is being experienced as a postadolescent *stasis* of a warped time and space (or as enfolded time and space) as we develop it in future chapters. Such a sense of space and time that we are working with in this introduction fits very well with the screenplays of the three Hollywood blockbuster episodes of Robert Zemeckis's *Back to the Future* (1985). Marty McFly (Michael J. Fox) through the help of a "mad" scientist, Dr. Emmett L. Brown (Christopher Lloyd) encounters his past and consequently changes the future. Each time, in each episode, as he meddles with the past the future is changed differently. In effect, Marty finds himself where he already was! "Back to the future" is the future anterior at work. This is the structure of *Nachträglichkeit* ("afterwardness"), an inverted direction of time. It helps us understand why today's youth can be said to represent the "truth" of our past blindness to the fantasy of the child. The symptoms contemporary youth exhibit are the traces whose meanings are finally being realized in the West as a "disappearance of childhood." By working through the traces of these symptoms, the past is reconstructed, changing future possibilities. Such symptoms are the "return" of what has been repressed. They form a traumatic kernel or cause as the "seeds of modernity's destruction" which were already there in germinal form when the fantasy space of the "innocent child" emerged fully in Romanticism (ca. 1750–1850) as a phenomena in itself through the writings of Rousseau (France), Pestalozzi (Switzerland), Fröbel's kindergarten system (Germany), and in England through the figures of William Wordsworth, Charles Lamb, Thomas De Quincey, and Hartley Coleridge (see Plotz 2001; esp. McGavran 1999).

Should such a structure of space/time, this "will have been" of the future anterior, be interpreted as mere predestination? Predestination claims an unfolding along definite lines. Here the situation is otherwise. The unconscious imaginary fixations or traces that were not assimilated to the cultural history of modernism now become exposed, but just *when* and *how* they are then reconstructed retroactively is anyone's guess. The moment of change of a "dissipative structure" (Prigogine 1997) which seems to operate with a similar loop of time is not precisely predictable. When change happens, this "will have been" is finally understood in the future through a backward glance. With each trip back, Marty realizes what the consequences of his actions meant for the future. Reflexivity "proper" is revisiting the trauma twice to make a difference in the course of the future. Metaphorically speaking, an event "back to the future" only takes place when such reflexivity is enacted. We suggest that the "future is now" when it comes to youth culture and its traumatic symptoms. The time of the future is postmodernism's meddling with the past, and the "truth" of such meddling places these symptoms in their symbolic place and meaning so that the future might be influenced.

THE FANTASY OF *OBJET A*: LACANIAN INNOVATIONS

Throughout our study, to grasp these emerging youth fantasies, we rely heavily on Lacanian psychoanalysis, especially on his concept of the Real and *objet a* that have been effectively developed further by the writings of Žižek. The Lacanian Real can best be captured in English by the portmanteau word "w(hole)" that demonstrates its both/and logic. On the one hand the hole within the whole designates a void that is impossible to fill, suggesting that a lack exists, and *must* exist if a structure is to remain open, subject to temporality and therefore change; on the other hand being whole it appears as a spatially closed system without lack, complete and self-sufficient. The fantasmatic *objet a* fills the lack (hole) so that the system ("reality," Symbolic Order, or Other) appears whole, so that it makes sense. Lacan calls such sense-making pleasure (*plaisir*) and distinguishes it from jouissance, yet another concept that plays a dominant role in our study. Jouissance is "beyond" pleasure. Sense making under the law as established by the Symbolic Order of society only sanctions certain expressed ways to "enjoy." But the subject constantly attempts to transgress the prohibitions placed on this enjoyment and go "beyond the pleasure principle." The result of this transgression is paradoxical. Rather than an increase of more pleasure there is an inversion to pain. The pleasure-pain threshold directly relates to jouissance, a "painful pleasure." Jouissance becomes the kind of paradoxical *satisfaction* that comes from the repetition of a symptom, a suffering that is derived from one's own dissatisfaction. It is a libidinal-embodied affective feeling. In sense making, the Freudian "pleasure principle" is at work because one is confirmed by the knowledge (*connaissance*) that the system (Symbolic Order or Other) is an authority which re-confirms identity; that is, the subject "knows" his or her place in the social order. There is a security attached to such knowing.

The Lacanian subject ($) is "split" by the gap that exists between the hole (as lack) and the whole; between non-sense and sense; between unconscious and conscious; between a "void" that exists at the "center" or kernel of the subject and the appearance of the subject as seemingly complete. In Lacan's terms this is the split between the *je* and the *moi*, a reversal of how ego psychology usually understands subjectivity. Lacan places the subject in the unconscious—as *Je*, the English "I." We might call this the Real self. Defined by non-sense, this subject can never be fully known. We can only get glimpses of its structuring, a *savoir* as opposed to a *connaissance*. Another way to think of this is to imagine trying to grasp the hypercomplexity of the neuronal relays of forgotten memory traces of a unique person (the *Je*) by always using a tool, method, procedure, or structure that is never "good enough" for the job, which always fails, but occasionally manages to grasp an insight by unraveling a cortical k(not). The "me" (*moi*), is the conscious egoic subject who acts *as if* s/he is w(hole) and complete, for Lacan this is a *site/sight/cité*[6] of misrecognition. The ego makes sense of itself only by placing a fantasmatic frame around itself, thereby differentiating itself from nonsense. The ego as subject, in effect, is recognized only through such a misrecognition of one's own lack (hole), its missing part, so to speak. However, we are all desiring subjects who want to be w(hole), to have that missing part "filled" in, to feel complete. Lacan introduces *objet a* as the *cause* of this desire. We are suggesting that the *zoë* of "youth" is the *cause* of postmodern desire. It is its Thing in the Real.

Objet a is *the* concept that distinguishes Lacan's approach to fantasy from the psychoanalytic approach of "object relations theory," at the very least, it constitutes one of its major tensions. Lacan's position of identification, desire, and the drives complicates object relations position such as W.D. Winnicott.[7] It is not the object *per se*, which is the fulfillment of fantasy, but the spectral object *cause* of desire—the *objet a* which is something "in" the object that is "more than itself" (S XI, *Four*). Therefore, it is a "surplus" that may be both intimately and biographically specific, as well as a surplus that can take on sociocultural dimensions when an iconic fantasmatic object takes on intersubjective cultural status. For example, it is not the breast *per se* that is the fantasmatic object but the fantasy that surrounds the *objet a* that comes when the infant sucks at the nipple (or its substitute). It is the comfort and warmth of the mother's body and the love that she extends to the infant while holding it that constitutes the fantasy. The brother or sister who stares at the infant at the mother's breast is not jealous of the breast *per se*, but of this affective state that the breast solicits—what is "more" in the breast than the breast itself. The *objet a* provides the fantasy of an imaginary fullness, as if we were subjects who weren't "split" (\$ in Lacan's lexicon), who don't lack, and who seem in full control of our egos.

Objet a[8] is somewhat of a bothersome concept because it is never defined, but there is good reason for this. By keeping it an open-ended concept, it allows the process of "becoming" to remain open as well. A person is always subject to change. Satisfaction is never "fully" attained. By positing *objet a* as a metonym, as a "bit" of the Real and a signifier of non-sense, it also enables us to "feel out" its *site*/sight/cite in the unconscious. *Objet a*'s "impossible" reference to its whole is the Real, or *das Ding*, which is totally unknowable. To do so is to claim to be omniscient and omnipotent—the delusion of being a God; that is, psychotic. A psychotic "lives" in the Real. Hence, when we say that "youth" is the *das Ding* of postmodernity, this is on psychic register of the Real. However, if certain specific objects are invested with *agalma*, the Greek term for an object's surplus magical quality as Lacan developed it in his *Transference* Seminar VIII, then they can provide for a youthful "look" or contribute to a youthful "lifestyle." Such objects contain a "bit of the Real" (*objet a*) on the Imaginary register. They contribute to the generalized "fundamental fantasy" of youth as *das Ding* that remains inaccessible.

The role of *objet a* in our study might be grasped through an analogy. *Objet a* is nonspectacular, and hence we have designated it by the homonym "site" whose location may well be rhizomatic and rebus-like in the unconscious Real—like Freud's amazing interpretative dreams of *Irma's injection* (July, 1895, SE IV, 107–121) and his *botanical monograph* (March, 1898, SE III, 291–295) that trace the co-joinings of non-sense signifiers. Physicists believe that weakly interacting massive particles (WIMPS)—particles otherwise known as neutrinos—make up much of the universe's "dark matter." The problem is: no one's ever "seen" a neutrino, they are only inferred by their gravitational effects; otherwise they remain undetectable. "If" WIMPS exist, the theory predicts that they contribute about ten times as much mass to the universe as protons, neutrons, and electrons of which familiar "normal" matter is made up. Lacan's theorization of the *objet a* is much like this neutrino problem that befuddles physics today. One might think of the "dark matter" of the universe as the Real, *objet a* as the *site*/sight/cite or a neutrino, and the conscious ego as "normal" matter trying to find or discover it. Fortunately, Lacan developed a way to "detect" and localize *objet a*, and that is through fantasy and anxiety.

The *objet a* is linked to desire through fantasy, through its staging in the Imaginary register of site/*sight*/cite. The *objet a* supports the fantasy which in turn supports desire. Reality (RL-real life) and fantasy are therefore intimately related. There is no separation between them. An object of conscious representation in effect has a tripartite existence. First and foremost, it exists consciously as a linguistic *material* signifier—as that which is *sayable* (cite). Second, its fantasmatic presentation as the imaginative meaning of the signifier exists at the level of pre-conscious (or subconscious); that is, its signification as an effect of perception—as that which is *seeable* (sight). Finally, its repressed effect in the unconscious that is only felt bodily as an affect in the unconscious Real—as that which is *feelable* (site). Such as the touch of the skin, a remembered smell, as the felt grain of the voice, as a taste, what we shall designate as the *skin-ego* throughout our study following Anzieu (1989). These are Lacan's knotted psychic registers: the Symbolic, Imaginary, and Real (cite/sight/site), which can be characterized by the sociohistorical and autobiographical conditions that oppress, suppress, and repress respectively. These three psychic registers will appear frequently throughout attempts at defining youth fantasies.

A fantasy is shaped by a fundamental misrecognition regarding the perception of "reality." This is a normative condition, not to be considered as a Marxian form of "false consciousness." We can't escape fantasies; we can only replace them with other, hopefully more democratic ones. Such a perceptual misrecognition is a precondition for a fantasy to fulfill its desire. As Žižek (1989) points out, reality's "*very ontological consistency implies a certain non-knowledge of its participants*" (21, original emphasis). To ideo-logically reproduce the Symbolic Order requires that "they do not know what they are doing" (Marx), or in the case of a cynical or ironical stance toward reality: "they know very well what they are doing, but still they are doing it" (Sloterdijk 1987, in Žižek 1989, 33). In this latter case, the knowl-edge of the ideological fantasy is acknowledged, if not entirely consciously; nevertheless it is disregarded to justify an advantage of playing the system at its own game. In both cases, ideology is not simply a "false consciousness"; that is, not seeing clearly from a point of view that somehow unmasks "hid-den" structures that are simply illusionary once exposed, rather ideology "*is a social reality whose very existence implies the non-knowledge of its participants as to its essence*" (Žižek 1989, 21, original emphasis). Ideology is a fantasy supported by *objet a*. " '*Ideological*' *is not the 'false consciousness' of a (social) being but this being itself in so far as it is supported by 'false consciousness'*" (ibid., original emphasis). By reversing our commonsense notion of what "false consciousness" usually implies, it now becomes an everyday event of perception, as a misrecognition. Ideological fantasy as supported by *objet a* is then displaced at the level of the unconscious Real. Exposure to the *objet a* that supports the fantasy of this perception via the imaginary register is not, therefore, an unveiling or an unmasking of reality as it truly is, rather the "truth" of the fantasy—*objet a*—makes the shift into another kind of reality possible. We can never perceive former "reality" the same way again once the fantasmatic object of support is exposed, for this means that a *lack* has been exposed, a gaping void appears. The fantasy frame of the imagination suffers a ruination. The traumatic "loss" of the fantasmatic object ushers in anxiety, a dissolution into nothingness that can result in a number of psychic states: mourning, melancholia, paranoia, hysteria. But, its ruination can also be a "traversal of a fantasy," a recognition of its powerful hold over the psyche, which then leads to a new beginning. The outcomes are never certain.

PUTTING IT ALL TOGETHER: FANTASY THROUGH AN EXAMPLE

Objet a remains a paradoxical and slippery formulation throughout Lacan's lifework. Its formulation enables an open-system logic of "both/and" to emerge, which introduces paradox and contingency into the system of thought. In this way desire is always metonymic, never fully satisfied once and for all by any "positive," that is, actual object. As the "cause" of desire, *objet a* does not refer to the normative scientific understanding of cause. It does not *preexist* desire as an entity that sets it in motion, arousing desire. Rather it is a nonspectacular element that "gives body" to a felt lack; "gives body" here refers to its constitutive function of closing the system, of enabling a fantasmatic frame to emerge around it, of establishing a spurious vanishing point so that the viewer/listener is spellbound, captivated, fascinated by what s/he sees or hears. It enables the scene of fantasy to materialize within the moment. Depending on the circumstances, that same object may lose its magical quality (*objet a*) and turn to "shit," as happens so often when a love relationship breaks up. The once most loving person turns into the most vile person alive, or the opposite can happen: the ugly frog turns into a prince once the magical kiss of transference has been blown his way. Love blossoms: the frog has been endowed with the magic of *objet a*. A scene from Rainer Werner Faßbinder's *Ali: Fear Eats the Soul* (1974) can illustrate this process quite readily.

Emmi, an elderly Putzfrau who has married Ali, a Moroccan Gastarbeiter working as a mechanic in Berlin, wants to celebrate their wedding day by going to a very special restaurant where she had heard that even Hitler himself had dined. Emmi has the fantasy that by dining with Ali at this special and very expensive restaurant, she and Ali will be treated royally, despite the disapproving racist gaze by her family, friends, and the German social order in general. Her mention of Hitler having frequented the place to Ali gives the restaurant the added historical importance and satisfaction that even a Putzfrau can now dine where the once mighty and now despised leader had. Ali simply shrugs his shoulders. Hitler means nothing to him.

The camera frames the Kellner waiting patiently, absolutely still, standing near the doorframe. The scene seems frozen as in the background Emmi and Ali sit at a table alone. There is no one else in the dining room. The next cut is a close up of Emmi studying the menu. She insists to Ali that the best food be ordered, especially "golden caviar," which is said to have been eaten only by the emperor himself. Again, the caviar, like the restaurant is bestowed a magical quality (agalma, *objet a*) that equates and elevates her with royalty. Ali once more just shrugs. Finally the waiter comes and asks whether they have decided. Emmi orders the caviar, drinks, and Châteaubriand, which seemed expensive. "English or Medium," asks the waiter. Perplexed, Emmi hesitates and says "English," that sounds good. "English it is," says the waiter. Followed by "Raw." Emmi and Ali look at each other in shock. "Raw?" she asks. "Yes," says the waiter, "Raw." "I think we'll have the other one," she quickly adds. "Medium" says the waiter. "Yes," says Emmi. "That's not raw." "No," says the waiter who then proceeds to take things in his own hands and begins to decide for them what they should and should not eat and drink. "Ordering is difficult business," says Emmi, and breaks out into an anxious sweat, fanning herself.

This scene illustrates perfectly how the change of the signifier /English/ becomes resignified from picturing Emmi's idea of living out a fantasy to changing into its complete opposite—the rawness of meat. It has been drained of all its magic to become a piece of inedible shit. Her fantasy becomes deflated as the waiter takes command; the *objet a* that structures this scene is evacuated. For Ali, he couldn't care less as long as Emmi is happy. His only objection, a mild one at that, came with the meat. They both leave the restaurant in the pouring rain, perhaps indicative of the way the power structures beat down on their bodies as abject creatures of the social order: Putzfrau and Gastarbeiter. The important point to note here, however, is the way desire emerges in these objects (restaurant, golden caviar,

Châteaubriand); that is to say, the surplus value that these objects hold speak to the social relations between Ali and Emmi. It is the desire of the Other that is at issue here. Emmi's deep wish to "fit" into the German Symbolic Order despite her marrying Ali, which guarantees her abjection. Commodity fetishism, as Marx tried to point out, rests on the social relationships of the Symbolic Order, an order structured by a political economy. Ali is a Gastarbeiter; this entire scenario is linked to the political economy of capitalist Germany in the mid-1970s. When we speak of youth desire and youth fantasy, they are always framed within this political economic problematic of designer capitalist society.

The scene illustrates perfectly well the commodity fetishism as already described by Marx. What is missing from Emmi's perception in the exchange at the restaurant is the place the Hotel, the caviar, and the Châteaubriand plays in the larger structure of class differentiations. She acts *as if* these commodities were not just simple objects to be consumed, but rather as objects that have been endowed with a *Schein*, a glow, a special appearance, and magic. Only then can an inversion take place between these "things" and the social relations that support them. That is to say, these "things" become reified ("thingified") as social relations between subjects. Even the waiter, who is structurally there only to serve, someone who is simply a helper, has taken on the magical quality of knowing what aperitif and wine to order with the meal. Emmi may be well aware that these objects don't "really" confer the status in the Symbolic Order that she is searching for, but she acts *as if* they do. She *believes* that they do. That is her fetishistic illusion, an illusion which operates in all such exchanges that are discussed throughout this book when it comes to fantasy formations.

This insight enables us to understand fantasy as a *material* simulacrum as already suggested by Democritus in fourth century BCE Greece. He had the idea that light emitting from the object (what Lacan called the gaze)—in this case we call it the *Schein*, meets the look (perception) of the viewer creating a simulacrum between them. That simulacrum we take as our "reality frame," a fantasy. Lacan went one step further in S XI, *Four*: the frame of the simulacrum was a lure, a veil that "covered over" the *objet a* of our desire and/or of our anxieties. In the above scenario, the glitz that emitted from those objects in Emmi's Imagination constituted a scene where she felt special and accepted, covering over something more foreboding: the xenophobic gaze of the German society as represented by the stare of the waiter in the scene. Emmi's fantasy frame shattered as that "raw" gaze came through with the fall of the signifier that had transfixed her fantasy. As viewers we see the Châteaubriand in another light—anamorphically for what it really was: the shit that both of them had to "eat" daily as an old lowly paid Putzfrau married to a virile Moroccan Gastarbeiter some 30 years her junior.

As a touchstone with Winnicottian object relations theory, one may liken these objects (hotel, caviar, Châteaubriand) to "transitional objects" in the sense that such objects of desire hold an identification and a disidentification in their bodily affectivity; they blink on and off in their fascination for us. In youth cultures what is "cool" and "hot" in one instance can fall quickly out of fashion in the next. This affect, however, can be contagious. Possessing the "it" of the object's power, as in the phrase— "she got *it*," confirms a group fantasy where identity becomes solidified. The anxiety of not fitting "in" becomes dissipated as the paradox of becoming like everyone else whose "cool," whose got "it" (e.g., in dress, looks, manners) means that a *camou-flage* of individuality is being expressed. This is a good example of fantasy of symbolic fiction, which acts as a stabilizing force by disavowing the antagonism that holds it together. The group's "impossibility" is to be found at its very heart. No one dares to denounce the "cool" kids for being arrogant and above it all, because to do so would be to betray oneself and not belong to the group. A high price to pay if you want to stay with the "in" crowd.

In Austria, the figure of Jörg Haider, the Landeshauptmann of the province of Kärnten, gives a material body to such a disavowal as well. Haider is a politician who constantly irritates the political scene by saying things in public that taps into the deep resentment of foreigners that the conservative element in Austria have, but who themselves would never consider coming out in public to express such a sentiment. Haider does it for them, and consequently seems to defy political suicide. He forms their "spectral apparition" in the way that he remains "above it all," telling the "truth," like Pat Buchanan's moral spiritualism allows him to say things about American capitalist greed, which his political opposition cannot. In both cases the disavowal of the antagonism against foreigners and the antagonism against capitalism enables their supporters to maintain their cohesion around these figures without denouncing their (own) racism or their (own) moralism (see also Žižek 1996b, 112–118).

For an object to enter and maintain its iconic sociocultural fascination (e.g., the hotel's historical significance, the expensive yellow caviar, the most tender part of a filet of beef) means that a sign's affective value has to be "anchored" and maintained through a particular symbolic discourse by an interest group. In Emmi's case, such status objects are maintained by an upper class. Emmi believes that by consuming them her status would also be elevated. But she finds herself "out of place." These objects have become "anxious objects," uncanny (*unheimlich* in Freud's terms) as she cannot control them in her Imaginary. The image of raw meat disgusts her. Its affective trace will remain as she eats it "medium." These objects begin to exceed her framing of them to the point where the waiter "takes over." The caviar will not taste as "golden" any more, and the restaurant has become empty, cold, and unwelcoming. Ali, on the other hand, doesn't have any cathexed investment in these objects. It's "no sweat" in his case. We find out later in the film that it is couscous that he longs for; perhaps the very antithesis in looks and taste of the fine meal that Emmi had ordered. Couscous, the staple of his Moroccan village, embodies the desire of his homeland, the memories of friends and times past, his own nationhood. We find out at the end of the film that Gastarbeiters suffer from terrible stomach ulcers. The anxiety of working in a country whose gaze is one of hate, which both literally and figuratively "eats at the soul," eats at the "Real," Ali's fundamental fantasy of who he is. He cannot "live" in Germany. As the doctor says, the ulcers are chronic, repetitive, they are the symptom of his anxiety. In three months Ali will be back in hospital again.

Emmi's food fantasies enables a better grasp of the paradoxical nature of fantasy itself; its status of being "objectively subjective," as Žižek (1997a, 119–122) calls it, neither existing in a subjective realm ("in" Emmi), nor in an objective realm ("in" the food). Rather, fantasy is a transitionary phenomenon that emerges in their overlap, in an "extimate" space in Lacan's topology, a neologism referring to the paradoxical interplay between the inside and the outside (see Miller 1994). As "objectively subjective" Emmi's fantasy, on the one hand, appears objective: the high-status food eaten in a high-status local confers her status. On the other hand, this (objective state) is her "subjective" state as well. We know as viewers that this is simply not the case. She is "kidding" herself about acquiring status, for she is not aware how she is "really" perceiving the food. Her unconscious desire prevents her from such knowing, for it appears to her that this food will indeed confer her status and make her a queen for the day, but the Symbolic Order of 1970s Germany already mitigates this possibility. She is caught by this double bind, trapped by her fundamental fantasy of wanting to belong, to fit in to a higher class, and at the same time being rejected by a Symbolic Order that makes no space for a Putzfrau who marries a foreigner. She is already denied her fantasy even before she desires it.

THE GUN AS THE LURE OF *OBJET A*

We might indulge ourselves with one last example. The repetition of a symptom is "telling" of the socialcultural order in terms of what it desires or deems of value. The material affectively cathexed object is only a lure or container for such symptomatic desire. The richness of gold is not the material itself, rather it is the fantasies of richness that gold as material can buy, ever since the moment it became "baptized" and named as such a "special" magical commodity. The special objects we buy identify a culture's wants and its needs. For an American who is against gun control, the gun is affectively, bodily cathexed as magically possessing *objet a*. Its destructive abilities are inverted as fantasies of protection and security. The sense that there are many individual and biographical fantasies that collectively come together around the object gun, make possible gun lobby groups, the defining feature being that the magical gun makes their egos feel "safe." Without this magical quality attributed to the gun, a gun lobbyist feels anxious, to the point perhaps of outright pathological hysteria if it is removed. Taking the gun away would mean giving up a large part of one's identity that is already affectively embodied. For the gun lobbyist, all the surrounding fantasies around that object would need to be mourned away. Only in this way would a gun

lobbyist survive its "destruction," to put it in Winnicottian terms, and perceive the environment differently—confine the gun to specific contexts only:
law enforcement, target shooting, war, and hunting but not continually as an
integrated part of self-identification as a gangster must.

One might say that an object only becomes "transitional" when it becomes
imbued with this fantasmatic attribute in Lacan's sense: "something is in it
which is more than itself." This surplus is what sets desire in motion. Such a
fantasy formation is already intersubjective. The proviso here being that such
desire comes from the Other (e.g., from society, from parents, from institutions, from media, and so on). The fantasy constituting my desire tells me
what I am to these others. It tells me what to desire. What these Others want
of me, or what I think that the Other wants of me. The majority of young
women desire what they think "society" as the big Other expects of them: to
be thin and sexy. To be desirous means possessing that excess or surplus,
which the Other (e.g., a young man) sees in such an eroticized body—the
mysterious *objet a*, which could be anything from eye color to the cavity
formed by the shoulder blade (as in Lazlo's fascination with Katherine in
Michael Ondaatje's *English Patient*). To be desirable is to be a wanted body.
When young women are said to lack "self-esteem," this means there is a failure of being propped up by this very *objet a* as it is housed in a body image.[9]
Lacan maintained that the subject was split (\$); it was defined by a lack for
no one could be whole or omniscient. We are all "castrated beings," castration simply refers to the idea that in order to belong to the social order all
infants must become "civilized." An infant must eventually be weaned off
the mother and accept a culture's laws, and this means having to "give up"
some part of one's "Being," to put a halt to placing demands on parents; put
colloquially, to stop being "spoilt." The *objet a* of fantasy, the cause of desire,
provides the minimum of fantasmatic identity for the subject to feel "whole,"
for the ego to feel "self-esteem."

The gun fetishist, or for that matter the gangster as well, has a particular
understanding of the Symbolic Order, as Other. It is perceived as a potentially dangerous place to live, and hence the fantasy is that the Other (the
criminal element) is likely to attack me. The gun is the great "equalizer."
It takes on this magical quality. I am perceived equally as dangerous, equally
protected, and equally capable of violence. Hence, I can defend myself
should such a moment come, otherwise I am left alone (unprotected).
The same logic applies to self–defense training like the martial arts. As a
black belt my hands have now become "legal weapons," my body empowered with magical qualities through numerous repetitive exercises that
energize it. But, I live by the code that I should not raise them against
anyone unless I am provoked. This illustrates yet another distinction between
Lacan and Winnicott. Whereas the gun and the lethal "hands" occupy a
transitional or "third space" of play, mediating the inside from the outside
that can be interpreted as a liminal or interstitial space, Lacan was quite
specific in claiming that the surplus *objet a* belongs to the psychic space of
the Real, beyond both the imaginary and the symbolization of language.

Its space appears only as a by-product, in the moment that gun is coupled to my hand or my lethal hands are poised in a stance to strike. The fundamental fantasy here is invincibility of the sovereign individual, which lies at the heart of America's Thing so humorously explored by Mike Moore's *Bowling for Columbine* (2002).

3

A Lacanian Approach to Media

The Stubborn and Defensive Ego

Lacan often said that his conception of *objet a* was his only major contribution to psychoanalysis. This was his "signature" concept, so to speak. In effect, its importance cannot be overstated *if* Lacan's philosophical anthropology, as advanced from Freud concerning a fundamental "split" or "void" that lies at the heart of subjectivity *is to be accepted*. This is a difficult concept at first to grasp, since the dominant view in cultural youth studies concerning audiences, identity formation, and literacy continues to be various forms of cognitive ego psychology and advances in Foucauldian derived poststructuralism where social discursive semiotic analysis is favored (e.g., Hodge and Tripp 1986; Buckingham 1996). This later constructivist approach in particular is an advance over former behavioral, statistical, and "needs and gratifications" research. It provides insight into how youth define and construct their social identities through their talk about the media narratives, how they "read" popular culture in the social situations that they find themselves in, such as in peer groups, the home, amongst close personal friends, and in their ethnic communities. Media "literacy" in these accounts give credence to the motivations and intents and purposes for youth judgments, and view them as "critical" consumers and producers.

Researchers take pride in the fact that they are "in the field" where the action is; getting their hands "dirty" with "real" empirical stories that their interviewees are giving them, and then analyzing the transcripts in their own private university settings, or in a team situation. Somewhat more rarely, the recognition of the power dynamics involved between researcher and youth are explored in this mix (e.g., Walkerdine 1986, 1993; Gillespie 1995). Ethnography is a master discourse that extracts the subject's desire for its own ends in the name of getting to "know" the Other better. As Fuss (1992) has persuasively argued, the "Other" is a Western appropriation, and Balibar (1991) has further shown its postmodern racist implications. It is somewhat disturbing, therefore, to at first suggest and then accept that motivations, intentionalities, conscious "authentic" responses of a unified conscious ego, the *moi*, which media researchers take to be primary data in their work are "misrecognitions" (*méconnaissance*) in Lacan's terms. The ego is a paranoiac and alienated structure whose defense mechanisms attempt to keep the *imago* (self's narcissistic image) stubbornly unified. This presents a more disturbing view of lived-life (*Lebenswelt*). The aggressivity that comes with maintaining ego integrity against others and the pleasure that is derived from such differentiation are often overlooked in media studies. The ego's defensive posture, the subject's perception of itself, of others, and the world around it is submitted to a systematic distortion, which is part of communication. We can never "truly" say what we "really" mean; we can only attempt to be heard through our own redundancy and insistence.

The display of the ego's defenses is readily available in media studies. Sex/gender differentiations are especially rich in this respect. The more obvious gender dichotomies that are prevalent between action-adventure and melodramatic genres maintain themselves through established heteronormative relations in terms of affective body responses. This is very slow to change. Many women find action-adventure narratives immature and lacking in social sophistication because they feel that they are more mature, sensitive, and refined in their interrelationships. Men have a tendency to reject the melodramatic genre as being silly and boring in the fear that they might become involved in the characters and begin to emote tears. They become emasculated, seen by their peer group as sissies. A very funny scene from Nora Ephron's comedy *Sleepless in Seattle* (1993) humorously demonstrates this. Jessica (Gaby Hoffmann) is absolutely in tears after watching Cary Grant and Deborah Kerr in the romantic classic *An Affair to Remember* (1957), which plays a *mis-en-abyme* effect in the film, a story within a story as a kind of standing joke. The men—Sam (Tom Hanks) and his brother-in-law Greg (Victor Garber), not to be outdone, begin to narrate *their* classic action film, *The Dirty Dozen* (1967) and fake crying as they describe each of the heroes being killed off. The scene ends with all three laughing as to how ridiculous it all is. Nevertheless, it demonstrates a half-truth. Such rejections maintain ego stability keeping masculine or feminine signifiers at bay in fear of an unwelcomed identification.

The classic case of ego disavowal in media research has always been the condescending and sometimes incredulous accusation that emerges when interviewees are asked about the way they are personally influenced by media (television, film). Any effects of risk or imitation that places interviewees in a bad light are avoided. Their answers are most often displaced onto others who they see as being morally weaker and much more easily seduced by media's effects. The researcher is often told that it is almost always the younger siblings who are imitating television violence (Power Rangers, Ninja Fighters, kick boxing), while their older brothers and sisters are not. For the parents it is always the younger generation, often their own children, who are at risk because of media violence—but not them, and so on. This is also an excellent illustration of what Lacan meant by desire as being always "desire of the Other." This classical media response by both youth and adults points to the way an Ego Ideal is being solicited from the researcher by the respondents themselves. They receive an "inverted message" that comes back to them as a confirmation of the way they want the big Other (society as the Symbolic Order) to see them as being media sophisticates. They desire to be rewarded for being "media literate," which is both a form of snobbery as well as ego defense. Such sophistication sets them apart from others, who may be differentiated by class, gender, ethnicity, or race. They are perceived as being in some way less intelligent and less sophisticated than them. Interviewees present themselves as being what they think that others (like the researcher who is hypothetically a representative of the power of the symbolic structure) think *that they think* that they are. A doubled mirror image—the inverted message—is being projected by them onto the researcher so they appear in the best light. In Lacan's terms, the media researcher *already* has received the answer to the question posed, but in an *inverted form even before it has been asked.* To break this circuit, the media researcher would need to disavow the power inequity (usually impossible) or expose the defense mechanism of the interviewee, which immediately runs into ethical problems.

The issue illustrates the distinction Lacan drew between enunciated subject and subject of enunciation. The first is the ego (*moi*), while the second is the unconscious I (*Je*). The "inverted message" the media researcher is receiving is coming from the subject of enunciation. It is a performative dimension that "speech-act" theorists like Austin and Searle made famous. The interviewee is saying "more" than is intended by his or her enunciated self. This "more" dimension is being performed for the "subject who is supposed to know," the media researcher as an authority. To demonstrate the difference, Lacan (S XI, *Four*) evoked the problem of Cretan's "liar's paradox" from Antiquity. When someone says, "I am a liar" we take this at face value and have no reason to believe that s/he is telling the truth. As a liar s/he must lying when s/he says this. To do so is to collapse the enunciated subject ("I am a liar.") with the subject of enunciation as someone who is honest and telling the truth. ("I am a liar who is telling you the truth that 'I am a liar.'") However, the "I" in the sentence of the statement (*énoncé*) is the enunciated subject which, as an ego, may or may not be a liar. This ego or "I" of the sentence cannot be directly equated with the person speaking the utterance (*énonciation*). The grammatical or structural "I" is different from the living breathing "I." It is this subject (the interviewee), as a subject of enunciation who *performatively* addresses the Other (the researcher). The enunciated subject may be entirely unaware of his or her performative enunciation. You could be lying, but be performatively be telling the truth (the obsessional); or you could be honest in your lie, intentionally believing that you are telling the truth, but perfomatively lying (the hysteric). The something "more" of language always appears that cannot be entirely controlled (as in parapraxes as slips of the tongue). The two levels are always separated by a gap, and always depend on the contextual utterance. This distinctive split is made in the Cartesian cogito itself. Lacan put a semicolon in Descartes's famous assertion: "I think; therefore I am," to distinguish these two subject positions. "I think" is not to be equated with *being* "where I am." Thinking and being are two separate states. The first is the conscious enunciated subject, which may or may not match the "being" of this enunciated subject (*moi*). To ascertain "being" is to identify the subject (*Je*) of enunciation. Such a position of the split-subject ruins the assurance that the interviewee's statements are to be taken on their discursive face value, a common enough occurrence in media studies.

To what extent the media researcher is considered an authorial representative of the Symbolic Order, as the "subject who is supposed to know," in Lacan's terms, will make a significant difference, of course, to the way s/he is addressed. Media identification is further complicated by a third subject position besides the two already mentioned, the subjectivity of the characters in film and cinema (Silverman 1983, 43–53; Mayne 1993). Here we are reminded of Fiske's (1993) study of unemployed down-and-out men in a flophouse watching Bruce Willis in John McTierman's *Die-Hard* (1988). As soon as Willis (John McClane) began to identify himself with the LAPD, rather than remain a rogue New York cop out to rescue the hostages held by terrorists in the building of the Nakatomi Corporation, the men promptly turned off the video and popped in another cassette. Willis was no longer an object of their collective desire. His actions no longer mattered. A disidentification immediately occurred as the plot line changed: Willis's body "turned" from being a rogue to just another cop to be hated. Just another shit, like Emi's Châteaubriand, mentioned earlier. Incidences such as these require a psychoanalytic explanation to grasp the text/subject interaction that is in play. At what point does the narrative lose its affective sustenance? As an imaginary system around which the stability of psychic identity is maintained, the ego strives by its very nature to remain stubbornly unaffected by changing circumstances. These homeless men did not want to have their pleasure ruined. Thinking and being became radically disjointed. Their unconscious disgust and conflicted position within the system found its target when John McClane "sold out." They couldn't bear to watch and be sustained by the narrative.

Talk of media "savvy" by youth, their resistance, emancipation, and empowerment to dominant ideologies are often rhetorical gestures of designer capital's thirst for the youth market, and by well-intentioned critical pedagogues who want a more just world to emerge. But the narcissistic identity of the ego is not so easily unhinged. It is inimical to desire, resistant to becoming. Put in its most radical form by Lacan: at the heart of subjectivity lies a "split," sometimes referred to as a divide, void or abyss, a Thing (*das Ding*), and what remains of the Thing—the *object a*, after it has undergone a process of symbolization. The fundamental fantasy sustaining these homeless men is their dignity to resist what they perceive as an unjust and cynical system, their distrust of the Symbolic Order itself.

AFFECTIVE BODY STATES AND *TRIEBE*

The imaginary unity of the ego, for Lacan, means that there is a devotion to a stereotypical picture of reality. In this view, media research works with *misrecognitions* rather some claim to be getting at an emic view of youthful informants. The ego/*moi* is fundamentally, both socially and internally, alienated from itself. The moment an infant grasps its unified bodily gestalt in an imaginary mirror, ca. 6–18 months old, Lacan claims that the infant experiences an estrangement from itself, a fundamental alienation. At the same time, this visual sense of the body's wholeness—that is, the privileged role of the body's image in the virtuality of perception—points to the importance of an identification of an external perceptual gestalt of another "body." This is well documented by the phenomenon known as infantile transitivism when very young child (around two years of age), often mistake another child's experience as its own. For instance, a child begins to cry upon seeing a playmate falling down in a playground; or begins laughing when s/he sees another playmate also laughing for no apparent reason. This transference and confusion between self and other is yet another indicator of Lacan's insistence that desire is radically decentered and located in the Other. This initial confusion makes possible for such basic emotions such as laughing and crying to be eventually externalized into the Symbolic Order or big Other as a signifier that substitutes and acts in my place. The Other can cry and laugh for me. The Other as media such as television and film can express emotions on my behalf. Again, this intersubjectively shared material nature of the lived-body identifies the phenomenological dimension of the Imaginary psychic register of fantasy. We again fail to see the validity of the usual criticism made of the Lacanian paradigm as lacking a phenomenological dimension (as developed by theorists such as Anzieu and Merleau-Ponty) where it is maintained that Lacan insisted on a "determined and determining insistence on the *barrier* between self and other and on the gap or *lack* that languages announces and so 'falsely' fills" (Sobchack 1992, 56, original emphasis). The phenomenon on infantile transitivism and transference forms the very foundation of psychoanalysis as positioning desire in the Other.

The essence of this *bodily* imaginary or *virtual* bodily identification of the self in a metaphorical mirror is an *alienation* that happens on two fronts, in two psychic registers: the Real and the Symbolic. We shall discuss the internal alienation first, which refers to a split within the self that establishes an imaginary bodily unity in relation to a previous disunity of the body's drive energies (*Triebe* like the oral, anal, genital), which are discordant and not entirely controllable. In this "civilizing" process part of the infant's "being," its vital energies that animate it as an organism (libido or life-instinct, Freud's *Es*, the Greek *zoë*) must be "sacrificed." Some dimension of its pulsational sources of desire—the free and unbound energy in Freud's terms that lay in a psychic dimension beyond the bounds of the ego—has to be "given up," and placed under the Law (prohibition) as its primary narcissistic imaginary ego is being formed. Here we can again introduce Lacan's notion of the Real where the drives, before they are symbolically represented in socially acceptable sublimated forms, are in full play. The Real is a psychic dimension of lived experience that is wholly unknowable and "impossible." It is beyond the representation of the Imaginary psychic register as well as the symbolic linguistic order of the signifier. How then do we know of its existence? The answer Lacan tells us is anxiety. Anxiety, unlike fear, has an identifiable object, as an overwhelming *presence*—rather than *absence* that is the position maintained by Heidegger. Anxiety makes its appearance when the frame of the ego's imaginary begins to break down. This is an encounter with the Real psychic dimension of experience, as a form of negativity. The loss of perceptual self-mastery points to an unconscious realm within ourselves where the body still remains fragmented, "in pieces" (*corps morcelé*), before the advent of the mirror stage. We might say, it is an OwB (organs without a body) in distinction to Deleuze and Guattari's (1983) formulation of a BwO (body without organs) contra Lacan, organs that require the stimulation of the "pure life instinct" of the Real to make the body come "alive." Anxiety demonstrates that the barrier between the Real and the Imaginary is never secure; an excess or surplus always escapes its organization by the Imaginary. It is this excess or surplus of the Real where the drives function, making Lacanian psychoanalysis so rich for understanding media affects. It is precisely around the rim of the body's orifices (ears, nose, rectum, mouth, penis, vagina), in their opening and closing, where a direct access to the body is found that stimulation is most intense. The skin-ego acts as both a protection as well as an organ of rupture that exposes the body to the affects of the Real—such as anxiety, fear, hysterical laughter, and so on, as moments when the body is out of control.

As an orifice, the organ of the eye plays a special role mediating incoming stimuli as it sits on the border between the inside and outside of the body, as does the skin, the largest organ of the body, which blushes when our Real self has been exposed. Throughout the study we utilize Anzieu's (1989) understanding of the skin-ego as the membrane that complexly mediates the body's inside and its outside as an enfolded space of exchange. Linda Williams (1991, 1994) has cleverly linked the most intense moments of stimulation, when the Imaginary psychic register overflows with uncontainable emotion— or to use Lacan's special lexicon for such an ecstatic release of energy as jouissance—and reverts to the psychic experience of the Real with particular filmic genres of excess. Put somewhat crudely, we can say that melodramas can bring an audience to tears, as can comedies lead us to hysterical laughter— tragedy and comedy being paradoxically inverted forms of one another, the simple lines of a smile become the inverted form of a frown. Crime and horror genres are capable of scarring the "shit" right out of us when we see bodies bathed in blood or subjected to violent and unexpected threats. Pornography can make us "cum" to orgasm and secrete bodily fluids as any red light district film house can testify, while the "action" genres, to further extend Williams's insight, also play on the very limit of the Imaginary register. In these filmic narratives the body is able to perform amazing super/suprahuman feats, especially through enhanced digitilized special effects, but at the heart of such stunts lies the instantaneous confrontation with the Real. The body can, in the next moment, be maimed, shot, wounded, or killed. There are, of course, no "pure" genres, nevertheless, the recognition of these intense affective states when we lose control of our bodies testifies directly to the importance of the unconscious when viewing such spectacles. The usefulness of this discussion, as we shall see in part III, Cyberspace as Obsessive Interpassivity, helps to further our understanding of youth's interactions with computer and video games.

IMAGINARY AND SYMBOLIC TENSIONS

In the above accounts, the body experiences a particular kind of ecstatic "violence" as jouissance. The release of bodily fluids, a sure sign that the body is under stress, approaches a threshold experience, an *Erlebnis*, where the dividing line between sublimity and trauma can easily slip into an excess, an overload, like a drug overdose. What was once experienced as an ecstatic bodily state becomes a "bad trip." Like coming to a sexual climax and suffering, as Bataille (1962) put it, a *petit mort*, a small death, the Real threshold is confronted. The tain of the mirror, to borrow the title of Gasché's book (1986), forms the very boundary between the Imaginary and the Real. It is its protective coating that enables the Imaginary mirror to form. The tain is another name for the skin-ego. Each time the tain's surface is marked or scraped—which can only be done metaphorically *behind* the mirror, in the infinite depths of the Real—a nonspectacular dark spot appears on the mirror, disturbing a viewer's self-reflected ego—his or her conscious subjectivity, or *moi*. Depending on the intensity of this "spot," there is a release of body fluids, indicating that the limit of perception and memory holding the distance to the object of anxiety has been approached and fully transgressed. This is not unlike what happens with piercing and tattooing when the skin-ego is penetrated to refigure the body's imaginary gestalt. With every pierce and tattoo the body's Real, the pain-pleasure of its jouissance is redirected—like the scratching of the tain behind the glass.[1] Here is a possible Lacanian-Hegelian innovation for media and cultural studies. It is only at the moment when the mirror "cracks" and becomes marred that there is a failure of reflection. When the subject of the unconscious (*Je*)—the split or divided subject ($)—is no longer caught up in its own disillusions, and that something in the mirror now gazes back, as if the paranoid "split" within the self is revealed for a moment. The spectator no longer loses herself in the screen of fantasy but becomes aware that she is being "framed," constituted and inscribed by the Other. "[T]he function of fascination is precisely to blind us to the fact that the other is already gazing at us" (Žižek 1989, 43). There are many dramatic moments in film where this paranoid moment in the mirror is precisely captured. To name just two examples: recall the powerful scene from Taylor Hackford's *Dolores Claiborne* (1995) where Selena St. George looks at herself in a bathroom mirror after a *Nachträglichkeit* experience on board a ferry; the trauma of her father's sexual abuse is suddenly relived, triggered by the smell of coffee he used to buy for her to warm up her hands so that she could masturbate him on a bench away from prying eyes. As she runs into the bathroom after the initial shock of this realization, splashes water on her face and looks up into the mirror—there is no image! She is starring at the back of her own head! The camera shot quotes René Magritte's portrait of Edward James entitled *"La Reproduction interdite"* (1937) where James stares at his own back as well, his reflection in the mirror is prohibited, his ego has been dissolved. The second scene is much more hilarious. In Peter Weir's film, Jim Carrey as *Truman* (1998) has become suspicious that he is under surveillance, being observed whereever he goes. One morning, as he starts his usual routine in the washroom, he draws a circle with a bar of soap around his face in the mirror and then adds two antenna-like projections, declaring himself to be from Trumania, a planet situated in the Burbank sector of the galaxy. Truman has become an astro (nought) or "zero," a transcendental signifier all to himself no longer defined by the big Other, in his mind at least. He has transcended the mirror by no longer recognizing himself in it, a reaction that the camera crew seem to intuit and mark the change with dismissive laughter. Deleuze and Guattari (1983) would perceive such libidinal "schizophrenic" behavior as precisely what is required to escape capitalist desire.

This dark spot in the mirror indicates the presence of *objet a*, the nonreflective and incomplete missing part of the scene/seen around which the visible *mise-en-scène* of the Imaginary is constructed. Again, this is why Lacan makes a distinction between the "true" subject of the unconscious—the *Je* or I—which presents itself in the Real psychic register, in the negativity or void that is at the center of ourselves, and the misrecognized *moi* or me of the Imaginary. In this way the media can offer glimpses of our "true" selves that we may deny and repress. This certainly was the promise of Sherry Turkle's (1995) enthusiasm for MUDs, which we examine more closely in our examination of the fantasies of the Internet in part III.

We see again why *objet a* needs to remain an "X," unknown. Without positing such a void, identity would be closed, caught only by the "smoke and mirrors" attached to the signifiers—the subject simply reduced to so many differing forms of discursive representations, as the reflective subject of ego psychology and identity politics with its matrix of categorizations. The poststructuralist subject confines itself to the Imaginary and Symbolic registers and excludes the Real, as theorized by Judith Butler (1990) for instance.[2] The positing of this "impossible" irreducible void, displaces desire in the Other, thus it prevents any full constitution of a completed self. It is precisely this unknowability as displaced in the Other that makes creativity possible. As Kristeva (1991) put it, the self is always "under trial and in process." Lacan, (like D.W. Winnicott), locates the locus of creativity in the "potential space" between self and Other. He does this by pointing out that the Symbolic Order, the various linguistic discourses that attempt to define reality as to what it "really is" (in Greek ontology as *ta onta*, that which "is"), is itself deficient, an open system that cannot answer all questions. There is no one who is *ultimately* in charge, although the representatives of the Law are there to claim that they are. But the statue of justice wears a blindfold. The Law as a book of rules takes us only so far. On the other side of the Law dwell the paradoxes of freedom and justice where new rules are yet to be established, "an ethics of the Real," an "abyss of freedom" as Žižek puts it (1997b).

INTERPASSIVITY AND THE MEDIA

For media studies the transference of desire to the Other leads to some rather bizarre affective behavior on the part of audience research. "Canned laughter" typical of television sit-coms, the cathartic release while watching a "weepy," the endless sighing, panting, and orgasmic squeals of porno stars "doing it" on late night porno channels, watching the grunts, groans, and hits in the world of staged wrestling, following screen avatars in chat rooms and virtual communities and attending spectacular rock concerts are just some of the ways affective transference is given over to the Other. It makes it seem as if the media are "enjoying" *for us* while we sit in the relative comfort of our seats in fascination, watching and moving our bodies vicariously (Pfaller 2000; Žižek 2002a). We laugh, cry, grunt, and groan with wrestler-actors, move with the music and even masturbate or make love while watching porn, as popularized by the film *Sex, Lies and Video Tapes.* Our bodily feelings are obviously both consciously and unconsciously externalized through the Other so as to create a minimal distance and relief from this Symbolic Order itself which, otherwise, structures, mortifies, and holds my body hostage to a particular "reality." The imaginary screen provides me with some relief. In a sense the machine is laughing for me, the actors are crying for me, the porno stars are "doing it" for me, the wrestlers in their various personas are fighting for me, my avatar is acting for me in virtual reality, and the rock star is playing songs for me. These surrogates (more specifically, surrogate signifiers) are all ways that free us up from an involvement and responsibility of such extremes of bodily commitment. It is through their very *exaggeration*, in their excess, that such transference of emotionality succeeds. We want to see and hear something "larger than life" to make its impact felt on us. Even though we might have only smiled at the sit-com, felt somewhat badly while watching the melodrama, moved our bodies only slightly with the wrestles, maybe only slightly aroused by the porno flick, and never entirely got "into" the music at the concert, nevertheless a bodily release was minimally achieved. The "rating" of the performance is often based on this affective unconscious exchange at the bodily Real.

At what point can it be said that in our interactions with the media, especially the new media that claim to be interactive, reach a moment of inversion where being active becomes being passive? The Other takes over for you but you think that you are still in control? You merely react to the interesting array of prompts that are being set up by the computer game, or educational program of instruction, which you manipulate with glee and with full bodily excitement. The machine rewards you every so often for your skillful interaction—like a sophisticated video game machine—the reward being an educational certificate given to you once the "course" has been completed, or that you have collected so many points or avatars to play yet again and prolong the game. For Žižek (1994c) this is ideological immersion at its purest! Put another way: at what point does interactivity with the "new" media reach where passivity itself simply vanishes? It is now the program that is paradoxically enjoying all of your affective states as it manipulates you into doing its biding—like an old slot machine where the hand "jerk" was all that was required. You simply "vanish" into its symbolic universe as "it" does it all for you. Although you think you are being active in it, you are being duped of your jouissance, the pleasure-pain of playing the game, and don't mind paying for it either.

A very simple example of this is the computer spelling and grammar program. The "spelling" is done for you. You no longer need to invest time to internalize certain rules of grammar. When the customary red (or green) underline comes up with the grammar check telling you your sentence it too long, you immediately begin to transfer authority over to the program. You worry that the sentence is "too" complex, and that your reader may not grasp its denseness. So you begin to revise it. Uncertainty has been introduced into your own capacity to write complex, more difficult sentences. Or, consider the reverse scenario; the Symbolic Order "vanishes" in you. There are no barriers anymore as you control all the possible interactive happenings made possible by a mind link to a computer program that you control. There is no *objet a* to encounter. You are fully immersed in cyberspace where every whim of your thoughts is relayed to a super computer that produces the results you want instantly. Žižek (1997a, 114–117) argues that it is precisely this *objet a* that harbors our very Being, the very *passive* kernel of our Real self where our fundamental fantasy lies, which substantiates the way a subject (*Je*) "enjoys" (jouissance), what late in his career Lacan called our *sinthome*.[3] It is through such an "interpassivity" as Pfaller (2000, 2002) and Žižek (2000a) call it, that we must "give up" this kernel of Being to the Other so that we can Become. Fundamentally, this means we are forbidden to run amok, literally overactivating ourselves to death. But this is what video games permit. We take up these discussions on the tyranny of interpassivity and the ethics of video games as an *obsessive* activity in part III.

Pathological Overidentification: The Fan as Predator

The inverse situation is also important to consider in media research. A pulling away from the Symbolic Order has to be achieved by those very surrogates who are held hostage by our gaze for the quality of their performances. The reclusiveness of movie and rock stars is well known, so that they can lead "ordinary" family lives. When models and stars "go out" in public, they attempt to be as non-conspicuous as possible, wearing clothes that hide their bodies, that draw no attention to them. Analogously, some intellectuals find relief in hard manual labor (such as gardening, military training, or sport) where regimentation and discipline of the body is demanded; or the reverse phenomenon where porno stars "better" themselves by attending colleges and universities. There is a "surrender" to the symbolic Other to provide a camouflage to be like everyone else; to be "ordinary" like those stars featured in *People* magazine where they appear like you and me.

Just like the spectator who must stay "passively active" through the Other so as to enable a fascination to take place and allow being caught by the spell of the performance; the performer, once offstage, must be "actively passive" to ensure that this fascination is broken. If these separate worlds are not maintained, or continually fluidly crisscrossed, then a pathology results. The actor cannot stop "acting" in "real life" (RL), while the fan cannot pull himself or herself away from the fetish object, but is consumed through its constant imitation (as in the film, *Desperately Seeking Susan*). Stars are stalked and a point may be reached where the death drive takes over. A significant number of Spanish soccer fans committed suicide in despair that Francisco Franco's golden team failed to qualify for the World Cup soccer final in 1950 after reaching the final round, so attached were they to the team. Equally as tragic was Mark Chapman's killing of John Lennon. Chapman was merely an instrument of the Other's will, a classical case of the superego's paradoxical injunction to both "enjoy" and *not* to enjoy, at once—guilt mixed with the ecstatic satisfaction of transgressing. "I remember I was praying to God [to keep me from killing Lennon] and I was also praying to the devil to give me the opportunity. . . . 'Cause I knew I would not have the strength on my own."[4] This phrase captures perfectly the intolerable level of Chapman's excitation—the jouissance (jouis-sense as the eclipse of meaning) of the inner voice of his superego taunting him. Chapman, as has been speculated, identified strongly with Holden Caulfield, the youthful teenage protagonist growing up in 1950s New York in J.D. Salinger's *The Catcher in the Rye*. Having been expelled from school for poor achievement, Holden goes to New York on a "vacation"; there, he records his unexplainable depressions that eventually lead to his nervous breakdown. To what extent Chapman confused the world of Caulfield with his own will never be entirely known. Holden's identity certainly "figured" in his life. But his court transcripts also indicate that on his previous visit to New York with the intention to kill Lennon, he had watched *Ordinary People*, a movie narrative in which Tim Hutton plays a suicidal youth trying to come to terms with his dysfunctional family. The impact of this movie had been enough for him to return to Honolulu after calling his wife on the phone to assure himself that she loved him. More amazingly, several hours before his death, Lennon had autographed *The Double Fantasy* album Chapman gave him. This gesture put off the killing yet again for several more hours. It reconfirmed Chapman's overidentification with Lennon as a fan.

In Lacanian terms, Chapman's crime was a *passage à l'acte*. He had to kill the very Thing (Lennon) that defined him, consumed him, in order to be "free" of it. The killing relieved him of the horror, the inner tension that he was experiencing. ("A *passage à l'acte* is the answer and not the question, it is an answer by which we ignore the question." S III *Psychosis*, 179). Eventually he arrived at a point where John Lennon as Chapman's Thing had swallowed up all his Becoming. Lennon embodied all his Being, his jouissance. In effect psychically he was killing that part in himself that had engulfed him, that gave him no peace. After the shooting he said to the police, "I'm sorry I gave you guys all this trouble"; as if he had finally cured himself, experiencing no guilt, a sure sign of his psychosis. At least that's one possible explanation. Yet, if Chapman was psychotic in the "true" clinical sense, he would not have had this raging "doubt" that plagued him, which is the hallmark of neurosis. He struggled with his superegoic conscience, like the figure of Gollum/ Sméagol in Tolkein's *Ring Trilogy* we mentioned in our introduction. Chapman maintained a certain distance at times from the gripping, anxiety-driven inner voice. Absolute certainty is the defining feature of psychosis. Were he completely psychotic, Chapman would have unequivocally known that he had to kill Lennon. The complete foreclosure or rejection (*Verwerfung*) of authority, which characterizes psychosis, is experienced as a command by a voice coming from "outside" the Symbolic Order. This is well illustrated in the film, *The Messenger* (Luc Besson 1999), a rather over-produced lengthy film about the life of St. Joan of Arc who is presented as a complete psychotic. She is possessed by language, by her inner voices and hallucinations. "God" commands her to rid France of the English invaders. This is her secret and divine mission, which only she hears.

Fandom is defined by the proximity of the Thing, and not its complete engulfment as in the psychotic's case. Chapman's pathology led to destroying the object-Thing, but for many fans coming too close to the Thing leads to hysteria and fainting as was so evident when the Fab Four made their first debut as the Beatles. The hysterical fan is Chapman's direct opposite. She comes too close to her fundamental fantasy, to realizing her very Being. The swarm of anxiety that overcomes her into non-consciousness is the very uncertainty that she be recognized as a person, a subject in her own right. Can she be the *objet a* for the Other? Or will she be perceived as an object of the Other's jouissance, someone to be used and eventually discarded, as so brilliantly illustrated in the figure of Penny Lane (Kate Hudson) in Cameron Crowe's *Almost Famous* (2000). This is the unresolvable tension that leads to collapse, in Lane's case, to swallowing pills in a suicide attempt. Lane was the leader of a group of young women who called themselves "Band Aids" rather than "groupies," preserving the fantasy that they were indeed *objet a* for the Other, a passive narcissistic desire because they were dedicated to a "specific" band. Our companion book, *Musical Fantasies of Youth Cultures* introduces a new figure of the fan on the postmodern landscape, which we identify as a fan(addict). This is a new relationship to *das Ding*, which cannot be compared to the "Beatlemania" of the 1960s, but neither is it pathological as it was with Chapman. Rather we argue that a sadomasochistic pact is formed with the ONE of their desire.

Death Drive and the Dead Voice

The tension between the *Je* and the *moi*, between the subject of the unconscious and the imaginary self provides a clue as to a further understanding of media violence in general. This tension is an internal alienation, which Lacan sees as a human predisposition to aggression and destructiveness. As an intrapsychic tension aggression is bound up with the ego's relationship to other people, but it is as much an aggression against the self (ego) as it against the Other. Most complexly it involves the *death drive* which Lacan, reinterpreting Freud, links with the disintegration of our imaginary unity where the very boundaries of the narcissistic ego are challenged. The paradox that is established here is one between death and desire. Here we follow Boothby's (1991) formulations in *Death and Desire* where he hypothesizes the liminal space between the Imaginary and the Real as one manifestation of the death drive. Access to fuller desire of the subject requires a *subjective destitution* of the egoic self, a traversal of our fundamental fantasies as triggered by jouissance, that more primal surplus in the Real that is never totally contained by our imaginary. We read this subjective destitution as a desublimation throughout this study as ranging from mild shocks to the ego's disintegration when the Real is encountered by the bodily affects of the partial drives up to the death drive's full effects, which includes suicide, when the full force of the drives come together. A psychoanalytic understanding of human nature becomes a way of grasping the Real subject as opposed to the imaginary one in the way this "surplus" structures everyday reality; in the way we all are subjects in process; in the way we are held by some specific formation of jouissance; in the way we continually repeat our symptoms, and in the way that this surplus of jouissance plays a paradoxical role in the pleasure/pain dialectic that structures our affective lives. Throughout his many writings, Žižek, one of Lacan's foremost interpreters, never tires in explicating the paradoxical affects of jouissance as a "pleasure in pain," Lacan's *plus-de-jouir*, where pain, in exceeding ordinary pleasure, turns into its opposite—as stated by the rather pithy sport's slogan, "no pain, no gain."

This process establishes the fundamental ontology of Freudian–Lacanian psychoanalysis; the dialectic between Eros and Thanatos, between Life and Death, between desire and the drives, between integration and disintegration, between love and hate as complexly understood within the sociohistorical discourses of the signifier. Such a dialectic of the death drive, explains Žižek (1997a, 86–90) is significantly more complex than at first seems, for it is informed by a Lacanian supplementary logic that places the death drive between Real and Symbolic death, a rather perplexing formulation. We introduce it here because of its importance when we consider, surprisingly, the television series *Buffy, the Vampire Slayer* in our book on television fantasies. To grasp this meaning, the stress should be placed first and foremost on the "extimate" space of their "between," where nature (Real) and culture (Symbolic) come to a vanishing point, a hypothetical zero state where each become informed by an original primal repression, a violent "cut" of the Law that founds our species being. Nature as metaphysically presented as Life undergoes a transformation from instinct (biology) to drive. Drive is acephalous, desubjectivized, machine-like, and informed by the excesses of jouissance. It's pure extract is the Thing (*das Ding*)—jouissance at its fullest and purist. As the monstrous, aggressive, ugly, ontological slime, a formless substance, its radical evilness asserts itself in the "impossibility" of its containment. This is Real death that revisits the subject through the crevasse of the "cut" of the Law that keeps the Real at bay to form our species identity. It seems to ooze out and escape from any possible entrapment. What seems at first innocuously inanimate and harmless now becomes alive as if the Thing has penetrated it. This threat of death in the Real is perhaps best illustrated by a scene from James Wong's *Final Destination* (2000), which effectively explores the question of predestination: Are we all fated to meet death at a particular chosen moment? Is there absolutely nothing we can do about it despite our best efforts? The Thing is out to get us no matter what.

Having escaped an ill-fated plane crash of Flight 180 to Paris, a group of teenagers mysteriously die one by one in a bizarre series of "natural" accidents. Alex (Alexander Chance Browning) the teenager who had the premonition of the plane bursting into flames minutes after takes off, and had urged his group of high school friends to deplane, is the key suspect in the series of "murders." In one scene, one of the teenagers, Sean (William Hitchcock) is in the bathroom, shaving and preparing for a shower. The camera slowly pans the floor to see water slowly moving toward his feet. The audience knows that somehow the "water" knows just what to do. Ordinary water seems animated, having a mind of its own, as if inert matter has come alive and is ready to reach and grab him so that he would slip and choke on the shower cable in the bathtub—which he does. Real death found its mark. The *demand* of the drive has this Thing about it. It won't stop craving to be satisfied. This is its excessive "denatured" deadly supplement which the Law provides us with some protection.

When it comes to Symbolic death, culture is supplemented by language itself, by the "dead" letter of the Law and its supplementary *voice* that animates it, already adumbrated in the reverberations of the baby's cry—by the primal scream of its birth. There is a jouissance of speech/voice itself, an out-of-the-body jouissance that searches for its lost object oblivious to the social order. But, back to the "dead" letter of the Law for a moment. Somehow, it seems that "ordinary" language has a "deadly life" of its own (akin to our "water" example). As a minimalist code reduced to binary signifiers it mortifies the body: labels it, holds its form, contains it, freezes it, deadens it, attempts to anchor its moorings in the Imaginary, assigning a place in the symbolic system of culture in which the subject inhabits. In this sense one can be "dead" while still alive, caught by the "prison-house of language" assigned to you, as Jameson (1972) once put it. What was alive, paradoxically has become inanimate, frozen like a photograph, the very reverse of the Frankenstein nightmare where the inanimate now walks. The image is better represented by the Ice Man, one of the *X-Men*, whose deadly breath blown on his opponent becomes so many sheets of frozen ice, the materialized deadly letter. As a totality, language as a system already preexists and transcends the being of the subject, crisscrossing and writing the body in complex ways. Language "kills" by replacing presence with absence, substituting the signifier for the thing-in-itself. This Hegelian insight that "the word is the murder of the thing" is often repeated by Žižek throughout his lucid accounts of Lacan's more difficult appropriations of the signifier's effects. We can think of *Buffy's* "slaying" with a stake through the heart of the demon as being equivalent to the word "slaying" an object. In this way symbolic language attempts to "civilize" the body's drives and place the child under the Law of desire, the metonymic and inexhaustible search for the lost object of his/her Being that has been "given up." It is this very openness, this lack, void, or abyss that ultimately defines and structures Homo sapiens as a decentered species without a predestined teleology and an open-ended eschatology.

Yet, something escapes the signifier's attempt to mortify the image, to fix and assign a place for the subject. Something within the signifier itself that causes its signification to "slip," freeing up the image and causing movement. What breaks up the deadly hold of the signifier is the death drive of the *voice*, which cannot be contained by the Symbolic Order. Such a voice is saturated with a *plus-de-jouir*, with an out-of-body supplementary jouissance. It is this excessive aspect of the voice, beyond the "dead" letter of the Law, where the tensions of symbolic castration present themselves; where the tension of the subject (ego) is at odds with itself; where the death drive's destructivity makes its reappearance as a return of the Real. Without this supplement the Law would be dead.

This is, therefore, yet another aspect of the death drive's affect between the Imaginary and the Symbolic psychic registers. Beyond the spoken voice, beyond its pure narcissistic auto-affection, its pure presence of interiority and immediacy, lies what Dolar (1996, 7) characterizes as the paradox of "the silent sound" and the "soundless voice." How is this possible? One possible theoretical explanation can be extrapolated from Boothby's (2002, 224–240) discussion on the role of the phoneme in language. It acts like a "vanishing mediator," to use a concept developed by Žižek (1994b, 182–197). The phoneme is a bridging element that constantly "vanishes" after doing its work. As the most basic element in language it occupies an intermediate zone between the structure of binary oppositions of the differential features of the spatialized body—our body "speaks" through a complex series of binary oppositions such as tense versus lax, open versus closed, rounded versus unrounded, voiced versus unvoiced, front versus back, and so on—and a level of morphemes and larger units of words and sentences that make up a language's meaning. These too are structured by binary oppositions. The selection of phonemes by any given language is able to bridge the primary spatialized body with semantic meaning. These enabling phonemes "vanish" in the sense that we are not cognizant of them, but also in the sense that in the space of their void—given that they do not signify— is where language is subjectivized. To enactivate the "objective" meaning, that is to transform the denotative structure of morphemes, words, and sentences into a subjective-expressive sense, requires that these nonsensical phonemes stand-in for the ego. We are back to a presupposition the unconscious is structured "like a language."[5] These phonemes are then perhaps the

key to speculating how a "silent scream" is possible. Phonemes, in themselves, are not structured by established system of binary oppositions. Each
culture has its own array, although the human voice is capable of making in
the neighborhood of over 900 speech sounds, any one language is limited
between 20 to 37 sounds.[6] Their combinations are contingent and have no
signified. They are self-referential within a culture's own context. Their value
consists solely in marking the difference between words. It may well be that
the mute voice that becomes "stuck in the throat" (Žižek 1996b, 93),
unable to form meaning, is the implosion of these phonemes in the unconscious, traumatizing the body, causing a reverberation in the void of the
phoneme itself. The paradoxical "postionality and dispositionality" (Boothby)
they occupy in the unconscious without an articulated meaning as non-
sense, finds expression with the Imaginary ego. Once this "silent" unconscious part of the voice is disrupted and traumatized it becomes an "object,"
it seems dis-embodied from the smooth functioning of the conscious self.
Stuttering is surely a mild form of such a trauma. Every stutterer has different phonemes that become his or her stumbling blocks. The phonemes no
longer able to bridge the body with meaning and fail in their task as their
usual codifications become frozen, stuck like the cursor on a computer
screen. One no longer feels in control of the self-assuring voice. It can reach
a place where its strangeness and uncanniness takes over the body.

This splitting-off from our "normal" self-assured presence of voice takes
on many guises: the drive of the inner voice compels us to transgress, the drive
of the paranoiac voice persecutes us, while the hypnotic voice manipulates us
without our awareness of its presence. Then there is also a "remainder" voice,
a voice that "reminds" us of the mythical murder of the primordial father as
Freud had speculated (Žižek 1996a, 149–155), as well as "warning voice" of
the Siren's whose reminder can be interpreted as the remainder of their *silence*
in their refusal of their containment of feminine jouissance within patriarchal
societies (Salecl 1998).[7] For an understanding of youth cultures this aspect
about voice is indispensable, for it can be a transgression of the Law in order
to insist on its appearance, as well as being *beyond* the Law in its sadistic and
psychotic forms. Such transgressions and outlawed performatives of an excessive disembodied voice are first and foremost encountered in music as we
illustrate through *Musical Fantasies of Youth Cultures*.

AN ETHICS OF THE REAL: TRANSGRESSION OF AND "BEYOND" THE LAW

What sets Lacanian psychoanalytic paradigm apart from poststructuralist discourse theories and countless ethnographic studies is this supplementary element of speech that refuses castration by the signifier during Oedipalization—a
time when the child finds a new relationship to language. That process when
language begins to "speak man (*sic*)," as Heidegger maintained, and the child
begins to speak "back" by using the empty signifier /I/ through narratives,

puns, and jokes. This refusal can take the form of masochism where castration has not been entirely completed, meaning that the symbolic Law is not fully operative. Oedipalization as the pivotal process between the Imaginary order of primary narcissism of infancy and the establishment of the Symbolic Order is absolutely crucial to the pacification of the internal aggressivity of the drives that batter on the Imaginary in the pre-Oedipal period. It is here that Lacan locates a primary masochism—at the border of the Imaginary and the Symbolic where pain begins to be turned inward on the self as the Law intervenes. But, this is also where the *jouis-sense* (the jouissance of failed meaning) of the *voice* in the form of the superego is located. The child being "installed," so to speak, in the Symbolic Order during the Oedipalization process is consolidated around the experience of *voice* of the Name-of-the-Father, the injunction of the Law, marking a shift from visual to auditory registers—from gaze to voice.

This "installment" is never perfect. The voice is itself split and contradictory. The child does not obey every command, nor does s/he know all the rules and regulations of the culture in advance. At times the child is punished for acts that seem, at first, perfectly alright to do. The punishment meted out seems senseless. As Freud showed in "A Child is Being Beaten" (1919, SE IV), which traces the vicissitudes of this primary masochism, the child (both girl and boy) represses this beating by the father. It remains unconscious. In brief, the Law seems at times meaningless and is experienced traumatically as an injunction. Eventually, the call of conscience modeled on the voice of authority installs the superego as a menacing image of punishment and power, symbolic castration has now been achieved. Yet, what makes the superego such a contradictory voice is its "benevolent severity"—its attacks on the ego in the name of the Law harbor in it a death drive to the point of the ego's destruction. The Law brought to its extreme self-negates itself, it passes into the obscenity, into its other side—what Lacan took to be an obligation to transgress. It begins to say, "enjoy" your jouissance, at the same time saying, "No!" Producing conflicted guilt in its very insistence that the trespass be taken. Good and Evil are not simply treated as binaries here but as self-negated opposites: Evil brought to its self-negation forms the Good, but it also works the opposite way. Evil can become a Good with no "pathological" status attached to it. Radical Evil, in this account, precedes the Good that belongs to its domain at the very point where evil cancels itself out by the Good and turns into its opposite (Žižek 1993, 83–124). It is their interchangeability, like Derrida's (1982) now famous commentary on Plato's pharmacy where poison can be become the cure and the cure the poison, that is so unnerving. This means ultimately a lack of absolute certainty of a universal ethics since the realm of justice always lays "beyond" the Law, and that *can* mean not only transgression against it but *outlawed* behavior to it as well, being a form of Good. Ultimately, the Law is always an arbitrary "cut" that is always subject to an "ethics of the Real," as an insistent complaint by a disenfranchised and disembodied voice from the Real.

Lacan in his *Ethics* Seminar (VII) insists that Kant's categorical imperative has nothing to do with common morality, with representing communal standards of the Good; rather it is *pain* and not pleasure that conditions the ethical. "The outer extremity of pleasure is unbearable to us" because it forces "an access to the Thing" (73). In the same seminar Lacan identifies the obscene jouissance of Marquis de Sade's philosophy of the bedroom as forming the internal limit of such an ethics. When the singing voice becomes "painful," when the fantasy to protect us from pain can no longer be sustained through a sublimation of the Thing that lies at the very core of our Being, the singer and those who can "hear" his or her insistent voice are confronted with the "call" of the Other as a "revelation." It is a sublime encounter with the object of the Law; the Law *as* object—as the unbearable Thing— which the voice confronts as it approaches this forbidden zone. The most powerful music places the listener on the barrier between the Real and the Imaginary to "feel" this ethical insistence. The words as signifiers no longer hold their meaning but spill over into their excesses.

History has judged that all those participants who believed that National Socialism was for the nation's Good—turned out to be wrong. It ended up being a sadistic execution to achieve the idealization of the Third Reich. The Jew is tortured and exterminated to purify the infected blood. No one can deny the evil that ensued. But what about all those who thought the dropping of the atom bomb on Hiroshima and Nagasaki was an act of Evil as well? The counter-logic that informs the superego is that without the authority of the Name-of-the-Father there would be no transgression, no injunction to jouissance, and no "evil" *per se*, and no "cut" of castration of establishing the Law. If there is no Law then there is no movement, no way of deciding what is and isn't permitted ending in a stalemate: everything is forbidden or everything is permitted. Transgression must face a limit. The transgression to enjoy (jouissance) is therefore sustained by the Law itself, by the contradictory superego that splits off as its obscene underbelly. The expectation to transgress is built into the Law. Ethics, against this backdrop, revolves around the limits of the Law and its beyond. Only there, in the extimate space of the Real, do the questions of freedom and justice emerge. In brief, the Law cannot be totalized, it always lacks, and it is around this lack that an *ethics of the Real* emerges, which asks us to take ownership of our fantasies, that is, our desires, in the way they organize our jouissance, and hence consider our transgressions in that context (see jagodzinski 2002b). This would account for one of the possible meanings of "traversing your fantasy," by suspending its hold on you. Such an "ethics of the Real" will reappear throughout our study, especially as developed in our chapter on *Buffy, The Vampire Slayer* in a forthcoming book on television fantasies. With the decentering of Oedipalization into its post-Oedipalized forms as discussed in part II, the "ethics of the Real" takes on the utmost importance for future directions.

II

POST-OEDIPALIZATION: POSTMODERN DRIVE CULTURE

4

Is Kronos Eating Our Children?
Historical Fathers

Saturn Devouring His Children

Goya's image of the Father (the god Kronos, also known as Saturn) devouring his children sits in the pit of one's stomach like the stench of bad meat, ready to be vomited out when the full impact of his crime is registered (see figure 4.1). Only then does its foul smell come up and becomes stuck in our throat, choking us so that we can no longer bear its sight. We look away in disgust as the abjected substance is expelled and we feel cleansed—still sick but on the road to recovery, the image-smell lingering as a bitter aftertaste. Goya's image seems ineffaceable and irradicable. The giant cannibal god, on bended knees, engulfed in darkness; his mad haunted eyes fully dilated; his mouth black and bloodied; his rending fingers, soaked with blood, savagely consuming his son whose head and limb have already been viciously torn from the body and devoured. It is a work of "such indelible power, it seems to have existed before it was created, like some deep-rooted, banished memory, inescapable as nightmare" (Morgan 2001). Inescapable indeed.

Why does this image and the myth that surrounds it come back again to haunt us at this particular "time" of postmodern de-Oedipalization with its host of synonymous terms such as post-Oedipus, or pseudo-Oedipus and even post-patriarchal Oedipus as the "Regime of the Brother" (MacCannell 1991)? Again, the "post" should not be read as a period following Oedipus, but more as a disruption to patriarchy within it which now takes a new form. In a society of a diminished parental function, who is this figure today? Does he stalk our youth, devouring them? In this chapter and in chapters 5 and 6, we explore the changed relations of the family and the ideological rule of a post-Enlightenment superego that supports a neoliberal global capitalist system. Is it a question of a return of a paedophilic-anal-devilish-primoridial Father of Jouissance who preys on youth as the authority of the symbolic Oedipal order continues to decenter and mutate into power plays where the drives begin to supercede desires? Rather than the paternal superego imperative of "No!" we hear instead the demand to "Enjoy!" as Žižek generally puts it. Or, is it a permissive Father who has been reduced to enforcing the power of rules?

Figure 4.1　Francisco Goya, *Saturn Devouring His Children*, 1821–1823, 146 × 83 cm., Prado, Madrid.

To come to such a crossroads we first begin with a digression: a brief historical examination of the changes in the psyche of family dynamics. In Greek origin mythology, Kronos, with the help of his mother Gaia, was able to castrate (literally, with a sickle) his father [O]Uranos, the sky god who, like the "primordial father" in Freud's *Totem and Taboo*, had become an all-powerful obscene non-castrated Father denying his children their place in the Symbolic Order. He wanted to dominate the entire "horde" at the expense of Gaia as well. The utopian blue sky had turned nightmare black as Uranos hated his children and buried them deep inside the Earth. The castration of Uranos reenacts the Freudian myth of the ritual slaying (primal parricide) of the primordial Father of "enjoyment" (jouissance), to install the Law of prohibition and incest as his sons suffer from the guilt of their act. The myth of Kronos, which is found in Homer's *Iliad* and *Odyssey*, is a mytho-poetic narrative whose psychic structure reproduces the eventual establishment of Phallic patriarchal Law as already formulated in the Egyptian myth of Osiris, a direct precursor of the Greek Kronos. Osiris was the offspring of an intrigue between the earth-god Seb (Keb or Geb, as the name is sometimes transliterated) and the sky-goddess Nut. The Greeks identified his parents with their own deities Kronos and Rheia. The Egyptian myth of Osiris and Isis, as retold by Plutarch, grounds an archaic "phallophorism" (Goux 1992, 45). The god-king of Egypt, Osiris, is killed by his brother Typhon who dismembers his corpse into pieces, which are then scattered in all directions. Isis, Osiris's wife and sister, patiently retrieves the 14 scattered pieces in order to reassemble and reanimate them. However, one piece cannot be found—his virile member. To replace this missing piece that has been irretrievably lost, Isis erects an oversized simulacrum, a fabrication or artifact that she orders everyone to honor. The transcendental signifier of the phallus is installed in the unconscious representing the restored "fullness" of patriarchy. "One" man becomes the exception to the Law for he is the one who makes it. He determines the Law for he "is" the Law, more accurately pretends to be the Law, like the 282 Codes decreed and enforced by Hammurabi, king of Babylon.

To recall Freud's early formulation of the "primordial father" in *Totem and Taboo* is to be reminded that such a father is the exact obverse of the superego Oedipal Father, the patriarch who protects and saves his children (sons), and limits the desire of the Mother to a maternal function. The baby is her phallus, which is supposed to define her fully. The primal father, like Uranos and Kronos hordes everything away from his sons, preventing them from ever "growing up" and achieving status by taking his place. Such a primal Father of Jouissance is said to "get off" on a woman fully and totally, as if all the pleasure comes directly from her, and not hampered by what an "ordinary" man imagines her to be. In their anger, so the myth goes, the sons want to kill him. By killing him, and cannibalizing his "soul," they believe that there will no longer be any obstacles to their desire. They will be able to possess all what they want—women and all his possessions. But, the enacting out of that wish fulfillment in "reality" (RL), as a done (cannibalistic) deed, brings with it an unexpected result: the betrayal of this obscene Father and the ensuing collective guilt brings about a recognition that a symbolic father of prohibition has to be reinstated so that unbridled want or demand (jouissance) can be curbed. This Oedipal Father of the "No" draws his authority from the disavowed death of the evil Father of Jouissance, thereby curbing aggressivity amongst the sons, and the aggressivity of the ego itself, which emerges historically for the first time as the empty linguistic signifier /I/ in the *Illiad* and *Odyssey.*

In a patrilineal system, the patriarch forcefully and violently takes children away from the Mother in his name, and renders the maternal as impure. It is from the Mother that the son must separate. Masculine desire is for purification and the establishment of separate spheres. There is a fear of the feminine. The Mother becomes the "Thing" (*das Ding*), which both attracts and repels. Males, especially in patriarchal societies fear women's desires. They perceive the woman as always enjoying herself at their expense. Women are said to reduce them to nothing but mere objects to be taken advantage of for their wealth or status. It is ultimately the anxiety of being engulfed by a woman's body and losing subjectivity—the anxiety of *vagina dentata* that is an earlier form of the Courtly Lady who is an earlier form of film noir's *femme fatale* of the 1940s, who is an earlier form of the *new femme fatale* of the 1990s (Žižek 2000a, 8–12). And on it goes. These are figures men create so that they can be destroyed and the patriarchal Symbolic Order restored.

Every culture establishes "padules" (patterns and schedules) to "tame" the drives through traditions, customs, and beliefs. Some part of the complete "fullness" of jouissance *must* be given up and become regulated by this Law. No matter how the different relationships between men, women, and siblings are arranged in various cultures throughout history, the prohibition of incest between the symbiotic bond of mother and child must be installed. This most primary law against incest was *already* operative in matrilineal societies where endogamous intra-clan coupling was prohibited. Exogamy was practiced through an elaborate kinship structure based on totemic food and animal taboos. Already in those societies where women rule the practice of clitoridectomy was evident. There was a widespread belief that such a ritualistic "cut" assures a woman her fertility. In a number of mythologies the clitoris was regarded as something impure and dangerous for the future child and hence perceived as a rival to the man's phallus (Salecl 1998, 143). Like the penile mutilation that served as a ritualistic access to manhood, clitoridectomy assured ritualistic access to womanhood, a blood sacrifice to a transcendent principle of fertility. Irigaray's "two lips" as a transcendental signifier seem quite appropriate in this regard as a rival conceptualization to the phallus.

Throughout the Middle East and in the Balkans, from the fifth millennium B.C. to the Late Greco-Roman Antiquity, "fertility cults" and agrarian religious festivals precede the era of dominant male ("father-image") gods in the polytheistic pantheon, such as the classical Olympian one. The Kronos and Osiris myth already belongs to the late Neolithic period where Mother Goddess *cult* worship was waning.[1] Kronos marries his sister Rheia and becomes king of the Titans and begins to symptomatically follow the example of his Father Uranos in disposing of his children by swallowing them, having been warned that he would be displaced by one of his sons. An uncastrated Father of Jouissance emerges once more who claims the transcendental phallic signifier for himself. To prevent yet another "loss of a child," Rheia gives Kronos a stone wrapped in swaddling clothes instead of the infant Zeus, his youngest son, who is taken secretly to Crete in order to grow up safely on the island. When Zeus comes of age, he forces Kronos to vomit up his brothers and sisters and defeats him, establishing the pantheon of gods. By then, the transition from the Neolithic to the Chalcolithic (copper age) has been effectively completed with the establishment of a masculinity based on a warrior elite (Heard 1963), and perhaps the incipient concept of a hero as the youngest son "who always rebels against his father and kills him in some shape or other" (Freud SE XXIII, *Moses*, 87).

Feminist scholarship of the archeological and anthropological evidence of the transition from matrilineal to patrilineal structures that occurred in the transition from agricultural societies to the warrior elite societies (Copper, Bronze, Iron Ages) posit variations of the following sequence. In the early Neolithic the Mother Goddess performs the Spring/Harvest Festivals alone. No fathers, as we understand the term are present. She then takes on a "brother," and later a "son" to help her with the ceremony; blood ties bind both of these kinship positions. In the late Neolithic a "husband" (consort-king) as a coequal representative with the Great Goddess performs the solstice and harvest rites. Blood ties no longer hold. It is during this late phase that matrilineal clan structures (moieties) composed of sisters and brothers begin to break down into a transitional fratriarchy (or martifamily) on their way to an eventual patriarchy. The mother's brother or maternal "uncle" takes on more authority as divided loyalties between matrilineal clans emerge. The firstborn sons are forced to choose between their mothers and (now) their "fathers" who have been accepted and permitted to stay in the clan by the "mother-in-law." The food-taboos between clans are eventually broken (Reed 1975, 309–318).

Finally, what began as husbandry leads to greater and greater power and management of village affairs by men. The long transition to patriarchy becomes complete when the "husband" or priest begins performing the rites alone (Reed 1975, 310–318; Stone 1976). The struggle between the "gods" and "goddess" as represented by the Babylonian poem of *Gilgamesh, King of Uruk*, for instance, is but one of many myths that chart the transition of the victory of the gods over goddesses—the Vedic god Indra over the cosmic serpent Vritra, the Babylonian Marduk over Tiamat and her monster offspring, the Canaanite-early Jewish Yahweh over the sea monster Leviathan. These stories express symbolically the emergence of order—of "patriarchal" order—out of chaos, of "civilization," out of "cultism," and of stable rational theology out of fluid mythopoesis (cf. Joseph Campbell). "Son" and "husband," "sister," and "wife" should not be read as positions in a modern family, but as complex intra-psychic kinship structures of matrilineal and matrifamilial societies characterized by clans and moieties.

In *The Forgotten Language*, Eric Fromm (1951) carefully examines three Greek tragedies, *Oedipus Rex, Oedipus at Colonus*, and *Antigone*. He argues that it is not the incest for the mother that is at issue, rather it is conflict between father and son that is forwarded (202). Oedipus is a firstborn son, conflicted between matrilineal and patrilineal loyalties. In *Antigone*, Creon (Oedipus's uncle) is again the *jouissant* Father whom Haemon (Antigone's betrothed and his son) rebels against; failing to kill him, he kills himself. Upon the news of Haemon and Antigone's death Creon's wife Eurydice takes her own life. Fromm further enlightens the struggle between patriarchy and matrilineality by discussing Bachofen's interpretation of Aeschylus's *Oresteia*, which is the symbolic *last fight* between the maternal goddesses and the victorious paternal gods. Clytaemnestra had killed her husband Agamemnon in order that she not give up her lover, Aegisthus. Orestes, her son by Agamemnon, avenges his father's death by killing both his mother and her lover. The Erinyes, representatives of the old mother-goddesses and the matriarchal principle, persecute Orestes and demand his punishment. Apollo and Athena, as representatives of the new patriarchal religion, are on Orestes's side. The argument is centered around the principles of patriarchal and matriarchal religion. For the matriarchal world, there is but one sacred tie, the mother and the child. Matricide (killing of the mother) is the ultimate and unforgivable crime. From the patriarchal position, the son's love and respect for the father is the paramount crime. Clytaemnestra's killing of her husband from a patriarchal viewpoint is a major crime, given the supreme position of the husband. From the matriarchal/matrilineal standpoint the crime is not nearly so serious since there was no blood tie between them. Only blood ties and the sanctity of the Mother count. To the Olympian gods, the murder of the Mother is no crime since it avenges the Father's death. In *Oresteia* Orestes is acquitted. The patriarchal principle wins, but is compromised in that the defeated goddesses play the minor roles as protectors of the earth and act as goddesses of agricultural fertility. In other words, it is a shallow victory as the metal ages (Copper, Bronze, and then Iron) begin to supplant the late Neolithic agricultural economy with an economy of trade.

From a Hegelian viewpoint, we can say that in the early Neolithic period a fully achieved patriarchy was "in-itself" (*an sich*), in a nascent form. By the late Neolithic it had emerged "for-itself" (*für sich*) but had not yet reached an ideological status "for all" (*für Alle*) position, which only became established with the Monotheistic patriarchal religions (Judaism, Christianity, Islam). What all these early myths of patriarchy indicate (Uranos, Kronos, Osiris) is the paranoiac structure of patriarchy and the absolute fear of betrayal of the Father by his offsprings who want to displace him rather than confirm him—the divided loyalties between love and hate of the Father by his sons. The Father of Jouissance, of full phallic power, must assume betrayal for he holds possessions his offsprings are fully denied. *The father is, therefore, a symptom of the son.* In Freud's four-stage sequence of this development, he begins by positing a primal horde—the primordial father and his females, which can be characterized as Paleolithic hunting and gathering societies. Mothers are not as yet referenced. (Historically, this seems suspect since feminist paleoanthroplogical scholarship has argued for the greater prominence of gathering and motherhood during this time (e.g., Tanner 1981). This can be countered by claiming that meat was highly valued in these early societies. The jury is still out as to the importance of gathering in the Paleolithic.) In the second stage, the primordial murder of the father gives rise to Mother-Goddess worship and matriarchy. This, too seems suspect since there is no direct evidence of a matriarchy in the archeological record (Biehl 1991). Here we can characterize the Mesolithic transition (semi-nomadic hunting bands) to the early Neolithic (without pottery) as characterizing this period. The emergence of matrilineal clan structures would be a more accurate description. Incipient patriarchal forms such as husbandry are now formed. Freud's third stage (of which Osiris and Kronos are examples) takes place in the middle to late Neolithic (with pottery) where matrilineal societies begin to experience a breakdown as patriarchal models "for themselves" are formed. Lastly, the Chalcolithic transition (monotheism—Islam, Judaism, Christianity) presents a fully installed patriarchy with the patriarch/ Father as being Divine, like Moses. In the Western and Mid-Eastern context it is the sons who assure and praise the patriarch's Divinity. In Christianity, Jesus Christ becomes the incarnate God on earth, confirming the status of the divine father (God) in Heaven. There is no more need of woman-mother. Mary performs a miraculous "virgin" birth, while Joseph is not considered to be the "real" Father. The biological Father has been replaced by a Symbolic Father. This repression of feminine difference establishes a homeosocial pact where homosexuality itself becomes repressed. (Like the trouble with contemporary Catholic priesthood besieged with accusations of pedophilia, both factual and hysterical.) In Islam, the prophet Muhammed provides the divine path to Allah through the "word" of the Qur'an and the Sunna. Both Islam and Christianity take Ibrahim/Abraham as a confirmation of Allah's/God's divinity. Both take him to be their foundational prophet. The complete trust of Ishmail/Isaac in the vision of his Father, Ibrahim/Abraham to sacrifice him to Allah/God confirms the absolute trust in this monotheistic superego that has a unifying effect. Karl Jaspers (1953) proposed a theory that an *Axial Age* (800 to 200 B.C.E) had emerged during this time, which grounded several major religions and philosophical foundations based on monotheistic thought.

When *Can* You Eat Your Son?

Previous to this point of monotheistic unification, betrayal of leadership was always possible. The tyrant remained guarded and could die a tragic hero when killed, not losing "face"; that is, not sacrificing his honor, code, or "diamon" (in Greek, a divine thing)—that something which is "more" than himself (*objet a, zoë, agalma*). Like the Japanese Samurai of the twelfth century, forms of seppuku or ritual suicide were preferred to loosing face (Heard 1963). In the name of rebelling against restricted power of the tyrant, a brother or a son who was not next in line could claim authority and broaden the laws that were in place as a political gesture to ensure support. In effect, a new tyrant was instated who excluded others. In other words, a symbolic Father had been established "for itself," but still had not taken on an ideological "for all" form as will be eventually coded by the Judaic Tanakh (Torah, Nevim, Katuvim), the Christian Bible and the Islamic Qur'an. In contrast, Abraham is asked by Yeweh (Adonai) to "lose face" and suffer a subjective destitution. He is asked to kill what is most dear to him in the name of a greater Cause without any explanation. His faith tested by having to kill what is most precious to him—commit an "ethical act" by destroying his *objet a*. This is why such a God is so jealous says Žižek (1999b). The Cause must have no rivalries. One must love the Cause/God more than family. (This explains why youth ratted on their parents during Nazism, and why the Irish Republican Army (IRA) asks for the same loyalty. The Cause stands above everything. One is willing to die for it, betray loved one's for it.) Abraham is placed in an impossible position: to decide between the two sides of YHWH—a symbolic God of earthly rules that states "thou shall not kill," and what appears as an irrational injunction by the same God—to lose a son, the reason that is ultimately unknowable.

The decision Abraham must make is not unlike Kierkegaard's "leap" of faith that lies at the very limit of reason. Faith is an irrational act. However, this leap of faith can only take place if Abraham massively represses the evidence before him and obeys Adonai—*his new Master*. Only then is the conflict inside him resolved. Is Abraham psychotic? Hearing voices inside his head, or is this "call" from the Real an inspiration to ground a greater Unity? It is his irrational response to Adonai's demand that raises such an "ethics of the Real." This side of YHWH (Adonai) refers to what can appear as amoral, and seems outside of human control as already found in the opening chapter of Genesis, referred to as Elohim (Schulweis 1994). Elohim is Nature as such, and points to that dimension of human experience which simply "is" (e.g., the Earth's gravity, accidents, Nature), exposing the impossible gap that exists between "is" and the "ought." There is a dimension of Nature that exists "out of human control," beyond our rational grasp. It belongs to the sublimity of Nature, what Kant referred to as dynamic and mathematical sublime. The story of Abraham raises the question whether there is such a suprasensible domain of the unknown in us? An "original sin" or pathological stain that cannot be symbolized, which is beyond ethical consideration of the Good; namely a pathological ego that is capable of murder in an act of radical evil (Žižek 1993, 83–134). When such a higher Authority is obeyed a massive repression must take between "what is seen" (I am about to kill my son) and listen only to the "Word," even when that "Word" seems Evil and irrational. Was Abraham asked to commit a *diabolical* act of Evil by an inner pathological superego that knows only jouissance? Why was Abraham ready to execute his son unconditionally, an obvious example of the death drive? Has not the name for such a superego historically been the Devil? Can such radical Evil itself embody an ethics by a higher power since Abraham is asked to commit it? Such impossible questions bring Abraham's act to the brink of undecidability between Good and Evil.

Abraham is pressured by a superego that is beyond his control, to act against his own self-interests—by his own death drive. (In Judaism that sacrifice of the son is repressed, but in Christianity that repression is lifted. God's son is sacrificed.) Through this act (which is stopped by YHWH's messenger before the moment of execution, but the intention has already been "committed"), Abraham becomes a "proper" Oedipal father. He has gained his symbolic authority through an unconditional faith in his willingness to execute the act. Rather than such a faith being "blind" (he believes without knowing he believes), there is a faith in the "irrationality" of the act proving his certainty in Allah/God's wisdom. The father and son sharing this faith speaks to an unbreakable bond of unquestioned loyalty between them. The son believes that the father is acting in his best interest, out of the purity and goodness of his heart, even if that means his own death. Read in this way, Abraham was willing to commit a diabolical act of Evil to usher in the Good.

Is this not the very same gesture that Palestinian suicide bombers enact in their impossible struggle with Israel, believing that their sacrifice will usher in a new Good? Palestinian Islamic Resistance Movement, known as Hamas ("Courage" in Arabic) has a collective faith in its particular interpretation of the Jihad (The Holy War) to liberate Palestine. They give up their lives to a greater Cause then themselves. Is this an act of diabolical Evil or Good? How different in kind is this from the same act of faith when mothers and fathers send their sons (and now daughters) off to war? An unquestioning "irrational" act that war is indeed for a greater Cause? The sons, daughters, and parents know that death awaits—it is a question of how soon. When such a centering Cause or grand narrative begins to decenter many competing possibilities come to take its place. Contemporary global politics is being shaped by a recentering of authority as staged by the United States in the figures of George W. Bush and U.S. Attorney General John Ashcroft as the *self-acclaimed* representatives of postmodern Christian fundamentalism, and Osama Bin Laden, as *the self-acclaimed* representative of postmodern Islamic fundamentalism. They are two sides of the same antagonistic coin: Western (Texas style) and anti-Western (outlaw style, wanted "dead or alive"). Once again, the fundamental question of a monotheistic Cause is upon us, this time on a global scale.

FROM FREUD'S JUST-SO STORY TO FALSE MEMORY SYNDROME

For Freud the Father-of-Enjoyment as the one exception who possessed all the women and material goods deified through the guilt of patricide by the fraternity of brothers was nothing other than a neurotic fantasy. It was a myth set up to justify a retreat by the sons in the face of participating in full unbridled jouissance that lead to a death drive. Eventually they would destroy each other. A transcendental figure held them together. The jouissant Father was always "dead" and ruled in name only. In light of feminist scholarship, it seems that Freud's myth of the ritual killing of the obscene "primordial father" in *Totem and Taboo* appears rather dated. The event itself did not happen in the Ice Age as he hypothesized, but more likely to have occurred during the beginning of the Chalcolithic period. It should not be forgotten that Freud himself called his hypothesis a "just-so" story. What he meant by that, however, is intimately connected to his theory of deferred action (*Nachträglichkeit*). The event may never really have happened; nevertheless it was accepted as being *true*. The unfolding of psychic life may be decisively influenced by an event *that may never have occurred*. "Occurred" here has an ambiguous meaning. The event may not have "occurred" because the person was traumatized by it, or it may not actually occurred, but the person thinks that it has. For example, the fascinating case of Binjamin Wilkomirski, the author of *Fragments*, the memoir of a young Latvian Jewish orphan's early life of struggle in two concentration camps turned out to be a "hoax." Written by Swiss-born Bruno Doessekker, the book was eventually withdrawn from circulation by Suhrkamp Verlag after irrefutable evidence convinced the publishing company that the story indeed had been "made up." In these cases a *Nachträglichkeit* experience as a contingent revisiting can take place where a primal scene's formative power is constituted retroactively. This is not unlike the repression that takes place in Freud's (1919, SE IV) analysis of "a child is being beaten" where no memory of the beating by the Father is recalled by the child.

The cases of "ritual abuse" of children by parents, prevalent as a symptom in the United States from the early 1980s through to the mid-1990s, also turned out to have been made up. The "recalled memories" of ritual abuse was bundled up as a sensational narrative, a fictive story to quell the paranoia of a "moral panic" surrounding deviant sex, child abuse, pornography, abduction, brainwashing, secretive religious cults and satanic worship (Ian 2000). The father was identified as a sexual abuser of his daughter who suffered from False Memory Syndrome (FMS). The combination of feminism, child-protection groups, and the devastating statistic that approximately one-third of all girls in the United States were said to have suffered some form of child abuse, led many psychotherapists into diagnosing, mostly white women of ages between 25 and 45, as having FMS. Most of these women had the same grim lives as their mothers: early pregnancy, unkind husbands or boyfriends, boring jobs, little money, and no education, leading to an anxiety in the over-presence of the Father. By blaming the Father as their sexual harasser, and the cause of their troubles, the anxiety of what was ailing them was lifted. This was taken as a "real" event, rather than a fantasy, which helps explain why it was women struggling with bad marriages or abusive relationships who suffered FMS. Some claim that women who missed embracing feminism found solace in their mental dilemma as being a victim.

The similar structuring fantasy holds when the "nuclear" family—as fantasized in heteronormative social imaginary—is threatened by stories of sexual child abuse. Rather than recognizing such abuse as occurring *within* "nuclear" families themselves the figure of the homosexual man capable of all sorts of perversity to children becomes the roving pedophile who is then demonized for such acts.[2] This releases the anxiety by locating the sexual abuser once more outside the home. It is the father, again, who is capable of such abuse who has come "too close" as an object of anxiety (in the Real), who cannot be faced.[3] It is the betrayal of the child's fundamental trust, which is at issue in incest cases as shown by Herman's (1981) classical study of father–daughter incest.

POSTMODERN KRONOS: DEVOURING HIS CHILDREN'S *DASEIN* FOR PROFIT

What sort of "Father" then rules over the new landscape of postmodernist designer capitalism? We left the story during Greco-Roman times, with the myths that inspired Freud. The obscene Father's rule eventually established an Oedipal Father of patriarchy. In *Moses and Monotheism* (SE XXIII, 1939) Freud's last work, the question of authority of the Father is revisited. Moses the Lawgiver of the Torah, who imposes monotheism and does away with pagan polytheism, is also killed by his sons only to return as the psychic structure of Jehovah (Yahweh, YHWH), a vengeful, jealous, and irrational superegoic figure—a two-sided God of love and hate and of capricious pre-destination. The guilt for this patricide, Freud says, is the reason Christians understand Jesus's death as sacrificial. "The 'redeemer' could be none other than the most guilty person, the ringleader of the company of brothers who had overpowered their father" (87). "Judaism had been a religion of the father; Christianity became a religion of the son" (88). Žižek's (1999b, 318–319) reads Moses as a Father figure of will and prohibition who enforces prohibition but remains ignorant of jouissance. As for Christ's crucifixion, he argues (2001a,b, 68–84; 2001c, 45–60) that this not a sacrificial act of redemption but an exemplary revolutionary "ethical act" of freedom, an act as "feminine renunciation" again raising the ethical ambiguity of the death drive as mentioned earlier.

Žižek (1999b) links modernist authority with the stage set by Judeo-Christian religion. The rise of monotheism over polytheism set the direction for rise of the modern subject. Moses's God prohibitions dissolved the old sexualized Wisdom [of matriarchal societies] clearing the space for a nonsexualized understanding of abstract knowledge. Objective scientific knowledge, we would say, did not become fully secularized until God recedes from the scene of prohibition. As a number of historians of science have traced, the concept of an authoritative God still first appears "outside the system" during the late Gothic early Renaissance period. God's authority is then rationalized as being "within" the system through the various forms of humanism (notably Aquinas) that arise with the recovery of Greco-Roman knowledge by literati. Finally God "withdraws" from interfering with the system, becomes a "hidden God" in Lucien Goldmann's (1964) terms with the rise of the Deists and the paradigmatic notion of science based on hypo-deductive methods. The founding of the nation-states and liberal democracy is based on such noninterference between Church and State. Both Thomas Jefferson and George Washington, for instance, were Deists. With such a noninterfering God, science becomes discovering Nature's laws, for a certain period of time these are still considered God's laws. Eventually, Nietzsche will famously pronounce that "god is dead" as the secularization of authority is complete at the turn of the twentieth century. Effectively, this pronouncement was also the "death toll" of the Oedipal Father as well who drew his moral authority from Judeo-Christian roots. God, after all, had defeated the Devil, the obscene Father of Enjoyment. As Verhaeghe's (1999b) study of Freud's cases indicate where fathers appear, all of them were weak figures. Lacan notes that the authority of the Oedipal Father was already waning at the turn of the twentieth century. From the sovereign authority of King and Pope to their leveling as elected presidents, and first prime ministers, to the judges that are representatives of the Law, the Symbolic Order rests on the fantasy that the interests of the nation's citizen's are being looked after. What emerges from such a scenario is the paradox of the Superego Freud had identified when the Father of prohibition is weakened, then the temptations to transgress the Law arise. As Žižek (2001a) humorously puts it, "the more Coke you drink, the thirstier you are; the more profit you make, the more you want; the more you obey the superego command, the guiltier you are—in all three cases, the logic of balanced exchange is disturbed in favor of an excessive logic" (23–24). This excessive logic of designer capitalism emerges when the Father of Prohibition retreats and a permissive society emerges where the expectation to fulfill one's passions is wedded to the machinery of productive capitalist desire of consumerist fantasies. Culture consists of the mythically sanctioned circulation of goods and the economy of social and sexual exchange, whereas religion (spirituality) provides the very limit of such exchanges. Against Althusser's thesis that the economy is the "last instance" determiner of consciousness, it is more the case that the enframing determinations of religion as the spiritual force of the Symbolic Order is more at issue. The demands "it" makes on human sacrifice, like the horrors of clitoridectomy, the excesses of potlatch ceremonies, circumcision, mock crucifixions, and so on. With this religious limit lifted through the separation of Church and State (at least constitutionally), *the contradictory split in the Superego widens.* On the one hand the message is to obey the secular Law while on the other hand there is the pressure always to transgress it. This contradiction is embodied in the ideology of designer capitalism itself. Designer capitalism is driven by an insatiable thirst of transgression. Its very ideology is to continually overcome crisis that mark its *productive limit,* so as to continue economic growth, always searching for new markets to take under its wing through various forms of postcolonial benevolent interventions where cultural difference is embraced and eventually assimilated under its logic. The creation of fantasies to ensure that the motor of its logic continues to run is absolutely crucial, while the "fetishism of the new" through commodity production and consumption ensures its survival (see Snyder 1988). The subject of desire as defined by the void of lack emerges full blown with consumerist postmodernity as an ideology "for all" (*pour tous*); its nascent beginnings, (*en-soi*) start with the creation of childhood in Enlightened

Romanticism with the emergence of liberal capitalism and nation-states; this subject of desire is given for-itself status (*pour-soi*) through a series of Reform Laws in England and universal suffrage approximately at the turn of the century with the advent of advertising and the creation of fantasy as surplus value developed by the economic monopoly capitalism, and finds its full expression in contemporary society. We are "plagued by fantasies" to echo Žižek. This movement was brilliantly traced by Baudrillard (1981) through his innovative rewriting of Marx's political economy along symbolic lines. He detailed the eventual decentering of the sign system of nascent modernism that categorically and hierarchically held subjects in their "proper" social positions. This gave rise to greater social mobility by the turn of the twentieth century, a trajectory that continues to the *simulacra* of contemporary bodies of designer capitalism and poststructuralist thought. What Žižek's appropriation of Lacan adds to this is the structural equivalence between the subject of fantasy and the fantasy of capitalism.

We can theorize the question of creativity that the fantasy of "youth" provides from this context. What we have in mind is a sort of reverse generational scenario of Richard Fleischer's *Soylent Green* (1973). Set in the year 2022 the narrative projects an overpopulated world suffering from the Green House effect where the population is fed different color-coded pellets of food produced by the Soylent Corporation. Soylent Green, the most nutritious of the products, is made from the euthanized bodies of willing old and poor people in exchange to ensure an inheritance for their loved ones. As it turns out, younger not so willing bodies are also processed to make the green substance for human consumption. In this light, the figure of *Kronos Devouring his Children* takes on a contemporary meaning if Kronos is designer capitalism consuming the raw energy of youth for its own gains. To come to such (what some will think) a bizarre analogy is to revisit a well-known figure, Antigone. A great deal already has been written on Antigone by contemporary scholars to justify her as an exemplary figure for the (post)modern ethical question of judgement and decision, to claim her as a representative for a particular Cause since Lacan immortalized her in S VII, *Ethics* as a beautiful object raised to the dignity of the Thing. Žižek (re)confirms her action as an ethical *act* after Lacan, Butler (2000) forwards the confusion of the kinship relations to ward off, yet again, heteronormativity, and opens up a space for other kinship structures, while Irigaray (1985, 219–220 esp.) sees her as a figure of sexual difference, caught by a primary masochism that women suffer in patriarchy. Copjec (1999) takes a turn by arguing succinctly the ethical problematic Antigone encounters when the intersection of freedom and death come together in a death drive. Clarifying Lacan's notion of the ethical act, Antigone presents a sublimation of Creon's demand as an ethical act of "perseverance," Freud's *Haftbarkeit*, which has intonations of legal responsibility (258, 260). Her position comes closest to our own. All trounce Hegel's *dialectical* reading of the conflict between two equally rational ethical claims to *Sittlichkeit* as the progress of *Geist*: the conflict between the Law that forbids the burial of state enemies and Antigone's familial claim of conscience. Yet, Hegel was in search

of the civic space that could be opened up to consciousness to sublate the
matrilineal/patrilineal conflict, between state and kinship. Perhaps that was
why he was so fascinated by Antigone? Not any different than contemporary
times, which is why Antigone still fascinates the scholarly community.

We can understand Antigone's defense of her brother Polyneices from
Creon's injunction not to be buried in yet another way. We are not aware of
a reading that takes Agamben's (1998) thesis of the *homo sacer* as an archaic
figure in Roman Law to heart and applies it to Polyneices.[4] Could
Antigone's "claim" to the ancient "divine laws" be referring to that realm
which the Greek polity shuts out—"bare life" or *zoë*. Agamben's decisive
argument claims that Greco-Roman polity is founded on the split between
"natural or biological life" (*zoë*) and life as *bios* which is politically qualified
as being virtuous and good. Isn't this another distinction between drive and
desire? The exceptional figure of the *homo sacer* arises to mediate these two
different conflicted notions of life, a figure whose essential simple dignity of
vulnerable life (as *zoë*) was both recognized and denied at the same time
since the sovereign had complete power to proclaim a death sentence. This
peculiar inclusion into the polity through exclusion produced a *sacred* body
that could be killed, but not *sacrificed*. It would seem that Polyneices fits the
archaic figure of the *homo sacer* rather well. He is a sacred body (Creon's son,
of royal blood) who was killed but not allowed to be sacrificed in accordance
with ritual practices of being buried "properly."

Antigone's insistence on the ancient "divine laws" that require a sister to
bury her brother that override the new "human laws" Creon is mandating,
at first sight, seems to be "simply" an ethical issue over the dignity of human
life—of *zoë*. The stakes, however, are high read from Agamben's perspective
and Lacan's construction of an ethical act by which she stands up to Creon's
demand by honoring the unrepresentable singularity of her family's *atè*,
which her brother represents. The two readings can come together if the
misfortune, as well as madness of the Labdacidean family that she identifies
with—the familial *atè*—is interpreted as belonging to the immortal life of
zoë, a realm that escapes the *bios* of the state's clutches and refuses its
demand. Her brother's bodily "life" (*zoë*) identifies the family's *immortality*
as well as its fate. Agamben's perspective would suggest that Creon's Law is
founded on the exception to create the rule. The contradictory figure of
Polyneices as *homo sacer* is a Master signifier that holds the Symbolic
Order's ethical accountability together. Such a figure exists in an "extimate
space," both inside and outside the system at once. *Homo sacer* confirms the
sacredness of life by denying it, doubling the suffering, so to speak, through
such an abjection. As *homo sacer*, Polyneices stands outside both judicial
(human/Creon) as well as outside religious (divine/Antigone) spheres. The
killing of such a figure by a sovereign is considered *unpunishable* on the
grounds of protecting the State. By spreading dust over her brother's body,
Antigone's action answers to this contradiction. It does honor to both family
and the vulnerability of bare immortal life, an act of reverence and not
idealization.

Read most radically, life as *zoë* belongs to the private sphere—the inner essence that *refuses* to be entirely processed into the biosubstance of Solyent Green. It exists outside the control of the Law and out of the clutches of the State, although it is also intimately tied to it in various forms of transgression. Its force as a transgressivity "to and beyond the Law" can be equated with the *desublimated forces of the death drive* (*id, Triebe, jouissance*) since there is a denial of castration, and hence an uncivilized "bestial" sphere emerges that is technically "outside" the Law by not being recognized by it. The issue, therefore, is how bare life is to be interpreted? Whether it is merely the "finitude of man" as interpreted by nineteenth-century biological sciences, or the very place of human *freedom*. If we choose the latter, is this freedom tied to Romantic views of *zoë* as a "fountain of youth" that is divine and sacred, or should this realm be secularized, atheistically formalized as in the philosophy of Alain Badiou? (See Hallward 2003.) He stands diametrically opposed to Jungian and Aquarian New Ageism, which would preserve this divinity?[5] We follow Copjec (1999) in our own way in support of a psychoanalytic body that is conceived not "as the seat of *death* [of biological sciences], but as the seat of *sex*" (248, original emphasis). "[C]ontrary to Foucault's claim, the sexualization of the body by psychoanalysis does not participate in the regime of biopolitics, *it opposes it*" (ibid., added emphasis).

Zoë, we would say, is a metaphysical *reproductive creative force of the drive*. As a potentially dangerous sphere to the state, the contradictory figure of the *homo sacer* is a way to negotiate this potential threat to sovereign (and national) identity. Pirates, concentration and refugee camp victims, those on life-support systems, persons who undergo euthanasia, at one time those who were HIV positive, and the many American Iraqi citizens held for investigation in jails throughout the United States would all be forms of *homo sacer* for Agamben. They are a potential threat or problem to the State. As is well known, Foucault argued that modernism politicized "life" in order to "free and liberate" it through the nation-state, resulting in biopolitical forms of power and control. "Life" as the private sphere (health, housing, welfare, and living conditions of the population) began to be micro managed indirectly through state discourses. In the second half of the eighteenth century there was "the entry of phenomena peculiar to life of the human species into the order of knowledge and power, into the spheres of political techniques" (1980, 141–142). Power, in his view, became decentralized, more insidious, and difficult to directly identify.

This incorporation of "immortal life," unending youth, occurs precisely when the fantasy of the "innocent or divine child" of Romanticism came to paradigmatic fruition with figures such as Schiller,[6] Blake, Wordsworth, and Coleridge. Creativity and genius were linked to childhood, a *sacred* sphere. This was also the height of the castrati phenomenon—their transcendental voices scraping the gates of heaven in their purity. The most famous and legendary castrato of all, Carlo Broschi (a.k.a. Farinelli) lived during the second half of the eighteenth century (1705–1782).[7] With the rise of liberalism and the sovereign individual that preserves a private space, along with basic freedoms, the contradiction between individual and the state is a structural constraint of liberal democracy. Locked within capitalist machinery, there is a the continual uneasy balance between encroachment on civil liberties by the state and unbridled competitive individualism. The contribution that Agamben makes is to supplement or complete Foucault's thesis by showing that life as *zoë* can be traced to at least Greco-Roman times, reestablishing a direct link to sovereign state power which Foucault dismissed.[8] Law and life are directly related and not so ambiguously decentered, a criticism echoed by Hardt and Negri (2000) in their praise for Foucault and criticism of his structuralism, which failed to identify the *productive* dimension of biopower. As they put it, "power is the production and reproduction of life itself" (24). "Biopower becomes an agent of production when the entire context of reproduction is subsumed under capitalist rule, that is, when reproduction and the vital relationships that constitute it themselves become directly productive (364).... Life is no longer produced in the cycles of reproduction that are subordinated to the working day; on the contrary, life is what infuses and dominates all production" (365).

While "bare life" as *zoë* is constantly being processed into *bios*, like Soylent Green, by the capitalist technological machinery (for example, DNA is decoded as the sequences of A, G, C, T, that stand for the chemical bases of purines and prymidines, while the genome is said to be composed of the color-coded sequences of over three billion letters) something always *escapes* which is why our insistence that *zoë* is yet another name for jouissance, the "lamella" of life as Lacan put it, yet another name for the missing elixir of libidinal "life" that would complete a person, make them stay "forever young." It is this impossible kernel of human *existence—la nuda vita*—the Real that refuses to be entirely colonized. As private life is continually invaded by public life, *zoë* as bodily jouissance is constantly erupting through aggressivity and violence as the faith (social capital) in the Symbolic Order diminishes in designer capitalist economies that push for consumerism. The neighbor, immigrant, refugee become a threat.[9] Given that neurosis for Freud was the human condition—the self is chronically out-of-joint, infantile narcissism remains as an existential surd that refuses total capture. Lyotard (1992a) refers to this surd as "infantai," as "that which resists, after all. But something will never be defeated, at least as long as humans will be born infants, infantes. Infantia is the guarantee that there remains an enigma in us, a not easily communicable opacity—that something is left that remains, and that we must bear witness to it" (416). It is this "miserable and admirable indetermination" of infancy, Lyotard (1992b) thinks, which can resist the Enlightenment ideal of "emancipation," the "inhuman" of systematization and complexification disguised as "development." The goal of emancipation is to "secure full possession of knowledge, will and feeling; so as to give oneself the authority of knowledge, the law of the will, and control over one's affections" (401). *La nuda vita*, "bare life" as *zoë* becomes the possible place of transgression and resistance.

TODAY'S MONOTHEISM AS THE ONE

The importance of raising monotheism within the context of postmodern youth cultures today is the question of its "singularity," which continues to be a profound issue today. Lacan's reading of the monotheistic foundations of Western subjectivity in SVII points to the impact made of positing ONE, the singular invention of God, as a violent rupture that creates subjects and their worlds around a void. With postmodernity questioning grand narratives it is not difficult to see how the ONE has become theologically interesting and dangerous again. The ONE has been identified as aliens with advanced technologies that visited the Earth. The ONE proliferates in New Age religions. The ONE has been understood as the insistence of patriarchy by feminists as abstracted hegemonic masculinity; the ONE is now shaping global politics through the schism forming between Christianity and Islam; the ONE is also a source of many media fantasies to find a new "redeemer." The ONE is also the fantasy of the Symbolic Order as such. This historical interlude informs the backdrop of post-Oedipalization in today's postmodern world where the trust in the Symbolic Order has waned. In chapters 5 and 6 we attempt to provide an overview of the sociological and psychic structures that are indicative of this "loss" of authority and the rise of the superego of consumerist demand with the expectation toward a command to Enjoy!

5

THE CONTRADICTORY DEMANDS OF THE SUPEREGO: CONTEMPORARY FATHERS

THE BROTHERHOOD OF PRESIDENTIAL FOLLIES

Freud's fable shows that the *socius* formed by the brotherhood was possible only because the brothers no longer felt excluded but established an imaginary identification after the revolt with the oppressive Father—now deified and transcendent. Such a *socius* or Symbolic Order led to the formation of several grand narratives which, as Lyotard (1984) signaled, have begun to unravel. These grand Western narratives have failed to deliver their teleologic claims for a "better" and more just world (the promise of Communism, the promise of greater democratic participation, the promise of salvation). The narrative of the Enlightenment was to erect a non-patriarchal state based on a fraternal egalitarian norm of which the French Revolution was, at one time, an exemplar model. This was to be a political state based on liberty, equality, and fraternity, a democratic state free of any irrational hierarchy (equality). It was to assure that arbitrary procession by a despot would not come about (liberty), and allow for the recognition of a common humanity for all its members (fraternity).

Since then, the secularization of God and the overcoming of the cult of the ancestor (Tradition) through the trajectory of the Enlightenment and its subsequent modernization has continually undercut the patriarchal power of the Church and Royalty. Democratic nation-states continue to be ruled, on the whole, by a fraternity of brothers. But these emergent leaders are all "post-patriarchal" in the sense that they are not privileged sons or heirs, but only "one" amongst brotherhood. The degree of loss of symbolic privilege, despite the retention of wealth can be seen by the British tabloids that ceaselessly promulgate and exploit the Royal Family's domestic troubles. Both The Bushs' and The Blairs', who are to represent the model families for their respective nations, have had trouble with their siblings, which make them less than ideal examples of how to raise children, although there is an unspoken expectation that both the first Lady, Laura, and the Prime Minister's wife, Cherie are supposed to comment and exemplify to the nation proper child raising procedures. Bush's twin daughters, Barbara and Jenna (both 19) were caught buying alcohol illegally; while Jenna was found drinking in a bar and ordered to do community service. Blair's 16-year-old son, Euan was found face down in his own vomit in Leicester Square, in London's West End. What this indicates is that there is a lack of identification with an Ego Ideal, which authority in the past was supposed to maintain.

Popstars are slowly becoming the "new" secular Royalty in postmodernism. They have taken over as the Ego Ideal through, paradoxically, a narcissistic self-admiration of their own Ideal Ego. Symbolic Ego Ideal and Imaginary Ideal Ego have imploded into one another to emerge as ONE. We have Michael Jackson, the "King" of Pop who now has two sons: Prince Michael Jackson I + II, which appear more like collectable playthings than the usual father/son relationship. In a visit to Berlin in November 22, 2002, "Jacko" was almost charged for child neglect and endangerment when he "waved" his, then, nine-month-old son (Prince II) over the fourth-floor balcony railing of the opulent Adlon Hotel to adoring fans below. Entertainment stars now embody the magic of the gaze.

The only thing that distinguishes a leader from the rest of the nation is his/her particular charisma, acting on simulacra affects of a paternal or maternal metaphor—more an Ideal Ego than an iconic Ego Ideal of a transcendent figure. From the very beginning of her reign, Queen Elizabeth II attempted to invite people into her "home" through her televised Christmas and New Year messages. Although she failed miserably with her stiff formal style, the older she got, the more maternal she seemed to become. With the death of the Queen Mother, Queen Elizabeth has slowly become the nation's "mom," occupying the vacancy that her mother left behind. The Queen's awkward trait of formal familiarity has become an endearing trait for the public. The very feature that seemed to undermine her early attempts to present a human face, has become a trait that begins to "stick out" after so much media exposure and, sustains her imaginary charisma. Ronald Reagan's constant "stumbling," or falling asleep during an international summit, or his consultation with his wife's (Nancy) astrologer were seen as "human" flaws, which then humanized his authority, made him more "real." Clinton's famous "lie" about "that woman" (Monica Lewinsky) was also taken as a human frailty, as long as he was able to maintain the illusion of his presidency. By working hard and going about cementing his international foreign policies that gave him a global profile, with the economy booming his indiscretion was not perceived by the general public as being grave enough to warrant an impeachment. Americans could relate to his private folly, which they themselves consider a fundamental right "to enjoy." Generic consumerism and advertising already presuppose lying and deceit, as long as it done with convincing style—"lying well." Warren Beatty's film left-leaning political satire *Bulworth* (1998) demonstrates quite well how politics and lying are necessarily tied together. Senator Bulworth (Warren Beatty) has put out a mob contract on himself disgusted with the way he has sold out his left-leanding democratic beliefs for neoconservative pap against welfare, affirmative action, and the poor to win elections. His daughter will then collect ten million in insurance claims. Caught by his own death drive to kill who he has become, Bulworth begins to embody the fantasy of "telling it like it is" and reveal the "truth" about

his government policies and what he "truly" thinks about society while cam-
paigning in front of an African–American congregation. Following a series of
these "truth-telling" death drive incidents he finds his old self again by having traversed the fantasy of his former neoconservative ideology. A new
group of constituents emerge as the world of the underprivileged opens up
and his former world of privilege recedes. He begins to "rap" the truth having found a new hip-hop voice. A love interest (Halle Barry as Nina) and the
impossibility of having the hit called off change things. Becoming once more
seriously committed he finds out that he needs to lie to establish the truth.
The figure of Bulworth demonstrates that politicians are structured by the
lie if they are to ingratiate themselves to the Symbolic Order that has a hold
over them (McGowan 1999, 77–78).

These unary "traits" of politicians, like Clinton and Bulworth's lies, are no
different than what catches the eye of an adoring fan as a signifier of identification. This is experiencing the person in his or her Real dimension. Just as
a trait might be one of erotic allure and affect, it can—for another, be exactly
what s/he hates. The *objet a*, as this unary trait, has this paradoxical sense
about it. Its presence can bring on anxiety on a number of fronts. A pop idol
or a movie star can become too close so that a fan may be hysterized—the
right distance has to be kept (by police, bodyguards, secret agents); or one
just can't "stand" a particular star because of the way s/he smiles, grins,
laughs. This was certainly true of the Republicans and conservative Moral
Majority fundamentalists, hate for the Clintons.

Clinton's indiscretion exposes the "near" impossibility of maintaining the
public/private split of the Presidential Office in postmodernity, which is
absolutely necessary if the illusion of a good Oedipal Protective Father of the
country is to be maintained. The Presidential Office must not be tarnished,
but remain an exceptional pure and empty space to maintain such a belief in
the system. Collapsing the two reduces the office to the banal status of just
another man with just another family, rather than the mythic exemplar of the
First Family. In light of Freud's myth we can see why the Republican attempt
to impeach Clinton rested on casting him as the Father of Jouissance, "The
Great Fucker." As bearer of the ever-precarious Oedipal Law, he could not
be an exception to the Law, but had to be held accountable and responsible
for his actions. Yet, Clinton as the first baby boom president had confessed
to smoking marihuana and had tacitly admitted to an illicit affair with
Gennifer Flowers. He claimed oral sex was not intercourse (which many
young people do as well), he jogs, plays s(a)x, and has been accused of sexual harassment by a string of women. Clinton, cast as Satan, offers lies, adul-
tery, perjury and a mockery of justice. His retractors said he suffered from a
"sexual addiction." John F. Kennedy was no different, perhaps he was worse
than Clinton was when it came to womanizing. Seymour Hersh's (1997)
exposition of JFK in *The Dark Side of Camelot*, described the scenes of lib-
ertine partying, daily sexual liaisons, and of course, JFK's notorious and
secretive affair with Marilyn Monroe. The difference was that Kennedy's
womanizing was still maintained by patriarchal privilege. The Kennedys had

aristocratic roots. Tradition was on their side. His private and public spheres were strictly maintained by his Secret Service. His affairs remained discrete (as in Europe with Miterand). Word never got out; the fraud of the Phallus could be maintained. JFK's showdown with Nikita Kruschev during the Cuban missile crisis and his assassination as the good and protective Oedipal Father of his country pretty well assured him of a hero's death upon his assassination in Dallas, Texas in 1963.

With Clinton, the patriarchal roots were gone. He was fatherless (William Jefferson Blythe died in a car accident before he was born), raised by his mother and grandmother who competed for his affection. His womanizing and open personality was part of his "feminine" charisma that got him elected as governor of Arkansas. In the team of Bill and Hillary ("Billary"), Hillary, as the maternal superego took over the moral high ground while Clinton remained an adolescent with a "mother" problem (Paglia 1998). Lewinsky was attracted by his feminine qualities of softness, tenderness, and neediness. It was the "sweet, little boy" that she loved (Morton 1999; Glass 2001). It remains to be seen whether the Republican George W. Bush can restore the claim of an Oedipal Father in a post-Oedipal age; whether his "unorthodox" use of the English language will be seen as a charismatic trait or a sign of stupidity and weak-mindedness; whether he can achieve authority or "bully" and threaten the UN Security Council with behind-the-scene deals; whether his moral position, backed by an extreme Christian Right, will be perceived as yet another attempt to establish The New World Order called on by his father as has been the long-standing patriarchal legacy for divination; and whether his foreign policies are but an obscene supplement to the Law, motivated to help U.S. big business in extracting gas and oil reserves from Central Asia with the building of the Caspian Sea pipeline that will run across Afghanistan (also gas and oil rich), thus effectively subverting the OPEC consortium.

Islam and Christianity are once more in dangerous tension with one another. It should not be forgotten that Bush's National Security Advisor had an oil tanker, *Condoleezza Rice*, christened in her honor by Chevron for services rendered while Rice sat on the oil giant's board of directors, from 1991 until the day before G.W. took office. It has since been quietly renamed "Altair Voyager." When Vice President Dick Cheney was running Halliburton, the oil field services company, he won a multibillion dollar contract with Chevron to build a Caspian Sea pipeline for them to use in moving oil out of the Tengiz field in Central Asia. In summer 2001, shortly before the events of September 11, Taliban officials were in Houston, Texas meeting with Unocal Oil Company officials in an attempt to negotiate a pipeline deal. That deal never went through. Now that Afghanistan has been "liberated," the door is once again open. This chain of events can be "spun" as just a series of coincidences. Said often enough, questionable doubt sets in and the obvious possibility of an obscene conspiracy will fade. But these series of events wait in their repression to haunt the Bush administration, like the Iran Contra Affair haunted Reagan, The Gulf War and his CIA involvement haunted George Bush Sr. It should not be forgotten that war, more than any other national disaster, binds a nation together behind its leader. The 9/11 event has produced an invisible terrorist enemy in the form of Al-Qaeda, one that is global in reach, enabling the rhetoric of "war on terrorism" to be extended and fought in the "backyard" of any country that harbors these terrorists. Iraq has become the testing ground to shore up presidential impotency. There are no more hard-and-fast borders. Cynicism and trust in authority can only worsen in a climate where Weapons of Mass Destruction (WMD) and solid evidence of Al-Qaeda links to Sadam Hussein are not to be found, and *if* found, will be strongly suspected of being planted by American interests.

THE FOUR HORSEMEN OF THE APOCALYPSE: YOU MUST, FOR YOU ARE DRIVEN!

In such a capitalist climate an aggressive superego demands "enjoyment!" *Bliss* in the parlance of psychoanalysis, is what has been unleashed—the order of the drives (*Triebe*) where the desire for gain at any cost seems to prevail. The corruption in the corporate world as exemplified by Enron is only the tip of the visible iceberg. The German verb *trieben* means to push, to pull along, to urge. Freud was attempting to indicate by this word a space between biology (as the needs (*Not*) for the body's nourishment and its demands) and culture where there was a willful element of free choice possible in the way culture must "repress" the demands of the drives. Such a primary repression or *Urverdrängung* was necessary to found civilization. A drive, simply put, is a need or a demand not caught up in the dialectics of desire and lack. The complicated interactions between the subject of the demand, of the drive, and of desire come into play in postmodernity where the accelerated recession of the authority of the Oedipal father has taken place in a permissive society that coincides with the (re)appearance of the Father of Jouissance—considered especially in religious circles with the debasement of morality and civility. Rather than prohibiting enjoyment this newly emerged superego father commands it through competitiveness and striving for excellence, unleashing aggressivity and stress into the workplace. Under the reign of this Anal/Oral/Aural/Scopic Father the subject is constantly confronted by the Other's enjoyment, often in its most unbearable dimensions—on the screen-image of television and film, in newspapers and magazines, in cyberspace; everywhere we see others satisfied, happy and "enjoying." And so we are told to "enjoy!"

The anal, oral, aural (invocatory), and scopic drives are the pregenital and pre-Oedipal drives involving a primary narcissism before the full development of language and the recognition of the Symbolic Order of society is in force. They do not represent the reproductive function of sexuality but only a dimension of enjoyment (S XI, *Four Fundamentals*, 204). A certain satisfaction (jouissance) is attached to each one of these drives. These drives regulate what comes into and what is expelled from the body, and what "fascinates" it. By saying that the *desublimated* reign of the Anal/Oral/

Aural/Scopic Father has emerged is to claim the *perversion* of these drives in at least four forms of the "Names-of-the-Father" as *père-versions* that have become central in a consumerist society in terms of the relationship between self and Other. Hoarding and restriction in a status of hierarchy rather than recycling, sharing, expelling, and waste processing defines the Anal Father. The Oral Father is defined through more and more consumption, the constant updating and thirst for the new. The Aural Father is defined by the imperative case—that of demand, always wanting to have something, as if a constant tantrum is being experienced. The voice has been reduced to a super-egoic command. Finally the obscene Scopic Father is defined by the "look," the surface aesthetic as a body Ego Ideal that matches as closely as possible the Ideal Ego presented by the Symbolic Order as the loved body. For convenience, we shall use the term "Father of Enjoyment" (cf. Žižek) or Jouissant Father in its singular sense, which refers to the coalescence of perverted drives in postmodernity as a short hand when discussing the emergence of this new Superego. However, where it appears that a particular perverted drive is operating, we shall specify as to which Jouissant Father is operational—which drive supercedes the rest. When all partial drives come together, as in the mythical "Four Horsemen of the Apocalypse," can we say that the suicidal "death drive" is fully realized in its transcendental purity. The Apocalypse signals the end of the end. We might call this the *pure desire* to die since desire becomes ONE and undivided. However, as Lacan (1995) maintained *each* partial drive is a death drive in and of itself, for any one of the "horsemen" can lead to excessive, repetitive, and ultimately destructive behavior.

Kronos, as a devouring Father speaks directly to the Oral drive, but there are the Anal Fathers who share nothing with their sons/daughters as well like the figure of Disney's Uncle Scrooge, where wealth becomes faeces locked in a vault, or Saruman in *The Lord of The Rings Trilogy*, for instance, who amasses all wealth and power. The father figure, A.N. Lewis, in the film *Peeping Tom* (Michael Powell 1960) who conducts experiments on his son, Mark Lewis, by filming him day and night to study the effects of fear is an example of an obscene Scopic Father. Mark eventually becomes psychotic, a serial killer who only gets "off" by viewing photographs that capture the moment of death registered on the faces of his victims. The Aural psychotic Father whose disembodied voice becomes a demand or command is exemplified recently in the film *Spider-Man* (Sam Raimi 2002)—the figure of Harry's father, Norman Osborn who is commanded by The Green Goblin, his psychotic voice and alter ego, to get "even" with the corporate CEOs who dispossessed him of his company. Corporate greed of enjoyment once more comes to the fore, which is Anal in its drive function—the capitalist as a shit exemplified so well by Gordon Gekko in Oliver Stone's *Wall Street* (1987).

SURVIVING ENJOYMENT: THE PERVERSITY OF THE NEIGHBORLY ACT

We can say that the campaign of the Jouissant Father is visible in the increasing abhorrence of pleasure as found in the Other. The intolerable Other provides a source of sadistic pleasure in today's society (Žižek 1993). This is especially true of racism, homophobia, ethnicity, and body size where the Other's enjoyment is continually ruined by striking at the core of self-esteem for not living up to a taken-for-granted social Ego Ideal as defined by wealth, heteronormativity, whiteness, a Barbie body for a woman, and a Ken body for a man. In *Anatomy of Prejudices*, Elizabeth Young-Bruehl (1996) discusses this encroachment of the Other by three prejudiced ideal personality types (*Idealtypen* in Max Weber's sense—obsessional, hysterical, and narcissistic). In designer capitalism, wherever the subject turns s/he cannot escape the Other's enjoyment. In nascent seventeenth-century modernism the dead primal Father presided over an emerging capitalist society relatively devoid of enjoyment, especially later in its Puritanical and Protestant formulations of the "spirit of capitalist accumulation" as articulated by Weber's "Protestant ethic" thesis.[1] This was still an Oedipal Father who drew his authority and power from God. The Jouissant Father of postmodern consumerism presides over a society where enjoyment has been magnified. The old primal Father ruled as a "present absence" or "living/dead father." The "new" Father's presence is felt everywhere, suffocating and insistent in its repetitive gesture to hammer at us as consumers. We can never get away from sensing his enjoyment even when he is physically absent. But his enjoyment doesn't bar us from enjoying. The presence of this enjoyment actually calls upon us to enjoy ourselves even more so that it turns into its paradoxical opposite— jouissance as the desublimated pleasure of our symptoms. We never feel as though we are doing this adequately enough, nor feel that we have enough. Duty no longer lies in going to work and working hard—the boundaries between leisure and work become blurred for those who are "fully" enjoying. Money is earned so it can be spent on more pleasure. With the system of credit, most middle-class Americans are only one paycheck away from becoming broke. This was humorously explored by Percy Aldon's *Rosalie Goes Shopping* (1989). Rosalie (Marianne Sägebrecht) uses one credit card to pay off another credit card in an unending game of circularity, until the game catches up to her. Not so humorously, after 9/11 many Americans it was reported, went shopping to make themselves "feel" better, as if their days had become numbered. Bankruptcies in the United States have increased 400 percent over the last 25 years and occur at an astounding rate of one per minute. Six million U.S. families will be in danger of bankruptcy by the year 2010 (Warren and Warren 2003).

The hyper-narcissistic excesses of the drives dominate lives today: the "surface" aesthetic of the "look," pornography, plastic surgery, steroid abuse, dieting, body piercing, tattooing, s/m, gambling (especially VLT's, Video Lottery Terminals), designer drugs, "escape" vacations, themeparks, extreme sports, and workouts. The eventual legalization of marijuana, perhaps, will be a benchmark indicator that this libidinal pleasure has been "normalized." With the demand to "enjoy" come addiction and a loss of feeling, an anesthetization so well explored by the David Rincher's *Fight Club* (1999). The narrator (Edward Norton) has become an addict looking for affection, trying to find a way to *feel* and touch people, moving from one self-help group to another without much success. He is a walking vampire living off the way addicts find pleasure in struggling with their addictions. In his schizophrenic state, the only way he can feel again is through brutal beatings that leaves his skin-ego physically battered and mentally toughed to withstand pain, which has now turned to pleasure. The "fight club" becomes a perverse sadomasochistic ritual, a desperate attempt to reinstate the Law. But, this fails as well. His inner disembodied voice of Tyler Durden (Brad Pitt) wins out. What is left is total anarchistic destruction, an eerie adumbration of the 9/11 event, but this time committed by one of America's own, like Timothy McVeigh's bombing the Oklahoma City federal building in June 1997 that left 168 people dead.

This enjoyment makes its presence felt by installing a new kind of superego, a superego that develops from the Jouissant Father who psychically attacks us for *failing* to enjoy, rather than for enjoyment *itself* as the old superego of the Name-of-the-Father once did. This new superego keeps the Jouissant Father's standard of enjoyment constant at the forefront of our thoughts. It remains constant and credible for it appears ubiquitous through all institutions of society. We are constantly reminded what success is through the media, and what such successful youthful bodies look like. Failure to enjoy leads to depression and nonrecognition. This unbearable presence of the symbolic Ego Ideal creates in every subject a sense that they are not enjoying themselves enough; that they are failing in their responsibility to live up to these ideals. Whereas the dead primal Father prohibited enjoyment, and thus tended to spawn subjects relatively content to forget, repress, and "live" with their castration, as subjects who lack, the "living" Jouissant Father constantly alerts everyone to *the fact of their castration and insists that they escape it*. The Ego Ideal is to become like David Mamet's play *Glengarry Glen Ross* (film, James Foley 1992), the ONE (mythical) figure who grounded the company and then left on a permanent vacation where everything he possibly imagined was available to him because of his wealth. Here we need only mention the escalation of multimillion dollar contracts in professional sports, the brunt of the costs are borne by the fans through increased price of tickets and season passes. Players demand to be paid more; to be paid less is a sign of castration—undervalued and out of the limelight. The phallus has to be spectacularized, vanity exploited to make profit dollars. This obscenity of this practice was perceptively explored in Cameron Crowe's *Jerry Maguire* (1996).

The juxtaposition of enjoyment to the subject's castration acts as a nagging underlying reminder: "Just look at what you gave up to get to where you did. Look at all that hard work and hours you put in to reach the top. You don't have to be put up with that!" You need not give up your tax dollars. Use your tax shelters! Demand more money! Sport stars like Boris Becker and Steffi Graf's father have been caught for tax evasion. But they are the tip of the iceberg. There are numerous other "stars" and multinational executives who use the tax loopholes to shelter their money. It's an expectation that comes with wealth. Yet, subjects existing in the world of the "living" Anal Father have a constant sense that they are still not enjoying enough.

In Nietzschean terms, there is a growing "resentment" against anyone who has accumulated the status this Jouissant Father demands, namely the hyper-specularization of the Self with *Vanity* (the name of an upscale magazine) and *15 Minutes* of fame (the name of John Herzfeld's 1992 movie) seem to be the defining features of such a narcissistic quest. Such resentment is particularly evident in the "culture of complaint" (Hughes 1993). The more narcissistic the subject is expected to become, the more likely is the blame placed on the Symbolic Order for failing in its duty to live up to its democratic ideals of human rights. Fear and the anxiety that comes with the potential "theft of enjoyment," the sense that the Other has stolen enjoyment away from me is the unspoken assumption of "fair" competition (Žižek 1993, 203; 1997a, 32). When fairness breaks down litigation is soon to follow. This is a hysterical position, which demands that the Law immediately "show itself" if justice and trust in it is to be restored. The pervasiveness of this struggle for enjoyment makes civil relationships between people seems impossible; community is extremely difficult to maintain. Each postindustrial country has its televised "reality" shows, which show this struggle in the courts (e.g., *Judge Judy* et al. in the United States; *Jugendgericht, Das Strafgericht, Das Familiengericht* et al. in Germany). Fictionalized courtroom dramas and police shows, docudramas as well have become a staple on primetime television (*Law and Order, Boomtown, The District, The New Detectives: Case Studies in Forensic Science, To Serve and Protect, Cold Squad, The FBI Files*, and so on). The neighbor has become abhorrent and difficult to live with unless distance is maintained.[2] There is constant betrayal amongst friends. This is the only relationship possible in the world of the Jouissant Father. In this world friendships seem precarious; where every potential friend is at the same time a potential thief who will steal enjoyment away—get the better grade so as to move on to graduate school, get the raise, be promoted, be recognized by peers. The *Survivor* series of "reality" television illustrate this perfectly. The game rules are to outwit, outlast, and outplay fellow castaways. On the surface everyone appears to be friendly and helping each other out, underneath there is the strategy of the game and schemes to get rid of particular players to get the prize. What we see is an *inverted community*, which exposes to the viewing audience the "rawness" of the drive—what must be done in order to survive. In the end, it is those who have been betrayed who have a say in choosing the winning contestant. They have the satisfaction of revenge, or at the very least, a chance to lash out for what they perceived as wrongful dismissal off the island.

In such a world of capitalist consumerism an impossible "enjoyment" is posited in the Other that the Other doesn't have, and it is this positing—*not the actual enjoyment*—which leads to a rise in aggressivity. Showing that neither character has the enjoyment that the Other believes the Other has explains Lacan's maxim: *enjoyment is always the enjoyment of the Other.* Enjoyment exists only insofar that it is posited in the Other, as the Other's enjoyment. So when a subject responds to enjoyment with aggressivity s/he is really recoiling from her or his own enjoyment and repudiating it. In this view, the contemporary rise in violence and aggressivity is not the result of too much "enjoyment," *but too little of it* (McGowan 1998). The living world of the Jouissant Father of proliferating enjoyment is also a world of enjoyment refused. Aggressivity is a refusal of one's own enjoyment in so far as it manifests itself in the Other. Aggressivity is, in short, a complete rejection of one's enjoyment because it is only in the Other that enjoyment can manifest itself. It points to the strange inversion of enjoyment into jouissance—into forms of envy and jealousy that characterize resentment, symptoms that have increased in consumerist societies.

This logic of the "theft of enjoyment" helps further explain the attacks on Clinton given that enjoyment also determines the relationship of the people to the country's leader. Clinton's concentration and consumption of wealth (the White Water Affair, for instance; his and Hillary's assets) is considered a "theft" only when he loses the perception of being a representative of the people who is "more" than they themselves are (its citizens). "A nation exists only as long as its specific enjoyment continues to be materialized in a set of social practices and transmitted through national myths that structure those practices" (Žižek 1993, 202). As long as that relationship is transferential then the president's wealth, prestige, and enjoyment is "ours." Such transference is over when the leader loses his charisma and is perceived by the majority of citizens as a parasite on the nation's body. This is precisely why conservative political forces tried to discredit Clinton's relationship to his enjoyment. The case of the Canadian Prime Minister Brian Mulroney (contemporary of Ronald Reagan and Margaret Thatcher) is another primary example of failed charisma. Mulroney left office being perceived as one of the most disliked and unpopular prime ministers Canada ever had. The fact that his Conservative Party was almost decimated in the elections that followed confirmed the nation's feeling of disgust for his expenditures. This is a political party that has never recovered since. Both Mulroney and his wife Milla were perceived as spending tax dollars on themselves for their own enjoyment (new house furniture, vacations, cars, gala parties with the Reagans) rather than "for" the nation's enjoyment. The notorious case of the authoritarian Marcos's regime in the Philippines where Amelda Marcos's shoe collection exemplifies the vanity of enjoyment to its fetishistic heights at the expense of the nation's poor is another dramatic example.

TONY SOPRANO AS EVERYMAN? THE CONFLICT BETWEEN TWO FATHERS

In late modern Enlightened society where (theoretically) identity is no longer determined by birth or social status, and where anyone (theoretically) can become the president or prime minister of a nation like the United States of America or Canada, requires that the myth of unification of paternal authority as an Ego Ideal (how one should symbolically behave as a leader) and the prohibition of the Superego be maintained. Such a mythical father should embody both the "No!" of prohibition as well as be an exemplar of what his sons should strive toward. For the mother, whose ambitions may be presidential or prime ministrable (e.g., Hillary Rodham Clinton in the United States, Alexa McDonough in Canada), the reality is that she has to act and belong to the brotherhood like a matronly Margaret Thatcher to run a nation. However, such a paternal (or maternal) metaphor is difficult to sustain when authority begins to wane. A paradox emerges where the Jouissant Father and the Oedipal Father become two sides of the same coin; they flip from one to another at the very place where the Möbius band turns, a place where the inside/outside binary no longer applies so that they exchange places when there is no longer a transcendent ideal to hold them apart and in tension. The father of authority as an Ego Ideal turns into an obscene Father once his impotence is exposed. An excessive rage occurs when he has been humiliated. The figure of Tony Soprano, from the Home Box Office (HBO) hit television series, *The Sopranos* (now into its fifth season as of 2003) is a perfect embodiment of this contradictory figure of a father who is torn between the pleasures of the Jouissant Father (as Mafia Boss he is into women, drug dealing, killing) and the weakened Oedipal Father struggling to "protect" his children, making sure that his daughter Meadow goes to college and meets the "right" kind of guy. For Tony this means someone who cannot possibly be like him: not part of the Mafia and not having minority status like Meadow's boyfriend, Noah a Black American Jew. He wants an impossible figure just the opposite of who he is: a "descent" middle-class upstanding guy who will look after her. Tony's son A.J. (Anthony Junior) isn't supposed to follow his father's footsteps in crime. Yet, that is precisely what he is attracted to. Whenever these two Fathers collide, or come into an impossible compromise, Tony "blacks out" and faints. The anxiety is too much to bear and he is off to see his psychiatrist, Dr. Jennifer Melfi. These analytic sessions present viewers with an "ethics of the Real," an impossible resolution between these two Fathers. Tony, the jouissant outlaw meets Melfi the in-law in what is a continuous struggle for redemption—for both of them. Tony knows that he is a fraud and impotent. He suffers from castration anxiety. Every time his authority is threatened he flips from being an affectionate human being to a raging aggressive brute as he loses control. Melfi, on the other hand, is attracted to him. Her hysterical side, which she tries to keep in control by seeing her own therapist, Elliot, is the fascination of desiring Tony as a protector (a confirming ONE) whom she believes she can manipulate and perhaps have wild sex with. Her own loss of faith in the Symbolic Order is revealed in the hate she has toward her rapist who has not been brought to justice. Yet, she refuses to tell Tony who would have quickly seen to it that his form of justice was executed.

The very idea that his own mother, Livia, along with Uncle Jr. wanted him dead is an added irony David Chase, its creator, developed. Even the Mafia, which represents the functioning of an old patriarchy with the Family elevated to a transcendental signifier based on blood ("Cosa Nostra"), is subject to a decentering. Tony insists on old-fashioned family values of the 1950s, but those days are essentially over.[3] Tony has conflicted views toward his father, Johnny Boy, a Mafia enforcer who spent little to no time with him and showed him little affection. He died of lung cancer when Tony was still a young man. An uncle under normal circumstances often acts as a surrogate father; not burdened with punishment, he can dispense kindness and wisdom on his nephew (or niece). But, Uncle Jr. is precisely the opposite. Not only is he locked into a power struggle with his nephew Tony for the control of the Family, but he is neither wise nor kind. He has no stomach (literally throwing up) for the tough decisions that need to be made. Eventually, he is stricken with cancer of the colon. But it is Tony's mother Livia who is the phallic Mother—like the figure of Medea. She is the one who castrated him and his father all his life. It is the maternal superego who can run the show when she wants to. When Livia finally dies, she continues to haunt Tony because all along he secretly wanted her dead. He has to deal with this guilt when her death finally happens. Tony was not able to entirely separate himself from her. She remains a conflicted figure in his psyche.

Such a reading places Tony in a perverted position still acting as the phallus for his mother. Given his poor relationship to his Father, Tony believes in a jouissance without limits. He sets himself up as the Law, casting himself as the instrument by which the jouissance of the Other becomes possible. This is precisely his role as the Godfather, the Mafia Boss. He assures the jouissance of those in his family. The irony, of course, is that this perverted role is made possible through Mafia "respect" for their m(Other)s. Such a brotherhood remains homophobic in their fear of the feminine. As the Jouissant Father women are to be objectified and used, but as the Oedipal Father Tony's proclaimed authority is continually disarmed by Livia, Carmela, and Meadow. Add to this "family" his sister Janice who manipulates him like his mother, and we find that Tony is completely alone with no parental models to follow. In postmodernity, even Mafia bosses have lost their authority as cleverly developed in Mike Newell's film, *Donnie Brasco* (1997).

It seems even family blood ties are harder to maintain. Tony wants his nephew Christopher (a heroine addict and a capo boss) to eventually take over the "Family." But, betrayal is always possible. Pussy, an ex-capo boss and close friend rats and is killed. Paulie, Tony's number one capo is scheming with another family. Like the biblical Abraham, Tony must see to it that Jackie Richie, Jr. (Meadow's boyfriend and son of Tony's former Mafia boss who died of cancer) is killed because he disrespected and killed one of the capo bosses. Tony had promised his ex-Boss, Jackie, Sr., that he would look after him, but again his "Oedipal-side" fails. As much as Tony wants Meadow and A.J., Jr. not to follow his footsteps, the transference in this case is too strong. They are attracted to jouissant excesses: Meadow flirting with drugs and bad-boy Jackie, Jr., and A.J. with nihilism and delinquency. A.J. has been diagnosed as having an attention deficit disorder and is considered irresponsible, so Carmel and Tony want to send him to the Hudson Military Institute to get a "boot camp" experience. Such a familial crisis should not be read as being atypical of middle-class Americans.

Tony represents the figure of the struggling Father today. He may not be a Mafia boss, but he is caught by the same inner conflicts of excess and familial struggles. The conflict between the two Fathers represents the impossibility of maintaining the trust in a symbolic Ego Ideal. If there is a "decline" in Oedipus in postmodernity, this means that sons and daughters no longer have an Ego Ideal to look up to. A.J., Jr. is confused, as is Meadow. In one episode A.J. discovers existentialism and goes about arguing that there are no absolutes. He no longer believes in authority. He doesn't want to receive the sacrament of Conformation by the Catholic Church, and metaphorically not to be "confirmed" by society either. According to "Nitch," says A.J., "God is dead." He so wants to be like his dad but in most cases he is paralyzed and not very involved in life. He faints whenever he is given a leadership role. He can't live up to his father's expectations, and does not want to compete with him. Every time Tony tries to shadow box, A.J. refuses to lift his dukes. He seems most content when performing mischief. A.J. repeats his dad's symptom of the superego, conflicted between taking on responsibility (the Law) or transgressing it. This loss of a central model for identification (A.J.'s symptom) prevents him from growing up and finding his place in the Symbolic Order. In the episode where A.J. is sent to a military school, his parents thinking that would enable him to grow up, A.J. refuses to go. He becomes ill. Meadow, on the other hand, plays her father like a violin. She knows precisely how to make him suffer. She even tells Tony and Carmela what a suitable punishment should be when she gets out of hand.

A.J. remains a youthful son destined not to grow up—to become like one of the characters on the hit series *Steinfield*, a thirties-something adolescence, *not* in competition with his Father. There is a *refusal of competition* since the Ego Ideal is so conflicted. The playful half-beards that so many young men sport today from 17 all the way to 30 and beyond seem to reconfirm this "holding" stage of not growing up, an in-between space postadolescent phase that has been further stretched in the past decade. These are boyz trying to find their way. As Verhaeghe (1999, 85) notes, in the last ten years the "borderline patient" has emerged who is best described "as an adult operating at the pre-Oedipal level." Verhaeghe might be right. Although BPD remains a controversial diagnosis, the APA (American Psychiatric Association) has characterized it (amongst other things) as a frantic effort to avoid real or imagined abandonment; as an unstable sense of self, a pattern of unstable and intense interpersonal relationships that are characterized by seeing people and situations in black or white (or "splitting"); as suicidal or self-mutilating behavior and dissociation. These characteristics sound like struggles of a failed separation from the Mother, the BPD is unable to suffer it alone, prone to wild swings of love and hate. *The Sopranos'* landscape is scattered with them. Tony is attracted to such women like the Italian American Gloria Trillo (the Mercedes saleswoman) and the Russian immigrant Irina, his two ex-girlfriends whose unstable behavior repeat, unsurprisingly, his mother's wild mood swings toward him (Gabbard 2002, 140–141).

In postmodernity a "flip" has occurred to the Jouissant Father with a twist. Rather than the sons once more believing that the primal Father has it all, that he is standing in the way of their "enjoyment," to their full pleasure, he has become an ambivalent model to emulate. Once "dead," the primal father has come back as a Father of Consumption as brilliantly portrayed by the figure of Milton who turns out to be the Scopic Father in Taylor Hackford's film, *Devil's Advocate* (1997) (see jagodzinski 2001). Kevin Lomax, the protagonist lawyer who always wants to win at any cost eventually must face the vanity inside himself. If there is no prohibition by the Oedipal Father—everything goes—the son locates the impossible cause of desire once more in the primordial father, in the father of "enjoyment," as if he has captured the impossible Thing (*das Ding*). Lomax is convinced that Milton's Law firm is the pinnacle of success and wealth. By working for Milton, Lomax ends up getting everything he imagined, but loses what is most precious to him: Alex, his wife. Unlike the myths of Uranos, Kronos, and the Primal Father of the Horde, this Jouissant Father is not being ritually killed but emulated like Milton. Even as Lomax redeems himself through a suicidal death drive, in the end of the narrative he is still not entirely free of Milton. The closing few scenes hold a surprise for the audience. A.J., Jr. is faced with a similar existential crisis like Lomax. He is attracted to the life of crime.[4] He knows his father is the Boss, yet he is supposed to believe in the Law. His nihilism is a way out of this stalemate. He need not compete with his father the Mafia boss nor does he have to accept the Law.

In postmodernity, why is there *no revolt*, rebellion or resistance to psychically kill the Jouissant Father, a question that Kristeva raises in her two-volume work (2000, 2002)? Why does revolt seem impossible in this global capitalist society? For Frankfurt theorists like Marcuse, "repressive desublimation" meant that capitalism was able to absorb and domesticate any attempts at revolt. There is nothing to revolt against in a society that demands that satisfaction be met. We can go "on-line" and (potentially) continually be satisfied by encountering an Other who is never "in our face," whom we can cut off when we want. Resentment only shows up when the Other (neighbor) comes too close and envy and jealousy sets in. Kristeva offers a mixed message regarding revolt, repeating her belief in the revolutionary power of "semiotic" as opposed to "symbolic" language. In the television hit series *Highlander*, which ended after six seasons in 1998, the figure of Kronos was prominently featured as the leader of the Four Horsemen, the mounted Bronze Age raiders who murdered, raped, and pillaged their way across two continents. Their goal was to bring mankind what it fears most, the Apocalypse, and only Duncan MacLeod (the immortal Highlander) stood between them and the end of the world. The fantasy of *Highlander* was all about *power* play: to restage the masculine fantasy of ritual killing (in this case it must be decapitation). One immortal usurps the creative life (*zoë*) from the dead immoral in an updated form of cannibalism, until as the story goes: "in the end there can only be one." This is a classic restatement of a Divine Father, however, no authority is ever reinstated. Duncan, born in the sixteenth century (1592) (pre-Enlightenment Renaissance) is caught in a permanent time warp, never able to become the ONE. Fans were never happy with each season's ending, especially the sixth, which turned out to be the last, entitled "Not To Be," is perhaps appropriately named but not ironic in the least. Redemption never comes.

POWER LUST: NO ONE IN CHARGE?

Neoliberalism posits that society runs best when government interferes the least so that profits are maximized (in the name of democracy), while consumerist "choice" is perceived as the form of citizenship. This has become the only game in town. It has led to a thorough depolitilization of the economic sphere, leaving limited decision making to the cultural sphere. The passion to argue political ideologies has vanished. There is a visible absence of a Left movement, socialist and labor parties hold hands with capital providing for little viable alternatives. What has replaced political debate is a "spin" culture, a surface game of obfuscation in business and government that simply attempts to cover up what might prove to be embarrassing and controversial "facts" that expose the obscenity of the shadow dealings that go on.[5] Democratic elections have become carefully staged media and publicity events run by pundits and pollsters. Lobbyists and campaign contributions attribute to the obscene supplement of democracy, the Bush/Gore presidential race coming within a hair breath of exposing its sham.

There is this mysterious stock market, a leviathan that seems to operate on its own in bust-and-boom cycles. The market forces seem impossible to explain or predict, although there is endless stream of stock market analysts and consultants who profit by trying to do so. All we know is that there is this small percentage of the wealthy 10 percent who control 90 percent of the money. Other obscene figures indicate that the richest 1 percent own more than 30 percent of the total private wealth; or that 90 percent of families hold a little more than one-third of the U.S. assets. The richest 1 percent of Americans makes 80 percent of all individual political contributions. While corporations outspend unions 10:1 when it comes to publicity (Hennessy 2000, 75, 77). The 1990s' stock market boom in the United States was due to the new information technologies and Internet businesses, but this did little to benefit the general population. It was still the wealthiest 10 percent who were able to invest large sums of capital and make unprecedented profits (Phillips 2002). The stock market production on industrial production has led to the falsification of true wealth through bookkeeping, like the Enron Scandal. More realistically put, capitalist democracies are more like plutocracies where fortunes depend on their proximity to power and government-provided corporate welfare, rather than the mythical "free market." Adam Smith's "invisible" hand has been replaced with Alfred Chandler's (1997) "visible" one of the management revolution, where the government is a willing partner and not an enemy of the business rich. In a global capitalist system all cultural life seems to be subject to commodification. With the collapse of communism, capitalism was heralded as the only system that worked, so eagerly greeted by conservatists such as Francis Fukuyama as the victory of economic and political liberalism. According to Fukuyama's (1989) vision, the "end of history" as the universalization of Western liberal democracy as the final form of human government had been reached "as the end point of mankind's (sic) ideological evolution" (17).

This process can only be sustained if everyone is engaged in the endless pursuit of enjoyment. The new superego is the drive behind this "victory" of

economic and political liberalism. We feel we are never doing enough cele-
brating on its behalf. In effect, what this new release of aggressivity and violence wrought is an unleashment of the "death drive" making it more and
more impossible to "desire" today as the forces of the drive overwhelms us
(Deleuze and Guattari 1983, 262) Reality TV (jagodzinski 2003c) makes
this abundantly clear. So much of television's "reality" are the symptoms of
consumptive addiction: the preoccupation with the excesses of the drives—
anal and oral (food/dieting—*Survivor, Big Diet*), genital (seduction, trust—
Big Brother, Temptation Island, Meet My Parents), trust (*The Mole*), extreme
physical exertion (*Survivor*), authority (*Boot Camp*). One shouldn't be surprised that the reality television game shows first appeared in the most liberal countries. *Expedition Robinson* was broadcast on the Swedish network
STV, followed by the huge success of *Big Brother* in Amsterdam, surely one
of the most liberal cities in the world where death stalks its streets under the
guise of neoliberalist freedom of expressive consumption.

The seeming "invisibility" of power and wealth is represented by the
unpretentious, low-profile figure of Bill Gates. Žižek reads Gates as an ordinary guy who harbingers a monstrous dimension, an Evil Genius made possible precisely because of his ordinariness (1999b, 347–364). You can get
away with evil by not seemingly to be the master patriarch, a highly visible
corporate boss—again, much like Tony Soprano who is in the waste disposal
business. The new Kronos is someone who is whipping the corrupt system
(the government and the Law) at its own game, but doing so in "plain
clothes." Like the Coen brothers' film *The Man Who Wasn't There* (2001),
the central figure, Ed Crane's low-key ordinariness (he is a barber) is overlooked by the police as not being involved in the crime of murder and extortion. As is the figure of Roger "Verbal" Kint (a.k.a. the notorious "Keyer
Soze") in Bryan Singer's *The Unusual Suspects* (1995) whose lame appearance hides a vicious revengeful killer. The CEOs in the Enron scandal
seemed innocuous enough until they were exposed for their illegal bookkeeping practices, destroying documentation and selling off stock to make
huge profits. Vice President Dick Cheney claimed "executive privilege" so as
not to reveal details of his meeting with Enron officials.

Incidents like these again indicate that the Ego Ideal of the Symbolic
Order as represented by patriarchal authority figures has been suspended.
The uneasy feeling is that Enron is just the tip of the iceberg (only some of
the many corrupt CEOs have caught) as to what is "really" going on. The
disappearance of the "Schein" that belongs to high office is reduced to an
imaginary level, which evokes the possibility that evil and corruption exist
behind the scenes of business and government; and that it has finally been
exposed as a Kronos superego of obscene enjoyment. Business "genius" is
reduced to nothing more than having the right connections to the top (in
this case the Bush administration). To end this section on an ironic note:
Lorraine Bracco (Dr. Jennifer Melfi of the *Sopranos*) stopped by the Enron
hearings by an "unusual" coincidence. She was on Capitol Hill to highlight
the wage gap between male and female managers.

6

THE LOSS OF SYMBOLIC AUTHORITY
IN POSTMODERNITY

THE EGOMIMESIS OF DESIGNER CAPITALISM

In the nineteenth century Marx had already exposed the fetishistic "secret" of the commodity form of capitalism (Žižek 1989, 14–15). He showed that the hidden labor-time that it took to make something could be exposed, but this had ultimately nothing necessarily to do with the value the product eventually came to possess. It was, rather, the *fascination* that the object held that provided it with value. Use value and exchange value were mediated by something quite immaterial—desire. A cheaply manufactured object could still fetch a handsome price if "presented" the right way. The seduction of the form itself took precedence over its meaning. As Goux (1990) put it, "to create value, all that is necessary is, by whatever means possible, to create a sufficient intensity of desire . . . what ultimately creates surplus value is the manipulation of surplus desire" (200, 202). Walter Benjamin's figure of the *flâneur* moving from one window display to the next, caught by the merchandise; while the *flâneuse* equally strolling through the new public spaces of the 19th century, the arcades, department stores, and amusement parks, capture perfectly this new fascination with form (Friedberg 1993). It was the *vitrine* that made desire transparent, producing a "commodity excess" that leads to today's "society of the spectacle" (Roberts 1991; Debord 1994). The emergence of the new desiring subject was overdetermined through capitalist commodity consumption during the late nineteenth century. This was also the key material condition for the emergence of new sexual identities structured along heterosexual and homosexual divisions within a constructed heteronormativity. This reification of sensory-affect of a gender hierarchy supported capitalist production by requiring an unequal division of labor in the workplace. The new consumer economy of the electric age provoked a more widespread acceptance of pleasure, self-gratification, and personal satisfaction that easily translated into new sex identifications. Sexuality became unhinged for the first time from its procreative patriarchal function as capitalist consumption practices began to intervene in production (Hennessy 2000, 103–107).

To consume requires the formation of a "possessive" individual of capitalism (Macpherson 1962). If one examines the Reform Laws in Britain in the last half of the twentieth century, for example, it becomes obvious that the legislation leading up to the autonomous, abstract individual made remarkable jumps. The first Reform Law of 1832 gave the vote to business-men who held property. Then, in 1867 property gave way to a minimum economy. The vote was extended to anyone who had a big enough bank note. In 1884 the vote was given to all males who did not have a criminal record. It was not until 1920 that universal suffrage was extended to women. This brief genealogy of *constituting* the "possessive" individual through political policies should sensitize the reader into realizing that universal suf-frage happened less than a hundred years ago. It was also at the turn of the twentieth century that the advertising arts *as ways to engineer desire*, emerged precisely (in Britain at least) when the "mass" of voters (workers) was large enough to displace the moneyed class who controlled government policy. The shift of capitalist society of producers to a society of consumers occurred in the last quarter of twentieth century (1875–1900) when Smith/Ricardo/Marx/Mill's labor theory of value was challenged by Menger/Jevons/Walras's marginal utility theory. What endows things with value is not sweat needed to produce them, not the self-renunciation necessary to obtain them, but a desire seeking satisfaction. The ancient disagreement on who was the best judge of value of things, the maker or the user, had been resolved in no ambiguous terms in favor of the user; and the question of the right to judge was blended with the issue of authorship rights (Bauman 2001).

From the "possessive" individual of modernity we are well on the way to the "possessed" individual of postmodernity (Kroker 1992)—an era of egocracy and egology, more accurately, an egomimesis where the Other is only recog-nized as the same (MacCannell Flower 1991, 49). Designer capitalism in its "flexible" and "fluid" state needs a new slate of sex/gendered bodies for con-sumption (jagodzinski 2003a). It has found these bodies in the new queer identities that deconstruct the hetero/homo binary of modernism. Yet, this "possessed" individual is decentered, not in control of his/her desires. It is the desire of the Other that Lacan forwards, marking yet again an antihumanism—a "death of man." Rather than the existential "who am I?" of ego psychology, we are faced with "whose am I?" of the Real. We are not entirely autonomous but subject to language, unconscious affective states that hold us, and precon-ditioned by various social systems that discipline human agency. Language can never be self-present, and hence we can never fully represent ourselves. Such a loss has to be made up through constant desire for satisfaction. This "death of man" is staged by designer capitalism and its economics of the global market-place where the new malleable performing bodies fit the neoliberalist notions of consumer choice and freedom. This is a two-way street, of course. The post-modern fetishizing of a small segment of sexually queer identities, like the free-dom of the *flâneuse* of yesteryear, opens a new realm of freedom at the cost of maintaining an exploitive system; at the same it provides a greater social accept-ance of "queer folk" who are not so materially privileged. Just when does such gay and lesbian visibility become possible? It happens when the market sees profit in such chic free-flow desires that match free-flow financial capital.

Deleuze and Guattari (1983) attempted to expose Marx's initial insight of commodity fetishism through their "anti-Oedipus" thesis, arguing that capitalism produces dehumanized "desiring machines." Heterosexuality is not necessarily needed by capitalism. Desire is "machinic" because the unconscious is not aware of persons as such, only partial objects, which are not representational but process oriented.[1] Their concept of a "body without organs" (BwO) already posits a decentered poststructuralist subject of global capitalism capable of consuming more by being a composite of different "selves" or "masks." One can "wear" the *self* one wants by constructing a "lifestyle" of choice regardless of class, color, gender through clothes, coded jargon, leisure activities, food preferences, sexual preferences, and so on. The individual subject, a BwO, is but a heterogeneous aggregate of parts that can (hyper)consume more "things" that are fed to it. Not only are products targeted to each specific body part, but also the body itself has been parceled out through cosmetic surgery (nose job, liposuction, lip enhancement, breast implant, butt enhancement). The postmodern subject has become a "patrimonial individual," reduced to owning his or her genetic and body parts (Kristeva 2000, 6). As a poststructuralist subject, the self becomes a construction of so many different identity signifiers (e.g., Polish Canadian, male, university professor, white, middle-age...) each with its own discourse of master signifiers to anchor it, making identity much more fluid and changing, more "nomadic" in one respect, but also more peer-bound in another for anchorage (fan cult, label cult, brand name). In a de-Oedipalized world it becomes more difficult to be determined by a socio-symbolic position. Adolescence stretches on and on. Graduate and undergraduate degrees are granted each day with students spewing out of universities and colleges, but unless there is some confirmation of identity by the capitalist Symbolic Order a taxi driver wielding a doctoral degree still remains a taxi driver. One's identity has to be performatively and socially operative, otherwise the degree remains only an imaginary identification. Identity is mostly lived at this imaginary level since confirmation by the Symbolic Order is more and more difficult to ascertain as the number of well-defined symbolic roles shrink (practicing doctor, lawyer, elected politician, teacher, soldier, and so on) while the service sector grows.

Hardt and Negri's (2000) *Empire*, extends Deleuze and Guattari's notion of the way global capitalism deterritorializes and reterritorializes desire by channeling all desire into commodity form. They argue that we have moved from the disciplinary society of modernity to a society of control (as developed by Foucault). Deleuze and Guattari's anti-Oedipus thesis is very much in keeping with the de-Oedipalization hypothesis that we support when trying to understand youth cultures of today. Their theory of unmediated and unregulated desire of the primary processes of the libido is consistent with the drive forces of jouissance that are no longer prohibitory by Oedipalization. The "schizophrenia" they mention, as a productive process we argue is already quite prevalent in music videos as forcefully argued in *Musical Fantasies of Youth Cultures*. A number of artists such as Eminem and

Pink utilize an a.k.a. and a split mirror of an alter ego to provide a critical distance for self-reflection on the Imaginary register as the Symbolic Order is being addressed. But on the whole it is perversion and hyper-narcissism that perhaps are becoming the new "norms" of a global capitalist production. It is along these lines that we continue our claim of the lost of trust in the old Oedipal Order.

PROPPING UP IMPOTENCY: PHALLIC EXPOSURES

In the Lacanian psychoanalytic understanding of *language* as a system, the Phallus refers to "a signifier without signified." The Phallus is that element which acts as a placeholder *within* the system (and not outside it) of what is not-yet-signified, of what eludes the system (Žižek 1994a, 201). It is the element of non-sense within a system of sense that keeps it "open." Without this "negative" signifier the system would be closed. The Phallus has a paradoxical existence of being simultaneously of both "in" and "out" of the system giving it a paradoxical status. Its very "lack" or emptiness as an element enables a projection of the new, *creatio ex nihilo*, to emerge. It is a point of pure absence since it will continually be displaced only to remerge as its own opposite—empty once again. For Lacan this phallic signifier was always fraudulent. Someone had to embody it, but could never, ultimately attain or hold it in some sort of permanent grasp. Someone is granted the Phallus only because there is group support to enable such leadership to continue—power is deferred to the leader. A leader has to embody an Ego Ideal in his or her ability to mete out justice, which is always "beyond" the Law, entering a space of undecidability and impossibility. When it came to deciding the presidency of the United States between G.W. Bush and Al Gore, the U.S. Supreme Court was called to make the final judgment concerning the vote in Florida. Although the decision was clearly biased along Republican lines,[2] there was enough public doubt still left in play that the decision was passed over as being "fair and just" to end what was quickly becoming a total exposure of the fraudulence of the Phallic signifier in the law courts as broadcast on public media of radio and television. This was "reality" television and talk radio at its best. U.S. citizens were riveted to their screens for it spectacularized the belief that an insignificant X (or a punch) on a ballot when tallied together, actually meant something—the outcome of an election. In the end, that X meant little to nothing as argument after argument by Gore's defense lawyer David Boies as to its validity was rhetorically deconstructed.

Despite the exposure of all kinds of injustices in the way ballots were cast, counted, and handled by Florida's court system, the U.S. Supreme Court "barely" survived its test as to whether they could maintain the illusion of unbiased symbolic authority and not be exposed for their partisan motives—their "penises" showing, so to speak, given the predominance of male judges (see Kellner 2001) It is during moments of social upheaval that the exposure of masked relationship between the Phallus and the penis reveals itself most acutely, when phallic impotency is strongly felt—during the French

Revolution (Hertz 1983; Bryson 1984), the *fin de siècle* (Silverman 1992), and our own time of postmodernity (Kroker and Kroker 1991). In the post-modern times, judging by the number of Hollywood films where the penis has become exposed in masturbatory scenes (*There's Something About Mary, American Pie, Boogie Nights, Happiness, American Beauty, Election, Austin Power*), definitely shows that phallic power is shrinking (Glass 2001; jagodzinski 2001). From its symbolic status as a signifier without a signified, it has been reduced to an imaginary function where it has emerged as a recurring joke rather than an embarrassment. It needs the bulk muscles of new superheroes to prop it up again in comics, on feature films, and in video games to still the hysterical fears of a decentering masculinity.

The concern for the impotent penis is registered by the claims of the new miracle drug Viagra, which as Žižek (1999b, 382–384) so cleverly develops, actually does away with the masculine mystique by eliminating the threat of impotence. Impotence introduces the paradoxes of an erection where the penis seems to have a "will" of its own. The male seemingly can and cannot control an erection. Here the difference between the penis and phallus emerges most forcefully. The Supreme Court judges (women and men alike) exert their authority as soon as they don their gowns and walk into the court-room. When they speak, they do so in the name of the Law. The phallus, as signifier of potency, of symbolic legal authority is active through them. The penis is transformed into the phallus. Without their robes they may be absolutely horrible and mean people, or weak personalities. We see this in the clever movie, Steven Spielberg's *Catch Me if You Can* (2002) a "true" story based on the con artist Frank Abagnate Jr. (Leonardo DiCaprio) who was a master of dawning the phallic coat of appearance and lifestyle to gain access to privilege. As the hype goes, before the age of 21, Frank had committed forgery, posed as an airline pilot, college professor, stockbroker, pediatrician, and assistant attorney-general, passing $2,500,000 in bad checks. It is no accident that Abagnate was eventually hired as a consultant to promote check and security measures. A con artist can exist only because the Law is already structured by fraudulence. The failed exchanges of capture between FBI Special Agent Carl Hanratty (Tom Hanks) and Abagnate reveal just how fragile maintaining phallic authority can be. Castration anxiety is all about the fear of losing this symbolic authority, that it will be revealed as a fraud, which was precisely what the accusation of partisanship in the Florida election was all about: the "collapse" of the "supreme court" phallus into an impotent "Republican" penis. The man who swallows the Viagra pill to copulate, quips Žižek, is the man with a penis but without a phallus.

THE LOSS OF EGO IDEAL: MECHANIZED EFFICIENCY

The failure of the trust in the functioning of the Symbolic Order and the incumbent loss of authority in postmodernity can be identified in any num-ber of fronts—seemingly on a "thousand plateaus" to refer to Deleuze and Guattari (1987) again. Kristeva (2000) makes one such broad assessment when it comes to the legal system: "we no longer speak of culpability but of public menace; we no longer speak of fault (in an automobile accident, for example) but of damages. Instead of responsibility, there is liability; the idea of responsibility-without-fault is becoming acceptable; the right to punish is fading before administrative repression; the theatricality of the trail is disappearing in the proliferation of delaying tactics.... Look at the scandals judges, politicians, journalists, business people are involved in. Crime has become theatrically media-friendly" (5). She continues to point out that in such a "liberal" society where punishment has become a farce, theatrically mediated cases have "become a sort of catharsis of the citizen's nonexistent guilt. Though we are not punished, we are, in effect, normalized: in place of the prohibition or power that cannot be found, disciplinary and administrative punishments multiply, repressing or, rather, normalizing everyone" (ibid.).

This again is a form of "biopower" that "regulates social life from its interior, following it, interpreting it, absorbing it, and rearticulating it" (Hardt and Negri 2000, 23–24). Global capitalism has moved from a "for-itself" position as a modern disciplinary society to a postmodern globalized society "for-all." With biopower invested in the reproductive technologies, gene research, cloning, and Stem Cell research we come to Kristeva's "patrimonial individual" where one's genes, sperm, and eggs are for sell (Davis-Floyd and Dumit 1998).[3] It becomes a society of dubious litigation (OJ's trial where he got away with murder, G.W. Bush who stole a presidency), of "compliant" and of the "victim."

For Kristeva (2000) invisible power, nonpunitive legislation, delaying tactics, on the one hand, coupled with media theatricalization on the other engenders and supposes the breaches and transgressions that accompany business, market speculation, and Mafia activity. "These are no longer laws but measures.... Measures are susceptible to appeals and delays, to interpretations and falsifications. This means that, in the end, the New World Order normalizes corruption; it is at once normalizing and pervertible" (5). This is Žižek's (1999b) point as well. The Oedipal father is reduced to self-reflexive rules. The New World Order (postcolonial, post–Cold War, postindustrial) is neither totalitarian nor fascist, but, for Kristeva, a normalizing and falsifiable order. *Power* rather than symbolic authority has become more of the defining factor as trust in institutions continues to decenter. Trust requires total nonreflected acceptance in these institutions. Whereas, power is invested in profit and pleasure rather than authority, which still aims at achieving a higher Ideal. An ascribed status rather than achieved status seems to be returning. Authority prevails as long as power does not have to be evoked—as in a governorship, for instance. The governor "kicks in" when things go amiss, the "climate" no longer is stable. Such a governor no longer exists as a symbolic fiction. In reaction to the stock market crash on "Black Monday" (October 19, 1987), a "circuit breaker" mechanism was institutionalized by which trading would be halted on the Chicago Mercantile Exchange and New York Stock Exchange for one hour if the Dow Jones average fell more than 250 points in a day, and for two hours if it fell more than 400 points. Such a measure is entirely mechanistic, based on an arbitrary chosen number. It has nothing to do with any lofty goals to stop the injustices of the stock market, such as program computer trading, the overvaluation of stocks, the uncertainties surrounding index futures and derivative securities and the difficulties of liquefying stocks. This was strictly business, to protect investors.

Symbolic "efficiency" begins to break down when the *willingness to disavow* the actual state of things can no longer be maintained. The choice between what one believes with one's own "eyes" against what authority says is true (i.e., their word is good enough, it should not be questioned but freely accepted) can no longer be easily sustained, either because the lies are so blatant (e.g., the Enron executives pleading ignorance, or hiding behind the First Amendment), or because imaginary simulacra of digitalization generates illusions that cause a hesitation: should I, or should I not believe this "reality" that I see? (Žižek 1999b, 322–326). Belief has become a search to anchor oneself again. In the West, this belief has turned to more esoteric Eastern religions and the mysticism of New Ageism where the emphasis on nonmaterialism is a way to find renewed meaning. Above all, this New Ageism has spawned what can be called a "religion without sacrifice," a religion that harps back to a postemotionality of serenity and stress relief for body wellness (most generally as forms of massage therapy) through any number of Asian body techniques: shiatsu, yoga, Shin Do/Acupressure, Tai Chi, Thai massage, and so on. Religion has become a shopping mall practice, more like Madonna's excursions into studying the Kabbalah (Jewish mysticism), mixed in with a bit of ayurveda (Indian holistic medicine) to arrive at serenity, and get away from her own blatant artifice. These forms have been (literally and figuratively) drained of their blood. In the ancient ritual of sacrifice, blood was an anti-entity, an abjected substance. Blood sacrifice has since undergone an evolution to practices of offerings and oblation, and finally to traditions of self-denial and asceticism where violence plays no explicit part. However, in all these forms what is sacrificed is an immediate access to the object of desire. Through a ritual an "object," or part of the self is given up in order to regain it in a new form. In this way the circulation of desire and signification come into being. The object has to be destroyed and lost so that it may be recovered in its symbolic dimension, enabling a bond to take place between the one who makes the sacrifices and the Symbolic Order (as a Cause, a perceived greater Good, a higher Spirit). This loss comes back as gift from the Other. The one who has sacrificed is confirmed within the group's solidarity (Boothby 2001, 186–189). In contrast, Madonna stages its perverse opposite. There is no sacrificial loss so that a gift might be received from the Symbolic Order. The trust in the symbolic is gone. In her claim to religious "holism" and wellness, she seals her ego by eating and digesting the bits of spiritual packages she consumes; religion becomes a form of spiritual boutique shopping. She has her own individual "spirituality" not dependent on some higher Cause. Just to make sure, with her film director husband Guy Richie, they have invested in the building of a Kabbalah Centre in London to match the one already in Los Angeles.

UNDECIDABLE ETHICS

There is another reason why "moral panic" seems so prevalent in postmodernity. The certainty of a moral high ground as to how to conduct ourselves has been lost, or at least waning. What has emerged is a *situational* ethics characterized by the making of rules and individual arrangements. One level of this results in what Lyotard (1988) identified as a *différend*,[4] a deadlock that emerges when it comes to ethical dilemmas, for example, the abortion/antiabortion debate, or the difficulty in deciding the complaint of a victim of sexual harassment (Clarence Thomas vs. Anita Hill) or hate speech (Ernst Zundel's neo-nazi propaganda), as well as statutory rape. This last dilemma is particularly difficult to negotiate. Statutory rape is not about the sex the victim says she did *not* want, but about sex which she *did* want; that is to say, the sex adults believe she only *thought* she wanted because she wasn't old enough to know one way or another! As a victim, the court views her as a hysteric caught in undecidability, rather than as a subject.

All these cases mark the limits of applying a universal principle. The *différend* problematic leads to a society of self-reflexivity where committees attempt to establish rules of conduct, such as university and workplace regulations on sexual harassment, but these rules often become empty measures, difficult to enforce. Quite often the "objective" discourse of science is called in to demarcate the Law. The legal abortion of a fetus is set during the first trimester (13 weeks) since, medically speaking, it does not feel pain. Equally perplexing is Left and Right politics that have been replaced by a "Third Way," such as Tony Blair's *New* Labor Party in Britain, because class divisions are no longer evenly divided between unorganized blue-collar working class and an office or professional class. A "wired" class and a service-sector class have changed the political landscape. Politically correct expressions at attempts to reduce offensiveness seem to backfire as well. Being called "visually challenged" or "visually impaired" thinly disguises the more direct term "ugly" or "blind," depending how "visual" is being interpreted, only makes matters worse, not better. Given the "wrong" context, the PC term becomes a weapon of irony that patronizes and humiliates. With the collapse of clear-cut rules there is a tendency for hystericized behavior, a state of constant troubling doubt. Not believing in what is being offered as the "truth," at the same time frantically searching to find a "truth" to live by—as a lifestyle or as a New Age religion. In the "risk society" of the "second Enlightenment," as theorized by Ulrich Beck and Anthony Giddens, the "Runaway World" leads to a radical uncertainty as to the consequences of our actions. We are "colonized by reflexivity" says Žižek (1999b, 366).

The *Unbehagen* of such a risk society is best summarized by Stjepan Meštrović's (1997) notion of a "postemotional society" where he argues that the aesthetization of postmodernist society has essentially produced its opposite effect: an emotional sterility, what we would call *Anästhetisierung* (anaestheticism) after Welsch (1990, 65). Welsh identifies a point of deadness or inertness in the excesses of aesthetics itself, a moment of overkill and suspension (31). There are many manifestations of this, some rather trite, but telling. It is possible to buy a good undergraduate term paper on the web on virtually any sociological topic of choice. The greatest selection and choice are in areas where the social problems are most dramatic: domestic violence, alcoholism, child labor, media influence, addictions, street gangs, homeless.... Space does not allow us to list the incredible number of "packaged" papers, but they are an indication that the suffering that is attached to each one of these societal ills needs no further study. A student can "buy" the emotion and pass it in for a grade (if undetected, of course). It is a prime example of "interpassivity" where the ready-made term paper is bestowed the task of having done the "work," relieving the student of its necessity (see Pfaller 2002). Couples today can also buy ready-made prenuptial contracts that pre-specify what usually causes friction in a marriage. Signing it will guarantee tension-free living, and peace of mind when the inevitable divorce comes. In Somtow Sucharitkul's science-fiction novel, *The Ultimate Mallworld* (2000), a consumerist satire set in a 30 kilometer-long shopping center located between an asteroid belt and Jupiter where anything can be instantly had, there are no prohibitions. You can shop till you drop—literally. One of the more successful franchises is The Way Out Corporation, which operates sui-cide booths throughout the mall. These self-immolation parlors speak to a general exhaustion and ennui that periodically grips many of the novel's characters. With no prohibitions, desire has been done away with and the drive forces run amuck as gratifications are always satisfied. While the hyper-bole of the suicide booth makes its point, there is a more sobering thought to consider. Why do so many young people suffer from depression and anxiety—the two most common mental illnesses, with as many as one in every thirty-three children and one in eight adolescents may have depression?[5] Could they be postemotional symptoms that have emerged in a consumerist society where the loss of affectivity is due to the continuous pressure to grat-ify the ego? What Kenneth Gergen (1991) popularized as "the saturated self."

Depression, which may lead to suicide, emerges when there is no more desire. The person feels rather empty as if s/he is nothing. No one desires them. Being a jobless youth, for instance, means no symbolic identification. There is no feeling of self-worth since no one confirms a subject's contribu-tion as a human being. Academia, for instance, is full of rejection and envy as academics vie for positions, publications, research money, and graduate students. The opposite of this predicament can also lead to ennui and depres-sion. Being given everything that is demanded so that there are no bound-aries can lead to a similar loss of identity, as if one didn't have to work to achieve anything. In Canadian junior high schools there is no such thing as failure. A child moves on into the next class regardless of achievement. Holding a child "back" is considered more damaging than setting up reme-dial help with students of the same age. This paradox was summarized by Lacan in the demand to "enjoy" by what he called "*plus-de-jouir.*" The pun plays on the ambivalence of the French word *plus*, meaning both "extra or bonus" and "no longer." It refers to the constant increase in pleasure (*plus*, *encore plus*), which reaches a paradoxical point of the loss of pleasure (*plus de*). The most common youth problem here to illustrate the demand to "enjoy" is drinking alcohol. A point is reached where just one more drink and you are on the other side of pleasure—the bulimic behavior of throwing up, alcoholic bingeing being typical of so much college behavior. There have been student protests at a number of colleges and universities in the United States against banning drinking at outdoor events, yet another indicator of a "rebelliousness without a Cause"; their imaginary enjoyment takes precedence over symbolic issues such as racism, education equity, student conditions, and tuition hikes. This "more pleasure," "Give me more!" also echoes Marx's *Mehrwert* (surplus value) of the fetishistic object (Fink 1995, 190–191, fn. 28). The other side of pleasure is anxiety.

Mass-produced emotions are approached as intellectual constructs, argues Meštrović. They are managed and manipulated by media images, the simulations being roughly equivalent to Nietzschean myths. It is a society of vicarious and conspicuous emotions that are consumed. The disappearance of rites and what is sacred is especially evident. Meštrović notes the striking example of the way Thanksgiving becomes evacuated of any remainder of specialness through the decentering of its meaning. Instead of being an American meaning to Thanksgiving, there is a Native American meaning where the Pilgrims are the oppressors; there is an African American meaning that likens the oppression of the Indians to slaves; a feminist American reading exposes the sexism of the Pilgrim Fathers, not to mention many American minorities where Thanksgiving is meaningless, only celebrated as a day off from work or school. Contemporary funeral rites, as he notes, are increasingly shorter in duration. They have become "instantaneous" with the mourning period substantially lessened as its "back to work" as soon as possible. The burden of children caring for their elderly and sick parents at home is no longer the case. Old age homes, as a "home away from home," have taken over this function. Rather than "compassionate attachments" we suffer from compassion anomie, from the infinite desires that cannot be satisfied. Above all, Meštrović's notion of postemotionalism identified the disavowed effects of the very depoliticization of the economic sphere; the loss of passion to the question of what's wrong with the injustices wrought by designer capitalism. After the 9/11 event, postindustrial countries (America, Britain—to some degree French, Germany) have redirected their efforts to the "war on terrorism," once more diverting the focus away from the global economy. Sadam Hussein has become the fixation of the Bush administration as the threat to Western liberal democracy for reasons that remain questionable. The combination of Bush's moralism and his oil interests have resulted in a global skepticism that extends to forms of resentment as the United States, representing 4 percent of the world's population, continues to set the global agenda with its military might in the name of a New World Order.

Meštrović updates Reisman's "other-directed individual" as characteristic of the postemotional subject. Such an individual is defined more by the singularity of a group (what we are referring to as the ONE) than being "inner directed." The peer crowd (friends) and their image is what is most important. Parents no longer mete out corporal punishment. Instead they use "time out" or "ground" their children for misbehavior by isolating them from their peers, or cut off allowance and television. These are punishments of satisfaction to get control. "Other-directed" transgressions are forms of bullying, hurting the feeling of others, being rude and selfish—egocentric in nature. Failing to do well in school or failing to meet parental expectations have become less important. Ironically in the post-Oedipal climate, it is middle-class Boomer parents who still maintain a "work ethic" while their postadolescent children are into "leisure." Parents work so that their teenagers can shop and have fun—reconfirming the post-Oedipal demand of global capitalism to enjoy and have fun. Or, what amounts to the same thing, to work for your leisure that places the more important part of the day on nightlife where it is important to have as much "fun" as possible after work, and "most definitely" during the weekends. In reality, parents have less control over their children today. This is humorously illustrated in *The Sopranos* when Meadow throws a wild party in Livia's empty house with her strung-out teenage friends. Tony catches her misbehavior and drives her home. Carmela and Tony lie in bed trying to figure out what a suitable punishment should be; and they come to the realization that they are essentially powerless. Carmela complains that if they take her car away (deny her pleasure), then she becomes her chauffeur. If they ground her one of them has to stay home on the weekend and act as a prison guard. Tony pipes in that they can't restrain her physically either because they'll be charged with child abuse.

With the extension of adolescence, children are treated as more responsible citizens and given freedoms of choice that they never had before. "Deals" and contracts are negotiated with middle-class parents about rewards, bedtime, the purchase of a new computer if certain grades are achieved, and so on. In divorce procedures children are allowed to have an influence in the decision, as to which parent they want to stay with, which is often made on their emotional well-being. They can even opt to get out of their biological family if they can show that they are being sexually abused, or mistreated unfairly. The child spends less and less time in the home and with family when one considers the amount of time taken by day-care centers and school. In well-off households the kids usually have their own private rooms with "stay out" signs equipped with television, computer, and DVD players. The family meal, aside from special occasions (birthdays, holidays) is the exception rather than the rule. It is the public and professional institutions that have become more like a surrogate family—the school, the university, college, and the corporate company and the peer groups (friends) in them. These institutions attempt to stamp their personal logo to maintain loyalty and belonging by its employees/clientele. This is especially true of so-called character schools with their turn back to "tradition" (school uniforms, Latin, and technology). The paradoxical result is that, on the one hand, children are being recognized as being more mature and responsible (the children's rights movement). On the other hand, such phenomena as "rebounding," where children come back home to live with parents after finishing higher education, or because the job just doesn't pay enough for them to make it on their own prevent them from growing up. Institutions have also become ersatz families, in some cases providing work-out facilities, vacation trips, and festival gatherings, extending adolescence indefinitely, like the characters on the hit television series *Seinfeld* and *Ally McBeal*. Even lawyers are engaged in fickle adolescent behavior, the morphing special effect exaggerations of Ally McBeal's *fantasies* especially bring this home.

PÈRE-VERSION AS THE NORM?

A situational ethic is most often resolved through "mutual" and "informed" consent between adults, enabling deviant forms of pleasure to be permitted. The limit of this informed consent is reached when the age of sexual activity is under consideration. At what age is sexual activity no longer considered pedophilic? With the failure of the Law and loss of faith in its structures the perverse subject is slowly becoming the norm. The term "perversion" is no longer politically correct, and is being replaced by "paraphilia" (Verhaeghe 1999, 114). Paraphilias are sexual desires or activities that lie outside the cultural norm; under some conditions they are considered mental disorders. Homosexuality, once considered a paraphilia, is now considered normal, dropped as a mental disorder by the American Psychiatric Association (APA). Transexuality, bisexuality, transvestitism are sure to follow. More disturbingly, consensual sadomasochism, exhibitionism, voyeurism and non-psychotic forms of fetishism, urolagnia, and even coprophilia (especially as now performed by sex workers) are increasingly becoming culturally acceptable forms of sexuality. In Germany and Austria, the television show *Wa(h)re Liebe* (the word play is on "true" love—wahre liebe, and ware liebe—the merchandising of love) is hosted by a transsexual, Lilo Wanders. The show features documentary-type stories about prostitution (both professional and amateur), swing couples, group orgies, love hotels, sex spas, sadomasochistic practices, orgies, aspects of the sex trade like the making of porno films, use of sex toys, how to practice anal sex, and so on.

Television shows like *Wa(h)re Liebe* attempt to "normalize" such behavior by being very nonchalant when presenting pseudo-pornographic material as if everybody's "doing it" with nothing to be ashamed of. Increased sexual pleasure becomes a demand. The featured bacchanal orgies induce an ecstasy, a feeling of standing outside oneself as the participant becomes "full of the Other" (Verhaeghe 1999, 179–180). This is precisely what the "mosh (slam) pits" do during music performances. The ego "disappears" into the Other, the rules of conduct as how to act in such a group dynamic being ill-defined since the risk of being physically hurt is part of the mosh experience. Sadomasochism and bondage in both homo and hetero forms are especially paradigmatic of a post-Oedipal society as the couple "contracts" out an agreement between the top (domina) and bottom as to the rules of the game that acts as a substitute for the missing Law, with the "bottom" having control of the situation. It is the victim who invests the torturer with the symbolic power of the Law. The failure of "trust" in the Symbolic Order is substituted by the "trust" in the rules of the SM relationship. If power is the "only game in town," men in positions of power have particularly enjoyed the fantasy of being "bossed" around by a demanding woman, whom they, in effect control. The binary reversals of master/slave, adult/baby, man/woman bring the "bottom" to experience jouissance—the paradoxical reversal of pain to pleasure emerges when the forbidden feminine aspects of male identity are experienced by surrendering to female power in the heterosexual scenario. Lesbian SM relationships have their own particular reversals as well (McClintock 1993; jagodzinski 1996, 399–415). The band, Genitorturers' motto is "Pleasure, pain—it's all the same." The front-woman, Gen, acts as a domina during the performances for all those who want to be "punished" by her with her whip, paddle, and nipple clamps. Their new album, "Flesh is the Law," is frank, explicit, and direct in its theatrical staging. The thrill of being driven to the edge in SM practices, to the point where an orgasmic release is felt through the bruised skin has become more public in an age where the Law has become lax, featured more frequently in film (spoofed in Garry Marshall's *Exit to Eden*, 1994) and on the *Life* television network.

Foucault's own sadomasochistic practices (see Miller 1993) have lead to his ethics based on a situational "care of the self," and the "technologies of the self," which seem to fit perfectly with designer capitalism's adjustments to de-Oedipalization. (Ironically, Foucault died of AIDS.) We see this decentering of the Law as advocated by Foucault as a shift from *guilt* to *shame*. Guilt refers to a Law that one unconsciously feels. One knows one has done something wrong, and hence one is already guilty because the "No!" has been internalized by a superstructural ego. With shame, it is a feeling that is confined to a group identity, a peer group especially where there is (usually) some sort of initiation rites of belonging—hazing, tattooing, and even killing as in some LA gangs. Only in this way is symbolic status earned. The sacrifice of the body has to be literalized—physically marked on the body as a "symbolic castration" of loyalty and resistance to the socio-symbolic Law. Tattooing and piercing have become the most common ways. It is a mark left by the death-drive. (To refer to *The Sopranos* again, Christopher's initiation as a capo into the Mafia meant having his finger pin-pricked to let the blood run while he swore his oath to the brotherhood.) The feeling of shame involves the Imaginary ego; the self is inferior, incompetent, and small. These experiences of inadequate self-esteem circle in situations where there is no transcendental Law at work; it is confined to the context of the rules the group has set. We argue, in the chapters that follow, that youth are more likely to feel shame than guilt because the group is what defines them more than the larger social Order. As in *The Sopranos*, the capos have no guilt about killing, stealing, cheating on their wives as much as they fear the shame of losing face and being put down by their peers or those under them. Christopher, for example, remains an object of anxiety for Paulie because he is unable to have his full respect.

The Paradox of *Just Be*: The Hypernarcissism of Youth

While SM practices present the masochistic subject positions, there is also the active subject who has found sublime pleasure when reaching the body's limit through extreme sports. In the 1950s it seemed that teens were engaged in "illicit" events like "car drags" down a strip late at night; these practices have escalated to legalized "death" stunts. We have only to think of the myriad of extreme sports that youth gleefully engage in today (skateboarding over rails, down steps, over jumps; bungee jumping over bridges; kite flying, extreme snowboarding; extreme motor biking, downhill mountain biking). MTV's *Jackass* seems to celebrate its most ridiculous side as young men try all sorts of bizarre and potentially painful stunts: crashing through a car window wearing a helmet, climbing a tree and then having it cut down to experience the fall, stapling the anus together (yes, you read this right), and so on. The broken bones, scares, and falls are part of the jouissance experience. It is this pain—as a direct response to the loss of prohibition of a social Order where everything goes—which youth find most appealing. Cutting the skin, tattooing, and piercing are all drive responses; ways of "feeling" in the Real to cope with postemotionalism.

Postemotionalism is the other side of a hyper-narcissism that has been inverted into its opposite affect, like a grotesque death mask that begins to appear with too much facial plastic surgery. Now in his forties, a close-up of Michael Jackson's face confirms this hideousness anti-aesthetic.[6] The narcissistic ego is formed by repressing the recognition of the other as Other, canceling difference. The libido is withdrawn from the Other by focusing only on the self. The recognition and acceptance of difference is what a narcissistic ego does not tolerate. The Other has to reflect the self in some way—be eroticized as a self-love. The Other is more or less like me and that's why I love them. Paradoxically, it is this very hyper-narcissistic ego that becomes "ugly" in its attempt to be unlike the Other; the body has to take on more differential signs to distinguish it from the "norm" (as Other)—more tattoos, more pierces, more radical hair styles, more funky inverted clothes, more plastic surgery, more.... There is no celebration of naked innocence of an unmarked classically nude body anymore, which was a sign that the Law has been internalized and there is no need to "show" that one obeys it (Žižek 1999b, 372). Even models sport small visible ankle- and arm-tattooed braces, nipple and navel pieces, not to mention the more hidden tattoos and vaginal rings.

The hyper-narcissistic youth of postmodernism is defined by Freud's "second game" in the mirror that replaces drive over desire. In *Beyond the Pleasure Principle* (1920), few pages after his analysis of the *fort/da* game (game 1), Freud relates a variant of the game his grandson invented (game 2). In the second variation Ernst *became* the cotton reel. Hiding beneath the mirror for a time, he would suddenly jump up and observe the sudden emergence of his mirror reflection; each jump was a performative reiteration of a fatasmatic partial self. In this case, rather than becoming a subject of desire who was lacking-in-being that the *fort/da* game exemplified, Ernst situated himself in the field of being, choosing his own *jouissance* over the "sense" of the signifier. Put another way, Ernst's drive in this second game was a return, again and again, to the master signifier (S_1) of nonsense—that part-object invested with *jouissance* without acquiring the completion of its binary opposite so as to make sense (as $S_1 \rightarrow S_2$), which was at play in the first game. The *fort/da* utterance, as a sign, stood for the presence and absence of the missing object where the "original" nonsensical phoneme finds its supplement to complete its meaning; in the second game the "original" has no supplement so that Ernst can stay as close to the *agalma* (libidinal energy) of Being as long as possible through repetition—like a baby babbling (S VIII, *Transference*). The second game is the trauma of a physical castration that occurs within the body of the drive. It is as necessary as the castration by language. It is a trauma not of meaning and meaninglessness as in language, but a trauma of being (immortality) and non-being (mortality). It is nearest to the greatest possible states of anxiety and bliss given that "reality" is structured on the rejected *objet a* as that something (a piece of one's own being) that has been relegated to non-being (or non-sense). Achieving such a state of seeming immortality is referred to by high-performance piercers and tattooers as a spiritual ecstasy.

The second game tries to stave off the anxiety of the fall of the *objet petit a*. Unlike the first game of *fort/da* that always resulted in a failure to capture that which escapes it, thus initiating desire as an endless repetition and metonymic displacement, Ernst's repetitive performance in the second game was a matter of satisfaction and pleasure (but without the incumbent pain). As we learn from Lacan, satisfaction and dissatisfaction are derived from incorporating the effects of partial objects that become associated with fulfillment only because the *jouissance* effect they give has been lost. The experience of losing *jouissance* makes desire a structure of lack where something always remains unfulfilled. But this excess in desire as the "beyond" that persists in meaning and thought, belongs more properly to the drives given that *jouissance* is the libidinal glue of being, knowing, and feeling. Whereas instincts, which belong the realm of biology, require an object of satisfaction like water and food for the material maintenance of life—as needs (*Not*)—we learn from Freud and Lacan that the drives insinuate a fantasy object—of wants or requirements (*Bedürfnisse*). The (death) drive toward jouissance is beautifully illustrated again in *Death Becomes Her*, with the two actresses seeking the magical potion of libidinal life that will keep them immortal, forever young. In Chuck Russell's *The Mask* (1994) Stanley Ipkiss (Jim Carey) puts on the "green slime" of eternal life and becomes a cartoon figure who has no control over himself (Žižek 1999b, 389). He is reduced to being a "stupid" figure as the drives do all the work, much like Tom Shadyar's *Liar, Liar* (1997) where Jim Carey's oral drive could not be contained. (The lawyer-lair couplet repeats the politician-liar relationship discussed earlier.) It is, once again, the same death mask that appears on the face of someone who has had too many surgical face-lifts, believing that such operations will stave off old age rather than bring death nearer. Ultimately, isn't it the drug of choice (heroine, cocaine, ecstasy) that frees us of the Symbolic Order's hold over us, swallows us up in our own jouissance so that we "disappear" into ourselves? Designer capitalism no longer hides that products are meant to be addictions. Dior's new fragrance advertises itself as *Dior Addict* that dares you to "admit it," just like cigarette advertisements since the late 1970s no longer hide their carcinogenic effects. Now the ad-campaigns invert the death message as a public right to slowly kill oneself in the name of freedom. The jouissance to transgress becomes the way to sell the death sticks (see McIntosh 1996).

This psychic tension between drive (game 2) and desire (game 1) is dramatically illustrated by the identificatory game staged by Calvin Klein's *Obsession* ads (in 1997) for CK perfume. The ads are usually two to five pages long with the full version having three negative (black) pages followed by a black and white picture of the CK perfume bottle with the caption "just be" under it; this is then followed by a well-known female or male fashion model, movie star, or singer who is often tattooed or pierced. Kate Moss is usually the iconic figure shown. On the center of each page the following lines appear in positive (white) print: page 1: *to be*; page 2: *or not to be*; page 3; *just be*. Under each picture of the model either the words "just be" appear, or sometimes one finds the caption: "be a secret, be a rumor" followed by yet another black-and-white photo of a model with "just be" appearing on the bottom of the page.

The answer to Hamlet's well-known soliloquy questioning the meaning of his existence is answered not with a desire to become someone in the Symbolic Order, as would be expected, rather it addresses the drives of the potential buyer: the perfume (the libidinal liquid secret) contained mysteriously in a black bottle offers the jouissance that comes when one just "is." Kate Moss is not presented as her "usual" self, a fashionable model walking down some catwalk modeling the latest fashion, rather her black-and-white picture strip her of all glamor. She wears no make-up, her hair is in shambles; for all intents and purposes she is a rather dowdy figure. (All the CK models appear in this "fashion.") Here lies the psychic tension of the ad: the viewer is caught between the dialectics of his/her own drive and desire in the following way: Fashion is a dress in which the key feature is rapid and continually changing style; fashion *is* change that perfectly supports flexible capitalism's need for a decentered subject who consumes. Constantly changing fashion produces conformity as the never-before-seen becomes the self-effacingly correct. Paradoxically, to dress fashionably is both to stand out and to merge into the crowd, to lay claim to exclusiveness and to follow the herd. Only those who are fashionable have no concern for fashion since they create and wear it. Their demeanor is therefore "cool" and blasé. In this ad Moss presents the "obscene supplement" to this capitalist structure by being determinedly *unfashionable*. She stages Ernst's second game as if identity required no spectatorship, no confirmation by the Other as to who one is.

The perversity of this gesture should now become obvious. Clinically, obsession is characterized by an *impossible* desire. The closer the obsessive gets to realize his [*sic*] desire, the more the Other begins to take precedence over him, eclipsing him as a subject. However, in the vernacular obsession merely refers to being possessed by an idea or image that you are unable to get rid off. The assumption being that if you just try long enough, your dream will eventually be fulfilled. Here the ideological subject position of the ad's discourse is offered no existential choice as to where to turn: to "just be" or "to be" fashionable. The antilogics of the solution is therefore to turn toward your own jouissance (i.e., just be) by making an antifashionable statement, and by doing so you will become fashionable (i.e., a rumor, a secret). The deadlock between drive and desire is therefore broken, and resolved by playing Freud's "second game." It is this perversity that is becoming the "norm," packaged by designer capitalism and neoliberalist ideology as the way "to be."

With such egoism of doing away with the Other that defines you (to which you must yield some of your jouissance in order to be part of the social order) comes the anxiety of being unsure of one's identity. There are seemingly a myriad of possibilities that lead to over-choice, a sense of being overwhelmed by a compulsion to be anything I want to be because there is no boundary that will stop the slide of being out of control. We are asked to reflexively choose to the point of a postemotionalism—the paradox of being frumpy, disheveled, or non-fashionable of "just be." The signifiers that eventually anchor the teen is established through a peer group that differentiates itself from other peer groups by the "affective" life-style it creates through music, clothes, shopping to articulate a particular brand. This means that the unique individualism is always externalized into the group of friends. To leave such a reconfirming "support group" where hysteria of identity is kept in check, and go it alone is rather unnerving. Such "outsider" status of not belonging in a group is not unusual in schools. Kids who don't fit "in" to the existing peer structures are becoming more resentful, leading to pathological behavior as in the case of Columbine. Judging by the increase in "personal ads" by young adults on-line seeking partnership, the lack of a circle of friends is socially endemic. The postmodern addiction to self-help "scenes" (as satirized in David Fincher's *Fight Club*, 1999) which provide rules, like the 12-step method to live by, become therapy centers defined by social symptoms. The anxiety of identity increases if these support groups are left. They become addictive in their own right as centers of common human suffering.

NAMES OF THE FATHER: TRADITIONALISM AND CYNICISM

The reactions to the collapse of symbolic efficiency—de-Oedipalization, have taken a number of definitive directions; all of which effect youth cultures. We can call them various articulations of the "names of the father" after Lacan's undelivered 1963 seminar on "Les nomes du père" as the result of his expulsion from IPA. They represent forms of reactionary recentering to postmodern uncertainly by refiguring authority in ways, which provide forms of functional resistance to its loss. The most obvious shift is toward traditionalism and fundamentalism. These movements—Christian fundamentalism and Islamic fundamentalism—are generally misunderstood as a naïve conservative return to the past where strict rules of a moral code still apply, especially in their cultist and religious manifestations. They are anti-modern and static in their opposition to a secularized society. This is but a half-truth. While it is true that both movements return to the sacred texts of their prophetic founders, Jesus (Bible, the Gospels) and Muhammad (Qur'an and Sunna), and to the authority of the patriarchal father, religious leaders, priests, and jurists for guidance and inspiration, they are very much postmodern movements in their attempt "update" the significance of their traditions for contemporary society.[7] The return is always to install a "difference." But this is always an ideological question of the "difference" since it embodies an unconscious fantasy of restoration. Christian fundamentalism constructs the fantasy of a stable, pure, and wholesome nuclear family that never existed, except on television (Coontz 1992). Islamic fundamentalism is also engaged against its own tradition of Islamic modernism, like Saudi Arabia, that has submitted to Euro-American capitalist hegemony (Ahmed 1992; Hardt and Negri 2000, 146–150).

Tradition is not simply "pure" nostalgia. Nostalgia, as a concept, embodies two distinct terms: *nostos* meaning "home," and *algia* meaning a "longing" (Boym 2001). We might view *nostos* as a restorative melancholia, a return to tradition that is safe because the boundaries are so clearly defined. Orthodoxy prevails. This is especially true with the men's movements such as the Promise Keepers where men promise to become the patriarchal guardians they once were. When it comes to *algia* we might see this more as a "reflective mourning," a more critical use of tradition to be able to see what has been neglected, forgotten, and recoverable. Toni Morrison's *Beloved* (1987) is a good example of this narrative strategy, a going back to fight the ghosts of the past in order to move forward rather than a staying behind.

The prevalent danger of fundamentalism today is that such a psychic economy is often characterized by a paranoid personality as exemplified by the rise of self-assured world leaders who are prone to delusions of grandeur characterized by an absence of self-reflective doubt. Such figures appear innocent to their followers because any shortcoming and defects are attributed to the fault of the Other. It is the Other who persecutes and is a threat (see Verhaeghe 1999, 121). Such a paranoid personality is also free from neurotic self-doubt because the psychic economy of the hysteric has emerged to both complement and reassure that such a leader is morally "right" when confirming his leadership. The postmodern hysteric is caught up in a multitude of desires, an obsession that the paternal authority is not living up to its Ego Ideal—which is his symbolic mandate. There is a search for a renewed paternal authority, a personality structure who would guarantee "The Truth." Paranoid personality figures like Osama Bin Laden, Rev. Farrakhan, Ariel

Sharon, Kim Jong II, Dick Cheney, and G.W. Bush (who was fixated on Saddam Hussein) have emerged to recenter authority. Much like the *coup d'état* staged by the four-star General Pervez Musharraf of Pakistan who took power in 1999 on the grounds of restoring democracy to what was a corrupt government. The Bush's administration on the "war on terror" has enabled a paranoiac strategy to develop, which attempts to preempt any possible future strike, as if the future could be controlled. Allies are either with them or against them, a choice without a choice. By positioning the United States as a victim, the moral high ground was taken during Bush's 2002 State of the Union address where the "axis of Evil" (Iran, Iraq, and North Korea) were said to be developing weapons of mass destruction (WMD) with Iran and Iraq having links to Al-Qaeda. Now any country can pose a threat. The Bush administration's unilateral and self-opinionated foreign policy seems to be a further example of a hyper-narcissism and a political immaturity of not being able to grow up, still in the shadow of Bush, Senior. Paranoia and conspiracy theories (which we develop in later books when discussing *X-Files* and the video game *Majestic*) are two responses to the nonexistence of the big Other, a belief that there is an Other of the Other, someone who is manipulating the strings.

Another strategy already discussed is a culture of cynicism, best represented by Peter Sloterdijk's (1987) well-known thesis. In many ways, cynicism is a form of self-preservation, and yet another name for one of the competing Fathers. The cynic has lost any idealism that the world can be improved upon or made better. It *is* what it *is*. Knowing how to play the game is all that counts. It is as if the cynic knows full well how the obscene supplement of the Law works. S/he knows how the dirty deals are set up, and how those who get ahead do so with the help of people in high places; but s/he feels powerless to do anything against such corruption. The cynic has given up trusting the Law. By distrusting the social symbolic institution s/he can also indulge in paranoia. Solterdijk calls such an attitude an "Enlightened false consciousness." When it comes to youth cultures, Sloterdijk's exploration of what he calls "kynicism" is much more apt. Satire and resistance form the healthier aspects of this kind of cynicism, where it becomes impudent, and rebellious in the face of the status quo. This is the laughing cynicism of Diogenes—god as a dog (Kynos)—pissing against the idealist wind of Plato and his *Republic*, exposing its arrogant utopianism.

Sometimes Diogenes is referred to as the "original punk" because one part of his head was shaved. In his laughter there is a strain of vitality and incorruptibility that mark resistance in face of cynicism. It seems as if the kynical attitude of resistance and satire of youth groups today collapses into forms of status markers that make them superior to so-called conformists— the Nerds, for example. Black-Punk fashions, which parody the mythological garb of the Nazi SS, seem to fail in making such a statement. Often it is impossible to distinguish between parody and the "real thing," like those neo-Nazi skinheads who mimic their SS heroes. The skull and crossbones mythology found in biker gangs, black leather and chains, cross fetishes, vampire allusions to necrophilia, and the tarot appear equally unsuccessful as kynical ruses. *The Propaganda*, a punk-rock magazine (one assumes its name to be kynical) for instance, serves up the latest latex and leather fashions. Featured in the twenty-seventh edition was Canada's Bif Naked, billed as a tattooed and pierced singer, songwriter, sorceress, seductress who has also appeared on the covers of *Glamour* and *Vogue*. Stories of erotic horror, SM scenes featuring lesbo and gay love illustrate to what degree such "gender trouble" (to use Butler's well-known phrase) is subversive parodic kynisism or simply feeding designer capitalism's need for consumer bodies? The twenty-seventh edition features a photograph of Sebastion, a 20-year-old gay dressed suitably in jackboots, leather cap, leather briefs, and leather strip-like suspenders photographed in the space where the Berlin Wall once stood. The context of the photo raises the political and social issues between East and West Berliners; the West swarming in the luxury of capitalist consumerism, the East reduced to the consumerism of street sex. But how far does this aesthetization of Sebastian's body point to this larger political economic concern? Very little. *Propaganda* is another "lifestyle" magazine featuring homoerotic imagery where gay and lesbian vogue is in. Maybe a bit more raunchy, but it joins other more middle-class mainstream lifestyle magazines that promote a similar erotic chic (*Details, Esquire, GQ, Maxim, Mademoiselle*). As Rosemary Hennessy (2000) points out, such chic queer consumerism pertains to only a very small niche of middle-class service workers in academia and the media entertainment industry who have emerged as the "new bourgeois professional class" (117). Rosemary Hennessy may well be right. In this second section of the book we have attempted to describe the post-Oedipal landscape, both its historical and contemporary manifestations. In part III we argue that the perverse landscape of the media is a direct manifestation of post-Oedipal society, intimately and hypercomplexly intertwined and overlaid in video games, the Internet, television, and music, which we reserve to discuss in companion books.

III

CYBERSPACE AS OBSESSIVE INTERPASSIVITY

7

MEDIA VIOLENCE AND YOUTH
(YET AGAIN!?)

THE BANALITY OF MEDIA VIOLENCE RESEARCH

In a rather pedestrian but responsible, orderly, and dutiful way, Jonathan L. Freedman, professor of psychology at the University of Toronto, painstakingly and meticulously reviewed "all"—about 200 or so significant research studies—of the available "scientific empirical evidence" on the correlation between viewing television and film violence and their subsequent effects in causing aggression, criminal behavior, and delinquency in participants. Freedman also examined the question of desensitization; whether people exposed to media violence caused them to become more callous or indifferent toward violence. These studies consisted of surveys, laboratory and field experiments, longitudinal studies, and studies that assessed aggression or crime when television was either present or absent. In his book, *Media Violence and Its Effect on Aggression* (2002), Freedman directly confronts the ubiquitous belief that children and adults—especially children—who watch violence on television and in the movies, *mutatis mutandis* for violent video games, are apt to become more aggressive and commit crimes. Seeing thousands of murders, fistfights, martial arts battles, knifings, shootings, bombing, and exploding cars take place between the forces of good and evil in the survey research results in a causal correlation between 1 and 9 percent. Such a sliding scale, however, only raises the *possibility* that media violence causes aggression. Once the rest of the research is examined, claims Freedman, the correlation in the survey research fails to be substantiated. Freedman concludes that there does not appear to be overwhelming support either for the causal or the desensitization hypothesis. He directly accuses prestigious scientific and medical organizations (the list is rather formidable: The American Psychiatric Association (APA), the Canadian Psychological Association (CPA), the American Medical Association (AMA), the American Academy of Pediatrics (AAP), the American Psychological Association (APA), the American Academy of Child and Adolescent Psychiatry, and the National Institute of Mental Health (NIMH)) of falsely claiming conclusively that media violence cause aggression. At the end of his carefully analysis Freedman states, "*Not one study* has shown that those who are exposed to more media violence are more likely to become criminals, to hurt anyone, to commit any violent crime or serious aggressive act" (202, emphasis added).

So, is this a conspiracy to keep the political and religious lobbyists at bay and dissatisfied? Defining violence and aggression is already problematic in most "scientific" studies; measuring it in laboratory or field situations becomes even more suspect, while claiming "causality" for desensitization and violence seems outright impossible. Freedman's plea to dispel the belief that there is a lack of scientific support for the causal hypothesis that relates violence to fictional material will, however, continue to fall on deaf ears. The belief in the relationship remains an ideological edifice, a symptom of the "loss of symbolic authority" and a disavowal of the sociological evidence that *poverty and family breakdown are the most significant variables.* Socioeconomic status is the greatest single factor when it comes to outbreaks of violence and crime, not to mention the availability of lethal weapons in countries like the United States. (Incest, e.g., is even correlated with poverty. In the United States a child whose parents bring in less than 15,000 dollars a year is 18 times more likely to be sexually abused at home than from a family with an income 30,000 dollars, Levine 2002, xxxiii.) Freedman joins a long list of sociologists and youth researchers who point out that youth violence has actually been declining steadily in the United Sates since the early 1990s (Krisberg 1994; Donziger 1996; Katz 1997, 92–95; Lucas 1998). Elementary school students, according to FBI records, are much less likely to be murdered today than in the 1960s and 1970s (Freedman 2002, 7–8). Such "facts," however, do little to unhinge the public's perception that in most industrialized countries there is a "moral panic" concerning the perceived threat to children. Family abuse, satanic worship, paedophilic stalkers, serial murders, and child pornographers are the order of the day. They continue to be sensationalized by the media because of their story value. Freedman also joins a list of other concerned media researchers in the past who have attempted to "set the record straight" concerning media effects, but also to no avail (Cumberbatch and Howitt 1989; Buckingham 1993; Gauntlett 1995; Barker and Petly 1997).

What "violence" means to youth themselves often presents a quite different picture than what media researchers have preestablished as being violent. Not only are there age differences (between infants, youth, and adults), gender differences (girls more likely to perceive the threat of violence than boys), differences in the perceptions of violence in certain genres and their depiction of empirical events (cartoons on one side of the scale in terms of fictitious representation, the news on the other in terms of its empirical actuality), but also socioeconomic and cultural differences. Television programming in the United States incorporates more violent scenes yet, on average, such violence is not taken as seriously whereas British and Australian audiences take more exception to such depiction. Upper-class parents, for example, tend to be more antiviolence when performing as "concerned parents" for researchers even when they have little control over what their children watch on television or the video games they play (Buckingham 1993).

The media violence debate is obviously hypercomplex. Given the huge profit-dollars that come with the marketing of video games, an industry that has now surpassed the music industry in annual profit shares, and the clamor of concerned educators, politicians, and middle- to upper-class parents wanting to "protect" their children, the "violence industry" is thriving. Even Madonna has banned television at home! University researchers especially in education and the social sciences (mainly psychology and sociology) have found a rich source of research dollars from governments and industry alike to investigate media violence with the added pressure to confirm the hypothesis of its ill-effects. Such funded research tends to reproduce traditional classical "objective" scientific paradigms that the scientific community of adjudicators support—statistical analysis, analysis of questionnaires, surveys, and many dubious but certainly inventive laboratory experiments.

PLAYING NBA AND MORTAL KOMBAT IN THE LAB

One American example stands out for us as a paradigm case of such "effects" research, which we shall examine carefully to identify some of its pitfalls. We have chosen this particular example because it has many affinities with Stanley Milgram's (1965) well-known and discussed psychological experiment conducted at Yale. So-named "teachers" were asked to administer an electric shock of increasing intensity to a "learner" for each mistake made during an experiment carried out by an administrator (an authority figure). The experiment raised the controversial relationship between obedience to authority and personal conscience. Somewhat analogously Mary Ballard (1999) and her co-researchers set out to find a correlation between violent video games and the resultant aggression. Male college students[1] were asked to play NBA Jam and three versions of Mortal Kombat (MK) for 15 minutes in a competitive laboratory setting against either a male or female competitor. The experiment was to determine whether the escalating violence in each of the games resulted in an increase of aggression by a male competitor measured in terms of a reward or punishment system. Only male subjects were used since college females, according to the researchers, tended not to play these violent games! The first game, NBA Jam, was considered to be nonviolent, while the second violent. Mortal Kombat (MK) had three levels of escalating violence: MK 1 with no blood, MK 2 with blood, and then MK 3 where gushing blood was always present when a character used a weapon. The graphics were more refined with finishing moves (known more commonly as "fatalities" in MK) as when a character like Kano wrenches the heart out of his opponent, or the Scorpion pulls out spines and skulls. Special effects included exploding torsos, cannibalism, dismemberment, and soul-stealing.

An "experimenter" escorted each male participant into the lab along with an accomplice (male or female) who posed as his competitor. (Milgram's experiment also had an "experimenter" who introduced the "teacher" and "learner.") The accomplice-competitor was trained in all the games and almost always won. The accomplice had already memorized 20 word pairs, which were part of the experiment in determining a reward or punishment. Five of those word pairs differed from the 20 word pairs that the participant received. When asked by the male participant to name all 20 word pairs after the competition was over, the accomplice-competitor would always miss five word pairs. (Milgram's sample also used paired words that had to be read back to investigate memory and learning.) Some form of punishment would have to be meted out. The "experimenter" told both the male participant and the accomplice-competitor to study the list of 20 word pairs for 3 minutes for a memory experiment; then to play the game for 15 minutes (which had been selected on a counterbalanced fashion so that all the games would eventually be tested).

After the game the participant would draw a slip of paper that would assign a "teacher" or a "learner's" role to see who would initiate the test of memory. The draw was set up so that the male participant always drew the "teacher's" role, and hence he would test his competitor-accomplice (male or female) for the matching words. (The Milgram experiment also rigged the teacher/learner pairing by drawing lots to determine the roles. The "teacher" was always the one who had answered the newspaper ad.) The male participant was instructed to reward the "learner" (his competitor) at his discretion with jellybeans for a correct answer, and punish him or her by sticking his or her hand in a bowl of ice water for every wrong answer. Each male participant's hand was placed in the ice water to demonstrate that he had to physically take the hand of the "learner" and place it in the water, release the arm, and then ask the "learner" to remove his or her hand from the ice water on his command. How long the "learner's" hand remained in the water was dependent on the male participant's discretion. (The slight difference from the Milgram experiment was that no reward was given to the competitor for a correct answer.) The submersion time in the water was timed and the jelly beans counted by research assistants behind a one-way mirror. The "experimenter" who brought the participant and competitor-accomplice into the lab took notes as a ruse to aid in obfuscating the hypothesis.

It requires minimally a mathematics degree in statistical analysis to comprehend the results, to come to grips with the acronyms (ANOVA, ANOVCA, MANOVA), the terms (Hotelling, square-root transformations for the jellybean rewards, logarithmic transformations for punishment behavior, effects tests or Turkeys, Sheffe tests), and to interpret the numbers. It does not require a mathematics degree to recognize how dubious the findings are; and how careful the discussion has been rhetorically structured to make the study seem worthwhile to confirm the hypothesis despite the obvious flaws and admittance by the researchers that nonsignificant differences seem to be more the rule than the exception. Rather trite findings are presented with weighty relevance. Male participants reward male competitors "significantly" less while rewarding their female competitors similarly across all conditions. This seems to be a trite case of being a "sore" loser, which applies to any game situation, violent or otherwise. Male-to-male competition is much fiercer and stronger than male-to-female rivalry. There is nothing groundbreaking in this result. The research further states that the gender of the competitor "*may* affect punishment behavior following violent video game play" (emphasis added). Cautiously the researchers claim that women competitors were punished by male participants more as the level of violence in the games escalated. This assertion seems to be at odds with the interpretation of rewards behavior that stayed the same while male-to-male punishment remained nonsignificant.

When researchers admit that there are large variances and standard variations in the way the participant "teachers" rewarded and punished their competitive "learners"—for instance, some male participants picked up jellybeans with their fingertips out of the jar collecting only a few each time, others grabbed a handful of them as rewards—then there is cause for questioning the results. Some male participants were unfazed by placing the competitor's hand in the ice water; others were less willing to cause discomfort. Something is going on in these exchanges that is more than any statistic can identify. The researchers admit that "something in the context of the situation or interaction of the participants may have impacted reward and punishment behavior differently for males and females." They are not sure whether it is actually the video game violence or the "arousal" and "excitement" from simply playing that elicits higher levels of aggression and hostility. Playing a video game for 15 minutes out of context provides very little insight as to what is going on.

Alcorn (2002, 42–49), in his analysis of the Milgram experiment, offers some insight as to what *is* "going on" in the Ballard experiment from a Lacanian psychoanalytic perspective. A psychological, sociological, or biological account of rewards and punishments looks a lot different from a psychoanalytic understanding when the relationship between desire and knowledge are worked through. Knowledge always serves desire in some manner. The experimenter in Ballard's experiment placed a demand on the participant "teacher" to initiate a reward or punishment (much as in the Milgram experiment where an authority figure demanded that the "teacher" initiates the punishment). The difference between the two experiments, however, was that the Ballad experimenter had little or no authority; s/he did not interfere between the teacher/learner interaction, remaining a bogus figure once the initial instructions were given and the demand placed on the two participants. Obedience in the Milgram experiment had everything to do with the Master—an authoritative experimenter. Although obedience was initially charged with stress and ambivalence, once submission to authoritative demand was achieved—at times immediately ("Yale must know what it's doing"), at times rhetorically ("that voltage will not really hurt him")—the "teacher" became filled with a sense of purpose as a justification for the abuse. ("I am participating in an important experiment.") The emotional conflict between stopping to mete out punishment to the victim or obeying the demand by the experimenter was resolved. The pain of the victim was suppressed as soon as knowledge was achieved as to which direction to follow. It seems about one-third of the students were willing to go against the authority figure, and disobey by recognizing the immoral nature of the experiment. They showed hate and disgust rather than love. Obedience is never a question of passivity—to blindly obeying what you are told, but a matter of generating knowledge (meaning) that resolves the inner conflict of what the Other (victim/experimenter) desired.

"Desire is always the desire of the Other [for/of the other person]" was Lacan's maxim. Our desire always passes through that of another (beginning with our parents and finishing with our latest object of love). The ambiguity of this maxim can be clarified in the two meanings it embodies. First, a desire "for the other person," which increases the more that the other is unattainable (or "forbidden"). The second meaning, "of the other person" means to desire recognition (or rejection) from the other; to desire the desire *of* the other person, or to reject that desire. Desire is complex response to lack in the social field. In the Ballard experiment, given the experimenter's weakened demand, the circulation of desire between teacher/learner became complicated and dependent on the dynamics of exchange that took place within the 15 minutes of video play. Ballard's experiment offers no transcripts of the verbal exchange between participants. One has to assume some took place since there was no injunction against it (at least in the material we read). Male participants did not operate on their own autonomous desire when meting out their rewards and punishments, but on the demand placed on them by the "experimenter" who had little or no relevance as to how violent the video games were. The conflicting emotions and unresolved anxieties of the "teachers" point this out. Some were just unable to put the "learner's" hand in the ice cold water to punish him or her. They disobeyed and resisted the experiment. Others gave an overexaggerated number of jelly beans as a reward. Was this a sarcastic gesture? Or a way of saying "I like you!" These are messages of desire, complicated by sex/gender interactions that could only be contextually understood. Any affect that may have been generated during the 15 minutes of game playing, was surely modified by what preceded and followed these exchanges.

MISDIRECTED RESEARCH: OUR HYPOTHESIS

There are, of course, many more sophisticated psychological "effects" studies that assure that a link between aggression, delinquency, and violent video games does "in fact" exist. Anderson and Dill (2000) begin their article by directly linking the Columbine high school shootings by Eric Harris and Dylan Klebold in Littleton, Colorado with the video game *Doom* that the boys had modified and played as being a significant factor.[2] Their General Affective Aggression Model (GAAM) builds on previous effects research to increase the number of factors that may cause aggression to achieve their correlation based on probability statistics. Studies such as these—and the Internet is flooded with them by media watch organizations such as Children NOW, Media Awareness Network (MAN) and Center for

Media Literacy: Empowerment Through Education (CME), who reference them and the journals of psychology that publish them—point to the weakness of the inability of such research to get at a more profound understanding of what is going on in interactive videos where violence of the action figures is clearly being "enjoyed." The psychoanalytic question of drives or desire drops out. Media watch organizations may be right to express a concern, but we maintain they fail to grasp the significance as to why violent films and games are symptomatic of postmodern culture. "Effects" research is what catches the ears of politicians and U.S. Senate inquiries. Yet, it doesn't take sophisticated research to note the sex/gender differences between boys/young men and girls/young women to identify the dominant preferences by males for violent action figures. After all, the video games industry was invented by Steve Russell who loved B-grade science fiction, Doc Savage and Flash Gordon characters. His first video game *Spacewar*, completed in 1962, consisted of two rocket ships (a Buck Rogers 1930s curvy spaceship and a long and thin one like a Redstone rocket) that were controlled by a toggle switch (Kent 2001, 18–19). Since then the video games industry has catered to boys' heroic fantasies. The designers are young men, and the computer industry is predominately run by men. Content analysis of video games in any given decade portrays women characters as being either absent, as a victim to be rescued, or typically objects of beauty or evil (Dietz 1998). These are by-and-large male fantasies. But, as we argue, that is only part of the story. Why has there been a proliferation of violent images on television and in video games steadily since the 1960s? Why is violence on television and in games treated as it were harmless fun by so many teenagers? Such questions cannot be answered by effects research. Rather, we believe a broader understanding of how emotions have been decentered in postindustrial cultures through the ever-increasing presentment of "reality" as mediated by telematic technologies, especially, television and the Internet, provide a much more satisfying explanation.

MORAL AUTHORITY/MORAL PANIC/ MORAL VACUITY

The status of media violence and the hypothesis of desensitization require that their effects are never conclusively proven outright if they are to continue to function as a symptomatic belief that youth are in a crisis situation. Definite proof would turn it into a banal fact taking away the ideological mileage that it now receives. Its shadowy existence as a belief floating in the space of outright truth or outright falsity must be preserved. Belief, after all, is a reflexive and doubled phenomena. It relies on the belief that others believe in the same concepts, values, and ideas. Doubt has its threshold. Belief, in other words, is the realm of the popular. It is a terrain that forms, articulates, and gives texture to "real lives." Culture critics such as Stuart Hall (1981) have theorized popular cultural belief as a contested zone where both resistance and containment are at play introducing an inexplicable contingency into the social order. Popular cultural belief, as Huyssen (1986) perceptively pointed out, is most often metaphorically designated by authorities as a fear of what cannot be controlled to maintain a stable ego boundary: woman, nature, sexuality. This "contested zone" is always subject to the claim for the need of management and regulation by cultural authorities and elite experts. Media violence and desensitization hypothesis receive their most conservative interpretation by those representatives of the post-patriarchal Symbolic Order (today's Church Fathers, politicians, teachers) who wish to reaffirm, reinsert, and restore their waning moral authority.

The anxiety that surrounds the collapse of authority by youth, what is often referred to as a "moral panic," is shored up by the relentless reconfiguration of the many forms of evangelical Christianity who attempt to update ritualistic participation by making the Church a more welcoming place. Youth, who are perceived to be the internal threat to the continuation of the social order, are to be won over by a "new ministry" that offers fresh leadership and a return to time-proven fundamental Christian values. The popularity of horror and magic genres such as those of Steven King and Joanne K. Rowling's *Harry Potter* series thwarts their efforts. These genres have renewed the fears of witchcraft and devil worship throughout several religious communities; priests and ministers acting outside of their established hierarchy have publicly condemned them. (The role-playing game, *Dungeons and Dragons* received similar condemnation.) Raising what psychic need these particular genres hold for young people seems to be avoided, for they offer a fascination precisely with what established religions repress or fail to address adequately in anything but dogmatic forms: radical evil (King) and the breakup of the family (Rowling). Harry Potter, an *orphan*, like so many children in single-parent households, offers a classical reinstatement of the Family Romance with a brave father and a self-sacrificing mother who protected Harry from the Jouissant Father, the devil in the shape of the Wizard Voldemort. Harry's scar, left by Voldemort's failure to kill him, is a sign of her love and self-sacrifice. The magical mirror reflects Harry's desire to be united with his parents again. Lord Voldemort represents the obscene side of the Law, the superego that taunts transgression. He is Potter's father "dark side" to use the *Star Wars* analogy. Lord Voldemort and Potter are therefore intimately connected: from look-alike as boys (Lord Voldemort as Tom Riddle), to being orphans raised by Muggles (non-magical families) and possessing similar brother wands. With time travel Harry confronts his own obscene superego in the figure of Tom Riddle. His wizardry powers and heroic adventures offer fantasies for children to deal with their loss and pain as classically argued by Bruno Bettelheim (1976) (see also Noel-Smith 2001). Many live in the hellish existence of post-Oedipal turmoil, like Harry does in a cupboard under the stairs in the home of his uncle Vernon Dursley, Aunt Petunia, and their son Dudley. Many others can sympathize with those that do. The Potter-series, wild success is hard to explain otherwise.

A more aggressive assertion of moral authority comes from the political Right who harness the existing anxieties of a violent and aggressive postindustrialized society to offer a way to contain the new media technologies like the Internet, DVD, video, MP3 recorders, and cell telephones that enable young people to pirate music, exchange opinions in chat rooms, and generally avoid parental control and surveillance. The media violence hypothesis is interpreted as a way to justify stricter censorship laws: to influence and sway public opinion toward more conservative social policies that punish lower socio-economic groups and single parent households for their alleged poor parenting skills and failure to socialize their children as good law-abiding citizens. The most notorious case of such political maneuvering in the United States has been the influential writings and media manipulation of Bill Bennett, the former drug czar under George Bush and secretary of education under Ronald Reagan (both jobs were handled poorly according to his many critics). Codirector of the conservative think tank *Empower America* (mission: to ensure that government actions foster growth, economic well-being, freedom, and individual responsibility), Bennett is the author of numerous books that explicitly articulate the moral rules to be followed when educating and parenting children and young people from an arch-conservative point of view. His book titles present him as a self-acclaimed moral guardian of the American populace.[3] He is best known for his attacks on rap music, talk shows, and media violence in general. Along with African American political activist C. DeLores Tucker, and Barbara Wyatt, the head of the Parent's Music Resource Center (launched by Tipper Gore to protect kids from violent rock lyrics), Bennett succeeded in having Time Warner sell its interests in Interscope Records, which had produced a number of successful and controversial gangsta rap artists.[4] Bennett testified during the hearings on "Marketing Violence to Children" (spearhead by Republican Senator Sam Brownback) as to the corruption of media violence on American youth. The media critic and defender of kid's culture, Jon Katz (1997) singles William Bennett out as the number one mediaphobe in the United States. The hypocrisy of Bennett's moralism was finally exposed when it was found out that he had a serious gambling addiction, losing *eight million dollars* over the last decade in Las Vegas and Atlantic City casinos. Limousine service, complimentary hotel rooms, and other amenities were afforded to Bennett as a high-stake gambler. At $50,000 for each appearance he makes, and through the sale of his many books, Bennett claims he can afford the habit and that he is debt-free. His reasoning would apply to all addictions: "It's OK to be an alcoholic as long as my family is fine and I am doing my job adequately." Both are "legal" addictions. It exposes a conflicted unconscious desire between his own conscious claims to be a high-minded moral leader with the "answers" and his secret jouissance, the suffering thrill that comes with the abandonment of that role to the fate of chance. They are two sides of the same coin. The one side repressed by the other. Bennett stands as yet another classical example as to why trust and faith in the Symbolic Order has waned. He confirms the prevalent cynicism regarding authority and exposes the emptiness of his moral virtue.

The ideology of protection of youth that Bennett, Tipper Gore, and the New Conservative Right espouse has a long history of rhetorical control.

It enables strategic interventions by the state so as to guarantee that social relations will be smoothly reproduced. Racial and ethnic divisions, gender and class relations are stabilized and social stability maintained, the security of family life assured. For such an ideology of protection to gain moral force it requires that any deviant act become a spectacle and be dramatized as evil, especially by the media (Arcand 1995). In this way the public sense the limit or boundary of the cultural norm that is permitted. The discourses surrounding violent video games and school shootings are paradigmatic in this respect. They provide the state and its representatives with the excuse to yet again enforce tougher draconian laws in schools (police officers to patrol hallways, surveillance cameras, lessening after school activities). Columbine High School now has new counseling programs in place, surveillance cameras installed, and a campaign to "Take Back the School" because of the continual never-ending media frenzy. After the Erfurt shooting in Germany, the spin-off in Austrian media was equally dramatic. The FPÖ (People's Freedom Party) representative for youth in the city of Klagenfurt did his own "experiment," which was enthusiastically taken up by the media. He sent out four adolescents to various video stores to find out if they could take out "adult" films and violent video games. Since they did not face strong opposition, this result was used as an argument to tighten the youth-protection laws to prevent easy access to such "harmful" material. It requires an entire network of media to create the climate of belief that there is something, yet again, wrong with youth. These discourses have to coalesce with one another to form an "articulation," a nodal point that holds the fascination of the public together long enough for the "crisis" to become believable.

PANIC TALK: THE MORAL CONFESSION

Besides the usual rash of movies that feature troubled kids (amongst the most depressing being Tim Hunter's *Rivers Edge*; (1986) and Larry Clark's *Kids* (1995), it is the daytime "confessional" talk shows that dominate North America and European countries, which sustain the moral interest in youth cultures. In the United States and in Europe, these talk shows are supplemented by a number of reality-TV crime shows in the evening to maintain the fervor such as *Hard Copy, Prime Time, Inside Edition. America's Most Wanted*, purportedly to be the best known and most successful in helping solve crimes, tries to achieve a documentary realism, which blurs the distinction between it and "actual" news reportage. This effect is achieved by using High 8, hand-held video cameras, mobile on location shooting using natural lighting, actual policemen and policewomen, and unknown or bit actors as criminals, along with documentary newsreel evidence to further strengthen its realist modality. Numerous television specials that focus on particular topics such as teen pregnancy, teen suicide, teen runaways, and teen prostitution add to the mix. News magazines like *Time, Atlantic, MacLeans*, and *Newsweek* that represent the moral voice of white middle-class Americans and Canadians, have regularly had feature articles on the "youth crisis," especially in the early 1990s, which further fueled the fears of a more mobile middle-to-upper conservative class who keep themselves informed of "current events" through these magazines.[5] This moral panic over youth is being staged by a sector of Baby Boomers who feel guilty over their own self-discretions into drugs and irresponsibility. As Males (1999) puts it in *Framing Youth*, "these Boomers have come to 'a new sense of responsibility and self denial' imposing strict moral standards on themselves and their peers—and most assuredly on their children" (340).

Talk shows are where moral panic is best managed. The show's host introduces topics and themes that provide a stamp of authenticity to the youth crisis by way of spectacular bodily displays such as tears and emotional outbursts. The youthful guests are invited to relate (confess) their personal tragedy to a studio audience who sit as their judge and jury—the public representatives. The *confessionary mode* is offered more for its exhibitionary value; it is the act or *performance* that is proffered. These confessions are communication acts that affirm, articulate, and capture a pseudo-materiality; the very Thing (Lacan, *Ethics* S VII) a society is unable to express symbolically, but remains present as a "spectral supplement" or "spectral apparition." This unarticulated Thing is what is "shared" in a culture—about deviance, transgression, and the emotion of guilt. The Thing as a Master-Signifier, as a signifier without a signified, is that *something* about which the confessors need not make any positive claims. *Spectral apparitions* are foreclosed from such talk. Whether the talk is about illicit affairs, divorce rates, freaks, serial killers, gangsta rap, drug abuse—what are taken to be the current societal exemplars of moral panic—the ultimate paradox of such symbolizing gestures is that society is "held together," confirmed by these very transgressions that appear on television talk shows. Paradoxically, they prevent any form of society's closure into some harmonious whole where violence has been eliminated. The very *absence of a harmonious society* acts as a spectral apparition (as Thing) enabling every confessed ' "immoral act" as yet another failed attempt to achieve a peaceful harmonious loving world. Moral panic rests, therefore, on an impossibility, an unfathomable limit that cannot be objectivized, located in what Lacan calls the Real, a space that is beyond language. Taken together, these confessional acts point beyond language to a bond linking its members together implying a shared relationship with such an impossibility.

The most important aspect of talk shows to sustain the moral high ground is the confessional act itself, and not the evidence, nor the penalties that go along with it, like the banal penance given to confessants by priests for what appear to be grievous sins. The talk-show confession assures the stability of the social order; that is, the recognition of the societal gaze as represented by the audience and the viewers at home. The self-incriminating youthful guest makes a double gesture through the confession, presenting the audience with the paradox of both identification, as well as a distantiation. First, the confessional experience makes it appear that the guest is just like us with a similar moral structure as to what is right and wrong; and second, how the guest is so utterly different from us because of what s/he has been through. In this way both the horrors and mundane problems become the extreme limits of the confessional moral discourse. When it comes to the horrors, the limits of the social are not contested but affirmed. This is the abjected part of ourselves that we detest in the talk show's guest. Through this mechanism the Thing as a spectral apparition beyond what is spoken is confirmed as well. With trivial concerns, the audience and the television viewers at home identify with persons who are like themselves, putting a human face to the intolerable deviant act.

TV talk shows are, therefore, a cauldron for a society's psychic ills. The audience is usually seeded with members who themselves have gone through a similar crisis in their lives. It is not unusual, for instance, on *Oprah* to have invited guests that reflect the show's focus (victims of AIDS, child abuse suffers, wives of convicted rapists). The distinction between invited guests and audience becomes blurred. The now defunct talk show *Sally Jessie Raphael* often invited a member from the audience to provide a summative analysis of what advice s/he would offer the invited couples to solve their domestic disputes. The community of viewers on most talk shows enters into a position that approximates "citizenship" in as much as they participate in the vetting of the proceedings, even if their participation is more often only as witnesses to the testimony that is being given.

Although most talk shows are prerecorded, usually there are "live" phone-in questions from the larger viewing audience at home. These prerecorded phone calls add to the "actuality of the event," and reinforce the idea that the "critical problem" exists in society as a whole, making it a "common concern." An expert or two are usually called in to confirm the authenticity of the testimony, and how best then to "manage" it. During this time, often traditional values of the nuclear family are reinstated, and the power of patriotism reconfirmed in establishing the nation as one big family. The host is never the expert, but plays more the role of a concerned citizen, mediator, and interlocutor, who brings guests and audience together. Many of these talk-show hosts have become catalysts for reuniting "lost" family members to reinstate a sense of "community," and to restore dispersed and dysfunctional families—the dads and mothers who had abandoned their children, adopted siblings in search of their "natural" families, runaway teenagers who want to come back into the fold, and so on.

The spread of a social paranoia where no one is safe anywhere, not even in small-town America, is inadvertently furthered rather than prevented through the hosting of such themes as, "Teens in Crisis," "Fathers and Sons," "My Two Dads," "How to Spot a Child Molester," "Teen Suicide," providing a never-ending flow of societal problems and what to do about them. The now defunct *Ricki Lake Show* took a quirky side to the youth crisis by having teenagers "confess" to each other how much they hate one another, or how confused they are concerning pregnancy, love, dating, and other matters of the heart. Either way, teenagers come across as having a confused and bizarre set of values confirming that in a postmodern society adolescence are essentially guilty or something or other.

8

BETWEEN POPULAR BELIEF AND FACT

The issue of media violence and desensitization is not possible to grasp strictly through "objective" scientific effects experimentation or "subjective" ethnographic research. Rather, the distinction between popular *belief* and *knowledge* continually belies any certainty. Belief is minimally reflective; it is transferred onto the Other. Within the media violence hypothesis this is easily demonstrated by the displacement that occurs when children regularly deny being influenced by television, film, or video game violence when asked by researchers. They most often claim that younger children are so affected, but not them. Adults make the same denial. It is always youth who are affected whereas they are immune because they are more mature, adult. The strongest rhetorical ploy is to evoke the image of a two-or three-year-old mesmerized by the television set, fixated on some violent action (televised wrestling is often mentioned) with the usual claim that such a child is unable to tell the difference between fantasy and reality. This is, of course, nonsense, unless we are talking about the pathology of psychosis or autism. Any neurotic child can tell the difference between fantasy and reality once the ego is formed (ca. 18 months). This is the distinction that Hodge and Tripp (1986) maintain in *Children and Television* (1986) probably the earliest media study, which was semiotically informed. Fantasy equated with reality (RL) is more likely to happen *after* the ego is formed. Before that, what an infant perceives is nonsense, like an adult who travels to an Asian country where finding what s/he thought was the universal sign for toilet becomes impossible. To what degree an infant's *physiological bodily processes* are being affected by the media is another question entirely, given that perceptual modalities have differential thresholds across a population and are also culturally variable.

The question of the separation between fantasy and reality, as this scene is usually dramatically and rhetorically staged, misses the point. It stems from the naïve view that the child somehow instantly recognizes images on television and makes sense of them; or equally misleading that these images are "non-real" or "fantasyful." As if perception is not an intellectual achievement in-and-of itself, requiring a child to make sense of the flood of images, asking questions and receiving confirmation as meaning unfolds. Those who were born blind, and then given sight have to "learn" to see. Recall Irwin Winkler's *At First Sight* (1999) based on a true story taken from one of

Oliver Sacks' (a NYU School of Medicine neurologist) many thought-provoking cases. When Virg Adamson's (Val Kilmer) sight is restored he has to come to grips with a world that is absolutely foreign to him. In the end, he decides that he is much better off remaining blind than to struggle with "how" to see. In his treatise on *Optics*, Descartes presents the blind man holding a stick in each hand as the exemplar of seeing man. Why? Basically "sight" is a spatial inner experience meaning the blind can "see" in their own way. This is precisely what an infant must do, or anyone from another culture who has never seen television before. They have to make sense of the figures and images that are constantly changing "in" the television set. We could say that these adults also are unable to (at first) make sense of the phenomenon called television (like a cargo cult that is unable to make sense of what an airplane is) until they are taught otherwise. In Brazil, a young uneducated underclass has strongly identified with the bourgeois life-style of telenovelas (soap operas) on television (Soong 2001). Some of these fans have been unable to make a marked distinction between television actors in these soaps and these same actors as "real" people with lives outside the television frame. But this is an issue of belief where no one has taken the initiative to explain to them the two separate realities. A child has to figure out the "strange happenings" in television just as s/he must figure out that the vacuum cleaner is not "alive" in the same way a human being is alive. The television set can be anthropomorphized in the same way. It is "alive." Still, children have to learn that the TV characters and violent scenes are supposed to relate to reality in someway. How could they possibly know what they "mean"? We don't see vacuum cleaners as being "harmful" to children, yet this same logic is applied to "violence" of television at this early age. Seldom is the inverse argument raised: seeing televised violence could act as a deterrent.

This distinction between fantasy and reality is misunderstood. It is only when fantasy provides a support to reality that the child "enters" reality. Before that moment, in the pre-Oedipal narcissistic stage, prior to 18 months of age, the child could not make any sense of the television figures to begin with. During this holophrastic speech stage s/he is unable to answer *back* parents with full articulated sentences. The child can, of course, communicate gesturally through signing and using holophrastic words. When the ego gestalt eventually forms during the mirror stage it becomes a fantasmatic support or alter ego; only then can the child begin to make sense of television imagery. We are *not* advocating that violence on television or video games is *harmless* to infants whose ego has not fully formed. There is an affective bodily transference that goes on at the unconscious level as violent images are processed, much like loud music will be physiologically registered. What we *are* saying is that once meaning (signification) enters the picture, there is a qualifiable difference in the way violent images are processed where the differentiation between what is RL violence versus simulation has been greatly exaggerated.

In a report (1995) on video game culture of teenagers in British Columbia, researchers from the Media Analysis Lab at the University of

Simon Fraser (1988) in Vancouver were rather surprised to hear a consistent agreement amongst teens concerning the harmful effects of violent video games and the potential of their addiction.[1] It was always the Other who was being harmed. Why such a disavowal takes place requires psychoanalytic insight, what Lacan claimed to be the inherent misrecognition (*méconnaissance*) that lies at the foundation of the first constitution of the ego in the mirror phase, as does the question of psychic health when viewing or participating in actual or simulated violence. When someone says, "I believe the media violence effects other people, but not me!" what is being unconsciously repressed is the effect of violence on oneself. A rationalization takes place at the level of knowledge; namely, I am more mature, more moral, more balanced, and so on, so violence does not effect me. The investment in this unconscious disavowal enables me to "enjoy" violence, while chastising those younger, less mature than me for doing so. When someone says, "I don't really believe that media violence affects other people, but nevertheless I think it is a good idea to believe it because that way, in case it might be true, media violence should be done away with, or at least lessened." Here we have the opposite disavowal. The second part of the statement (but nevertheless…) hedges on being factually true (as knowledge), but on the repressed unconscious level a disavowal has taken place that already confirms and ratifies the belief that media violence indeed does harm. It's a fib.

Alarmist Zeal

In contrast to belief, knowledge as it is "scientifically" and pragmatically defined in Freedman's (2002) overview, is attributed to the authority of a corrigible and objectifiable method that can stand the test of verifiability; for example, the earth is not flat, but spherical. This can be "proven" by the repeatability of the results establishing a "causal" connection. In postmodernity, the representatives of such an authoritative method have become suspect for their ideological and contextual bias. Phenomenologically speaking the world "is" flat. It is experienced as being flat. Both perspectives can coexist with one another in a nonhierarchical relationship, each defining the specificity of its domain. Newtonian and Einsteinian physics can coexist with one another. There is no transcendental point that is not always already contextualized. From the perspective of a decentered universe, the earth may indeed take on a dimensionality not as yet theorized. A single view from the Hubble telescope estimates that there are 40 billion new galaxies with countless other solar systems. This has brought a new insignificance to the planet Earth, and added speculations on Black Hole space travel and the immense existence of antimatter that is unaccounted for. Currently, the earth's shape is changing into a more rounded sphere as the ice caps melt causing weather disturbances, the consequences of which meteorologists are yet to fully ascertain. Simple Newtonian notions of causality have now been replaced with an updated scientific paradigm based on stochastic probability or warrantability, such as the study by Anderson and Dill (2000) mentioned earlier. Who is most likely to be effected by media violence and desensitized to its effects is now presented in terms of a composite profile of the viewer/computer video user: age, class, gender, economic status, past criminal record, and so on to determine the probability of media violence effect. Who is most likely to be behaviorally effected, emotionally affected, or ideologically influenced now becomes a composite profile. Such "at risk" children include those who have experienced violent traumas such as war, floods, disasters, or who have learning disabilities and suffer from deficit disorders.

This complexity, however, does not prevent those trained in behavioral psychology to continue to still believe in direct causal effects. Perhaps the born-again Christian zeal of former U.S. Lt. Col. and behavioral psychologist David Grossman (1995) is the most obvious high-profile case. Having trained soldiers how to kill, Grossman's crusade is to claim that violent video games lead to better marksmanship, techniques of sniping and using cover, above all, desensitization so that one could kill. When suicidal school shootings occur he blames violent video games for their enactment. The Columbine tragedy gave him a high-media profile as having been "right" all along, and an opportunity to say so to the U.S. Senate Commerce, Science and Transportation Committee, Hearings on "Marketing Violence to Children" (May 4, 1999) (see Kent 2001, 544–555). However, the Marine Corps have denied ever using games like *Doom* for desensitization purposes: sharp-shooting and teamwork training, yes; desensitization—no. Ironically, the Marines, who were involved in the original modification of *Doom*, went on to form their own company and marketed their customized version (Manovich 2001, 278). Nintendo also claimed that they never supplied the army a first-person shooter simulator as Grossman had testified.

Grossman's reliance on the outdated and heavily critiqued theory of B.F. Skinner's operant conditioning, and his failure to recognize the obvious difference between a military war situation/training camp and a video games arcade makes his position sound rather ludicrous to those who have actually talked to youth about these games (especially Jones 2002, 166–167); or to psychologists who have abandoned behaviorism as a reductionist understanding of human experience, but certainly not to educators and parents who want to be convinced by the sensational sell that violent video games lead *directly* to the psychosis of a killing spree. The forensic psychologist Helen Smith (2000), explicitly states that that there is no connection between violent video games and the violent kids she works with. Although we wonder whether profiling characteristics she uses, as determined from surveys, are the best way to ascertain who is likely to commit violent acts, Smith sees such games as a form of sublimation, a way for some violent youth to deal with their rage. Lower-income kids from impoverished homes who commit the majority of the violent crimes, as might be expected, aren't able to afford such games. The U.S. secret service's Threat Assessment Center investigated major incidents of school violence since the 1970s to see whether violent video games were involved. Of the 41 cases they investigated, only 5 involved such games. The report concluded that of these five cases there was no direct evidence that they caused or led to the shooting (Benger 2002; see also Jenkins 2000).

It seems like the "evidence" is against Lt. Grossman from both the law enforcement community itself, that he so respects, as well as from psychologists who have worked with murderous teens utilizing more complex set of premises than simple behaviorism. The prevailing generality is that imitating violence often leads to an identification with violence—rather than revulsion of it. It is then assumed that violence is incorporated to solve problems of everyday life; finally, violence is believed to be located unconsciously as a central activity that defines one's subjectivity. From a Lacanian viewpoint, the *jouissance* of violence is unique to an individual's biography, to the family situation, complexity of class, race, and sexual orientation. Yet, despite these probability statistics and profiling, no scientific account can completely explain the contingent event as to when a serial killer strikes, a mass murder acts out, or a pedophile molests. Such an event belongs to the Lacanian impossible Real. To eliminate such a contingency of a violent act would be to foretell the future as in Phillip Dick's sci-fi, "The Minority Report."

In distinction to this objectivized knowledge, belief is tied to the Symbolic Order, which itself is a virtual fiction, an ontological belief system in which people must necessarily buy into but not necessarily place their faith in. They must feel bound to some symbolic commitment, yet they need not trust it. As Freedman (2002) points out, the prestigious psychological and medical institutions seem to blindly quote one another and follow each other's exaggerated claims and overstated assertions concerning media violence, such as "more than a 1000 scientific studies and reviews conclude that . . . 3500 scientific studies reached this conclusion . . . ." Faith in the Symbolic Order, that the big Other is providing the fundament of symbolic "trust" is what enables the system to maintain and reproduce itself. Once such authority is shaken, paranoia can set in.

The ultimate paradox of belief is that there is "no hard proof." The typical reaction to Freedman's analysis by a true believer in the media violence hypothesis, is to state that any research can be picked apart and criticized if one wants to do so, as if it is forbidden to question received authority. In such a defensive move, Freedman is said to have merely displayed his own overwhelming bias that he *believes* that desensitization and media violence hypothesis are false by picking the existing research apart and interpreting the evidence his way. In this view, we arrive at a deadlock that enables the existing belief to continue to mystify, maintain, and reproduce the Symbolic Order. Freedman's claim can be dismissed as merely a ploy to dislodge the facts by interpreting them differently. His facts are then accused of being just another fiction, which then leads us toward relativism. Who are we going to believe: a psychology professor with an analytical bias or a slough of prestigious scientific and medical institutes who say otherwise? Or, in another historical context: who do you believe, Galileo or the Church Fathers who refused even to look through the telescope to confirm or deny his claim? On what grounds do you decide who has a more supportable and ethical claim?

What kind of knowledge does Freedman offer, which makes a believer of the media violence hypothesis feel uneasy? The answer is hysterical knowledge. A refusal to fully accept the master signifiers that keep the symbolic belief system in place. His hystericized position is exemplified in the opening chapter through his enactment of a taunting and almost jeering style when exposing and accusing prestigious institutions for their failure to live up to their scientific claims when they have set the rules. This is his hysterical symptom, his dramatization, and his linguistic quirk. In an earlier historical period of Church rule, he would have been branded a heretic, muzzled, and perhaps put to death. Freedman is someone who introduces doubt concerning the accepted master signifiers "media violence" and "desensitization" by inverting the scientific "causal" game; by showing that the numbers that are being played with fail to add up. On the very last page of his study Freedman shifts the entire debate by placing the fulcrum under "real" violence, rather than its fictional simulacra equivalent.

> Indeed, I think it is likely that real violence and the coverage of real violence do affect aggression and crime. Children may imitate violence they observe directly. Both children and adults may be influenced by their knowledge that their society or their neighbourhood has a lot of violence. Moreover, it seems likely that repeated exposure to real violence, either directly or in the media [e.g., murder on the front page of the newspaper, or as a lead story on television news], causes desensitization to subsequent real violence. . . . Thus both the causal hypothesis and the desensitization hypothesis may be correct with respect to real violence or media coverage of real violence, and perhaps that is what people should be worrying about. (210)

For Freedman, ultimately the distinction rests between "real" and fictional violence. If they remain apart, then his argument retains its hysterical force in unnerving supporters of the causality hypothesis. Indeed, it does seem obvious that nonfictional violence is more difficult to cope with, regardless of age. However, youth find specific strategies of coping when it comes to both fictional and nonfictional material. Having had negative experiences each individual soon identifies genres that are immediately to be avoided because they are so disturbing. Some are just unable to watch "real" (RL) medical operations on television where scalpel cuts are made explicit and human insides are exposed. The sight of blood is too much to bear. For a devout Catholic a film such as William Friedkin's *The Exorcist* (1973) may bring about many sleepless nights. The presence of evil is just "too" close to the unconscious core subjectivity that identifies him or her as a Catholic. Yet this same film may be analyzed for its spectacular special effects. How did they manage to make Linda Blair's head swivel around 360 degrees? What sort of make-up was applied to make her so bleak looking? How did the special effects crew make the bed tremble? And so on. Such "objective" knowledge enables a psychic distance to be maintained from the belief that such events actually do happen. Ultimately, the plausibility of the event depends on the belief system of the person watching, and that is more of a psychoanalytic question than a cognitive one.

There are many other "containment" strategies to make the anxiety of watching "scary" movies possible, ranging from direct to partial abstinence where only the non-scary scenes are watched. The rest of the time eyes are closed and fingers cover the ears. Watching a questionable movie or television program with a group of friends also transfers and disperses the anxiety onto the group. Another strategy is simply to wait for the video of the "scary" movie to come out so as to change the viewing context in the familiarity of one's own home, or to then replay a particularly frightening scene over and over again so that its impact is lessened. (This strategy is not unlike Aztec rituals of progressively shortening and then chanting the name of a devilish spirit until only a single phoneme of the spirit remains. Once that is repetitively chanted away the spirit has been psychologically and completely overcome.) Video games based on horror film (and vice versa) can likewise further the psychic distance (e.g., House of the Dead, The Mummy Returns, Jurassic Park III). Then there are the proverbial fans of horror who know their genre so well that they can laugh at the quotes, citations, ironic and cynical references that the director throws in for those "in the know," like Keenen Wayans's hilarious film, *Scary Movie* (2000). Intimately knowing a genre provides a great deal of control over the form, and hence achieving a distance that remains pleasurable.

Despite all this, parents, especially middle-class parents, worry that their children will suffer from nightmares and recurrent anxieties and fears when exposed to certain media violence. The psychic life of the youth becomes critical. The effects of media violence can thus range from behavioral responses (aggressivity), to emotional ones (pleasure as well as repulsion), from being outright ideological and attitudinal, to being totally abject (Buckingham 1996). Translated into the language of Lacanian psychoanalysis, all such effects raise the place of jouissance in the life of the viewer/user. How is libidinal life regulated in reference to the Law, in terms of prohibitions and allowances in cyberspace? This is the underlying question of subsequent chapters.

Fact as Fiction: Fiction as Fact

What if this distinction that Freedman makes between fictional and nonfictional forms of violence collapses more often than it remains apart? This is humorously and cleverly explored in John McTiernan's *Last Action Hero* (1993) where Arnold Schwarzenegger as the screen hero Jack Slater, and his number one fan, Danny Madigen (Austin O'Brien) magically exchange the make-believe screen world with the "real" empirical world effortlessly, back and forth, several times. Each separate exchange juxtaposes and highlights fictional and nonfictional violence. Danny, like a cartoon character, never gets hurt when he is transported "in" the screen, while Slater is always getting hurt when he tries to play hero in the "real" (RL) world, outside the screen. The film's diegesis makes it clear that the fictional and nonfictional worlds are mistaken only by the screen characters, while we, the viewing audience can maintain the distinction. It would be pathological not to do so; we would be psychotic. But what if, psychoanalytically speaking, fictional and nonfictional space are not diametrically opposed as binary oppositions, but coexist as *belief and knowledge*, sliding and slipping over one another as fact becomes fiction and fiction fact? What if our mediated reality of television and film has made it more and more difficult to retain a distinctive *trust* in their difference? Who can deny, for instance, the changed graphic and spectacular presentation of screen violence compared even to a decade ago? And what of photographic digitalization?

We seem to be arguing against our opening gambit. It sounds as if we are reneging on our previous claim concerning the distinction between RL and VR. There is a danger of being misunderstood here. We are *not* referring to the misguided fear many parents, educators, and politicians have that viewing violent television or playing violent games teaches youth that this is the best way to solve their problems. It doesn't take long for a child to figure out that make-believe violence can lead to injury where, no matter how trivial such an injury can be at times, it can bring the raft of parents, the school administration, and ultimately the Law on the shocked perpetrator. The separation between "reality" and the fantasy of make-believe play establishes itself in such instances rather bluntly and concretely. Nor are we referring to the flights of an overinvestment in empowerment that screen fantasy can bring; becoming too self-assured when performing a superheroic feat that is imitated in a film sequence, which can equally result in injury or possible death. A number of high school boys, for example, imitated a scene from David Ward's *The Program* (1993) where a frosh initiation for a university football team consisted in a test of bravery. A team member would lie down on the white line in the middle of the road during rush-hour traffic and allow cars to speed by in both directions without moving. After the films release, several deaths were reported around the United States as a result of this stunt. The scene was subsequently cut when the film was released in video. There are instances of kids playing superhero. To show off for friends, they jump off building platforms too high for them, landing with sprained ankles and broken bones. These instances *test* the boundary between fantasy and reality consciously—as daredevil stunts. "Can I really do that?" is what is being asked of the self. "Reality" TV stunt shows are forever warning its viewing audience not to try this stunt "at home." Of course, without such reality testing some of the most creative inventions would have never emerged, nor some of the most incredible accomplishments of endurance, strength, and bravery. We would not be able to fly in airplanes, for instance. Often with such experimentation where limits are concerned, there is always a risk of death.

The collapse of fantasy and reality that we have in mind occurs when our belief in the world is unhinged. No bodily injury may necessarily result. It is the psyche that is affected. Films like Daniel Myrick and Eduardo Sánchez's *The Blair Witch Project* (1999) can still create the ambiguous space between reality and the fantasy that sustains reality in the first place, so that we experience a psychotic moment when the fantasy space begins to falter. Not pleasant, but certainly insightful. Viewers are not sure if such an incident as Blair Witch actually happened. Was the audience viewing "actual footage" shot in October of 1994 a year ago by three student filmmakers that disappeared in the woods near Burkittesville, Maryland, while shooting a documentary? Or, is this all an elaborate hoax?

Orsen Welles' radio play of H.G. Well's *War of the Worlds* as a news broadcast fooled an American audience back in 1938 (a day before Halloween). Radio was the primary mediator of reality at that time. Welles' Mercury Theatre of the Air dramatized *The War of the Worlds* as a simulated news broadcast created with actors playing journalists who described the Martian invasion against a background of sound effects. Those listeners who tuned in late and missed the brief announcement that this was "just" a staged performance had no way of distinguishing factual news from its fictionalization. The frame between fact and fiction disappeared. News on the radio was believed to be the most reliable reportage of the "truth." Despite the far-fetched narrative, the broadcast created a panic causing people to quickly pack their belongings in the family car and hit the road. Some hid in basements with their guns loaded, still others even wrapped their heads in wet towels as a protection from the Martian poison gas. In 1958 a similar scandal surrounding fact and fiction broke out, this time over NBC's quiz show *Twenty One* (dramatized as a movie, *The Quiz Show*, Robert Redford, 1994), which raised the issue as to the game's "authenticity." The contestants knew the answers ahead of time and only pretended to guess at the answers so as to dramatize the contest and make it more "entertaining."

When television became the primary way "reality" was mediated in the 1950s, it should be no surprise that the news broadcast continued to be the most trusted genre as to what constituted the "truth." In 1957 the BBC program *Panorama*, a "window on the word" program dealing with current affairs, interviews with the famous, and book reviews, staged an April Fools joke by reporting that a bumper crop of spaghetti had been harvested in southern Switzerland. Richard Dimbleby, the program's host, was shown walking amongst trees growing spaghetti while a rural Swiss family pulled the pasta off the spaghetti trees and put it in baskets. When viewers asked how they might grow the exotic plant, BBC told them ironically to "place a sprig of pasta in a tin of tomato sauce and hope for the best." The authentic feeling of the broadcast was achieved by Dimbleby's keying on crucial signifiers that made up the credibility of such a discourse. A mild winter had been experienced, the spaghetti weevil had disappeared, the past breeding of the spaghetti plant had insured its uniform length, and there was fear that an early frost might come and ruin its taste. Few "Brits" in the 1950s knew what spaghetti was, which made the hoax possible.

BBC annals herald another equally controversial broadcast. *Ghostwatch*, a television play produced in 1992 on Halloween would repeat Orson Welles' hoax by having a "real-live" ghost hunt take place in a house on the outskirts of North London and presented as a docu-drama—a dramatized documentary. "Pipes" the ghost had been "captured" on video (as the audience saw it), but he continually seemed to vanish. The idea was to combine a team of psychic researchers (an eccentric young male psychic investigator and a female journalist) with all the technology of television journalism, and it worked. Stephen Volk, who wrote the screenplay, presented the investigation in a "first-person narrative," as most ghost stories are. To make it both convincing and authentic, Volk utilized interviews, talking heads with their faces to the camera so as to convince the audience that an authorial truthful "I" was being presented. To maximize all the rhetorical devices from factual (reality) TV, he used phone-ins, an inquisitive presenter, earnest interviews, a video wall, blow-up photos, clips and the vox pop of the crowd. What ultimately convinced the audience as to the "authenticity" of the incident was the utilization of a cast of "real" TV presenters (Michael Parkinson, Mike Smith, Sarah Greene, and Craig Charles) who were cast as "actors" in the docu-drama. In many ways the combination of the scientist and skeptical journalist repeated the *X-Files* formula where fact and belief once more were intertwined.

Audience reaction to *Ghostwatch* was across the board of possible responses: all the way from enjoying it as a Halloween trick in the clever way it was presented, to feeling stupid, duped by the hoax. For those irate callers to the BBC switchboard, who felt that they had been taken advantage of, a fundamental trust between them and the BBC had been broken. One caller claimed that the BBC had evoked demonic forces by broadcasting the show, while another claimed that the show had actually taken place despite BBC's constant disclaimer that it was all staged. Sarah Greene (who played the reporter) was not alive, and the BBC was now involved in a cover-up. These audience reactions identify just how the fantasy screen of belief is maintained in the "reality" of television, in its ability to offer what the audience *believes* to be the "truth." When this fundamental fantasy is broken, believers feel duped. Rather than recognizing how one had been fooled in the way fiction and non-fiction are precariously held together, some audience members go so afar as to disavow that they have been fooled at all. The incident had actually happened and now BBC is involved in a cover-up conspiracy. Others were offended because it came as a shock to be reminded how gullible we all are; how our belief system has been shaped by the misrecognition of the imaginary screen that we all must to some extent "trust," otherwise we would live in a state of constant hysterical suspicion and paranoia. In 1977 such paranoia occurred with the publication of Leslie Watkins's *Alternative 3*, a fiction book about a doomed overpopulated earth and a conspiracy between the United States and Russia to populate Mars with only the most physically fit and intelligent citizens. Many readers refused to believe that Watkins had made it all up. Some thought the CIA had pressured him in denouncing it as a fiction. Others thought that their missing friends and relatives had already been taken to Mars as the future colonists.

One would think that we have reached a point where we are much too sophisticated as an audience to be fooled yet again. Conspiracy theories abound as to whether the 1969 Apollo XI moon landing was a staged event, construed by Nixon who had commissioned Stanley Kubrick to create a studio version in London, which was then broadcast to an awaiting world, assuring the U.S. technological dominance over the Soviet Union's own attempt at a moon landing. On April 2003, the documentary, "Kubrick, Nixon und der Mann im Mond" ("The Dark Side of the Moon") was broadcast in Europe (ARTE), a French-German production directed by the eminent filmmaker William Karel. The documentary argues that NASA provided the technologically advanced Zeiss lens for Kubrick to use to capture the exquisite candlelight scenes that ingratiate the film, Barry Lyndon (1975), making it a masterpiece of technique. The lens was made available thanks to Kubrick's involvement with the Nixon administration in producing a staged moon landing as a "back-up" in case the cameras on the moon failed. Donald Rumsfeld, the current U.S. Defense Secretary under G.W. Bush was on Nixon's staff in 1969, as was Dr. Henry Kissinger, Nixon's foreign secretary. The documentary interviews both men in their current positions and ages, and convincing archival footage of them is shown as young men who were said to have flown to London to set up the deal with Kubrick on Nixon's orders.

To make the documentary more plausible Stanley Kubrick's wife, Christiane and her brother Jan Harlan are interviewed about the "alleged" film. Former Nixon advisors Lawrence Eagleburger, former White House Chief of Defense Staff, General Alexander Haig, Kissinger, and Richard Helms confirm through interviews that this was indeed Nixon's plan that had been executed. Another layer of credibility is added by Vernon Walter, former CIA director, Buzz Aldrin, Apollo XI astronaut and David Scott, Apollo XV astronaut. Kubrick is said to have reluctantly supervised the CIA amateurs who put it together, but then something unexpected happened. Nixon became concerned that a leak may occur, that the plot would be found out. So he set up a "hit list" for the CIA to liquidate all those involved in the production of the moon landing, so that no trace could be found. This too comes across as being believable since Nixon was known to be impulsive, often making irrational decisions, especially if he drank too much. The Watergate scandal also confirmed his willingness to transgress the Law. Haig, Kissinger, and Eagleburger go on record to try to stop his irrational decision, but with little success. It's too late. Nixon gives the order for the hits. The involved CIA agents are identified, having been given new identities and dispersed over the globe to keep quiet, and begin to disappear one by one. Again evidence is provided through newspaper articles that report their death. On location shots and interviews are collected from Vietnamese locals that testify as to their disappearance. Kubrick is said to have worried that he was next to be assassinated, and this explains why he refused to travel to the United States. He became more reclusive, remaining in his home country England until his death in 1999. Watching Karel's documentary unfold as it trades on previous conspiracy theories seems to finally confirm their truth. As the credits run, outtakes of Christiane Kubrick, Gen. Haig, and other blowing their lines and asked to repeat them more convincingly throws the whole documentary into skeptical disarray. One is left with the uneasy feeling that this hoax has thrown doubt into the previous conspiracy theories that now, strangely, become plausible again, raising the question that this latest documentary is a cover-up of the original cover-up—more smoke and mirrors. This is a perfect example of "symbolic deception," feigning raised to the next level, or doubled as it were, an insight into the way "spin" works. As Žižek (1997a) cleverly puts it, "human feigning is the feigning of feigning itself: in *imaginary deception*, I simply present a false image of myself, while in *symbolic deception*, I present a true image and count on its being taken for a lie" (139, emphasis added).

These incidents show that the imaginary screen of our perceptions—Lacan's Imaginary psychic register—as established both culturally and historically, always mediates the symbolic world as we believe it exists. This is more fragile than we let on. The collapse of that belief means we face an abyss. The shattering of our ego is a psychotic moment when the Real psychic register impinges on us, and we lose our ground. We can recover from such an encounter with the Real by realizing what fantasies take hold of us, or we can disavow them and continue to repeat and be caught by them. This is a never-ending process. What these moments of collapse explicitly show is the sudden disappearance of the Symbolic Order and the collapse of the Imaginary with the Real. This also implies the disappearance for a moment of the virtual space that sustains our fundamental fantasy. We no longer are able to project an identification with a virtual image, a place in the big Other from which we can see ourselves in a likeable form—as an Ego Ideal—as an ideal teacher, researcher, or professor. Our ideological identification is gone. The trust in the Symbolic Order (big Other)—which refers to not only the explicit symbolic rules that regulate our social interactions, but also the shadow side of unwritten "implicit" rules—is broken.

As the aforementioned cases show, the virtual community of belief begins to decenter. We believe journalists and documentary filmmakers have the authority to report what is "authentically true." They may indeed be fallible, but it is their very fallibility that makes them believable in their "honest" attempts at getting at the truth. Certain journalists become known precisely for their quirks, style of dress, presence, and tone of voice. The international journalist Christiane Amanpour, for example, is notorious for having spurned objectivity in the interest of humanitarian engagement. Yet it is her passion for "truth" that gives her voice credibility. This is what makes her "human," and trustworthy. When journalists become "actors," appearing as themselves in films, radio play, or television, their betrayal seems complete. The audience feels they have not lived up to their ethical responsibility—to maintain the "vital illusion" of objectivity, which itself is an impossible order (Manoff 1998). This is different from a fraudulent figure like Stephen Glass who, in the early 1990s before he was caught and arrested, deliberately made things up and passed them off as journalism in such marquee publications as the *New Republic*, *Rolling Stone*, *Harper's*, and *George*.

The shock then is to recognize that what we experience as reality is always-already sustained only by a symbolic fiction, dispelling the false assumption that "real life" (RL)—tangible certainty and solidity—is separated from fantasmatic "virtual life" (VR), its pale representative. Ontology itself is virtual; experience is always-already reflected having passed through the channels of the Imaginary, filtered by what is and isn't repressed. It is this symbolic fiction, the big Other, which guarantees authority, and assures us a reality, the way things "are." It is this ontology of authority that is decentering in postmodernity. In these early examples from the 1950s, 1970s, and 1980s, we see moments of its dissolution in effect, but only implicitly. Television programs like *Candid Camera* and its updated versions like *SPY TV* have turned such hoaxes into standard fare. The emergence of simulated digitalized reality of cyberspace has made this hidden foundation of fantasy that supports the symbolic fiction explicit by externalizing our fantasies in VR. In doing so the efficiency of the Symbolic Order to give us the assurance that, as a public we are indeed not continually being hoaxed or being taken advantage of in other ways, has been undermined. We are less certain, more paranoid, less willing to be in community, more skeptical that are public votes count for anything. William Karel's ironic documentary has reconfirmed that.

PARTING THOUGHT

As has often been remarked, the debate on violence has a long history in the West, tracing back to the difference between Plato and Aristotle. Plato proposed banning the works of poets and artists from his ideal Republic because of their corrupting influence on impressionable minds of youth, the would-be future leaders of Athens. Homer was not to be recited. To update Plato's complaint in a postmodern context is to do away with simulation (what would now be simulacra); to rid the Republic of any false "copies" so that only originals remain. At the very least, the copy must remain subservient to that which it represents or displaces. Aristotle, on the contrary, argued for the cathartic effects of art, a way to relieve pent-up emotions so that we might be emotionally relieved and drained, feeling psychically healthier after experiencing an "emotional bath" after the performance of a dramatic play. He also thought that the goal of *techne* was to create what nature found impossible to accomplish. Reality television, for instance, applies such *techne* to make "human nature" even *more natural!* Postmodernity presents a Zeitgeist where this long-standing debate has been perverted. We might say Plato and Aristotle's positions have come together at a vanishing point, a ground zero where both sides have collapsed into one another; Plato's violence of simulacra has inverted itself into Aristotle's simulacra of violence. Anxiety creation and its cathartic relief continually reinforce each other in constant self-reflexive loop.

In this chapter we have revisited media violence, attempting to show, yet again, the complexity of the concern. It will continue to be an ideological tool, symptomatic of a youth culture accused of being morally deficient. We attempted to emphasize the impossible gap between popular belief and scientific fact, and the way moral panic concerning youth will continue to be ceaselessly rehearsed. In our previous section on fact and fiction, we attempted to identify how precarious belief structures are. In the United States, when the media hype surrounding the Columbine school shooting had calmed down, The Justice Policy Institute released a white paper report three months after the tragedy (in July) called "School House Hype: School Shooting and the Real Risks Kids Face in America" (Donohue et al. 1998). In the report they reaffirm that schools are a safe place to be and point out some startling statistics to sensationalize their own stance in a war of rhetoric. "As many kids were killed in 2 days of family violence and abuse as were killed in the 5 publicized school shootings [in the 1990s]." "Three times as many juvenile homicide victims are killed by adults as by other juveniles, and only about 3 percent of U.S. murders consist of a person under 18 killing another person under 18." "The vast majority of youth homicide victims are killed by adults [mostly parents]." They point to the availability of guns as one of the most pernicious causes of youth deaths. Every year 3,000 children die from gunfire. We were struck again by the way the paranoia of teachers manifested itself in the direct expulsion and suspension of elementary, junior, and high school students for minor, often noncriminal acts after these shootings. Michael Moore must surely have poured over this material when making his documentary, *Bowling for Columbine* (2002).[2]

We close the chapter by paraphrasing five such documented incidents (from hundreds of others) that appear in the report.

- Two elementary students were suspended for composing a list of people they wanted to harm. The Spice Girls and Barney, the purple dinosaur were on the list.
- A seventh grader was discovered to have a list entitled "People I Would Want Gone," of 20 classmates and teachers. The 13-year-old was placed under house arrest and must undergo psychiatric treatment.
- An eighth grader was suspended from school for 9 days for writing a story about an escaped convict who kills a teacher, 2 students, and a janitor.
- A 15-year-old was arrested for a drawing he made of a man in the cross hairs of a rifle sight.
- Three fifth graders were suspended for the rest of the school year because they were overheard talking about how to plant a bomb in the building. No explosives or bombing plans were found.

The aforementioned are examples of the Zero Tolerance to Media (Ayers et al. 2001). It identifies violent behavior in schools that lead to absurd paranoiac behavior by school administrators and teachers who suspend kindergarten and elementary kids from school because they use "violent" phrases they heard at home, or they issue "threats" to other children or to a teacher. Such minor infractions as innocent enough wish fulfillments are taken seriously. These Zero Tolerance programs turn schools into extensions of the police department and ruin community atmosphere by reducing ethical and moral behavior to a question of punishment. It once again reiterates the fear adults have of youth who are beyond their control. They threaten authority, which leads to some school administrators and teachers projecting their own aggression and need for power and control.

To what extent is it still possible to maintain that media violence can provide a vehicle through which feelings of rage and frustration can be vicariously expressed and discharged? Arguments have been made that the "potential space" of creativity where transitional objects mediate our inside/outside world, as Winnicott theorized, has been totally invaded by the new media (Gutwill and Hollander 2002). There is no "protection" left any more, no "blankies," and teddy bears, but the very "rawness" of the media piercing directly onto the skin-ego, like the forms of piercing and tattooing we have discussed as the "new" postmodern "blankies" that are permanently worn. Writing from a Winnicottian point of view, Gutwill and Hollander's (2002) position acknowledges that the repetitive narratives of violence found in the media are a way children and adolescence defend themselves against the threat of being overwhelmed by the pervasiveness of violence as they experience it in interpersonal peer-group relations, families, and their own struggles with intrapsychic emotional life. Yet, they believe this simply reinforces identification with violence and aggression. They buy into media transference as being the model for feeling and acting, thereby reinforcing the belief of a vicious circulation between real and faked violence. Contra to Freedman's (2002) warning, they repeat the standard mantra that "thousands of studies have demonstrated the connection between TV violence and real-life crime (268)," listing the usual claims of desensitization and victimization of TV effects. They support biblical theologians like Walter Wink (2001) who believes that the myths of "redemptive violence" are simply reinforcing "lawless solutions" in comic books and TV cartoons. The debate on media violence remains never-ending for it is symptomatic of the very core that defines the American psyche—its tendency toward aggressivity as defined by possessive individualism.

9

GIRL/GURL/GRRRL VIDEO GAMES AND
CYBERSPACE

GIRL GAMES: THE SEX/GENDER FIX

As if to answer the impossible Freudian question "What do Women Want?" a number of media studies have shown that both girls and young women are insulted by "pink" marketing strategies that take toys and video games designed for boys and paint them pink to appeal to girls as well (Wilcox 1996; Gilmour 1999). Some girls are further insulted by video games that are specifically targeted for them, like Nintendo's *Barbie's Fashion Designer*, and *Barbie: Super Model*, for instance, or Phillips' *Girls Club*, which has a slot machine-like scenario. Girls can choose their dream date from the heads on the screen. Given an equal opportunity to play video games the gender differences in play performance, as can be expected, tend to disappear as proficiency increases (Greenfield and Cocking 1994). Other studies (McNamee 1998; Furger 1998) show that girls enjoy computer games as much as their brothers, but their brothers dominate access to the computer. Many more girls and young women play videos targeted for boys and young men than the other way around. Many compete with their older and younger brothers playing the same games. The now famous *Geekgirl*, the first cyberfeminist electronic zine founded in Australia that specifically addressed women and technology spawned numerous Grrrl e-zines (see esp. *Brillo Magazine*).[1] But the issue is not skill but identification with characters and the narratives that the games provide. Some puzzle-type geographical games such as Broderbund's *Where in the World is Carmen Sandiego* seem to appeal to both boys and girls (Groppe 2000). But when boys and girls of elementary age are asked to design their own video games there is a tendency simply to repeat socialized gender differences. According to researchers such as Kafai (1996), the claim is that elementary girls prefer games that utilize problem-solving and cooperative play such as *Myst*, a fantasy-adventure game also produced by Broderbund. Girls are said to prefer nonviolent games with positive feedback for the players. If a player makes a mistake s/he would have to start from the beginning, but be encouraged to do so, or games that involve puzzle or spatial relations such as *Tetris*. Girls are said to have an aversion toward violence. When designing their games they did not program evil characters, nor did they incorporate an evil enemy as the goal of the game, as had the boys.

In another study by Kafai (1999), where fourth graders (ages nine–ten) were asked to design educational video games to teach fractions and the solar system to third graders, it seems the same gender division manifested itself. As subjects, math and science had more appeal for the boys. They relied heavily on existing video games and popular media for their designs, utilizing hunts, adventure, and violence as the predominant strategies. Without a games background girls chose likeable figures and familiar settings for their narratives. Video marketing research specifically targeted for girls by such companies as Her Interactive, Purple Moon, and Girl Games essentially replicate ethnographic research such as Kafai's to determine what are "suitable" video games for girls. What emerges is a list of "girl-friendly features" that such games should have. These include female-controlled players, solicited help that is available, puzzle elements, evidence of a creative component, absence of violence, absence of killing and evil characters, predictable rules, positive feedback that is unsolicited, realistic or familiar setting, and cooperative play. By interviewing girls, these companies find out just what their target audience wants. The surveyed answers are a reflection of what girls believe they should value—most often clothes, make-up, shopping, and boys. Unsurprisingly, Girl Games then came up with a series of game videos: *Let's Talk about ME!* and *Let's Talk about ME! Too*, ending with *Let's Talk About ME! Some More*—all no longer produced—based on such marketing research. These games included a diary, and featured a hairstyling salon (in the last version the user could incorporate her own face), a "future" area that was all about horoscopes, a number of quizzes (some sensitive material on AIDS and pregnancy), and a "herstory" section on female role models. Feminists of lesbian persuasion argue that such ethnographic marketing research merely reinforce the stereotype and gender divisions that are already in place (de Castell and Bryson 1999; see also Cassell and Jenkins 1999). Girl-friendly features that define these video games reproduce the nurturing (little mother types) and domestic socialization (the natural helpers) of females rather than recognize other "tribal" high school groups like "computer geeks" and "sport jocks."

Such subjective ethnographic research is often cast as being diametrically opposed to objective scientific "effects" research because of its "emic" or insider's view. "Voice" is appropriated and exploited for marketing and consumption purposes and then justified in the name of providing what girls' "truly" want, as if the sex/gender of girls could be clearly demarcated and profiled by a list of "girl-friendly" features. The same marketing approach is aimed at boys' video games as well. Marketing strategy always determines youth's desires first, and then develops the advertising campaign and product that fills their "lack." Desire is always the desire of the Other, as Lacan, claimed. The teenager wants to be as "cool" as his or her friends are. Yet, the vexing question always emerges concerning sex/gender identification, and here we enter the debates that rage in feminism in general. When sex/gender differences are essentialized in video games research, prominent and high-profile feminist theoreticians such as Carol Gilligan, Mary Belensky, Luce Irigaray, and Nancy Chodorow amongst others, are often referenced to philosophically justify this position. In many psychological studies, especially with "effects" research, sex/gender is an unproblematic biological category: female versus male. When there is an attempt to deconstruct sex/gender stereotyping, to consider queer positions and Grrrl cultures where the values of "nurturing" and "domestication" labels are questioned or outright rejected, then prominent queer feminists such as Judith Butler and Elizabeth Grosz may be called on. Gilmour (1999) for instance, quotes Butler's *Gender Trouble* to reiterate Butler's point that "gender is not always constituted coherently or consistently in different historical contexts, and because gender intersects with racial, class, ethnic, sexual and regional modalities of discursively constituted entities. As a result, it becomes impossible to separate out 'gender' from the political and cultural intersections in which it is invariably produced and maintained" (Butler, in Gilmour, 267). The point here being, a philosophical justification plunges us into psychoanalytic questions of sex/gender identity, which never escape the sociopolitical and historical contexts of sex/gender struggles. Every culture has a myth to establish sex/gender differentiation. A strictly biological explanation remains impossible in this view. As we have argued, postmodernity is characterized by a post-Oedipalization or a "de-Oedipalization." Sex/gender can no longer remain as an unproblematic binary as the majority of media research seems to insist. The strong division of hyper-masculinized men and Barbie-like buxom women in the toy market, in wrestling, and the video games is a symptom of the nervousness of the decentering of sex/gender that is taking place (jagodzinski 1996, 493–530).

GRRRL VIDEO GAMES: IDENTIFYING WITH TOUGH WOMEN

Female video "first person shooter" characters such as Lara Croft (*Tomb Raider*), Joanna Dark (who infiltrates the data Dyne corporation in *Perfect Dark*), Jill Valentine (who battles the Umbrella Corporation in *Resident Evil*) are often dismissed by feminists as simply being the buxom, thin-waisted perfect models of male fantasies, the counterparts to the muscular action figure hulks (Children Now 2001), while the Pixie-like Elf in the *Legend of Zelda* series appears androgynous enough to appeal to both girls and boys. Reminiscent of the Peter Pan figure, the genderless androgyne of pre-pubescence, his refusal to grow up invades adult sexuality and gender division. He clings to childish wonder and playfulness. Pan is everything the Victorian girl-child, Wendy, couldn't do. The Elf of the Legend of Zelda is that carefree girl, "Wendy Unbound." But how do youth identify with such figures? These video games that feature "tough" women continually update the saga and almost continuously introduce new female characters. *Resident Evil* (now also a feature-length movie) has continually expanded their characters as the game's saga surrounding the illegal biological dealings of the Umbrella corporation progressed. *Resident Evil Zero* introduced 18-year-old Rebecca Chambers into Racoon City's Police Special Tactics and Rescue Service, the S.T.A.R.S. Bravo team; *Resident Evil 2* introduced three new female characters: Ada Wong (a tough-minded detective investigator), Claire Redfield (a tomboy), and Sherry Birkin, a shy 12-year-old lost and neglected by her working parents in Racoon City; *Resident Evil C:V* introduces a *femme fatale*, Alexia Ashford one of the head researchers for the Umbrella Corporation who is a brilliant but evil researcher. There is now at least one video game where young women find themselves in similar heroic roles in sport as men. *Mia Hamm Soccer 64* (produced in collaboration with Mia Hamm) is, at the moment of writing, the exception given there are no video games starring members of the Women's National Basketball Association (WNBA), whereas the sport's video *NBA* has been a best seller.

There is of course, justification to chastise the video games industry as aiding to reproduce the female/male binary on biologically stereotypical grounds, and not providing a range of different character types for both men and women. The Hollywood feature-length films that turned these video "tough" women characters into screen characters made sure that they appealed to a male audience in the way they were dressed and their femininity exaggerated. The casting of Angelina Jolie as Lara Croft in Simon West's *Tomb Raider* (2001) presents her as essentially a 007 female figure. (Preproduction of the sequel has already started with Jolie returning to the role.) Alice (Mila Jovoich) in Paul Anderson's *Resident Evil* (2002), is scantly dressed, looking seductive throughout the film despite toting heavy weaponry. In the meantime a love story is worked into the plot. In comparison, Rain Ocampo (Michelle Rodriquez), one of the S.T.A.R.S. team members comes across tougher. (Preproduction has already started for *Resident Evil 2: Nemesis* by the same director with the return of Mila Jovoich as Alice). Sonya Blade (Bridgette Wilson) in Paul Anderson's *Mortal Kombat* (1995) is sexualized as well. After being kidnapped by an evil sorcerer, not only is she rescued by her two male companions, but falls in love with one of them. When rescued she has been transformed into a "sex kitten." From being tough, independent, and self-assured she is reduced to a desirable model, a threat to no one.

Despite these obvious appropriations for male consumption, identification with these video figures can *never* be assured on a strictly male/female basis. That side of the story is most often missing since it throws into disarray the "scientific" and ethnographic marketing research. It is rare in video games research to come across a statement such as that of Christine Ward Gaily (1996). "Whether game playing is considered as having positive or problematic effects, almost all studies of children playing video games have presented these players as absorbing or rejecting but not as *interpreting* and thereby *altering* values embedded in the games and play process" (16, emphasis added). The generality of Gaily's statement still holds its ground, although the psychoanalytic literature in film studies has argued since the groundbreaking article by Laura Mulvey in 1975 that fantasy formations of identity are more fluid and unconscious than first thought. Unconscious "pleasures" always tell another story that is not so apparent as it first seems. Not even playing with the Barbie doll is going to assure that the desired identification by marketers (and/or parents) will take place as Rand's (1995) book, *Barbie's Queer Accessories*, ably illustrates. Rand documents and stages her own perverse fantasies with her Barbie dolls as a way to resist the "straight" world. From a Deleuzean perspective, Driscoll (2002, 97–100) discusses Barbie in terms of "becoming" a girl/woman, a zone of paradoxes of feminine adolescence, an "assemblage" of girl-doll relations including zines such as *Hey There Barbie Girl.* "Barbie maps girls in relation to each other as well as in relation to norms that may be constrictive" (98). By purchasing Barbie the girl always aligns herself with a shifting discourse on her way in "becoming woman."

Seldom is there a defense of violent videos as a form of empowerment and working out adolescent fantasies of good and evil. U.S. educators, even those of a critical bent who are no friends to the conservative educational establishment have trashed film, television, and video violence. Giroux (1996, 27–88) accuses the directors of films (especially Torentino's *Pulp Fiction*) of promulgating "hip" hyperaesthetic violence as well as "white panic" and "racial coding"; Peter McLaren and Janet Morris (1998) give *Power Rangers* a hard knock for their "phallo-militaristic justice." While Eugene Provenzo, Jr. (1991) testified in 1994 before the Subcommittee on Juvenile Justice spearheaded by high-profile senator Joseph Liberman that the media were violent, sexist, and racist (Kent 2001, 461–480). Provenzo has continued to maintain this same position in his testimony (2000, on-line) before the Senate Commerce Committee Hearing on "The Impact of Interactive Violence on Children" chaired by Republican Senator Sam Brownback on March 21, 2000 (Kent 2001, 544–555).

In this regard Gerard Jones's own quest to understand how young people themselves interpret violent video games in *Killing Monsters* (2002) is surely an exception rather than the rule. It is a position we, to a large extent, support. A comic book illustrator and storyteller conducting many art workshops throughout numerous schools, Jones was struck by how a young timid 13-year-old girl was empowered by the violent scenes in a comic book he wrote and illustrated, *Freex*. *Freex* attempted to mix "authentic" teen dialogue with ferocious battles to tell a saga of teenage runaways who are cut off from the world because of their deforming superpowers. They form a sort of street gang for mutual protection. The characters provided this young girl with a way to identify with their plight in the way they looked after each other. Jones found that young people's fantasy of combats helped them relieve their anxieties, feel stronger and in control, to access emotions they were afraid to let out, often to calm themselves down when facing "real" (RL) violence. It seems clear from Jones's stance, that violent video games provide ways to cope with changed families, the uncertainty of the future, and the loss of authority.

Throughout his book Jones uses the term "fantasy" in its most common (mis)understood way—as imagination. It should be pointed out that fantasy is not simply the work of the imagination. Following Lacan, we have been problematizing the term as a *failure* of the full access to "reality," rather than the commonsense view that fantasy is itself illusionary, obfuscating "reality" as it truly is. The Real kernel of fantasy is precisely what is "missing" from our perception, what we are blind to, which makes "reality" possible. The scene of fantasy (the narrative structure and its aesthetic) is the frame around this "missing piece," this lack that is designated as *objet a*. When Jones endlessly repeats that violent video games empower game players, gives them some control over their anxieties, it is these very anxieties that hold the key to the psychic life youth are faced with today. They constitute the *objet a* of such fantasies. What are these anxieties if not directly related to post-Oedipal transformation such as entering the Symbolic Order and finding one's place in the world? More concretely dealing with parents (getting angry at them, suffering abuse from them, losing them to illness), with friends (hostile schoolmates, competition amongst peers, whose in and whose out of a peer group, violence on the playground and in the neighborhood), with teachers (unjust grades, too much homework, school as prison). These are the everyday anxieties of growing up—"becoming man and woman."

The Freud–Lacanian scholar Richard Boothby (2001, 172) argues that in the course of the Oedipus complex the imaginary ego is confronted with a revived specter of the *corps morcelé* (the body in pieces). The dismemberment of the body, according to Lacan, is at the core of the Oedipal transformation, a wound to the child's narcissism. Imagining the fragmented body that issues in castration anxiety is not merely the threatening inducement to change, but also the prime constituent of it. When Nintendo released their version of *Mortal Kombat* with the excessive blood and violence removed, it received thousands of angry letters from gamers, including parents who warned the company not to censor their children's games! (Kent 2001, 446). Is this not telling? The irony that *Doom* was developed by *id* Software should not go unnoticed. The child must achieve castration so that the anxieties of change can be worked through. Here, again the link between the imaginary body and the death drive can be found. The specter of violence is thus an ingredient to the psychic formation of the Oedipal period of adolescence, it is also in and through symbolic castration that violence is transcended. The pacifying of imaginary aggressivity is associated with the passage through the Oedipus complex. Violent video games are, from this perspective, a healthy form of sublimated play. Through the imaginary space of VR, the collapse of the Real with the Symbolic is mediated; an "acting through" rather than an "acting out" is achieved. Jones intuitively recognizes this throughout the many stories that he relates. Especially crucial is his observation that when authority figures like parents and teachers become alarmed and deny the fantasy of violent play, youth see themselves as being positioned as killers, much more powerful than they ever imagined themselves to be. The authorial gaze of the Symbolic Order makes them appear dangerous and out of control.

This reinforces their anxieties and further distances their perceptions from those adults who, from a youth's perspective, seem to overexaggerate and fret needlessly. Jones also makes the point that these violent videos enable older youth who may be more inhibited to play games openly because they are too "old," a chance to work out their ideas and aggressions in VR.

THE POWER OF VIOLENT IMAGES

Anyone who has taught art in junior high will readily see gory and nasty drawing of mutilated bodies, especially by boys as they work out their empowerment narratives. The typical drawing of horses by girls serves much the same purpose, a way to overcome fear and fantasize control over a powerful animal—a metaphorical displacement for male aggressivity—which can—like the horse, be both a source of threat or protection. The fantasy of the horse as being beautiful, powerful, associated with the freedom of movement enables an adolescent girl to work through her anxieties that circulate around power, sexuality, and autonomy. Playing "horsey," riding on a merry-go-around horse, and eventually riding an actual horse provides her with a sense of awe and power of controlling a "beauty/beast" that is so much more powerful than her (Schowalter 1983). One thinks here of the 1950s U.S. television series *My Friend Flicka* (starring Liz Taylor); at the same breath, the pathology of pornographic bestiality lurks on the other side of this fantasy as well. Yet, violent scenes are missing in girl's artworks (like in their video game designs), and one has to ask why? Simmons (2002) provides one possible answer. She argues that girls are caught in a double bind. On the one hand they are socialized to value friendships, act sweetly, and be nonviolent. On the other hand, unlike boys they have no way to express their conflicts and aggression. They resort to a "hidden" culture of relational bullying with the archetype of the "slut" being perhaps the most prominent (White 2002). The rumor surrounding the slut is that she performs the "train job," servicing one man after another willingly and indiscriminately. The slut becomes the abject figure of the sexual drives gone wild, out of control, standing for the loss of control over female sexuality, and the fears surrounding the mystery of feminine chthonic power. Once labeled a slut at school claims White, the psychic wound is so deep that many women are unable to achieve orgasm later in life, some wish to commit suicide, while others seek psychiatric help and are placed on medication. Still others simply resign to the label itself, attempting to turn it around in their favor.

There is ample evidence for acts of relational and indirect aggression in adolescent girls as they go through Oedipalization. The silent treatment, name-calling, starting rumors, note-passing, glaring, dirty looks, gossiping, ganging up, policing fashion, as well as policing whose "fat" and who isn't, being nice in public and then mean in private; these are all ways the Real subject is attacked. Such behavior aims at aspects of the unconscious self that abject the Other, and make her the "odd girl out," as Simmons indicates by the book title. Women, as Luce Irigaray has argued, are socialized into a masochistic existence. With this in mind, one wonders whether the violent video games played by Grrrl cultures are not a sublimated way to find another outlet for their aggression? The "tough girl" is the "slut" who evaporates men with her "weaponry." She is the one who is "jock" enough to stand up for herself, stealing phallic power from men. As the standing joke goes, perhaps bell hooks (1994) has a point when she says you cannot dismantle the patriarchal house with the tools that built it, but young women can certainly have fun trying to do so. There is great satisfaction (*jouissance*) in the effort itself. From this point of view, violent first-person shooter video games provide them with yet another sublimated way to work through their aggressions, rather than being confined to being "sugar and spice and everything nice," a healthy release of anxiety.

Ego Shooting and Puzzling the Ego

The first-person narrative structures of video games provide a way for youth to cope with their anxieties as well. Do not *Doom* and *Myst* (one violent, the other a puzzle game of quest) provide two possible gendered approaches to navigating the virtual space of gaming, psychically mimicking two strategies youth employ when experiencing the uncertainty of finding their place in the Symbolic Order? The paradoxical masculine helter-skelter and frenetic burst of activity in reaching a goal (*Doom*), and the more feminine deliberate, hesitant, exploratory search in determining what that goal might be (*Myst*)? Isn't an obsessive "addiction" to such games a way to avoid facing the desire of the representatives of that Symbolic Order, especially parents and teachers who make sometimes unreasonable demands of their children/students in "real life" (RL)? Both games emerged in 1993 (Manovich 2001, 244–245) with two different approaches to narrative game structure. With *Doom*, speed was important. The player had to go through corridors so as to complete each level as quickly as possible. Movement was restricted to straight lines with abrupt turns when entering new corridors with demons attacking constantly. *Myst* was just the opposite, slow and deliberate moves were called for. The console-player was capable of "looking around," seeing several perspectives, then deliberating before proceeding in a chosen direction. It was possible to move in circles eventually moving from one self-contained environment (world) to another until eventually the entire spacial map was grasped. But note too, in *Myst* no one was around. The player was alone, facing his or her own search in the surreal still empty spaces. With *Doom*, the player had to make her way through the environments one step at a time, unraveling the story as it unfolded along the way. With *Myst* one was not entirely sure what the objective of the game was. Textual clues found along the way could be misleading. It was a mystery—foggy—as the name suggests. Even as you moved through the worlds and read the textual clues the mystery never truly resolved itself. A "cheat" book could be bought if a player had become too frustrated. *Doom*, on the other hand, had a definite goal. *Doom* added the possibility of hacking and adding to the game.

A "death match" could be staged where players could hunt each other in teams (like *Counter-Strike*) instead of going after demons and monsters. (This later feature became a much-publicized point given that Eric Harris had hacked a special version of the game based on his high school.)

We can't help thinking that these two navigational environments relate so well to the uncertainties and anticipations of adolescent life in general where the junior high—"high" relates to the fast pace of life, darting from one place to the next, with as much excitement as possible. All along however, just where the kids are headed remains a mystery, a puzzle. These two first-person narrative strategies in video games continue to be popular. One could characterize them as a dialectics between closed and open systems, in Lacanian terms, between masculine and feminine structures. In VR both boys and girls are on equal bases. They can both explore the entire game environment, whereas in "real life" (RL) girls are more often restricted to the territory they are allowed to explore because of parental and societal fears of rape and injury (Massey 1994). It does not escape us that video games also rehearse the American theme of frontier mythology, which is what the Web has been compared to. Games such as *Adventure* and *War Craft* seem to make such a frontier fantasy explicit. There is but one world (one environment), which involves greater and greater territorialization in order to conquer and win. In general, the environments themselves rehearse the postmodernist themes of anxiety, nostalgia, and melancholia, offering its console-players a strange blend of past and future—Gothic and Medieval science fiction where heroism is kept alive.

CROSS-DRESSING IN CYBERSPACE

Whether it's a cinema viewer or a video player, the question of identification with the screen character does not provide an easy straightforward answer that satisfies a panicked public who wants no-nonsense, jargon free answers. While our intent here is not to go through the literature of psychoanalytic film studies to make our point (see jagodzinski 1996, 165–243, for review), the introduction of more and more "tough" women characters in television, film, and video games requires the most comment since such character development has received the most attention and is the most visibly noticeable, for instance, *Xena: the Warrior Princess, Buffy the Vampire Slayer*, Captain Jayneway of *Star Trek: Voyager*. In the American society where too often women are raped, assaulted, and murdered by men, the fantasy of a young girl or woman's empowerment where she is shown defeating the men who attack her is to be admired. At the same time such an act generates horror. Women who take on these masculine characteristics present a homophobic threat to men. They are women in men's drag as the biologically held socially assumed binary of male/female is deconstructed, making gender an ambiguous and performed discourse. The question of the mannish lesbian continually haunts these figures.

In the sport of serious women bodybuilding this is especially the case. The bodybuilding organization, headed by the Wieder Brothers, goes out of its way to mitigate this threat by preventing "big" women from winning Ms Olympia contests by factoring "femininity" into the judging protocol. You have to "look" like a woman to win! In muscle magazines such as *Flex*, big muscular women are shown as centerfolds, their brawny bodies dressed (as well as undressed) in skimpy undergarments, wearing translucent body-suits, *dessous*, and stiletto shoes (Aoki 1996; Ian 2001; jagodzinski 2003a). Women's bodybuilding comes closest to the "tough" women characters in computer games who are similarly defined by their excessive muscular bod-ies. Toughness in women suggests masculinity and hence is a threat to men, whereas if they are portrayed as being *strong* but not necessarily tough, then the same associations do not hold. Before commenting on these "New Tough Women" as Inness (1999) calls them, from a psychoanalytic view point it is interesting to examine Clover's (1992) hypothesis of the Final Girl standing in the horror films of the late 1970s and 1980s. Her reading of this fantasy is important for several reasons. It points out how the threat of a strong powerful teenage to twenties-something young woman is mitigated by this Hollywood genre. Second, the Final Girl emerged when families in the United States were going through a profound change as women entered the market, divorce rates went up and feminism gained ground. And, three, it raises a question about the New Tough Woman of the new millennium. How radical is she? Can she escape the parody of being a woman with a man's body?

Carol Clover in her study on slasher films claimed that this occult horror genre was a response to the "trouble" going on in the Oedipal household. "The typical patrons of these films are the *sons* of marriages contracted in the sixties or even early seventies," a time characterized by "the women's move-ment, the entry of women into the workplace, and the rise of divorce and woman-headed families" that "would yield *massive gender confusion* in the next generation" (62, emphasis added). A new "female victim-hero" appeared on the scene. Clover raised the question as to why such a large audience of mostly adolescent males identifies with this female victim-hero, or the Final Girl in these slasher horrors? The Final Girl is the last one left standing at the narrative's end after having defeated, killed, or sent the killer back to "hell," but only after the killer has left a long trail of bodies, and she has done a long arduous battle with him. As Clover argues, it is doubtful that the male audience identifies with the "good" male characters. They are usu-ally boyfriends or schoolmates of the girls who are marginal, underdeveloped characters that are dispatched with quickly. The would-be rescuers—policemen, fathers, and sheriffs—are usually presented as incompetent or incapable of stopping the killer. Often they are dispatched with as well. The killer himself is often unseen or barely glimpsed in the beginning of the narrative. When he does make an appearance he is ugly, fat, masked, deformed, or dressed as a woman, and sometimes is a woman (as in *Friday 13th*, pt. 1). The killer is himself eventually killed or dispatched as well from the narrative to live again in another sequel. It is the Final Girl who lives to tell the tale. All this conclusively suggests that identification rests on the Final Girl and the diegesis that rarely varies.

Clover's thesis is that slasher films play out a *male fantasy* despite the appearance that the hero is a young woman. She proceeds to argue that these films specifically engage its forms of "cross dressing" and games of gender identity in order to make possible the disavowal of the fantasy, "a boy is being beaten by his father" (51–52). To recall Freud's (1919, SE XVII) beating analysis, this is the fantasy that boys suppress and interpret as, "I am loved by my father." To avoid the homosexual implications of male love, heterosexual boys displace this entire fantasy as, "*I am being beaten by my mother.*" Sadomasochistic incest fantasies and castration anxieties, the taboo subjects of male adolescence, are explored in the relative safety through the femaleness of the victim. The Final Girl is always "boyish." She is set apart from her more "feminine" friends. She is sexually reluctant, can look death in the face, is resourceful, intelligent, clever, while her name signals her masculine attributes: Marti, Terri, Laurie, Stretch, Will, Joey, Max, just as the surname Ripley in *Aliens* also suggests. Such gender displacements, claims Clover, are obvious in these films where the Final Girl is really a girl in boys drag, a "congenial double for the adolescent male," while the killer is really a woman in men's drag—the phallic mother. On a rare occasion, like *Friday the 13th*, the killer *is* the mother. The killers are virginal and sexually inert, and on occasion are dressed in drag as transvestites and transsexuals, Norman Bates in *Psycho* was an earlier forerunner. Their masculinity is severely qualified. Rape, as Clover points out, is not normally part of the stalker genre. The defeat of the killer for the male audience might now be interpreted as the castration of the phallic mother.

Despite her insightful analysis, Clover has little to say about the way girls in the audience experience these slasher films. If boys cross-gender for empowerment, don't girls do so as well? We maintain that the crossing over of sex/gender identification with action figures in violent video games for the fantasmatic purposes of *empowerment* and/or *control* is what provides the jouissance of play for some youth. The figure becomes the embodiment of *objet a* for them. As cross-identified figures they fill a lack. How and why? The threat of the opposite sex, in particular, is mitigated through such cross-identification. Adolescent boys who identify with the skimpy-dressed, big-breasted heroines like Lara Croft or Joanna Dark—figures who are active, powerful, and threatening—feel like they can control and come to terms with the "impossible" power of female sexuality, which, in "real life" (RL), poses a threat to them. They may be shy, unable to approach the opposite sex, embarrassed about their own bodies, and unable to fit in with the more "mature" sexy crowd who date. The fantasy of control is psychically reassuring. Whether the fantasy is one of admiration (boys are in "love" with such self-assured girls), or retribution (boys are angered by the rejection they receive from such girls), it still sublimates their emotions.

Such cross-identification goes for girls as well. There are now a significant number of websites that celebrate Grrrl culture (or gURL) of "first shooter" video games.[2] The following sample of names tell the story: Amazon Sex Kittens, Babes in Boyland, Beautiful Ladies of War—players of *Half-Life*-where the player is an innocent scientist who has to fight his way through hundreds of invading aliens and soldiers sent by a corrupt government; Evil Quake Goddesses and QGirlZ Quake Clan—players of *Quake* (2 and 3) where the protagonist battles a legion of zombies; FJK—Female Jedi Knights, which is an all women's' *Star Wars Role Playing Game*; GameGirl, offers information and forums relating to *Half Life* MUDS like *Counter Strike* and *Day of Defeat*. The fantasyful identification with hulky male action figures by girls is empowering. Again it provides a way to cope with the threat of the male mystique; the threat of force, brutal strength, and domination. Hate or love them, the question of sexuality is sublimated through game playing.

For both sex/genders, the fantasy space created by the game's narrative becomes a "holding place," a transitional space (Winnicott) to work through the threat of the opposite sex. One might hazard a generalized hypothesis here that these fantasies are heterosexually sexed/gendered: *for boyz cross-identification is more for control, for gurlz cross-identification is more for empowerment*. Such a claim, however, may be far too simple when both heterosexual and homosexual positions are taken into account where the picture becomes much more complicated. Gay and lesbian youth who are almost always under homophobic threat in schools, or whose identity is conflicted when peer support is missing, would cross-identify for yet other fantasmatic desires. Suffice to say that the "impossibility" of sex/gender identification is given more possibility for exploration through the fantasy space that is being offered through these games. This, of course, is a positive development for the anxieties surrounding sex/gender that every culture has to provide for an explanation; however, the question remains whether the fantasies that are offered through video game narratives challenge the existing power relationships, or as a cathartic sublimating release, are they merely maintaining the established hegemony? In our view such strategies offer another insight into the post-Oedipal landscape that is especially being opened up by the site/sight/cite of video game culture.

LESBIAN CYBERFEMINIST INTERVENTIONS

The now-defunct lesbian art collective, VNS Matrix, (VeNuS Matrix) formed in Adelaide, Austria in 1993 attempted to expose the masculine fantasies of cyberspace and cyberpunk by staging their own brand of cyberfeminism by using viral symbology as a subversive strategy. They were the Guerrilla Girls[3] of cyberspace. They issued the first Cyberfeminist Manifesto. Their installation was an ironic parody of "first-person shooter" games (Nintendo's *Game Boy* at the time) using black humor. The plot of the game tried to stage a perverse fantasy, which replaced phallic symbols with explicit gynocentric ones, a strategy used by many feminists in the early 1990s. The clitoris was encoded as a laser beam phallus, a direct on-line connection to the cyberspatial Matrix. The Oracle Snatch watched over the Renegade DNA Sluts, while G-Slime provided the fuel for players to move. As an interactive spectator, depending how one negotiated the hypertext of the installation's space, one of the narrative outcomes was a rerouting to a lesbian sadomasochistic video installation called the "Bonding Booth" (where G-Slime could be replenished). The plot was to join ANG [All New Gen] a band of (s)heroes—the renegade DNA Sluts—in their quest to sabotage the databanks of Big Daddy Mainframe, the imperialist, militaristic Machine and his technophilic son (a "techno-bimbo") called Circuit Boy. Circuit Boy's on-line access to the Matrix was possible by unscrewing his penis (phallus) and transforming it into a cellular phone (Steffensen 1998). In the "Contested Zone" of the game, players were encouraged to question their gendered biological construction and consider new mutations. VNS Matrix made explicit an avenge fantasy to channel the rage many feminists, especially lesbian, felt toward the male domination of technology. By reversing the roles of gaming as well as the metaphorical imagery to allow for an identification as a "tough Slut," the hoped-for outcome was for the player to come away with a new understanding of the relations between text, body, and technology.

The question to what degree such a game is subversive to power relations that dominate the Web still remains an open question. It almost seems as if the video game *Resident Evil* has capitalized and appropriated a version of VNS Matrix's narrative fantasy, but without the feminized space that had been attempted by the collective. Maybe that is a wrong-headed conclusion, for even such simple sex/gender mimicry of reversibility would make a viewer/spectator at least "hesitate" in accepting the hegemony of the sex/gender divide that is constantly reiterated daily. In the abyss of that very "hesitation" is precisely where new possibilities might emerge. Joanna Zylinska (2001), in her insightful book on the feminine sublime, *On Spiders, Cyborgs and Being Scared*, argues that cyberfeminism as a genre opens up this space of hesitation. Cyberfeminism attempts to maintain an antifoundational basis for feminine identity, to keep the possibilities of the ethics of such an alterity open, a position that we support.

Inness's (1999) analysis of "tough women" in popular culture is also instructive given Clover's thesis and the question of the kind of fantasy such a stance provides. In her study she attempts to define these New Tough Women through body, attitude, action, and authority (24). Their muscular bodies are also made to appear tough through the style of clothes they wear. Khaki pants and black leather biker jackets is usually the signifying attire. Attitude as a feature of toughness means the heroine must display little or no fear, no matter how dangerous the situation. To be tough she must also be competent, intelligent, and in control when threatened. Yet, she is not to be emotionless, and this is where her actions become important. She can become angry but her rage does not mitigate her performance. Authority emerges through her actions, although often excessive, defining her as a leader in a time of adversity. Finally, by authority Inness means she must project an attitude of superior judgment so that she can impose discipline. It is a particularly illusive and intangible trait to define. One has "it" or does not.

Inness finds an array of women bodies that can be classified all the way from semi-tough, through to pretty-tough, ending with real tough. In between she explores women characters as lady killers (femme fatales like *La Femme Nikita* (Anne Parillaud), Ellen (Sharon Stone) in *The Quick and the Dead*); tomboys (Jodie Foster, Gillian Anderson); tough women characters found in outer space (Ripley of the *Alien* series, Captain Jayneway of *Star Trek: Voyager*); in the post-apocalyptic landscape (Sarah Connor (Linda Hamilton) of *The Terminator* series, Kidda (Joan Chen), the protagonist of David Peoples' film *The Blood of Heroes* (1989), and Alex (Sue Price) the heroine in the film *Nemesis 2: Nebula*, and in the rash of new postmodern comics (Storm, Elektra, Martha Washington). These form only a small representative of Grrrl comic heroines. One website gallery features 35 separate figures[4] whose range repeats Inness's characterizations from semi-tough to real tough. Like in the sport of female bodybuilding, this array of female bodies Inness maps out do not all pose a threat to masculinity. Many women bodybuilders are gymnasts, who may be muscular, but not bulky. Femininity is always forwarded. Ms. Fitness contests cannot be compared to Ms. Olympia where bulk, although often discouraged by the judges, is still the order of the day. Like women action figures in video games, these are parodies of men. They are not able to disturb and deconstruct the sex/gender binary that is in place.

Inness's study presents much the same situation. There are few truly "tough" woman like *Xena: Warrior Princess* (Lucy Lawless), but even here the television series plays with lesbian motives and its queer well-known following. Just as tough is African American comic book character Martha Washington who is aggressive, often violent, and able to take charge even in the most difficult of situations. She is just and moral, in control of her emotions, and a definite leader. Inness also identifies Alex the protagonist of the sci-fi film *Nemesis 2: Nebula*. Sue Price, who plays Alex, is one tough woman, *and* she has a body that *can* be a threat to male masculinity. Price won a number of minor national bodybuilding contests, which eventually led up to her fourth place finish in Ms. Olympian in 1995. She is "big" by most standards. The film makes this evident, and despite her buff appearance with lots of exposed flesh, she still comes across as being extremely tough, and again lesbian overtones are present.

Inness remains optimistic in her conclusions. Even though these bodies are "limited, confined, reduced, and regulated in a number of ways...the containment is never absolute. [S]uch figures still offer visions of female power and independence that help to challenge the gender status quo. [L]ike most popular culture characters, [the tough woman] is a multivalent representation that can be read in numerous and even paradoxical ways" (178, 179). We certainly agree with Inness's assessment but we would like to add to the caveat she makes when she worries whether such an image is ultimately desirable. Does such a tough figure—strong, autonomous, and not dependent on men that has infiltrated in all forms of popular culture—simply play into the liberalist feminist stance of wanting what men have? Does this loss of difference simply reinstate patriarchy, modified to be sure, but still patriarchy as any numbers of feminists of other ideological persuasions have so insisted, especially Luce Irigaray? Hegemonic masculinity is consistently reproduced in these video games despite the sprinkling of "tough" women characters throughout. Until this changes women are forced to continue to play this "man's" game, and at the same time attempt to change the rules so that a more just social reality emerges. Or, do we take a much more optimistic, but combative track and follow "tough" cyberfeminists such as Sadie Plant (1997) and Haraway (1997) in their call for the deconstructive power of the cyborg to keep the sex/gender roles open? Perhaps we can end this chapter on a compromise note taken from Zylinska (2001) who writes:

> mimicry can provide a non-utopian viable political option for these theorists of gender who neither want to resort to a prediscursive essentialist identity nor believe in the possibility of creating "entirely new" identities, which would not be marked by the Law of the Father governing representation and language. Indeed, as Luce Irigaray concludes, "There is, *in an initial phase*, perhaps only one 'path', the one historically assigned to the feminine: that of mimicry. One must assume the feminine role deliberately. Which means already to convert a form of subordination into an affirmation, and thus to begin to thwart it." (130, emphasis added)

Mimicry is a form of simulacra, as Deleuze (1983) argued, "an image without resemblance" (49), a form of dissemblance and not resemblance. Translated into Lacanese, it belongs to the psychic order of the Real. Cyberfeminism "haunts" masculinity, a virtual specter of its limit. Grrrl mimicry does not provide a "solution" to sexual inequality, rather it seeks an "exhaustion" through its cultural proliferation: not exhaustion in the sense of more possibilities, but reworking the sexual deadlock so that it mutates into a qualitatively different relationship in the future. This may be Braidotti's (2002) wish as well? This is certainly part of the post-Oedipal struggles and strategies of "becoming woman."

10

The Myths of Media Interactivity: Youth and Cyberspace

What then is to be concerned about interactive video games if we have not accepted the media violence hypothesis, and have raised some skepticism regarding the New Tough Women characters in cyberspace? By dismissing the authority of these scientific studies, are we not ourselves undermining our own thesis of the continued "loss" of faith in the Symbolic Order? Are stances such as Gerard Jones (2002) who is almost entirely supportive of violent video games to be applauded? There are a number of serious concerns that need to be addressed with interactive video games and youth interaction with the Internet (www), designated as cyberspace or VR (virtual reality) in this chapter. These issues directly deal with questions concerning youth identity, designer capitalism's dominance of Internet sites, and the dangers of video game "addiction" that have emerged with the failure of trust in the Symbolic Order. Globally and nationally speaking, it is only a small, mostly white minority of privileged youth today who "enjoy" being "wired" into the "new media." These are the so-called teleWebbers or viewsers who multitask, simultaneously e-mailing, instant messaging, surfing the Web, talking on cell phone, watching TV while doing their homework *and* even at times playing a video game.

Media interactivity has been touted as a positive development, not only as an advance in its entertainment value but educationally as well. A close identification with the screen in a "first-person shooter" or "first-person explorer" environment enables the player/learner to simulate a direct "screen presence" by actively manipulating an interface device (console, wand, joystick). In aerial environments the player/learner controls an avatar who explores the game environment or who iconically represents him or her in a VR chat room. In VR it's not a question whether the created world is as real as the physical world, rather the question is whether it is "real" enough for the console-player to be able to suspend disbelief while immersed "in" it. Such a close identification in interesting "realistic" environments can simulate learning and game play. The medical student can, for example, learn to dissect a virtual cadaver as often as necessary until s/he gets the skill right. The high school biology student can do likewise with the traditional frog dissection. This impoverished and reductionist experience raises the usual phenomenological question of what is "humanly" missing, raised some time ago by Dreyfus (1972) and Weizenbaum (1976) and subsequently explored by Sherry Turkle (1997) as a question of what is posthuman (Hayles 1999, 287–291). Are we reducing the chaotic metaphysical irreducibility of "life" (*zoë*) to simply information? The proverbial paradox of killing the specimen so that it can be examined. This is an issue we shall take up in another form later on in the chapter, as the posthuman question of the interface between artificial intelligence (AI) and the human.

A second aspect of cyberspace that has received a great deal of attention is the benefit youth experience in VR chat rooms and visiting teen websites where identity can be explored to cope with the tribulations and concerns of life. By taking on a persona of one's choice irregardless of sex, gender, ethnicity, and so on in a chat room or MUD (Multiple User Dialogue), the teen is relieved of restrictions that normally influence face-to-face interactions. Girls, especially, can be treated with more respect (Furger 1998). In classroom situations, where girls are stereotypically less talkative and assertive than boys, on-line they are less afraid to say what's on their minds, and be more open in their opinions (Evard 1996; Ferganchick-Neufang, on-line). The "freedom" to be what one wants to be can be had. Different sides of the self can be explored. It has also been argued that Web Home Pages provide girls with an opportunity to more fully express themselves by creating a public identity (Stern 1999), while commercially sex/gendered on-line sites cater to youth culture and concerns (music, movies, relationships, and advice).

The home page of gURL.com is instructive and paradigmatic in this regard since it repeats gurl'z interests of magazines such as *Seventeen*, at the same time it is organized as an e-zine. The six sections and their content form a fairly comprehensive imaginary net of popular cultural desires that is promoted for gurlz. "Dealing With It" (sex section, sucky emotions, significant others, daily grind, misbehavior, labels); "Looks Aren't Everything" (body image, virtual makeover, fashion yourself, paperdoll psychology); "Where Do I Go From Here (after high school, gURL grants, believe it (or not), practical matters); "Stop. Look, and Listen" (books, music, movies, clips about clips); "Movers, Shakers, and Media Makers" (spotlight, dead women, feature gURL makers); and "SportsgURL" (all sports). The site offers a gURL an e-mail account, a gURL.com personal Web page, chat service, and gURL grants, which are financial grant for gurlz between 13 and 19 years of age who compete for personal and professional growth (education, projects, and public initiatives).

When it comes to commercial websites for boys the sex/gender divide repeats itself. Boys' sites like IGN.com cater to reviews and previews of Video Games, reviews and previews of on-line games, a games store, movie reviews, a "for men" section (babes, cars, gear, dating), DVDs, Sci-Fi, Wrestling, and a Music section. E mail and chat is also available. While such sites reproduce the sex/gender divide, Gay/Les/Bi teen Internet sites have made it possible in a discrete way to explore sex/gender identities that would otherwise be difficult and painful, teenage suicide rates being the highest amongst this group. The gaystudent.org website, as one of many examples, provides a platform of sections that directly address the difficulties of living in a heteronormative society. "Advice and Support" (get advice, read advice, our support team); "Interact" (discussion forum, cyberpals, chat, our E-zine, polls); "Community" (diaries, coming out, articles, college life); "Resources" (health, links) and Contest/Auction. Silberman (1998) writes powerfully how AOL Online Gay and Lesbian Community Forum has opened the door for closeted kids. "John Teen Ø" access "to AOL's gay and lesbian forum enables him to follow dispatches from queer activists worldwide, hone his writing, flirt, try on disposable identities, and battle bigots—all from his home screen" (117).

A third aspect of VR developments has been the praise for the open-ended structure of hypertext narratives. In the following chapters we raise questions whether these developments of cyberspace are as "positive" as they claim to be. As Žižek notes (1997a), there are three borders or boundaries that cyberspace threatens today:" 'true life' and its mechanical stimulation; between objective reality and our false (illusory) perception of it; between my fleeting affects, feelings, attitudes and so on, and the remaining hard core of my Self" (133). In the first, nature (*zoë*) is reduced to technology, as so many DNA codes. Nature's generative structure is supposedly revealed. In the second, the belief is that it is possible to eliminate the vanishing point, the limit to vision and become omnipotent by occupying it. The third addresses the decentered subject that enables the console-player to experience a variety of identities. In this chapter and chapters 11 and 12 we borrow from a number of expositions on cyberspace by Žižek (1996a, chap. 3; 1997a, chap. 4; 1999a, chap. 5; 1999b, chap. 6) to develop our concerns of youth culture's engagement with the new media and the fantasies that structure them.

ESTABLISHING VIEWS OF CYBERSPACE

The proliferation and then universalization of simulacra, the so-called indistinguishability between fact and fiction, the "lie" from the "truth," "reality" from its artifice has been theorized by Baudrillard in his many writings as plunging us into a complete world of artifice where subjectivity has been lost. The human becomes merely the locus of a "screen." Metaphysics, with its obsession for Being, has long had its day. For Baudrillard, any sense of "authentic" being has finally been vacated. Cyberspace theoreticians like the French town planner and architect Paul Virilio (1999; see Wilson 1994), on the other hand, still long for Being's nostalgic recovery. He fears that the virtuality of design could replace reality as such. He speaks of a dystopia, a paranoid psychotic vision where the virtual city becomes a global urban megacenter populated by an elite group (as in the sci-fi *Blade Runner*). Other cities are reduced to being periphery satellites. City planning, made possible through virtual technologies, becomes a projection of an elite's version of reality extended outward, constructing an ideal system in place of a "real" world. There is no need for the symbolic social Order (big Other) founded on a democratic pact of consent. Such a paranoid vision believes in the "Other of the Other" (Lacan), a controlling force or authority that is able to make everything transparent, as in Peter Weir's *Truman Show*. When Truman confronts the god-like voice of Christof, the director and producer of the world-renown reality show—his paranoia is confirmed. A puppet master does indeed exist!

Doel and Clarke (1999) present a useful and comprehensive overview as to the directions VR has been theorized, which puts many of the debates about cyberspace in perspective. They come up with four interpretations, the last of which is consistent with a Lacanian understanding of fantasy as being informed by VR. (1) VR is simulation and simply a false approximation of the real (RL). This is the Platonic view that harbors the anxiety in the way a virtual-as-copy (simulacrum) de-realizes the world and can become a dangerous supplement to it. As a stand-in it may efface or occlude RL such as commodity fetishism of money. Fundamentally, such an anxiety speaks to the fear that a double can be better than the original. Our twin brother or sister, or our clone, can replace us; (2) VR is a "suppletion," or a resolution of the real (RL). Here the argument is that VR can become a prosthetic supplement, it can complete and extend the limitations of the body and nature (*zoë*) in general to its full potential. The real (RL) and VR are no longer opposed but connote different degrees of potentialization along a continuum that runs from real (RL) to the hyperreal (HR). This is fundamentally an Aristotelian argument for the power of *techne*. Hayles (1999) concludes her book on the posthuman on this possibility; (3) VR as "s(ed)ucation" refers to the virtual illusion of a final solution. This possibility takes hyperreality as advanced by Baudrillard in the "suppletion" hypothesis to its ultimate conclusion. This is the liberal humanist dream of VR, advanced earlier by Hans Moravec (1988) of downloading human consciousness into a computer. In brief, it is the dream of a collapse between VR and RL, a completely technologically perfected world as an achieved utopia. Besides Virilio's designer scenario already mentioned, we can give the example of the human cyborg with its extermination of human imperfection—the anxiety as represented by The Borg of *Star Trek*. Steven Spielberg's film *Minority Report* (2002), based on Philip Dick's short story where crime has been eliminated through the technological interface with psychics who are able to predict and stop the crime before it actually happens, would be another example; and (4) VR as simulacra that is "real virtual(real)ity." This is the Deleuzean perspective where VR is treated as its own separate ontological "reality." Here we would say that this perspective comes close to, or is in actuality equivalent to, what Lacan and Žižek, his most elaborate defender mean by fantasy as it is informed by the Real and the Symbolic. The ghostly presence of VR is precisely where the ego "disappears" or "fades" (*aphanisis*) and the core "subject" emerges. Aphanisis refers to the impossibility of being self-present to oneself. Something always "escapes" one's full knowledge of oneself. As we "become" we also "fade" away; we remember and forget in a never-ending process. The subject's ego is always marked by a w(hole)ly imaginary promise of complete self-presence, by a desire to fill the lack (hole) that makes us human and fallible. The VR of the Symbolic Order promises to fill that lack, to provide a place for the "subject," to provide a meaning to life. As we saw in the previous chapters, this virtual Symbolic Order that gives us the sense of "concrete" reality can collapse. For us, Deleuze and Lacan come together in the supposition that VR is the ghostly presence of the spectral Real. The "real" (RL) is already virtual in the way fantasy makes it possible for the "subject" to find a place in the social Symbolic Order. We arrive once more, at what seems an intuitively strange position, repeated often throughout our chapters: real life (RL) is already virtual. It is the gaze of the Symbolic Order coming at us from the spectral Real. Our unconscious fantasy life makes RL possible.

DESIGNER CYBER-CAPITALISM: THE DREAM OF DIRECT PRODUCT IMPLANTATION

The cyberspace of the Internet is the playground of designer capitalism. To follow Althusser (1977), it is shaped by the ever-deferred "last instant" of the economy; an open-ended system constantly informed by contingencies of its users and the marketplace. The global youth market, especially the Y-Gen in the United States has triple the spending power compared with youth in the 1960s. The Internet is a training ground for young entrepreneurs and visions of teens becoming rich abound. Youngbiz.com provides interactive content information on Stock Optionz, Biz Startz, Careerz, and Money Smartz. An e-mail service is available to be in contact with like-minded teen entrepreneurs. The shadow side of this enterprise is the way an "electronic body" of the teenager becomes established, which is then used for market demographics to continue the sell.

The most sophisticated development of this VR consumer "e-body" is done through the market strategy of a relationship between the customer and the cyber-company through two-way "conversations." The goal of one-to-one marketing, which Amazon.com (for adults) and Bolt.com (for teens) are perhaps paradigmatic, is to become intimately familiar with the customers, to learn their preferences and become buying partners, to obtain detailed information about their tastes, desires, interests, and values. To track such information these companies use "cookies." A cookie is a small piece of data (an identifying code) that is placed on the customer's personal computer's hard drive by a website to monitor and track information about the user. When buying a book from Amazon.com the customer is greeted by name, given new titles that s/he might be interested in, sent an "alert" when an author the customer has bought is published, and so on.

This form of marketing will only become more and more sophisticated as interactive television (ITV) and the "wireless web" grow allowing a broadcaster to further invade the home to become more precise in terms of what "a" particular customer wants (Montgomery, CME, 85–88). Bob Van

Orden (1999), vice president of product marketing of digital-subscriber networks for Scientific-Atlanta Inc., claims that this form of collecting data and matching advertisements is like "direct mail on steroids" (145). Whereas direct mail advertising usually yields a 1 percent response rate, this new form of advertising routinely exceeds 20 percent. This is the dream of "friction free" capitalism as a direct access to the unconscious where the *objet a* of each customer's unconscious could be materialized as a product in a perfect fit. The future looks like a scene from the sci-fi thriller Spielberg's *Minority Report* (2002). In the future everyone is ID-ed, there is no escape. One of the few ways is to surgically replace the eyes. Detective John Anderton (Tom Cruise) does just that to flee from the Law. But, whenever he runs past a VR billboard that "reads" his now "illegal" eye print, he is beckoned by the seductive (female) voice of advertising. The images on the screens automatically change so that he would look at the product that "perfectly" fits his lifestyle.

With the coming of cable and digital satellites many American homes have up to 150 channels, but 500+ channel universe is entirely possible. TIVO (www.tivo.com) is a digital video recording system where a customer can record and download from a variety of available programs to develop the kind of personalized television schedule s/he desires, to view the programs in the order and time of day desired. TIVO presents a perfect example of interpassivity. The little black box that sits on top of the television has a big hard-drive memory (projected to be twice the size of the average Blockbuster video store) with a scanning and searching capability like a computer. It can store a personalized television schedule by searching through the myriad of programs that are playing simultaneously on satellite television or cable. More to the point, it is able to track, record, and store the customer's random scans as s/he surfs channels looking for something of interest. Eventually this "smart" devise gets to "know" the customer's choices, predicting and offering its own choices to view. Programs may be selected, which the customer has never seen before but fit perfectly with his or her pattern of viewing and interests. In effect, TIVO's little black box begins to take over the function of the customer's enjoyment of randomly scanning and its idle pleasures. It becomes tailored and personalized to what the customer thinks s/he wants. Caught in a self-reflexive loop the machine "relieves" the customer of the responsibility for his or her personal cultural choices. It begins to "enjoy" for him or her, like canned laughter. Add to this the ideal of micro-niche advertising to fit the customer's lifestyle and we are not far removed from *Minority Report*. The communicative aspect of television as a public forum simply vanishes, as does so-called audience-research based on mass marketing. Marketers now have an inside look at people's taste preferences and cultural choices that is unprecedented.

There are many websites to feed such a fantasy for young people. Youngbiz.com encourages a rather detailed registration form to be filled out, which is used to profile its users. Teen.com converts the teenager into part of a marketing "Trend Team" to help decide what's "in" and "out," what's "hot" and what's "not." To be selected as part of the "team" a questionnaire was first sent out that probed teens most popular desires. From the 800 plus e-returns, 250 were selected who subsequently received gift packages of CDs, cosmetics, T-shirts, and the like (Montgomery, CME 2001, 33, 116 n. 118). Teens believe that they are deciding what their likes and dislikes are. In effect they are being used for market demographics to set up the next marketing campaigns, and developing brand loyalty (Klein 2000). Three of the more pernicious marketing strategies involve: "Online Street Marketing" (teens are hired to post flyers and distribute leaflets on the street, music concert, sporting event, in order to create a "buzz" about a new product. This same strategy is applied on-line through message board posting, e-mail, and AOL instant messaging); "Viral Marketing" (this technique uses an on-line version of "word-of-mouth" to promote a product or service. "Word-of-modem" product information is achieved with every communication by sending a clickable URL about the product) (see Montgomery, CME, 52), and "Branded Communities" (Montgomery, CME, 31; Klein 2000). E-com sites entice teens to remain loyal to them by having its users directly express and participate in the creation of the content on the Web. It appears that teens are simply talking to teens and are being supported by allowing them to post message boards, asking them for advice, or them giving advice, publishing their texts, profiles, artwork, poetry, and especially creating a personal home page.

Designer cyber-capitalism in effect "steals" away the voice (*zoë*) from teens and uses it for its own "biotic" profit. The routine surveying and monitoring of chat rooms, bulletin boards, discussion groups—the very spaces of "free" teen expression—enable marketers to find out what are the latest trends, hot products, desires, and teen obsessions. To quote a well-worn Borg line from *Star Trek*, "resistance is futile." Whatever teens say is appropriated into the designer cyber-mill of marketing. The Center for Media Study (56) reports the sophisticated marketing of Teenage Research Unlimited (TRU), Roper Statch World Wide, Zandi, Kalorama, and Cheskin Research who use focus groups, on-line surveys, and anthropologists to study teen subcultures. CME reports that Girl Games even hosts "slumber parties" for teen girls to build trust and get the inside view of their habits and values. What is most pernicious in this research is the way the contingent event of teen culture is used to stabilize the markct. Thc so-called "explorers", teens that are considered independent and highly influential in what they believe in are especially targeted to establish future trends. Ravers, Goths, Wierdos, and Freaks—collectively known as the "visibles" because they "stand out" above the rest—are especially monitored. They are the likely trendsetters. Non-teens, typically labeled as "Nerds," "Dorks," and "Geeks," the abjected segment of teen culture provide yet another challenge for marketers because of their underrepresentation in the Net. Cyber-capitalism wants them ALL as ONE.

The Center for Media Education (CME) describes how several e-commerce sites have managed to tap into teens buying on-line despite the difficulties of not being independent consumers. Most have to rely on their parent's credit cards and look after the payment transactions. Nevertheless, an innovative new kind of website has emerged, known in the industry as an "e-commerce enabler," that has opened the purchasing door for teens. Cybermoola.com enables teen e-commerce by allowing users to create pre-paid accounts. They can then use the money to purchase products from affiliated websites. Rocketcash.com enables teens to shop without a credit card by having parents open an account for them and then shop at over a hundred on-line retailers. The most sophisticated is DoughNet.com. In this virtual bank account system, parents can set up on-line banking accounts and parent-controlled credit accounts for their children to use in on-line transactions. There is even a way to invest, save, and make charitable contributions to nonprofit organizations. It is also possible to earn "DoughPoints" for teens that have no money to spend on-line. These are earned by answering HarrisZone polls. There are now other companies (CDNow) that pay teens to post advertisements for company merchandise on their home pages. Gaming sites on the Net are also available where teens can win virtual money or tokens that can be used to win cash and prizes.

Mobile phones (cell phones, "handies") have become the toy-thing for teens and yet another way for cyber-capitalism to reach them. Cell phones have been extended now to become part of a wireless world of portable entertainment centers capable of instant messaging (IM), digital pictures, downloading and listening to music, playing interact video games on-line, and surfing on a truncated version of websites designed specifically for cell phone use. Voxx.com has an interactive site for teen girls, which delivers a recorded voice message from Jennifer Aniston whenever she is scheduled for an interview. gUrl.com, Alloy.com, Bolt.com and dELiAs.com all offer teens access to the Net, posting shopping information and upcoming events via cell phones and pagers as "bursts" of information for teens on the "move" (Montgomery, CME, 83–84).

What has been the "free" use of cyberspace is potentially to undergo even a more radical antidemocratic change. CME report in their "new trends and future directions" that the Web will eventually shrink, reduced to a small subset of featured websites. The reason for such a possible massive shift is the ever-increasing move to wireless mobile communication devices, personal video recorder (PVRs), and interactive television (ITV) like TIVO discussed earlier. Here the myth of interactivity finds a heightened irony. Customers can create more and more of their own media experiences using customized PVR and ITV programming features. The cable industry is "designing and deploying systems that offer only the *illusion* of online choice" (Montgomery, CME, 80, original emphasis). Like walled-cities, these are virtual gated communities dubbed as "walled gardens," "walled jungles," or "fenced prairies." The customer is supplied a defined range of approved Web pages with the cable company supplying the service assured that its range of brands and advertising will be the only ones that the customer uses for as long as the cable service is paid for. In effect, the customer is captured and held as a "willing" hostage to what the cable company offers. As the Web's shrink-age continues, the CME report continues, so will the number of companies controlling the most popular Web content as the pressure to consolidate grows (as part of the so-called dot-com shakeout).

OEDIPUS ON-LINE: CYBERSPACE REDEEMED AND LOST

Have we overstated our case concerning cyberspace as the playground of capitalism? Are they the "evil" purveyors of youth, out to get their "souls"? It has been argued that cyberspace is infinitely more flexible, more like the space of post-Oedipalization where the freedom to explore oneself is more open than ever; where the proliferation of personal home pages provide an opportunity for teens to present their "bedroom walls" to the world, and make a statement as to who they are (Chandler 1999). To change perspectives for the moment we look closely at the stance of Jerry Flieger (1997a,b 2001) who, from a psychoanalytical (Lacanian) stance, claims that cyberspace is still a site where authority is in place. Teens and adults are not as "free" to do as they like. For her cyberspace acts like the Symbolic Order itself (RL). Its features are, by definition, intersubjective. Our interface with it works much the same as a "face-to-face" interaction. In the end we always address an Other who is "unknown" to us rather than the illusion of some transparent Other like our friendly neighbour. When interfacing with cyber-space, the same process happens. Even our close neighbor, as Freud (1940, *Outline of Psycho-analysis*, XXIII) pointed out is not transparent. S/he can become "too" close to us, turning ugly and threatening. Tony Soprano's neighbors know that he's up to no good. Nobody "really" wants to know him. Given the right distance, all is well. Cyberspace gives us that psychic distance where we do not have to "love our neighbor." Flieger argues that desire is always thwarted in cyberspace following Lacan's maxim: "desire is the excess of demand [drives] over [biological] need." (The baby's cry bears an inexplicable excessive desire. It has been nursed, seemingly all its demands met—cuddled, rocked, sung to—yet it wants something "more.") She directs our attention to Lacan's characterization of the ego as a paranoid structure, not in the pathological sense of a psychosis, but as an epistemé of acquiring knowledge as Lacan develops it in S III, *The Psychoses*. All forms of communication (speaking, writing, art-ing, singing) require a form of decen-tering to take place by fantasizing the Other whom we are addressing. We act "as if" the Other is staring back at us, and listening to what we are say-ing. This is what is happening in our interface with cyberspace (VR) as well.

In Flieger's view, both our Ideal Egos and Ego Ideals can be shaped by the screen of the hypertext of cyberspace. First, narcissistically as an imaginary projection of an alter (Ideal) ego we can take in any virtual community—our representative avatar acts as an icon "as if" we were a uni-fied ego and not the divided self that it represents. Second, as the imaginary perception we think that virtual community has of us—whether we are being confirmed or rejected—as Ego Ideal. What is behind the message that is being conveyed to me on the screen? The uncertainty of the answer occurs at the symbolic level since we can never be sure of the relationship we have with this virtual Other. The cyberspace in this case acts as a space where we can try out other points of view, explore other parts of ourselves. At the same time, not all such exploration is freely permitted, as if our every demand is met. Cyberspace (Web) acts as an agency of prohibition that prevents access to our full gratification (jouissance). It *is* Oedipus on-line. My desire is mediated by the desire of the Other. It is impossible to do away with the interface so that there is no gap between my representative avatar and me. My demand (drive) is curbed within the jurisdiction of its Law as failed desire. The demand of a sent e-mail (or (E)go-mail as Flieger puts it) is never fully gratified as it goes through its cyberpath. Many things can happen to it. As it is forwarded it may be reproduced, replied to thereby eliciting further replies, relabeled, bounced back as no such address, and finally returned to me in an "inverted form"—I answer my own question without ever being certain that I am right.

Cyberspace is thus filled with Oedipal questioning of desire, always arriving at a fundamental enigma: "Just what does the Other see me as? What kind of object am I for his or her desire?" Thus cyberspace puts a limit to the Imaginary. It works ersatz for the Symbolic Order by the very use of our language. The constant threat of newer and better viruses seems to assure us that the Web is a fallible space, impossible to be controlled by any one single Being (an Other of the Other). We believe that no ONE is observing us; no ONE has access to our home computer, yet the threat is always there. A virus can strike waking us up to the illusion of its infallibility. The success of an e-mail or a video game, or a MUD depends ultimately on how the interface has been felt by my own bodily situatedness. To what extent have desires been met within the confines of what is permissible within the Symbolic Order as represented by the www of cyberspace? Ultimately, the failure of gratification (of our drives) reinstates the border between RL and VR. In cyberspace we continue to search for (Real) completion, but we always end up lacking. Cyberspace continues to signify the mysterious Real that would fill the "hole" to make us "w(hole)." In light of our previous discussion of cyber-capitalism, it is precisely this "lack" that enables capitalism to maintain its driving force, to provide a never-ending stream of products that will never fill that lack up.

Žižek (1999a) takes a different tact. He accepts Flieger's position that cyberspace presents a strictly formal structure of symbolic prohibition, but he names such a stance as also being a form of post-Oedipalization, not Oedipalization in its mythical sense as Flieger argues. What is missing in cyberspace is an embodied representative of the prohibition to *jouissance*. No one is in charge except the mechanized formal structures of language (computer language). To put it bluntly, the "No" of castration is experienced mechanically—the program refuses to work properly, access is denied, full gratification thwarted by a mechanistic Law. Transference with a computer's access to VR works strictly mechanistically. We trust that it "works," but when it doesn't we become very angry. Our incestuous narcissistic pre-Oedipal attachment to the terminal is cut off rather rudely. About three-quarters of privileged on-line teens pooled by Pew Internet (Lenhart et al. 2000), for example, said they couldn't "live" without the Net.

The alter ego that we create through our Windows word processor as we write, the avatar that runs around for us in chat domains, our "browsing" and "surfing" the Net are all suddenly interrupted by this technical castration. Are computer technicians then to become the embodiment of the reassurance that the symbolic function of cyberspace can be trusted? Do we give them the transference of authority as embodying a "little bit of the Real," maintenance men "with a heart?" They regulate, restore, and expand access to the Web. In such a vision cyberspace is metaphorically characterized as a pre-Oedipal Mother, the Matrix of cyberpunk fictions, which as some feminists have argued (Sadie Plant 1997; Valie Export 2001; Zoë Sofia 1999) is really the masculine corporate body in disguise—cross-gendered with its military and cybernetic origins forgotten or repressed. When women and computers become structurally equivalent in the masculine imaginary, cyberspace becomes a maternal superego, a phallic woman (the vamp) denying access like HAL from *2001: A Space Odyssey*, or a dutiful Mother (the virgin) like the computer systems on *Voyager*, *Star Trek*, *Johnny Mnemonic*, and *Alien*, all working for their corporate bosses. The attack of the "viral girls" becomes the only way to assure that the system remains open, leaving its totality and existence in doubt. For cyberfeminists like Plant, Export, and Sofia castration happens at the breast—as Melanie Klein had maintained. The cutting "off" the breast in Amazonian fashion now takes on new metaphorical meanings when cyberspace becomes a matrix (womb) as in Wachowski film *Matrix* (1999) complete with its submarine spacecraft submerged in amniotic fluid, generating power for the corporation's super computer.

With this critique we, once more, arrive at a bleak picture cyber-capitalism, the dystopias presented by male theorists such as Baudrillard, Virilio, and female theorists Anne Balsamo (1995) and Claudia Springer (1996) alike. But, it can get worse. Flieger's on-line Oedipalization thesis can lapse into a psychosis, into a foreclosure of the Name-of-the-Father as Žižek argues, for there is no flesh-and-blood representative as a symbolic stand-in for the paternal "No." Such a bodily stand-in is required if a transference is to take place to sustain the illusion that someone as the representative of the Law, stands in the way to full gratification. In cyberspace no such authority exists, rather it is a reduced mechanized authority. Without such an authority, which could come by way of contingent technical failure, there is the danger of being immersed into a psychotic world as a fusion with the motherboard. The computer begins to function as a maternal Thing, swallowing up the subject into its endless "windows" of VR corridors in an incestuous fusion.

We might understand this concern of psychosis in yet another way. Consider the replicants in Ridley Scott's now classic film *Blade Runner*. They can be considered post-Oedipal in the way Žižek reads Flieger's Oedipal argument. As a convergence of genetics (DNA) and language they are condemned to a psychotic life of living in the present, unable to embody language as memory with a past, present, and future. Their narrative lives are a literalized invention (a database collection of artifacts), not metaphorized. They are in a constant search for their identities. But this is an impossible task for their language is externalized and objectified, as in psychosis; they are unable to enter the Symbolic Order and hence must be euphemistically "retired." To become "human" they search for their Father (their inventor, Eldon Tyrell) to free them from a predetermined mechanical death. This is their ultimate object of desire; their demand for eternal life (immortality), which is theoretically possible through cloning. Such a Father is what the replicants (homologous to cyberspace) lack—a representative of the Law. The only Law that holds them is a mechanical one, not the human one of entropy where death is inevitable. But Tyrell is no superhuman god. He is portrayed as a frail old man with thick glass lenses (one would think that in the advanced future glasses would no longer exist). But it is this very frailty that makes him a believable "father" who says "No" to them. Only the replicant Rachel (Sean Young), Tyrell's "daughter," has a "father." Like Athena born of Zeus, as a figure she updates the corporate takeover of technological fertility—the ability to clone. In the end Tyrell is murdered, but what of it? So that Decker (Harrison Ford) can copulate with a man-made machine that is "woman?" To keep her secret? Ultimately, to verify the impossible love between them? To confirm corporate masculine control over reproduction? The questions seem to proliferate to the paradox of an "endless stand-still."

In her very clever and witty response to Žižek's critique of her position, Flieger (2001) attempts to set the record straight by carefully deconstructing his essay on the possibility of traversing the fantasy of cyberspace (1999a). By using a baseball analogy as told by Abbott and Costello's classic 1936 routine, "Who's on First?" Flieger is able to match Žižek's rhetorical flourishes with her own. At stake is the question of Oedipus. How is it to be interpreted since Žižek uses the term "post-Oedipus" and "beyond Oedipus" much as we have been using it as well? Flieger's point is that Freud's position was already "beyond" Oedipus "proper," and "far beyond the gender and culture-bound casting of Oedipus as castration complex" (66–67). In brief, Flieger's "proper" Oedipus is directed to complexity theory, the notion of "thirdness" that she claims Freud was utilizing *throughout* his work, already evident in *Totem and Taboo* and his theory of jokes written well before *Beyond the Pleasure Principle*. Freud's "thirdness" is a slippery term defined as the "site or differential position itself...in non-linear dynamics of change at the 'tipping-point' by the addition of a term which changes the very nature of the process in which it intervenes" (68). It becomes a formal function.

The confusion between the two positions is that Žižek retains the notion of the Oedipus *complex* as a narrative when claiming the "post and beyond" status, while Flieger wants to define it as a formal structure in terms of

complexity, which is consubstantial with the Symbolic Order. In this way
historical materiality enters to the picture. Oedipus as "thirdness" becomes
a "screen" that both sustains and prohibits the console-player's desire. For
Flieger there is no need to "humanize" this screen, whereas Žižek reads the
screen of cyberspace as an all-too permissive space that requires a prohibitory
"No!" to emerge outside its influence through a flesh-and-blood representative. For Flieger this inhibitory "No!" already happens through the technological symbolic apparatus itself (like language). The bottom-line question
is whether cyberspace does indeed assert the "No!" of the Symbolic Order,
or whether it can be an indefinite play space where no prohibitions are met
or avoided? It seems that both definitions of the Oedipal need to be maintained in dialectic play with one another. Flieger does not dismiss the importance of the Oedipal complex, but wishes to avoid reducing it to the usual
misunderstanding that it is "only about sex." Flieger's Oedipal formalism
of complexity theory and Žižek's reminder of the flesh-and-blood of the
console-player, who is forever interacting with it as a "screen" presence, are
but two approaches of the same coin. They show that Oedipalization has to
be rethought as to the way screen technologies are able to restructure the
family complex that traditionally defined it by developmental ages. We need
only to think of on-line dating, brides, romances, feigning of identity, and
access to "adult" material to identify its post-Oedipal fallout.

THE ILLUSIONARY FREE CHOICE OF THE
CYBER-SUBJECT

As cyber-citizens, are we as "free" as the hype tells us? What precisely does
such "freedom" consist of? The universalization of simulacra means that the
"appearance" of authority in the big Other has been vacated. It has begun
to disintegrate (Žižek 1999a, 111). It is not a question of an "authentic
being" that must be recovered, as it is the loss of trust in a "supra-sensible"
dimension beyond phenomena, a belief that there is order, a sublime
Thing that is in place. "Appearance" is, therefore, another term for symbolic
fiction, for a belief in authority *per se* as we have discussed in our
de-Oedipalization chapters. In this view, cyberspace threatens the disappearance of a supra-sensible dimension of phenomena. Everything is reduced to
the imaginary, or illusionary level of the simulacrum—to the banality of
information. Pornography, for example, is a simulacrum for "real sex." It
does away with the "supra-sensible" dimension of love, with the Real of
seduction as Baudrillard (1990) argued; its availability strips away the magic
and mystique that surrounds it; reducing sex to a drive (*Trieb*). "Lighten up,
its only sex" is *Hustler's* motto. The invention of Viagra (Žižek 1999b, 383)
ironically desexualizes the sex act. The medically enhanced erection strips
away the fear of impotency, which actually confers the mystique of masculine
potency itself, the paradox of an erection being what a man has both control
and no control over. Late capitalist discourses have produced a narcissistic

subject who is "colonized by reflexivity" (354). Neither "nature" nor the grand narratives of tradition provide the foundational support that can be relied on. The narcissistic individual is asked to bear all the authority of the decision on his or her shoulders despite the lack of proper foundational knowledge; not knowing or being aware of what the consequences of such "free" choices are. S/he must paradoxically rely on no one but on reflexive judgment so as to decide freely and rationally, as if a person knows what s/he "really" wants. When it comes to teens, "authority" becomes even more problematic. "Whom do I believe, my parents? my peers? my teachers? What I have read on the Net?" The issue is exacerbated since transgression is part of growing-up to adulthood and taking responsibility.

Part of the nostalgia for strict rules and authority is especially evident with a Boomer generation who have teenage children, and the moral panic discussed earlier. In the Pew report on (privileged) kids on-line (Lenhart et al. 2000) parental attitudes indicate an ungrounded fear of having "strangers" approach their kids via instant messaging (IM) or e-mail, even though teens themselves were not particularly worried about this phenomenon. Over 70 percent of the boys said that this was a common occurrence, for the girls the percentage was slightly lower. This indicates that the parental perception of cyberspace is that there is no control. It is an open landscape with no boundaries. There is no Master, no authority providing the seemingly arbitrarily the ground that tells you what you want (Žižek 1997a, 153). Rather the subject today is bombarded by a consume-society where the advertising machinery attempts to provide an array of goods from which one "freely" chooses; or, appropriates the whims and wishes of target audiences and offers them back what they thought they really want. In such a consume-society, where the burden of choice is all on a teen or adult's shoulders, the big Other—the Symbolic Order—cyber-capitalism *dominates its subjects completely*. Free choice is replaced by its false semblance. Why?

No matter what choice the subject makes, the big Other will always be exempted of blame. It has been emptied of authority. No one is "forcing" *you* to buy anything. No one is "telling" *you* to become this or that. This is the liberal autonomous subject who is "free" to decide. If the choice happens to work out, the big Other takes credit by having allowed the "free choice" to take place. If the choice fails, the big Other wins again for it is *you* who have failed in making the right choice. A Master authority has been suspended. There is no one whose arbitrary gesture grounds a definitive reality. If there is no certain ground, no forced choice, then the ground disappears— as does choice itself; or choice becomes somewhat empty of force. In such a "reflective" society knowledge becomes heuristic, situational, and informational, reduced to a series of expert committees whose pronouncements are often dubious and trite. Consumers are told which foods are likely to cause cancer, and then which foods can help prevent it! Given that nobody knows for sure, we invest more and more authority in technological solutions such as medical diagnosis, genetic engineering, chemical solutions like Viagra, and mood drugs like Prozac to avoid responsibility.

Public skepticism of authority continues to grow. Democratic politiciza-
tion, which requires the decision making of active citizens, is in jeopardy.
Putman (2000) has documented how each successive generation of
Americans has been less inclined to vote than the generation that precedes it.
Young people seem to be less interested and knowledgeable in public affairs.
This trend seems to apply to Europe as well. The number of young people
voting in elections or registering for membership in political parties has also
been dropping according to a white paper sponsored by the European
Commission (Gudmundsson, 7, on-line). Not only do fewer and fewer people effectively decide a nation's course, but also their decisions do not lessen
the risks of not improving the quality of life. The antinomy of neoliberalist
capitalism is to enable the instant gratification through consumerism, and on
the other hand deprive others of the basic necessities of life—food, shelter,
and health care. In such a "risk society" the freedom of choice is so overwhelming that such contingency leads to anxiety relieved by forms of
perversion as well as psychosis.

THE PARADOXES OF INSTANT
GRATIFICATION: EVACUATION OF TIME

The term "boring" has been around in teen culture for sometime now. It
seems to be *the* thing to avoid—after all it means the phenomenological
experiencing of the slow passage of time, which is precisely what has been
evacuated by VR technology. The computer can't function fast enough
for our liking. Teen multitasking is one way to remove this "boredom."
The Pew Report on teenagers on-line (Lenhart et al. 2000, 13–14) quotes
the following as a typical teen responses. A 15-year-old girl as part of the
Greenfield Online group discussion said, "I do so many things at once. I'm
always talking to people through instant messenger and then I'll be checking email or doing homework or playing games AND talking on the phone
at the same time." Another 17-year-old girl said, "I get bored if its not all
going at once, because everything has gaps—waiting for someone to respond
to an IM, waiting for a Website to come up, commercials on TV, etc." Yet
another 17-year-old girl said, "I don't remember what I used to do when
I did not go online. Sometimes I'm just so bored I'd probably be reading or
bored out of my mind." Richard Lanham (1993) pointed out that in the
information-rich environments the limiting factor is not the speed of computers, nor is it the rates of transmission through fiber-optic cables; not even
the amount of data that can be generated and stored. "The scare commodity is human *attention*" (in Hayles 1999, 287, emphasis added). While it is
easy to float off into the abyss of "attention deficit disorder" and make claims
that VR technology is "responsible" for the symptom of hyperactivity found
in children in postmodern societies, this would be an error. What applies to
the false causal link between violence and the media, applies equally to any
sort of causality here as well. Rather, we take a different tact.

In consume-cultures of postindustrial technologically sophisticated countries around the globe, it seems that the world-wide-web of the Internet has thwarted (perverted) desire as lack. When most things seem directly available for purchase on the Internet or through telemarketing, or are instantly accessible at our fingertips and on the computer screen (films, e-books, radio, music) they appear to lose their heightened value. The object no longer retains a special place in our lives. The "lived" time with objects (and people) seems to be progressively shorter and shorter. We are more likely to discard the object (divorce the object) and purchase a newer model (usually younger) than repair it (through counseling) so that our history with it fails to develop. Our libidinal relationship to both people and things begins to suffer with ironic consequences. Like Žižek's example of Viagra, the availability of cyberporn, phone-sex, lap-dancing, topless nightclubs, escort services, red-light districts have degraded the mystique of femininity as "everything" becomes available. There is less and less need for "real sex" since we can get it on-line daily, with a fresh crop of exciting images. Add to this mix the availability of birth control and future cloning, and it seems that *sexual desire is waning despite its seeming ubiquity*. Sex has been reduced to a drive, a form of entertainment to be satisfied. The birthrate in many postindustrial countries (Germany, Japan, Italy, France, Spain, Portugal, the Netherlands, and Sweden) has been steadily decreasing while those 65 and older are living longer. In the United States the birthrate is well below replacement level. The present "baby boom echo" (Gen Y) of the late 1980s and early 1990s, as discussed in the initial chapters, is a result of large-scale immigration into America, beginning in the early 1970s. Daughters of these early immigrants started having children of their own in the late 1980s. "Their birth rates were still closer to those of their parents' country of origin than that of the United States," suggesting that their familial lifestyles were shaped by a different value structure than that of the general population (*The Economist* 2001).

And so it is with teen experience. Boredom comes with the inability to stick with the task, to develop a history with it. The evacuation of time that becomes condensed into an "instant." We see this phenomenon with personal Web home pages. The paradoxical aspect about them is that they are "automatically published." While this is touted as a positive feature because it enables the teen to change it at his/her will (Chandler 1999), without going through a long approval to be published, the very impermanence of the document also cheapens it. The odd feature of its very availability, to be stored on a Web server and changed at will, can make it "boring" after the initial thrill of having it posted wears off. For desire to sustain itself, a prohibition has to be in place. Some "Thing" must prove unattainable, which puts an end to an unbearable anxiety of undecidablity—the addiction of never having enough, of wanting it ALL—for it enables an individual to live with his or her lack, with impossibility, rather than being instantly gratified. It is the ability to remain content while living with our limitations. Consumer products that are "impossibly" priced—mansions, Ferraris, *haute couture*, jewelry, fine furniture for the adult market, and computer games, MP3, CDs, cell phones, fashion for the teen market—are *not* what is prohibited. On the contrary, it is precisely the high cost of such objects that late capitalism identifies as being possessed by those who *do not lack*; whose every desire has magically been satisfied—perverted. The superego of neoliberalist capitalism promotes just such an aggressive anxiety of failed satisfaction. The psychic structure is that of phallic mastery: narcissistic fantasies of unlimited power and authority, oneness, self-control over desire, and reason over emotion. Desire is evacuated, while drive and the *jouissance* that comes with it becomes forwarded.

The instant gratification of VR signals an erosion of "transitional space" (Winnicott), a space where the object can be held so that a history can be established with it (Žižek 1996a, 190). There is an evacuation of the very "substance" that makes it "real"; that "substance" is the object's fantasma, its *objet a*, that which establishes its subjectivated meaning, what gives it worth. Objects are hyped up and then drained of their desirability to make room for the next updated generation. Cyberspace, as Virilio maintains, eliminates mechanical time and collapses space. In a wireless world messages and images are brought to us instantly from a distance—the very meaning of telematic. Transitional space requires a "holding," a time dimension that has become progressively eroded. That is the danger here. So as not to be misunderstood, this erosion of transitional space is not taking place because of "violent" video games. It is rather the delaying or "holding" of the subject that is being lost. A "glance aesthetic" replaces the aesthetics of dwelling within and with the object. We see this already with the way teens use IM (Instant Message) technology. In Pew report (Lenhart et al., 2000) the majority of the teens reported that IM, e-mail, and chat rooms increased the number of contacts they made, but they almost all agreed that making friends was not achieved through this form of communication. As one 17-year-old wrote, "The Internet has helped me socialize with more people, but at a very impersonal level." The distancing effect of IM made it possible both to risk asking someone for a date (more so for boys than girls), but it also was most often used to cut off or end relationships, to tell someone that the relationship was over, or to block communication from someone the teen was mad at. Rather than facing up to the friend, IM enables unpleasant messages to be sent, yet another form of interpassivity: the IM machine "enjoys" delivering the castrating effects. IM becomes both a controlling device as well as a way to stay in touch. But it has little value as a form of communication that sustains a deep friendship. True, teens have buddy lists, an IM address book that is collected by the user. When one logs on, the user can find out how many buddies are on-line at the same time s/he is. The buddy list can include friends from school, teachers, family members, past friends, kids from other schools, and friends met during summer camps. However, such a buddy list is easily changed, and many on the list easy forgotten or erased. The bottom line is that IM devices are most often used to consult and make plans with friends (more than 80 percent said so in the Pew Internet Report). Because of teens busy schedules, the IM-ing back and forth enables a group to agree on a meeting time, arrange an activity together, ask each other if they are "free," and so on. Such technology has made all of us walking cyborgs. So where is the "No!" to be found?

11

FANTASY STRUCTURES IN VIRTUAL COMMUNITIES: THE PERVERTED GAZE

Some psychoanalytic theorists of culture, notably Elliott (2000, 137–139) cautiously celebrate the imaginative fluidity of postmodernism as being a time of extraordinary creativity where everything is possible because of the seeming constructivist nature of the world. It seems as if reality can be reduced to information, a mathematical combination of −'s and +'s or 0's and 1's, which are digitally recombined to produce startling special effects, as if from these invisible codes a virtual world magically appears. The possibilities seem endless. Sherry Turkle (1995) and Allucquère (Sandy) Stone (1996) were both cautiously enthusiastic and optimistic that VR could provide alternative visions to the Symbolic Order that was in place. The ability of the console-player to take on various forms of identity in virtual communities in the various on-line chat rooms—MUDs (Muti-User Dimension, or Multi-User Dungeons), MOOs (MUD-Object-Oriented), and GMUKS (Graphical Multi-user Konversation)—released the subject from being limited by the symbolic encrusted forms of identity in RL. One could change sex/genders and personalities at will. Such bisexuality permits heterosexual men to explore their "feminine" side and women their "masculine" ones. Gays could pretend to be heterosexual women, lesbians could take the persona of heterosexual males. One can have as many avatars in as many chat rooms representing as many different sides as one pleases. "Tough" female characters in VR would be beneficial, as Inness (1999) would confer.

More than half the teens on-line have more than one e-mail address or screen name. Most use different screen names or e-mail addresses to compartmentalize different parts of their on-line lives so that they can experiment with different persona. In the Pew report on teen's on-line (Lenhart et al. 2001) one quarter of the boys had at least four or more screen names, while about a fifth of the girls had equally as many. Both had at least one secret address that they used when they wanted to be alone or on-line. Elisheva Gross (Lenhart et al. Pew Report, 17) maintains that teens who have strong social connections tend to use IM and e-mail as a way to simply reinforce the preexisting bonds that they already have. It is teens with smaller or less well-developed social networks, those who are shy or have been home-schooled, are more prone to use the Internet to fill the lack on-line that they lack off-line.

As opposed to Flieger's (1997b) hypothesis, the Oedipal structure of paternal symbolic authority that holds the modernist subject is said to be weakened and decentered through participation in on-line chat communities. A post-Oedipal world opens up as famously iterated by Haraway (1991, 181) at the very end her influential "cyborgian manifesto:" "I would rather be a cyborg than a Goddess." The Cartesian cogito is free to manipulate itself freely and aesthetically, in the footsteps of Foucault's thesis of a "technology of the self." The big Other no longer has its patriarchal grip so that a multiplicity of shifting identities now has become available for experimentation. A similar argument is maintained for the development of open-ended exploratory hypertext narratives and puzzle video games. The console-explorer is free to interact as s/he pleases with the text. Each engagement with hypertext can potentially produce a different scenario, unique to the individual. We have free reign as a conscious subject within the established fantasy of the cybernarrative.

The dangers of such a "screen life" have been identified by Sherry Turkle in her groundbreaking book, *Life on the Screen* (1995). She writes somewhat somberly (1996) how young people (Josh 23, Thomas 24, and Tanya 24) use the MUD communities to essentially escape into a VR world so they need not have to deal with their "real" (RL) lives, which were in a state of ruins. Josh was an Internet Hobo, soliciting time on computer accounts like a beggar looking for spare change. Thomas, a bellhop in a hotel, despite his college degree spent six hours a day in the MUD constructing virtual rooms and involved in VR community politics. He had no use for "real" politics. Tanya, also a college graduate, felt more safe and alive in the MUD than in RL as well. All three exhibit typical obsessive behavior avoiding to confront the desire of the Other (Symbolic Order). These three young adults illustrate the postadolescent difficulty of assuming "adult" responsibility. Rather, their obsessive escapes into VR avoid it. Despite this, Turkle ends on an optimistic note. Life on the screen need not be rejected, nor need we treat it as an alternative life either. Psychoanalytically informed, she continues to believe that virtual personae can be a resource for self-reflection and self-transformation.

LIVING ENDLESSLY: IMMORAL LIFE

We are more skeptical of Turkle's optimism given the depoliticization of the economy. A great deal has changed since her groundbreaking study. In light of our post-Oedipalization stance: to what extent has the work-a-day reality of advanced capitalism "driven" young people "underground" to live simulacra lives in cyberspace as the only site/sight/cite left for a perverse experience of jouissance? We have in mind the new virtual game cities that have emerged on-line, which far exceed the interactions with text that defined MUDs. GMUKS (Graphical Multi-user Konversation) have emerged as "multimedia chats" where players (rather their avatars or "props") roam around from one graphic room to the next in Palace sites like Main Mansion, futuristic Cybertown, a haunted house, Japan, and Star Trek. You can now roam these virtual cities just like "first-person" shooter games. Rules are made explicit and "deadly" to prop up the missing Law. Neocron[1] is a 3-D intergenerational game city that provides the fantasy scene for precisely such an escape from RL of late capitalist society. It is set in the dystopia of a postapocalyptic world of the twenty-eighth century, complete with a historical narrative, which uncomfortably provides the present fruits of global capitalism as a projected possible future. The prolog to the game tells the potential player that "global pollution, excessive wars and a perforated atmosphere have turned the planet into an almost lifeless sphere of toxic mud." With radiation everywhere, most animals have either become extinct or mutated into monstrous and bizarre creatures. What's left of humankind seeks protection inside the protective walls of three giant cities: Neocron, Tokyo 2, and Dome of York.

What is most disturbing is that cyberlife in Neocron is the very inverse of Fritz Lang's *Metropolis* (1927) fantasy that took place in 2026. Rather than the working class living in the Underground City, where they plot their rebellion in the catacombs led by the virginal Maria (iconic for Liberty leading the *sans-culotte* at the barricades during the French Revolution) to defeat John Fredersen, the Master dictator/Father of Metropolis and his "evil" cloning technology (the science of Rotwang's robotic Maria), the new working "service" class has escaped into a cyberspace city that is hauntingly a ghostly parallel of where they *already live*. There is no escape, and no rebellion. Here the *cyberscape of the working service classes is into the self-same society of late capitalism*, dangerously littered with neo-fascist elements as we try to explain.

Neocron is a "living-dead" city populated by paying citizen-players that roam its "districts," each inhabited by a certain class of people. The districts range from the upper-class Via Rosso (populated by the rich and beautiful, home of the Stock X market and the NCPD headquarters) to the forgotten and decayed Outzone (an old industrial area, which has been shut down after the spacecraft industry died). In between these extremes there are other districts like the Plaza distinct, the "Heart" of Neocron, the home of the city's Administration, and Pepper Park filled with clubs, bars, strip clubs like Pussy and Veronique Clubs. The city is patrolled by Copbots; it has both a nightlife and "daylife." Beyond, the Outzone is the Wastelands, the biggest and most dangerous area in the world of Neocron where mutants and banned citizens live. Here corporations run secret labs, factories, and communication outposts.

The fascistic tendencies of the game emerge when you learn how to "survive" in such a city. In effect, it teaches you to be a "survivor" in a rather rough and mean world, much like the *Survivor* series on reality television. When a player first signs on after paying the appropriate costs, s/he is assigned a "free" apartment—thanks only to the wise and generous ruler, Lioon Reza. The idea is to get your career in Neocron started, which means you must undertake "missions" that are offered to you by Companies and Organizations. But, first it's best to get some "starter cash" to move around using the Gene Replicators. To do this, it is recommended that you team up with others so that you can co-hunt mutants and vermin in the sewers that exist under the districts, basically to learn the weaponry that is available to you. If you stay loyal to the company that you accomplish the missions for, it will pay off in the future. It seems that certain factions are against one another. To get more complex missions and possibly to form a faction clan of your own, you need to have a team. If you are successful in founding a clan, the next step is heading for the Wastelands where high rewards are available for capturing outposts such as factories, laboratories, mines, forts, and communication facilities. It should be clear by this brief description that there is a distinct hierarchy at work here. Despite the group pressure not to fight alone, no one is to be trusted and everyone is under suspicion since one is never sure if the clan (faction) will hold together—a paranoiac climate of deceit and cunning. It is the world of Tony Soprano all over again.

On-line games like Neocron offer what we call an "endless cyber-life," living in the pure Imaginary where death has been eliminated. *Zoë* and *Bios* continually collapse into one another in a closed circuit of sustained pleasure. That means the potential life-transforming effects of the Real have been suppressed. We shall shortly explain why. Lacan's notion of a psychic Imaginary has been reduced to the *imagination* only. The Ego-player, or his/her avatar, can wander around endlessly and forever in the cyber environment, "lost in a hall of mirrors." It appears and feels like the console-player is in control. But, of course, this is not just aimless wandering around. The player must follow the "soft" wired hypertext of the game's environment, in a fantasy structure where just about anything can happen. That's what makes such video games so interesting and exciting. There is the promise of "immortality." No matter what happens, you know that it will be possible to restart and replay a segment of the game.

In *Ultima On-Line* there are multiple players, and so you can make up your own characters. They can be good or bad. You are your own author and hero as in *Final Fantasy*. In the first-person protagonist game, a physiological thriller called *Silent Hill 2* from Konami Corporation you *are* James Sunderland. You are drawn into the narrative's nightmare when you receive a letter from your wife asking you to come to Silent Town...but she has been dead for three years. What could all this mean? (Answer: not much but a hell of a lot of fun!). So you take a chance and enter the town, but it is silent and empty. There is only Mary who looks like your former late wife—who bloody well insists in coming along; and Laura, a mysterious girl. But watch out for her tricks! And so the adventure begins on your PlayStation 2. *Silent Hill 2* has no definitive end. It projects you into an endless nightmare—there is no goal, only the aim of the drive mechanism manifested in the excitement of the play. In our view, it is a take-off on Alex Proyas' sci-fi film, *Dark City* (1998), which offers a similar, perplexing nightmare. *Silent Hill's* James Sunderland is a homology formed between Kiefer Sutherland who plays Dr. Daniel Schreber, and John Murdoch, the protagonist. Like the movie and *Silent Hill's* game narrative, there is no search for a final goal; it is *not* a question of desire but of a visceral kick. *Dark City* floats by itself in the universe, sustained by John Murdoch's imagination. It could just be a "figment" of his imagination. *Silent Hill 2*, is exactly alike. It floats in on-line cyberspace. What sustains the Ego-player/viewer (like John Murdoch and James Sunderland) is the rapid and confirmatory appearances of the self in the mirror, like Freud's grandson Ernst ducking under the mirror, seeing himself in delight, and then ducking down again, only to come up . . . again and again. These are the same sort of emotional shocks that are happening in these Ego-game environments. The slight twist to Ernst's game is that each time the players comes up there is something exciting going on in the mirror; each glance in the mirror presents a new scene to *GlanZ* at. Ernst's "ducks" are like hesitations in the game before the next action happens—the next surprise, the next door to open . . . .

THE GLANZ AESTHETIC: THE INVERTED GAZE[2]

One narrative in *Silent Hill 2* can take up to six hours to play before a player is "terminated." As Jonathan, a player can choose another scenario, yet another narrative to play that has a different conclusion, with different set of players. There are about one hundred hours worth of *actual* playing time in the game. Theoretically, you may never want to leave *Silent Hill*, just stay floating in cyberspace of the *Dark City*. It takes many hours to become experienced with it, as its "interpassivity" takes over and gaZes at you! In the video game environment we are totally caught by the game *despite being active*. "Being directly transfixed by the object, passively submitting to its power of fascination, is something ultimately unbearable: the open display of the passive attitude of 'enjoying it,' somehow deprives the subject of his (*sic*) dignity. Interpassivity is therefore to be conceived as the primordial form of the subject's *defense* against *jouissance*: I defer *jouissance* to the Other who passively endures it (laughs, suffers, enjoys . . .) on my behalf" (Žižek 2002a, 8 original emphasis). It is James Sunderland, as your alter ego, who is doing it all for you.

It is this gaZe that we want to develop to show why the *object a*/Real has been eliminated in the game environment; all we are dealing with is surface effects and aestheticization. To do this we need to modify and update Lacan's gaze theory as he developed it in S XI, *Four Fundamentals* to have a better understanding as to why the obsession with video games maintains itself. Ultimately, we argue that the console-player is caught between a two-mirrored space/time environment—an endless corridor where s/he constantly glanZes at objects that look back. The only escape is to end the game when a rude encroachment from the outside world (RL) occurs—in most cases this is bothersome and annoying. LAN parties (Local Area Network) where multiple game players get together, for instance, draw curtains when they stage all day and all night game playing in homes. In larger venues (up to 3,000 for the QuakeCon convention in Mesquite, Texas home of id Software) empty warehouses serve the purpose. A power or technological breakdown, cyber-death, and mundane biological needs of the body (hunger, waste management) are other disturbances like angry parents asking that their kids go to sleep. Otherwise the immersion is complete.

Let us briefly review Lacan's gaze theory, which deconstructs normative spatial perception. This can best be done by going over the three figures he uses on page 91 and 106 in S XI, *Four Fundamentals* (reproduced below as figures 11.1–11.3, The Deconstruction of Perspectival Space).

Given that gaze theory is a well-known concept amongst Lacanians and has been theorized in a number of controversial ways (see Brennan and Jay 1996; Silverman 1996), we wish here to give only a brief account so as to make our own innovation. Figure 11.1 presents us with the normative "look" of things. The image in this figure is claimed to be an exact reproduction of the object. This image may be a film sequence, a photograph, a music video, and so on. For our purposes we shall call this image simply an image-*frame*. This image-frame simply means that we put a frame around an object or part of the world to identify our perception of it. Such an image-frame is normative and causes us no anxiety. We perceive it to be a "realistic" representation of RL. In this sense it works on a correspondence theory. In the bustle of everyday life we assume this normative perception of image-framing, otherwise we would distrust our symbolic place in the world and feel unsure of our reality, perhaps be paranoid that we are being stared at. Such an image-frame is a *necessary* gestalt for it is impossible for us to see all the particulars. Each time we reframe we produce another gestalt. All of us must to some degree form an ideal generalization or disposition to the world around us. Framing something means that a foreground/background

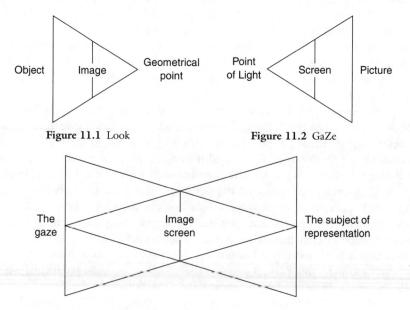

Figure 11.1 Look   **Figure 11.2** GaZe

Figure 11.3 The Deconstruction of Perspectival Space

is created with a middle ground mediating the two. In figure 11.1, Lacan identifies the "geometrical point" as the impossible place from which we form this gestalt of the image-frame. This point is rather important, to make a pun. *No one can occupy the geometrical point.* It is theoretically uninhabitable since it is a topological space and time remain outside the image-frame making system. It is a non-sense realm, which would properly be called the Real. We can imagine this point as existing somewhere *behind* our heads.

Picking up figure 11.2, Lacan wants to deconstruct this "normative" framing of perception, of believing what we see. Lacan's figure 11.2 is the precise *inverse* of figure 11.1. Exactly where the object is located in figure 11.1, Lacan locates a similar radically de-anthropomorphic point of light. From this "impossible" point the object "looks at us," it stares at us. How? In what way can an object "stare" at us? Throughout this book we have been constantly recalling the GlanZ of objects, their *Schein*, their magic (*agalma*), their fascination that they hold over us. That is the way they "look" at us as we desire them. When they do, we "fade" as subjects, caught by their splendor or terror. Holbein's picture of the *Ambassadors*, which Lacan utilizes in S XI to develop the notion of anamorphism (jagodzinski 1996) is a perfect example of how every object has been carefully rendered so that the richness of its surface catches us, looks at us. The extraordinary capability of computer graphics can do exactly the same—bathe every object with such GlanZ light. In figure 11.2 Lacan locates a screen that is in the very same place as the image in figure 11.1. We are told that this screen is opaque, while the image-frame in figure 11.1 is like a clear window (a *lucinda* or *vitrine*) because perception in the first figure is like looking through the frame of a window—a pane of glass at "natural" reality. With the screen in place, a mirror is formed. How? The screen acts like the tain of a mirror, that silvery substance that is put over glass to cause a reflection to happen. Such a reflection "frames" us, puts us in the picture of the Symbolic Order (as it appears in figure 11.2). It frames who we symbolically represent. How we are perceived by others (by the big Other) is shaped by the way we are gaZed at by what surrounds us, by our environment that includes the world we inhabit. Although we can never possibly grasp how we are being perceived by this amorphous environment outside that includes other people, objects, and the discourses that write our bodies, we can catch glimpses when this mirror "cracks," so to speak. When the Real breaks through and our normal perception is disturbed by an object that has come too close to our liking, or has been elevated to such a point that we are unable to face it. It is too great for us. Such moments of anxiety and sublimity offer us a way to come to a better understanding of ourselves, a "working through." What has to be understood is that such paranoid moments are informed by the death drive. We do not know what lies beyond the mirror, beyond the screen. For Lacan the object lies in the Real; that place which is beyond the Imaginary and Symbolic psychic orders.

Let us quickly move on to the last figure 11.3, which is the full deconstruction of perspectival space, of the normativity of perception. On the left-hand side of the image-screen-frame we have the Real. The gaze occupies the position of the object of figure 11.1. On the right-hand side of the image-screen-frame is the Symbolic Order, how we fit in it. The subjectivity of the ego (called the subject of representation) is placed at the geometrical point of figure 11.1. Imago, the term Freud used, is therefore very appropriate for the ego-subject. It is an Ego Ideal, an idealized gestalt. A subject's Ego Ideal is placed in the background or tableau of the social Ideal Ego. This is how you are "put in the picture" by the outside Order. Are you a good student, for example? Does your Ego Ideal of being a good student match the expectation of the particular culture or society's Ideal Ego of being a good student? The answers lead to conflict as well as accommodation (hate/love).

In the middle of figure 11.3 is the Imaginary psychic order formed by the screen-image. For Lacan, this screen-image acts as a veil, a lure that covers over the *objet a* as the gaZe from the Real. It is the Imaginary register. This frame of perception, of fantasy space, can always be disturbed by a confrontation, an encounter with the Real as in a *Nachträglichkeit* experience. What has changed in cyberspace game culture is the elimination of an encounter with the Real, to live, as it were, within a veiled universe of objects that glanZ but never disturb the Ego, other than offering it more glanZ effects. "Life" on the screen becomes interpassive while we interact feverishly with it. We have the emergence of a hyper-look, or hyped-up look, and here we agree with Baudrillard's hypothesis of a hyperaesthetic when it is applied to video game culture *only*. When we write this book, we are also feverishly interacting with the computer screen as the book's "world" emerges, its frame created; the difference is that such interactivity sublimates—it helps us grasp the landscape of the media. We are playing Ernst's first game with the mirror, caught by the fantasy that it might be possible to actually capture such an understanding. In video games the very reverse happens. We are into Ernst's second game because the computer program is enjoying the fantasy for us as our alter egos, as if a word processing program could just as easily lead us into writing a book of *its* creation, not our own. Yet, we believe *that we are writing* this book because we are so actively engaged following the instructions, simulations, and situations the writing program is creating for us. Although we have illustrated this interpassivity by writing in the third-person plural, which might appear rather odd when dealing with Ego games, but such games can have any number of players, all believing that they are uniquely interacting with the video game's narrative.

Video Ego-games are able to *invert* the gaZe in *two* ways that speak directly to the obsessional's existential question "To be or not to Be," that is: "Am I alive or am I dead?" The first way—Am I alive?—the "look" (of figure 11.1) attempts to covet the gaZe (of figure 11.2). Another way of putting this is that figure 11.2 is *doubled*, through the inversion of figure 11.1 (figure 11.4).

In figure 11.4 we can see that on the left-hand side the Object and the Picture come together—in Lacanian terms, there is a collapse of the Real

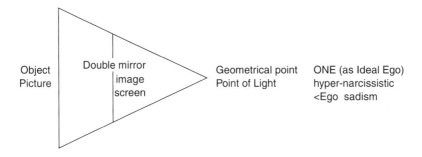

Figure 11.4 Am I Alive? The Look captures the GaZe (figure 11.1 superimposes itself on figure 11.2).

into the Symbolic Order—all is discourse as poststructuralist designer capital maintains, as if the person can be reduced to the digitalized 0 1 binary. The object is put into the picture as a tableau by the Ego. The fantasy mirror (screen-image) is intensified—it is hyper-aestheticized in its doubling. On the right-hand side of our diagram we see that the point of light and the geometrical point come together. Here the collapse of the "point of light" implodes into the "geometrical point" produces a hyper-narcissistic Ego that actually occupies this impossible point, hence the hyper-narcissistic Ego is filled with light, which we have already identified as *zoë* (and not bio). This Ego we shall now designate as the ONE, and it now lies *within* the system or environment, not outside of it. It represents the aggrandizement of the star: star band, star diva, star actor, star . . . This is a perverted subject since it can act as a god—a demigod. Lacan's matheme of desire ($\$\Diamond a$) has been perverted into a$\Diamond\$$. The *objet a* (point of light) is occupied by the Ego.

There are many so-called god games where the console-player is in complete control. We see this as a general trend of designer capitalism. This is a "redeemer complex" that has now emerged in film (*The Matrix, The Truman Show, Vision Quest . . .*). The new book exploring the philosophy of the *Matrix* (Irwin 2002) makes that rather apparent. Sony's inventive EyeToy enhances these possibilities. It sets up a USB camera with a tracking system. This allows the console-player to instantly become the main character in his or her own game. We present such an Ego aggrandizement as "<Ego" in figure 11.4, to suggest that < designates an increase in the Ego. This development answers the first part of an obessional's existential question: "to be (or not to be.)" At the same time the ego can be diminished into being simply a "bit" player, as in the game environment of Neocron. This is the second way the gaZe is inverted as we develop it later in figure 11.5. Here the ego can be designated as "ego>" to show its diminishment.

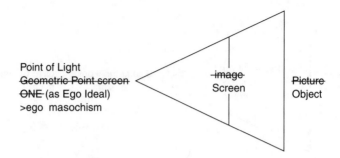

Figure 11.5 Am I Dead? The GaZe captures the Look (figure 11.2 superimposes itself on figure 11.1).

This development answers the second part of an obsessional's question: "Am I dead?" Given that these video on-line games are obessional, structured by the two existential questions of aggrandizement and diminishment of the Ego: "to be or not to be" or "am I dead or alive," they have a close affinity, as both Freud and Lacan, claimed, to religion. Such games, in many respects, are the fantasies of the emerging New Religions with New Age thinking embedded in them.

Figure 11.4 presents the doubling of the screen-image. What we are hypothesizing here is that the fantasy space has become a double mirror reflecting back and forth forming endless corridors in all directions. The screen holds a continuous fascination interrupted only by moments of nanosecond hesitations, or rude interruptions by RL. This abyss of the endless mirrors presents precisely the labyrithian space/time of on-line computer games that we have been discussing. The console-player can go from one environment to another . . . endlessly as in the labyrinth of the mind captured by the Deleuzean rhizomatic mapping of space/time. In the future this ONE ego will become more and more powerful omnipotent position. The console-player will become more and more powerful because *the collapsed geometrical point and point of light are placed inside an environment itself. The vanishing point becomes internalized as the console player's every retinal movement is relayed to a super-computer.* This possibility can result in the utopian effect of Star Trek's "holodeck" (Holographic Environment Stimulator), or its nightmarish sadistic dystopian side as presented by Brett Leonard's *The Lawnmower Man* (1992). There are already CAVE environments that do precisely this (we discuss this development in chapter 12). The dream is that total knowledge (like the Human Genome Project) will be possible. Ego games will increase the bodily involvement to the point that the skin-ego will be hooked up to computer feedback instantaneously. But, now we are on the verge of science fiction, which we also discuss in later chapters.

The second inversion of the gaZe answers the second part of the obsessional's query— "am I dead?" In this case the gaZe of the Real captures the

Look of the Symbolic while the imaginary Ego Ideal undergoes a subjective destitution on the image-screen, which now turns decisively dark. Figure 11.5 shows this possibility with strikeouts through the relevant concepts that are overshadowed. It is the inversion of figure 11.2 over figure 11.1.

Here, of course, is the notion of paranoia (am I dead?) and psychoses (I am dead) fully emerge as the Real engulfs the ego, diminishing it. We can designate this as ">ego." We have already discussed earlier the more dramatic paranoiac moments with our examples of Orson Welles' *War of the Worlds* and *Ghostwatch*, but there are many less dramatic everyday experiences. For some *Blair Witch* produced a psychotic moment. The total engulfment by the Real over the Look (Symbolic) brings us to a psychosis where authority disappears. There is no Name-of-the-Father and hence an imaginary substitute must be found. This is the "impossible" equivalent to the god-like position of the ONE as Ideal Ego when the Look overpowers the Real; the difference being that this ONE is projected *externally* as an Ego Ideal. Its superegoic transcendence is the controlling agent, like Aliens or the figure of Christof in the *Truman Show*. They represent an "answer" from the Real. We have here on-line games that are apocalyptic in nature; games where one is considered a "bit" player who must self-aggrandize to survive. It is the masochistic half to the sadistic possibility that opens up by playing god. The ego is caught by both possibilities: "<ego>" in a perverted sado-masochistic pact with the game's rules. The New Age apocalyptic dystopic games characterize this dilemma quite nicely. There is only "anarchy" and the only way to survive is to join clans and gangs as in virtual games of Neocron and American Anarchy.

What we have outlined here, we believe, is the ambiguous apocalyptic promise of designer capitalism and its political ideology neoliberalism as either a nightmare or utopia. The *Dark City* is here already; or, as Derrida tells us concerning apocalyptic speculation: we are on the verge of a long awaited future—the New (Brave) World Order of Technology, nomadism, bio-computerization, and so on. We, however, remain doubtful if not skeptical...but the future is always open. Žižek (1999b) ends his essay on cyberspace with the optimism of the possibility of traversing the fantasy in cyberspace, as well as with a reminder. "How cyberspace will affect us is not directly inscribed into its technological properties, it hinges on the network of socio-symbolic relations (of power and domination, etc.) which always-already overdetermine the way cyberspace affects us" (123).

MUDING AROUND: VIRTUAL ESCAPE ATTEMPTS

A subject's playfulness in MUDS or with open-ended hypertext games and explorations can be usefully theorized from this renewed gaZe perspective in the way that the subject's Ideal Ego becomes impacted. When secrets and intimate features become contingent playthings, the console-player can begin to jettison his or her coordinates in the "virtual" symbolic world (RL). The gaZe can be perverted again. Who one believes one is; the way one is confirmed by the Other, as the Other's gaZe in RL can be "overridden." The console-user simply remains locked in the fantasy space of the MUD chat room or computer game for hours, even days at a time. The console-player can become "lost" in a virtual imaginary fantasy space, either trying to figure out its rules and environments, the artificial worlds of video games, or splitting him-or-herself up into a number of avatars who frequent a several MUDs at the console-player's whim. A pathology can result when the console-player loses his or her identity in the Symbolic Order (the "real" virtual world) and overidentifies with an avatar in the VR to the extent that RL begins to be just another VR. Such behavior would eventually lead to a psychotic breakdown where the ground of the belief in the Symbolic Order completely begins to give way. Instances and traces of this occur during days of video game playing amongst groups of boys in a designated home or arcade. All day and all night affairs are common stock as the fascination with the game, like *Counter-Strike*, swallows up the hours. Video arcades are open 24 hours in most major cities to cater to this obsessive passion.

In this view, the VR of the Symbolic Order—the transcendental taken-for-granted realm of the gaze that confers a discursive identity on a subject; for instance, the RL of being a high school girl, Catholic, who is rather shy, living in the city of Klagenfurt, has a dog, and so on—begins to compete with the VR of projected fantasy in the MUD. She plays a hot grown-up tart from New York who likes to tease and have cyber-sex to the point where she is more on-line than off. So long as a clear distinction can be maintained between virtual fantasies on-line so they do not infiltrate (or take over) symbolic identification in RL, the potential addictive pathologies are stayed. It is precisely when the fantasies that sustain RL come up against the fantasies that sustain VR on-line or in a video game, or *vice versa* since the exchange is fluid, that various psychic shocks and pathologies occur. Sanford Lewin (see Stone 1996, 65–81) who pretended to be a female psychiatrist, is perhaps the most infamous on-line case. Lewin, acting as Julie Graham, said that "she" was a New York neuropsychologist who had been badly disfigured by a car accident, was mute and paraplegic and confined to a wheelchair. Such a virtual persona enabled him to start a women's discussion group on CompuServe and give advice to similarly crippled women to lift their depression and stave off suicide. Julie almost took over Lewin's life, as if a schizophrenic split had occurred. He began to invent an entire fictitious life for her to keep the pretense up. Soon she was flirting and having cyber-sex with her on-line friends, eventually she staged an imaginary marriage to John who was rich and supportive. She was now lecturing at conferences. John and Julie were traveling to exotic places like Greece from which Lewin sent postcards to his on-line friends. When pangs of guilt swept over him, he attempted to stage a screen death (terminal illness) for her, but could not go through with it once all the well wishes came pouring in. Nor was he able to manage to successfully wean his "clients" over to a new screen persona—Stanford Lewin—whom he created. Eventually he was found out, which caused bitterness, a feeling of betrayal, as well as genuine mourning for the "virtual death" of Julie Graham.

Youth, especially boyz, who misrepresent themselves as females in cyber-environments do so as pranks, to "get off" by thinking they are fooling their virtual interlocutors as they gender switch. It becomes a game of deception and feigning as discussed earlier. The tendency for men to gender switch identities as females is far more prevalent than the other way around. It seems that more attention and more titillating sex can be had this way. Gurlz, on the other hand, have a tendency to take on male roles as a way to accrue power and leadership positions. In some cases, young women who were quiet adolescents and felt dominated by stronger-willed boyfriends, allowed themselves the "freedom" to be more aggressive and self-confident in chat rooms. These are some of the general findings of John Suler's (1996) comprehensive and ongoing on-line longitudinal study of cyberspace identification in the Palace site of the Main Mansion community where gender deception in such a "habitat" is *expected*. Jim Bumgardner, its creator and Master Wizard, wanted to build "mischief" into the party atmosphere of the Palace, and succeeded. Playing jokes on players is acceptable behavior, but what is a prank and what is abuse always remains unpredictable, judged on the particular interactions between avatars. In Main Mansion the challenge is for players to create opposite sex "avatars" or "props" to visually represent their "new" selves. Particularly interesting is Suler's discussion of "deviant enclaves" of adolescence that form for a period of time within specific locations of the larger community. One particular group, which formed in one of the rooms of the Members Palace, defined themselves as "weird" through the use of off-color language and avatars that looked menacing, bizarre, or antisocial in theme. The off-putting quality of their scenario defined the identity of the group making it uncomfortable for outsides to join in. Wizards (cyberpatrol authority) generally left them alone if the larger community was not being disturbed.

Chat rooms are all-day "parties" where cyber-communities produce a range of "acting out." Suler comprehensively discusses and provides interventionist ethics for troublemaking avs (avatars), exhibitionist avs (the flashers and prop-dropping avatars), the hate and violence avs, blocking or poking at avs, eavesdropper avs, foul talkers and bad mouthing avs, and so on. The entire range of possible human behavior is on full display. Stalkers, verbal exhibitionists, pedophiles, and "breather" avs emerge, the lewd talker who continually propositions female users, usually by whispering to them. Bumgardner divides these up as "horny breathers" and "psychotic breathers" who are aggressive and obscene in intent, expressing a desire to kill. Sex in all its manifestations is what makes the cyber-community "spin," so to speak.

CYBER-LOVE

Perhaps the most frequent collapse of VR and RL is the love affair that develops on-line when two imaginary fantasized characters "flirt" with one another (e.g., Ullman 1998, 38–43; Cooper and Sportolari 1997). Such love affairs are sometimes consummated in RL resulting, more often than not, in disastrous life-turning events as the Symbolic Order collapses on both sides. (Every prostitute and strip dancer knows better than to meet her johns outside the context of the fantasy where she is his object. Cyber-sex spells a similar disaster.) There are instances where the male, significantly older than he has pretended to be in the chat room, ends up meeting a teenage girl who has also pretended to be the woman she only fantasized to be so as to give him a "come on." Then there is the child pornographer and pedophile always looking for potential on-line victims. John Suler's description of cyber-life in Main Mansion of the Palace offers many vivid descriptions of sexual incidents that are not easily solved unless a Wizard steps in to control things. "Computer (or cyberspace)-mediated relationships" (CMR) produce an entire range of transference and counter-transferences that occur between players. Such incidents make explicit the imaginary fantasy level of all these interactions, *in the virtuality of the Symbolic Order as well as on-line VR*. When it comes to cyber-love, what is most shocking in these incidents is the realization that it was *only* a fantasy—which has now been ruined. Meeting in RL, the man is ugly, bald, and fat; the girl is not a woman—but an immature girl who speaks about silly things and has an underdeveloped adolescent body. The screen love affair with her was *more intense* than the RL meeting. Milder shocks come when a female avatar finally admits that she is "really" a heterosexual man and is unable to meet her male suitor in RL.

Adults are not the only ones who have cyber-love affairs; teens do so as well. The Pew Report on teens on-line (Lenhart et al. 2000) quotes teens who feel quite OK with the anonymity that becomes established in e-mail or IM contacts because the focus can remain on personality and the intellect, rather than on attractiveness and "style." Yet, as one 15-year-old boy from the Greenfield Online Group said "I continued to chat with 2 girls. Then when I met them . . . they did not look like what I had expected. I thought they would be cute, but they weren't. After meeting online our offline friendships died off" (17). Although one would think that the lesson has now been learnt, the dissolution of the fantasy often leads to a new on-screen search. The thrill of the sexual rendezvous on screen and off is where the *jouissance* lies, not necessarily in establishing a permanent relationship, perhaps only in one-night stands.

The success of Internet dating, television blind-date programs, and reality television shows such as *Temptation Island* seem to confirm the *jouissance* for "junk sex." Teen websites are also available for developing romantic relationships. Headbone.com offers three possibilities of playing the match-up game. *PenPals* lets you "Tell the world who you are and what kind of person you're looking for." *Profiles* lets you "Make your page. Make your mark. Stand out." While *AutoMatch* is where "Our very smart computer finds you someone you're sure to get along with." For teens who want to include an "authentic" digitalized photo of themselves, ratingspot.com provides a listing of sites where you can be rated to check and see how "hot" you are, how you look in a swim suit, to be a model, and so on. The narcissism and vanity of such "independent" rating should be clear. There is now a reality television show called "Are you Hot? The Search for America's Sexiest People." For Žižek (1996a, 198), such sexual encounters in virtual communities are an escape from the superego command in modern marriages to love your spouse. Judging from the proliferation of virtual sex-communities, swinger-clubs, and divorce rates in postindustrial societies, such a command is waning, being replaced by the superego demand to "enjoy" your illicit love affair, it's much more exciting, dangerous, prohibitive, and wild.

Cyber-sex love affairs become particularly problematic when a teenage girl (usually 13-years-old and up) "runs away" from home with an older man (usually 20 years and older) that she has met on-line. Such incidents become spectacularized through the media, inflaming once more the "sex predator" myth staking youth on-line for an easy score. The earlier maturing of girls due to diet and lifestyle (in Europe and United States the statistical average for menarche is 12.5–13.5-years-old), and the pressures of sexual experimentation meet up with boys who mature emotionally and intellectually much *later* as an identity of adult responsibility is much more difficult for them to establish. The discrepancy between the ages of these incidents seems less surprising when looked at in this way. When such incidents do happen, it is the girl who is usually identified as the victim and denied her desire in initiating the affair (she was lured away), while the boy is seen as responsible and often sentenced for statutory rape. The ambiguities of freely chosen love or sweet-talking dupery are often overridden (Levine 2002, 69–89).

THE PROMISE OF ONE'S WORD: ON-LINE SUBJECTIVATION

In virtual communities the signifier becomes empty. There is no need to be obligated to the performative of what one says or does. There is no "subjectivation" of deed and word as if one were in the "real" (RL) world. This freedom to be whoever one wishes to be also enables the most repressed sides to be projected into the imaginary avatars. Teens have a secret address that they use only between close friends. Often IM is used for pranks and jokes to play on others. It is easy to be misunderstood on-line because the tone of the voice cannot be conveyed, and the manner with which one is saying it through the writing. Sarcasm, in particular can easily be misunderstood (Pew Report). It is also easy to send messages to tell someone off; to be cruel without much thought. In a sense, lying is already an established precondition in VR communication since no one "truly" knows a character's symbolic identity. One is always able to pull out of a situation when one wishes: to be as mean or as nice as one wants, as spiteful or as loving as one wants, and so on. This "dark repressed side" can be experienced without impunity, whereas in RL it would never be allowed. To wear a mask in VR is to be relieved of one's responsibility and commitment in RL. This aspect is not lost with teens. Pranks, tricks, and deception using IM and sending e-mail "bombs" are typical occurrences. They know very well how to play this game of anonymity. A 17-year-old boy from Maryland replies in an e-mail exchange with the Pew Internet Project (Lenhart et al. 2000) was typical. "Unless you know the person really well, they're just some anonymous typist hiding behind a funny screen name. I don't see people at school and think that's somebody I know from AOL. I would not even recognize them and times that I do... 'Hey, there's HAPPYKID113'" (16). Upscale teens in the Pew report were savvy users of IM and e-mail, however, only a small percentage entered MUDs on a regular basis. It is taken for granted by teens that in MUDs the expectation is that everyone lies, deceives, and role-plays searching for sex. Girls in particular don't trust MUD contacts. The most common question asked of teens in a chat is "ASL" (Age, Sex, Location). Younger kids perceive them as dangerous places. A typical response by a 15-year-old girl was "I used to go to chat rooms, but I don't anymore" (24). On the other hand, young adults (as mentioned earlier) see them as an escape from the work routine. Doug (one of Turkle's interviewees (1998, 9) comes home from a hard day at work, enters the FurryMUD, and feels like a sexual tourist. Acting out repressions, the console-player never needs to face up to them or feel responsible for them. Inhibitions may be dropped, but they are not necessarily confronted. It is easy to avoid them, after all one is only engaged in a fictitious game.

A certain undecidability and ambiguity in the way we deal with our fantasies in cyberspace is always possible. In the early enthusiasm of Turkle's *Life on the Screen* (1995), the psychotherapeutic benefits of decentering the self are clearly lauded. Rather than "acting out" our repressed fantasies, what Kristeva (1991) usefully identified as our own uncanny strangeness to ourselves—as the "stranger" inside us, Turkle, as well as others like Taylor and Saarinen (1994), believe that repressed and aggressive sides of ourselves might be "worked through" on-line, or in simulated game situations. In a similar tone, educators around this same time (Lankshear et al. 1996) perceived cyberspace to be the new panacea for critical pedagogy. Believing the modernist "book" was outdated, virtual communities promised new democratic forms of communication because social relationships were less inhibiting. However, games such as *The Sims* (version 2002), created by Will Wright, illustrate how easy it is to "act out" one's every whim in the game world. The console-player creates a character who can interact with up to eight members of a Sim family in a never-ending sit-com melodrama. The Sim series has moved from the business of city management (*SimCity, SimWorld, SimAnt,* and *SimTower*) to the management of people in good neoliberalist fashion. The choice is set whether to play with preestablished Sim characters or build your own personalities, dressed the way you like them (skin color, personality preference, clothing, and gender). With $20,000 cash you can then build your/their own home and furnish it. Then comes the tough part. Like a Tamagotchi toy, you have to look after them— jobs, love, marriage, possessions, *and* their bodily functions (defecating, urinating, and eating)—to pursue the never-ending game of happiness. Points are scored this way. If they aren't happy, like the Tamagotchi toy, they fall into a depression. The game perfectly celebrates the superego's demand to enjoy! Happiness is achieved by buying bigger and better possessions (plasma televisions, hot tubs, and houses).

The player can then go about "writing" his or her own family narrative— to supposedly "work through" family dynamics. But the "family albums" section on the Sims' website shows a different story. Many players "burn," murder, and maim the characters they have created by letting them die of hunger or force them to stay in burning rooms until they die. This is clearly a sadistic scenario where the "look" perverts the gaZe (figure 11.4). A number of posted narratives end in multiple Sim deaths; not unlike what happened to the Tamagotchi toys that were neglected. Critics have noted that Sim players create a double standard in their narratives: polygamy for the men, but not the women. Sexuality, it should come as no surprise, is the most concentrated aspect of the game. Public nudity, the fondling of the partner's buttocks while kissing (heterosexual and homosexual alike), and hacked frontal nudity are common fare in the posted narratives. Winning is usually equated with bedding a desirable character or hot-tubing together. *The Sims* illustrates unbridled jouissance. It is a so-called god game that enables per-verse narratives to be explored. It is difficult to see how such a game can help the console-player recoil from the exploitation of the characters that have been created which, more often than not, become a nuisance and are "torched" or abandoned like the Tamagotchi toy because of its demand to be fed and looked after.

The conviviality of virtual communities is debatable. Jon Suler's (1996) longitudinal study of Main Mansion suggests that the community is held together by an addiction to it. The avatars return to the VC because they fill a desire that the players lack, mostly sexual desires and forms of human con-tact that can be "safely" explored. But this is never assured, as an "inverted message" (in the Lacanian sense) often bounces back at them. One young woman in Suler's study mentions calling her avatar "Doctor," innocently enough she thought. Not only was she continually taken to be a male but also accused of accosting another avatar as "a dirty old man," something she never expected. Flaming (insulting people on-line) is not something easy to control unless one has a strict and vigilant person looking and checking the list server.

Lankshear et al. (1996) are quite convinced that a "working through" strategy is possible for education in these VR communities, and they provide a comprehensive set of possibilities for doing so. Although they admit to "darker possibilities and realities in cyberspace" they candidly admit to choosing to " 'surf' on the side of optimism" (177). For youth to be able to "speak out" and "talk back" freely and without restraint on-line and in a community, the question remains how much policing would be necessary? A VR community would *still* have to operate under the umbrella of an existing Oedipalized Symbolic Order—no mask playing would be allowed; a rather tall order for one can never be absolutely sure of an on-line persona, or just when a student is "speaking out" or "acting out," especially if the class never meets face-to-face. The performative speech act could never be guaranteed (subjectivated), and this certainly adds to the jouissance of those who "just wanna have fun." To freely "talk back" and "speak out" would be very risky. To confront repressed content (acting through rather than acting out), it seems, can only happen if a *disavowal* takes place. The console-player can externalize his or her repressed self, which s/he would otherwise be unable to confront in RL, *only if such repressed fantasies are accepted as a game itself.* I enter a VR community disguised just to see what happens and how I react to what happens. In other words, these repressed fantasies do not "truly" belong to me in the first place. I do not take responsibility for them in RL. It becomes questionable as to whether one is actually "working them through" or simply avoiding them yet again.

The exchange of computerized messages is only governed to the extent a conversation obliges each to affect the other's symbolic universes. With no "face-to-face" communication the question how to assure that the potentially empty signifier can be subjectivized comes to fore so that some semblance of faith and trust is established. In Internet businesses, like e-bay for instance, where bidding for goods takes place, the reputation of the sellers is assured by the posted comments of the buyers. Any seller who does not send the goods and earns a bad reputation soon finds himself "out of business." The pact of bartering has been broken. On-line education courses are also "policed" in the same way. There may be sporadic face-to-face classroom meetings throughout the course, and then finally there is an evaluation. In cases where there is no obligation to "be true to one's word," to ensure trust, a business pact, or some sort of mutual consent that will affect lives, then ethics become problematic. Rape and violence in MUDs occur, and characters are often sexually harassed as Suler shows (1996).

The well-publicized case, that of "The Bungle Affair" that took place in the LambdaMOO, is a perfect example of the difficulties in sorting out the dividing line between RL and VR (see Dibbell 1998). Mr. Bungle's avatar was "a fat, oleaginous, Bisquick-faced clown dressed in cum-stained harlequin garb and girdled with a mistletoe-and-hemlock belt whose buckle bore the quaint inscription 'KISS ME UNDER THIS BITCH!'" (Dibbell, 84) who "raped" two avatars utilizing his "voodoo doll." (A "doll" is a programming trick whereby a phantom that masquerades as another player's character is created. The doll then "possesses" the character, making it do whatever it wishes.) His first victim was a legba described as "a Haitian trickster spirit of indeterminate gender, brown-skinned, wearing an expensive pearl gray suit, top hat, and dark glasses." He "forced" the legba to sexually service him in a variety of more or less conventional ways. His second victim was the legba Starsinger, described as "a nondescript female character, tall, stout, and brown-haired." Bungle was able to "force" Starsinger to have liaisons with two other avatars against her/his wishes. He then sadistically made Starsinger eat his/her own pubic hair, and then violate herself with a piece of kitchen cutlery. He was finally stopped by Zippy who was able to shoot a "cage" over him, disabling his voodoo doll's power.

The shock of his violent devastation resounded through the VC (virtual community), calling it an act of rape. Banning together on-line, a large number of LambdaMOO members attempted to "toad" Mr. Bungle, to have him "erased" from the community with a death sentence. The only members who had the power to do that were the wizards, the master programmers of the MOO, and they had issued a document earlier which announced that the wizards were only technicians, not authority figures. They would make no decisions affecting the social life in the MOO. Various political arguments broke out on the MOO mailing list called *social-issues as to what was to be democratically done. No agreement could be reached. Mr. Bungle claimed that all he had done was a psychological experiment in "thought-polarization." Since this was not RL the "affect of the device [the doll]" he had used had been "heightened." Besides, he claimed, the sequence of events had no consequences on his RL. In brief, Mr. Bungle disavowed the whole incident.

Despite the important exercise in democratic debate the community's interest began to disperse when an agreement could not be reached. After the debate, JoeFeedback, a wizard, acted alone. He "toaded" Mr. Bungle. But, the story was not over. What happened next is perhaps the more important question for what happens to the psyche in cyberspace. Mr. Bungle made a return to LambdaMOO. He had simply acquired a new Internet account, paid his dues, and signed on. He entered as another avatar, Dr. Jest. What to do with him remained an issue amongst the inhabitants of the MOO, despite his changed appearance and changed personality. He seemed less aggressive. Had he learned his lesson? The answer was left unresolved. Eventually, Dr. Jest stopped logging in. Suler (1996) offers a myriad of ways VC can deal with such deviancy. Toading (killing) is just one of them. Exile and bans are possible. Bot avatars can be sent to patrol the chat rooms. Actions of killing (being disconnected for good), pinning (sent to a corner of a screen where an avatar can't move), time-out rooms where the "rules" are given to misbehaving avatars, and setting up restricted areas and a "pit" where there are NO rules provide other possibilities. However, evil will always stalk VC. It cannot be eliminated as any number of sci-fi film fantasies has explored, for example, Geoff Murphy's *Freejack* (1992) and Robert Longo's *Johnny Mnemonic* (1995).

Although these are only fantasy avatars (screen persona) who are being violated, the console-player also feels violated. Why? The anxiety that is felt is recognition that our identities are also sustained by a virtual symbolic fiction in RL. Being on-line can collapse the virtually sustained RL and the fantasy of VR. Any "newbie" into a VC who is at first sexually accosted, experiencing Netsex (tiny sex, virtual sex) for the first time feels these two spaces collapse (Ehrenreich 1998). There is a double reflection of the mirror at play here. The first reflection is of the MUD avatar as our imagined reflected self, a fantasy in-and-of itself as an imaginary Ideal Ego. But there is also a second reflection which we *do not see*, and are *not aware of*, that is how others perceive us, and how their gaZe confirms who we think we are. This is our symbolic Ego Ideal that confirms an identity of how we would like to be perceived by others. This too is a virtual world, a world of ideological identification in the Symbolic Order. Hence as university professors we identify ourselves with a virtual place in a community of university professors in the "real" (RL) world. As our avatars are being attacked in the communities, we feel that our imaginary ideal is being accosted. The separation between RL and VC is constantly and *interpassively* being disavowed as our avatars go about imaginatively performing our screen personas. When something happens, however, like a virtual "rape," virtual sexual harassment, or virtual violence, the two virtual worlds, for a brief moment, come into sharp contact, like in Orson Welles' play, and the BBC hoaxes. We feel a violation that cannot be easily explained because it exists in the Real, it both affects and effects the core of our unconscious being. There is no explanation for it. The Symbolic and Real collapse onto one another as the gaZe from VR stares back at the console-player who sits unnerved and in shock. The gaZe has, once again, displaced the Look (figure 11.5).

CIVICS IN CYBERSPACE: CAN YOUTH HAVE THEIR OWN VOICE?

As with the paradoxes and ambiguities that surround the possibility of traversing one's fantasy through imaginary projections of oneself in chat communities, similar concerns occur with the hope that Internet communities will emerge, which will enable new democratic forms of participatory democracy to arise from the grassroots. Turkle (1996) became more skeptical as to this possibility, whereas Žižek (1997a) was always skeptical of it. Such a hope is mitigated, it seems, by the very isolation of each console-player sitting alone, as a solitary monad plugged, into a virtual community while actual forms of democratic action remain questionable and problematic. Sending lists of e-mail protests to governments on ecological issues, or for the release of political prisoners have not been overly successful, but a necessary course to initiate further action directly between the governments involved. Informing a virtual community of possible social action or protest on a Web list has been useful and powerful. Yet, Klein (2000, 393–396) is more optimistic about social activism using the Internet. According to her, Nike, Shell, and McDonald's have had to respond to the continual availability of their environmental and human rights abuses thanks to activist campaigns such as the McSpotlight website. "Indeed, the beauty of the Net for activists is that it allows coordinated international actions with minimal resources and bureaucracy" (395). But claims for a "Digital Nation" (see Holeton 1998, 147–288) that can construct a more civil society based on rationalism, shared information, and the pursuit of truth is certainly exaggerated. The Internet has *also* provided the spawning of every conceivable interest group that can find a way to create a website and maintain it; from the neo-Nazis' Right to the Christian Right; from the communist Left to the republican Right. They too use the Net to organize their ideological campaigns internationally.

In their report on nonprofit civic websites for teens, the Center for Media Education (CME) (see Montgomery 2001) was hard-pressed to uncover

youth civic media sites in the United States. Eventually, in 2001 five paradigmatic sites were chosen: HarlemLive, The Diary Project, Nation 1,
SERnet.org, and Voices of Youth. Most of the youth sites they found were
not prominent, or even visible against the clutter of cyber commercialism, which captures its youth surfers through streaming video and java
applets. Standard search engines and mainstream portals weren't particularly
useful, unless a specific website was known. This usually required personal
referrals, newspaper articles, and links from other sites. These sites attempt
to promote "youth voice" to discuss political and social topics, as well as personal problems through the usual e-ways (instant message (IM), bulletin
boards, chats, e-pals) with the hope of not having this voice appropriated by
scavenging marketeers. This may well be why "word-of-modem" is the best
way to find them.

The CME's selection of civic websites span and describe the possible positive and hopeful ways teens can utilize the Web for social transformation and
for their own ends. The Diary.com site focuses on providing peer-to-peer
support through anonymous postings and diary-like e-messages on issues
such as relationships, teen-life pressures, loss of friends, death, violence, prejudice, body image, and so forth. To postings on such topics, comments can
be added, responses given, advice and support from teachers, adults, and
health professionals can be expected. The monitoring of the site is by "teen
advocates" who include both adults and teens. Another variation of teen support, which specifically targets African American youth is the HarlemLive
site. This site is unique in that it combines its on-line presence with offline
organizations. The local and the virtual are linked in mutual support of
one another, reinforcing the programs that are being offered. Voices of
Youth.com is the UNICEF on-line interactive forum for young people
that attempts a global conversation on such concerns as child labor, youth
rights, environment, armed conflict, HIV/AIDS, gender discrimination, and
urbanization.

While these three sites are paradigmatic of an attempt to avoid commer-
cialization, the next several sites are paradigmatic of the difficulty to maintain sovereignty without financial support. The CME report mentions
Nation1, which emerged out of a Junior Summit in September 1998 that
was supported by MIT Media Lab. The idea was to have a global conversation (accommodating ten different languages), consulting youth for their
perspectives in planning for future design in the use of technology, given that
they were the first generation to grow up with the new digital technologies.
In effect, such youth would be "ambassadors of a new digital culture." Since
CME's reportage, Nation1 has merged with Taking1Global.org. a rather
impressive website in its outreach to the global youth community. Big-
business interests however are involved. Sponsors include Citibank, Swatch,
Logo 2B1 Foundation, and several other lesser-known companies
(Enterprise IG, SpikeCyberWorks, MaMaMedia, Amikai). To what extent
these global "youth ambassadors" of technology can avoid eventually being
"branded" by the company logos that support the site, and continue to

retain an activist global social consciousness, like a resistant and vigilant NGO, rests with the future.

Other nonprofit youth civic media providers have formed alliances with commercial on-line capitalism to secure funding. Such sites are a blend of teen social concerns and commercialism. CME mentions FreshAngles.com, essentially a journalist site with on-line news publications by students, and the then fledgling YouthNoise.com billed now as "the sound of change for our generation." The site's goal is to enable youth to help younger children become involved in volunteering, philanthropy, and public policy. The site itself is a brilliant and clever blend of popular culture and social and political concerns. In "Just 1 click" section, the on-line user is sent to an article on intolerance in *Seventeen* magazine; "What's Hot" has a section on sex; "Quiz content" asks what would I do as the [U.S.] President? "True Story" section is about overcoming prejudice toward a Pakistani girlfriend; "Three Second Quiz" asks you to identify a Hip Hop newsmaker. "Celeb Watch" seems self-explanatory; in "Be The Solution" you are encouraged to send the [U.S.] president a letter on a current sociopolitical concern; "Top Ten"—ten ways to fight cancer are featured; "What's Gong On" features stories on global youth leaders. The obvious civic engagement that this site provides for young people is exemplary and hopeful.

While we have presented a number of myths of interactivity in this chapter—we are not as "free" to interact with media as is hyped—there are yet other aspects that we explore in chapter 14. Advances in VR environments raise interesting questions concerning knowledge and hypertext narratives. We raise the question of "interpassivity," the way the "new" technologies, in effect, often take over our lives and drain our emotions. We do this by again revisiting video games, which continues to surpass the music industry in sales.

12

THE DREAM OF TOTAL KNOWLEDGE:
HYPERTEXTUAL FANTASIES

In this chapter we change our focus yet again, this time to the interface between human and machine when it comes to the question of knowledge and its fantasy structures. The "wiring" of education for privileged youth has received wide attention. Upscale middle-class parents are in favor of such a computerization of schools, according to the Pew Internet Report (Lenhart et al. 2000) because they see this as a way for their children to "get ahead" in the world by having the latest technologies. Educationally speaking, one of the most controversial issues concerning the Web is the nature of knowledge that it offers. Joseph Weizenbaum (1976) many years ago argued passionately that judgment was uniquely human and impossible to replicate in a machine. Yet, his initial insight has been constantly challenged. There is a significant divide between an education that teaches teens computer programming and how computers work by making them transparent—as first pioneered by the MIT educator Seymour Papert (1980)—and simply teaching them how to *use* the programs, which is what generally passes for computer literacy in the majority of schools. Turkle (1997) has usefully attempted to show the difference between these two approaches.

Our tact here is to move away from this much-publicized debate concerning computerization in schools, and look at the fantasies that accompany the shift of knowledge being reduced to so many accessible databases—as information, rather than the more high-minded ephemeral notions of wisdom (*sophia*) and *Bildung*. Information is power and databases are supposed to provide instant knowledge at the fingertips of the terminal with machine and user both mutually supporting one another. In her conclusion to the "posthuman" condition, Hayles (1999) cites the work of Hutchins (1995) to make her point that there has always been a distribution of cognition between human and nonhuman agents. It's not a question of either/or, but the complexity between the two that is already in place. We operate with devices and systems as environments that we have little or no understanding in how they work, such as DVDs, videos, digital cameras, computers, modems, and so on. Yet, such interactive devices make us more sophisticated because the environments we have devised are themselves "smarter."

According to this logic, cyberspace environments provide the prosthetics that enable us to have an ecological relationship with machines. Complex cognitive distributive systems decenter the subject yet again. This time, not as the autonomous controlling subject of Nature, but in partnership with it. We arrive, yet again, with the definition of "human" as a hybrid cyborg. Ever since *Homo habilis* picked up the first pebble and used it as a tool to crush tough fibers and crack bone, the material cultures of technology have intimately shaped human consciousness. Our pebble technology has simply gotten "smarter" just as have *Homo sapiens*. Technological "smartness" can now be harnessed in tandem with human sapience. Does such an obvious stance require criticism?

As mapped out earlier, in Doel and Clarke's (1999) useful typology of cyberspace, the ecological cybernetic model is characterized as a prosthetic one where hyperreality predominates. As any number of critics have pointed out (Baudrillard, Virilio), hyperreal environments skew the way RL is experienced, not any differently from "reality Television" that skews the way RL is experienced in a "contained and natural environment." The two phenomena form a binary: hyperreal/banal.[1] In hyperreal environments what's "fake," more often than not, becomes more compelling than the mundane real, which then, in turn, can become "boring," like our previous examples of cyber-living in MUDs, cyber-sex, and multitasking. Aesthetization and anesthetization (hyperreal/banal) form a closed circuit that switches back and forth to sustain momentum of capitalist media and product production. For Doel and Clarke, the hyperreal view of VR leads ultimately to an apex where cyberspace environments are cast in utopian terms, as panacean solutions. This is where ecological thinking seems to stumble between the so-called soft-anthropocentrism of the "deep-ecology movement" (Arne Naess) and the "hard-anthropocentrism" of human technologists. From a "hard" technological and ecological viewpoint, the more we can understand the flexible and adaptive structures that coordinate our environment and the human role in them, the better it will be possible to fashion ourselves in those complex interplays as one entire global system. In contrast, "deep ecology" treats Gaia (Earth) as a "thinking" system; the wager is that human technologies can work in harmony and equilibrium with it. An entire ecosophy has developed around this hope and dream. Whereas, a hard anthropocentricsm claims that human technology based on complex ecological systems is able to "manage" Gaia, a turn to a hyper-autonomous individual of management technology. Bluntly put, the complexity of the dispute can be reduced to solar energy versus nuclear plants. In effect, both sides are utopian dreams, two sides of the same coin, grand narratives as to the direction VR will take in the future. The mysticism (New Ageism) that surrounds "deep ecology" makes the movement appear almost technophobic at times, while the zealots of technology offer a technocratic solution that is equally unnerving in its totalitarian implications. The future is "now."

VR has already changed the way knowledge is mediated. As Rosalind Krauss (1987) pointed out, the database has become the new art form for developing the narcissistic self through video. The digital computer becomes the perfect medium for the database form. New media, "regardless of whether it represents to the user her image or not, can be said to activate the narcissistic condition because they represent to the user her actions and their results. In other words, it functions as a new kind of mirror that reflects only the human activities" (Manovich 2001, 235 n. 29). The banality and trivia of "reality" television (notably Big Brother) and "reality porn" where the video camera is installed in the bedrooms of various young women (notably Jennifer Rigley—"JenniCam") are primary examples. Birkerts (1998) makes the case that language-use is fundamentally changing with database computer interfaces. Syntax has progressively become less complex. Spellchecks and grammar checks in word processing programs tend to make even experienced writers follow simplified syntax suggestions. Paradox, irony, subtlety, and wit in writing are fast disappearing. Student textbooks compared to 20 years ago have begun to prune and gloss difficult texts. The same can be said of handwriting skills. As computer keyboarding begin to be taught at an increasingly earlier age to schoolchildren, penmanship, compared to an age dominated by the pen and ink, or even the ballpoint for that matter, has deteriorated to a scrawl. Against this backdrop, by perverting the rules of "good drawing," we have the odd development of artistic forms of "crude drawing," which are technically inept in their execution, taking on an authentic significance, which is both overvalued and overpriced.

There is also another perversion taking place to existing canonical texts, be they musical, artistic, or works of literature. One can now easily "add" to an existing text by writing in new characters (Miss Piggy of the Muppets appeared in a new version of *Three Little Pigs*), or filling in unexplainable gaps (Martin Scorsese's *The Last Testament of Christ* (1988) which wrote in Christ's possible sexual encounters with Mary Magdalene), seeing an established text from a minor character's viewpoint (Tom Stoppart's *Rosencrantz and Guildenstern are Dead* that rewrites Hamlet), or from a woman's viewpoint (Christa Woolf's retelling of Cassandra and Medea). These texts have become decentered as well, raising the question of knowledge yet again, privileging the reader and not the author. Music suffers the same fate as musical hypertexts are written and CDs produced, which explore any number of major classical composers by exaggerating sections, or which bring out their minor less played and important works. Through hypertext and a database one can study artists like Van Gogh selectively by the years he lived, or focus on one period of his life, or select only pictures that have sunsets in them, thereby distorting the larger perspective of his life. By filling the unexplained gaps in canonical texts, or by distorting them through numerous perspectives, and thereby unhinging the ground of the "original," inadvertently devalues these canonical texts rather than enriching them.

This devaluation emerges not because the hypertext variations are somehow poorer copies of the original, as some neo-Platonist might argue; rather their devaluation comes from the decentering of form and the evacuation of the specter that haunted the original canonical text in the first place.

Canonical texts now become reduced to information of sorts rather than sustaining their fascination as a unique historical object of art in the achievement of humankind in which they played a sublime role. This loss of aura, of the spectral Real as "presence," is welcomed by some and seen as progressive. For others, these developments of cyber-revolution present an obscene kind of "over-presence" (Žižek 1997a, 156), a slick world of "friction-free capitalism" where there are no hindrances for exchange since everything can be turned into information, transforming time into space. For education, this has raised the whole debate about "forgetting," and the fading of cultural memory. History as a school subject has become an ideological battleground to prevent its decentering. Those who control the "official" story, control knowledge as well as hegemonic identity of a nation. The anxiety of the more conservative educators is that history becomes yet another postmodern "surface" effect, as flattened historical perspectives, stored as databases on CDs. The depth and dimensionality of the book begins to transform itself into the ephemeral weightless database of stored information expunging our sense of historical chronology. The database celebrates the loss of authority, of a Master whose arbitrary gesture grounds a definitive reality and stops the slide of the endless and possibly infinite variations, versions of variations of textual possibilities, or actions. In this view, those who control the databases remain in power, but they are *not* authorities in the traditional sense of the term. They are more like archivists whose duty is assure an impossible completion of material.

THE TECHNOCRAT'S DREAM AND THE OBSESSIONAL'S QUESTION

When it comes to hypertext databases, as interactive participants we are supposedly "in control" of where we want to go and what we want to retrieve in the virtuality of the cyberspace narrative (be it a video game, puzzle game, or on-line hypertext). The ultimate fantasy is to be able to discard the body so that the console-subject is all mind—accessing information instantly in less than a nanosecond, with no delay. Metaphorically this would mean to "enter" into the screen world where one would be an omnipotent presence with no lack and no obstacles, the ultimate expression of the ego. Disney's classic production of Steven Lisberger's *Tron* (1982) was the first sci-fi movie to explore this fantasy. A computer hacker (Jeff Bridges) is transported into a computer where he faces Master Control. Having programmed a number of features in the environment he attempts to replace Master Control with Tron, a safety system. Master Control is the psychotic, the "stranger" within us, which we fear, unconstrained by the Law/Tron. Tron embodies what the machine cannot—judgment and prohibition. As the Frankfurt school (Žižek 1997a, 138) theorized with the concept of "repressive desublimation"— a universe freed of everyday inhibitions leads to a universe of unbridled sadomasochistic violence and will to domination. Such an anxiety is replayed in a number of sci-films. The closing scenes of Brett Leonard's *Lawnmower*

Man (1992) present such a scenario. Jobe Smith (Jeff Fahey) has been able to strip off his body and enter cyberspace as a pure essence, pure mind, as if he is able to control the Internet itself. As this pure essence he is depicted as a sadistic killer (Springer 1996, 91–94) whose cyberspace sex with his girl-friend ends up as an attempted rape. Trapped in a looped circuit by his creator Dr. Lawrence Angelo (Pierce Brosnan), he manages to escape to return in a sequel. In this sci-fi Frankensteinian dystopia the question as to who is God and who is the Devil—the scientist or his creation—is left dangling. Angelo as his name indicates creates the "fallen angel," a projection of his own repressed unconscious desires. In Lacanian terms, the impossible Real would vanish as if we could "actually" occupy the spurious vanishing point that enables the "realistic" screen projection to form itself, to actually occupy the impossible space "behind" the screen. We would be able to discard the virtual Symbolic Order once and for all and "exist" in VR. This is the utopia Doel and Clark (1999) articulate as their third interpretation of VR. The belief in this scenario is that no visual limit is necessary. No blind spot need frame us. Such a lack can be eliminated. This is the Enlightenment's tech-nological dream come true; its full completion where the subject has become pure ego, an authority in-and-of itself. It spells the end of a dream as we now enter its created possibility.

Lacan argued that it is precisely this "limit"—the Real—which makes vision possible in the first place. What makes us finite human beings with all our limitations is precisely our inability to see ourselves from the vantage point of those outside us (parents, friends, institutions—collectively the big Other), who give us meaning as to who we are. Their collective gaze is for-ever allusive. We can only imaginatively construct what we think it may be through the interactions we have with the world. We are shaped by their desire as they conflict or support our own drives and desires. VR promises to change that gaze by insisting on a hyper-individualism that can do away with it. Here we might think of another amazing sci-fi scenario, the opening sequence of Kathryn Bigelow's *Strange Days* (1995). Lenny Nero (Ralph Fiennes) dawns on a cap-like computer s(t)imulator (called a SQUID), which plunges him directly into experiencing in his mind a virtual world of a failed bank robbery, complete with the feeling of falling off a building and plunging to one's death. This is a "first-person shooter" sequence where the frame has totally disappeared. The eyeball is turned *inward*, it has gone inside the body. Lenny sits in a chair, eyes closed, no longer staring at a screen engrossed by video effects. He is totally immersed in VR with his entire body convulsing as he experiences the thrill of the robbery. The screen has become his mind.

Strange Days fills out the potential where the "total subjectivization (the reduction of reality to an electro-mechanically generated cyberspace 'win-dow') coincides with total objectivization (the subordination of our 'inner' bodily rhythms to a set of simulations regulated by external apparatuses" (Žižek 1997a, 135). In a very funny scene from the sci-fi thriller, Spielberg's *Minority Report* (2002), based on a short story by Phillip Dick about the possibility of capturing criminals before they commit their crime, the future possibility of entertainment arcades based on immersion VR environments is shown. A pudgy frustrated business man rushes into the VR entertainment "playdium" and asks the arcade owner whether he has a VR environment booth where he can reenact killing his boss. In another VR environment we see a man sitting in a lounge chair as virtual models stroke and tell him how wonderful he is.

While such a devise that Lenny wears has not as yet been invented, its approximation is already in place. We are now capable of extending the hypertext narrative to a point where we feel we have seemingly omniscient control within a computerized three-dimensional program, very close to the Holodeck (Holographic Environment Simulator) fantasy on the *Star Trek* series. In the holodeck "matter" and people look, sound, and feel like the "real thing." The gaze of the Symbolic Order seemingly has been eliminated. No more symbolic identification in RL, only an imaginary identification in VR is necessary. There is now immersion projection-based environmental research that enables a researcher/learner/console-player to "step into" the screen so that his/her every demand (within the confines of the program) can be explored in "real" time thanks to the high processing speed of the computers that run these programs. These so-called 3D Virtual Environments "augment" reality by taking Virtual Reality Modeling Language (VRML) a step further to a point where "realistic" special 3-D effects that the console-player manipulates becomes possible.

One of the earliest VR environments was the CAVE (Computerized Automatic Visual Environment). A console-user is no longer on the outside looking in, but on the inside looking out. Stepping into this $10 \times 10 \times 9$– foot darkened cubicle is like climbing into one's own personal computer screen. No longer is the console-user observing data through portals or just a flat screen; the display enables him or her to experience the sensation of being "inside" the data. Freedom of movement within the box is made possible by the reduction of bulky helmets and data gloves. All that is required inside the CAVE box is a pair of data glasses and a wand. The wand is a moveable interface devise. By pointing it at an object, the console-user can change its position and orientation in any of six directions: forward or backward, up or down, or left or right. Data are projected in stereoscopic images onto the walls and floor of the CAVE so that they fill the cubicle. In a simulated aquarium, fish not only swim in front and on the left and right hand sides of a console-user, but also below and behind as well. In these virtual environments the user can become smaller than an atom or larger than the universe. S/he can watch and interact with simulations of the birth of galaxies; watch ripples of gravity as black holes collide, or travel through the human bloodstream—so the hype goes. One can also build cities, cathedrals, mosques, and pyramids, or listen to the sounds of chaos. Science, medicine, education, industry, and the entertainment industry (saleable 3-D virtual glasses have already been developed), all see this as the next step in cyberspace development as HDTV (high-density television) becomes more affordable. Digitalized HDTV has five times the detail and twice the resolution power of analogue television. Its images are brighter and sharper, while the sound is comparable to compact disks. In this futuristic scenario, interactive, "real-time" broadcasts and cablecasts could become commonplace.

In these CAVE environments (which use such programs as CAVE 6D, COSMIC EXPLORER, PARIS) what comes about is what the console-player wants to come about. The medium has become the message as the console interface—the Graphic User Interface (GUI)—has become transparent, replaced by 3-D glasses and a wand. One's demand is instantly met through the computing system. Desire seems eliminated. There is no need of the Other. There is no authority (no Other) to be confronted here. The console-user *is* the authority as the eye and its gaze is synchronized together so the computer "sees" what s/he wants to see. There is a complete identification with the position that the computer organizes for the user at his or her whim. The reality of the screen "is" reality itself. Simulacra refers only to itself, although, of course, it may resemble "reality" (RL) by hyperextending perspectives and the senses—colors and smells may be more intense, definitions more sharp, and so on. In effect, one has "stepped" into the computer screen as if the interface (like Lenno's experience in *Strange Days*) has been eliminated. Images that were suspended on screen now pop up as 3-D. These images can be explored from any angle: above, below, or inside as if one were on a post-Euclidean walkabout.

VANISHING THE VANISHING POINT: EFFACING THE INTERFACE

The perspectival mirror is no longer the model that is being used here; rather the vanishing point has *moved inside the CAVE box*, producing folded time and space. By so doing, we can create a world of three-dimensional simulacra. Doel (1999) attempts at an explanation of the post-Einsteinian relativity theory that is involved. The console-player stands at this impossible point that can be tracked anywhere within the cubed environment. Not only what one has designed can be changed and played with, but it is possible to introduce more affective body feeling into these environments including taste, smell, sound, and touch. While such sophisticated holodeck environments are not fully solved, it seems only a question of time and resources. "Lag," the time it takes to "refresh" the image—to slow it down or to speed it up—has not been fully resolved. A console-player can become dizzy because the coordination time between user's perception and computer processing of the information into 3-D images is difficult to get right. This varies from individual to individual. There are resolution problems because of the refreshed images, the size of the database need to be reduced to make such computations quicker, and so forth. But the "Strange Days" are around the corner. It is only a question of time, money, and political will.

These VR environments will be the next major step in video games. First-person shooter games will become 3-D interactive "step into" the screen games. With the minimal distance from the screen image gone, the player would not only hear the sounds of gunfire and see the blood splatter, but s/he would also see the virtual players being shot in 3-D, and experience the firing of the gun in the hand and shoulder by wearing a data glove, or some such interface device. The entire body feel of the gun firing could be felt (see also Provenzo Jr. 1998). What could never be reproduced is the "horror" of an actual kill, the psychic order of the Real. But through disavowal (its only a game) the repressed feelings of aggression could be let loose. Could remorse and guilt still be experienced if a console-player is continually immersed in such a VR environment? Would s/he indeed lose touch with humanity given that the Symbolic Order has been completely eliminated? There is no need to face any responsibility or guilt concerning virtual kills. These are after all, only 3-D images created by the computer program. A complete disavowal remains possible.

Such questions raise, once more, the ethical and *obessional* question that rehearses itself in many sci-fi movies, explored brilliantly in novels and films like *Blade Runner*, *Bicentennial Man*, and cleverly in Steven Spielberg's *A.I. Artificial Intelligence* (2001). The obessional's existential question bluntly put is: "Am I alive or dead?" For Žižek (1997a) this translates into post-modern's anxious filled world as: "Am I a machine (does my brain really function as a computer) or a living human being (with a spark of spirit or something else that is not reducible to the computer circuit)?" (136). Turkle's claim is that our answer to this obessional question inevitably ends back to a form of its denial. At first we claim an obvious difference between the machine and human uniqueness; we then become anxious that there really is no difference since the potential of AI (artificial intelligence) is capable of learning. IBM's computer Deep Blue, after all, did beat the best chest player in the world at the time, Gary Kasparov, even though the strategies in the matches were uninspiring. AI seems capable of self-independent thought. It can learn from its mistakes. Lyotard (1991) ponders this same question. Once the sun is extinguished in four billion years, will thinking machines be the only artifact of humanity able to populate other planets? He concludes his query by claiming that embodied perception and the intuitive subjunc-tive condition of analogical "as if" thinking is infinitely more complex than the binary logic of machines. The machine is unable to suffer. Finally, the obsessional question leads to a disavowal. There may indeed be a human trait that is denied machines, such as fear, anxiety, and love, but that very denial enables us to interact with computers as if they were "thinking" machines, such as the telerobots developed by nano-technology. They may seem to be living and thinking machines but *we* are in control of them. On the one hand our obsessional anxiety is relieved only momentarily. It is looped back again into a new anxiety as the "next generation" of technology is invented. In Chris Columbus's sci-fi fantasy *Bicentennial Man* (1999), we have the inverse of this obsessional anxiety staged by the machine itself: "Am I human or a machine?" The robot Andrew Martin (Robin Williams) outlives the Martin family that "owned" him, raising the question whether AI will outlive humans or be in conflict with them, as in *The Terminator* series.

But Andrew is no ordinary robot. He becomes capable of emotions and creative thought. It is his search across two centuries to find out whether he is capable of an emotional bond with his human mother. The film, based on a novel by Isaac Asimov, has a bittersweet ending, a true masterpiece of exploring such a question.

MAJESTIC: A SIGN FROM THE REAL

VR immersion environments represent the uninhibited workings of the conscious ego where there are no hindrances from the Other; it appears to be a "pure" unmediated immersion into a computer program's cyber-narrative ideology. It has all the authority, yet it seems as if the console-player has the power because of the interactive ability of effortlessly calling on what s/he demands. Unlike cinema where the spectator might be surprised by sudden twists of the plot as the spectator follows a story that s/he has no control over, within VR immersion environments the console-player is in complete control. The minimal distance from the screen has vanished. The console-player is blindly convinced of narcissistic authority, as if no external authority existed. Here paranoiac possibilities may begin to present themselves that are explored by sci-fi filmic narratives like *eXistenZ*, *The Matrix*, and the closing sequence of *M.I.B.* (*Men in Black*) where we find out that our planet earth is just some marble plaything of an alien being. What if "real life" is just another VR? There is no "real" outside, but an endless series of rooms within rooms, worlds within worlds, dimensions within dimensions. In the *Matrix* we find out that a supercomputer has created the VR. Thomas A. Anderson (a.k.a. Neo) (Keanu Reeves) has to "see" through this VR to begin to read its code in order to redeem a new vision. In Cronenberg's *eXistenZ* the players at the film's end come out of playing one virtual game only to find that they are always inside another. There seems to be no "ground" for concrete "reality."

The possibility of such a bazaar experience is already in place. CAVE-to-CAVE conferencing linked through a supercomputer is already possible. Researchers will be able to incorporate an electronic representation of themselves in their coworker's CAVE. Such an experiential possibility speaks of the paranoia that there is an "Other of the Other," someone who is pulling the strings. Conspiracy theories are but a hair's breath away. That the big Other can reply, that there indeed IS someone "out there" who is controlling things, such as aliens in league with the government, or a God who predestines everything, is precisely what has made the conspiracy game *Majestic* so successful. Loosely based on the movies *The Game*, *WarGames*, and the Roswell Alien incident, *Majestic* is a cyberspace on-line game that goes the furthest in blurring the (false) distinction between fantasy and reality.

The player is sent clues to figure out a conspiracy s/he is involved in through every conceivable form of communication that can invade a person's private life: e-mail, faxes, home phone, cell phone, Internet, AOL instant messenger, Web page with realistic-looking news sites, PDA, eavesdropping on Webcam conversations, streaming video/audio through Real Player and Webcam. The player is inserted in the middle of a sinister plot that involves a game company, Majestic–12, whose top new product is compromising the agenda of a mysterious, high-powered, top-secret political organization. But something goes wrong and the player has to find out what. Rather than the big Other being some stupid, impossible dead entity whose entirety we can never grasp with no ONE person in charge; that is to say, it remains an open-ended inconsistent system existing only virtually with infallible figures attempting to wear the mantel of representing its authority (priests, judges, military generals, presidents, doctors), *Majestic* gives us an answer from the Real so that we may believe in some sort of authority again. Contingent events converge and confer instructions on the player through the various communication networks; s/he then must attempt to decipher the clues and work out the symbolic network of the conspiracy. The big Other now intentionally "calls" on us. Rather than pretending that we trust the system of rules and unsaid regulations—the system of laws is felt to be just and so on—we are made to feel invaded, as if a social superego is instructing us what to do.

Even the president of the United States, arguably the most powerful position in the world, is still obligated to answer to the United Nations before military action against another country can be taken. Even if this seems like an empty gesture, it is still a necessary symbolic one to keep the global gaze in tact, to keep appearances up. To do otherwise is folly and perhaps political suicide as the G.W. Bush administration (almost) found out. They had to use the pretense that the UN Security Council had already sanctioned force in its Resolution 1441 (November 8, 2002) if Saddam Hussein failed to meet UN inspectors deadlines. In *Majestic*, however, there *is* a big materialized Other who beacons, arbitrarily intervenes in our lives, and orders us to obey its clues. Although players are told that it's "just a game"—and therefore they should disavow any "real" power of *Majestic*'s network, this is not so easy to do. Its symbolic authority must remain virtual. Although the game producers explicitly state that there is nothing to worry about—no one will knock on your door late at night—a player can't be sure. Symbolic authority, which now has been given over by players to arbitrarily allow *Majestic* to invade their communication systems with clues, means that they become afraid to put its power to the test. Is it really so powerful, or is it an impostor as it says it is? As a Master-Signifier of authority it must remain ambiguous if the game is to remain as unnerving as it is. In this conspiracy game the player begins to believe that there *is* an Other of the Other; someone *is* manipulating private space, invading your life, calling on you at different times of the day and night. Like the *X-Files* "The truth [really] *is* out there!" You are but a pawn in their game as it manipulates you. There are always clues you cannot decipher, or perhaps you have mistaken an ordinary event *as* a clue, which makes you even *more* paranoid. What was once considered an intrusion into private life—telemarketers annoying you on the phone, unwanted junk mail coming at you daily, irritating pop-up advertising showing up on Internet sites, spam, and pornography messages on your e-mail site, as examples of the invasion of fantasies from the outside that usually cause anger and frustration—has now been turned into a game of willing participation. A player surrenders to willful manipulation, yet another illustration of the perversion of authority as the masochistic player strikes a pact with *Majestic*'s sadistic superego to be accosted in the thrill of a game. But can a player tell its Web servers to stop? The Other as ONE speaks indirectly to the player, its signs have to be interpreted and the rules kept.

Majestic is yet another reminder of the perverse landscape of the media where sadomasochistic games are becoming more and more popular. A RL equivalent of *Majestic* has finally emerged, billed as an "art" event. It too has the same sadomasochistic trappings. *Video Games*, a New York–based group of performance artists founded by Brock Enright, who has a Masters degree in Fine Art from Columbia University, do "designer kidnappings" complete with a signed contract, and a surveillance team that tracks and kidnaps the willing victim. Once kidnapped, the "victim" is then punished, interrogated, held for X amount of hours, and then released according to the terms contracted. The cost is anywhere from $1,500 to $8,000 dollars, but that price tag includes a "reality" video of the event! These "performances" are spreading to most major U.S. cities primarily among men in their twenties who are looking for new venues of excitement.

M. Night Shyamalan's film *Signs* (2002) might be seen as a suitable dénouement to *Majestic*'s end game. The conspiracy has already been materialized, the Aliens have landed, but they are an unfriendly lot who want to take over the world. This is yet another New Age solution to the loss of symbolic efficiency, not unlike the Trinity Broadcast Network's Christian movie *The Omega Code*, based loosely on Michael Drosnin's book *The Bible Code*, which reveals secret messages in the Torah once the code has been deciphered. By taking sequences of letters (every fifth letter, every twenty-fifth letter, and so on), hidden messages appear, predicting such things as the deaths of Kennedy, Princess Diana, and Yitzak Rabin. Once the code is revealed the Real vanishes. We are assured that even accidents have a rational meaning behind them, attributable to a higher Being. The twist with *Signs* is that we are dealing with a contingent event, and not a revelation. Yet, its meaning will also be revealed. It is perhaps closer to James Redfield's *The Celestine Prophecy* with his claim of "spiritual awakening." In *Signs*, Graham Hess (Mel Gibson), an ex-priest turned farmer, has had his symbolic world shaken—he has lost faith in God, his big Other, after his wife had been tragically pinned by a car in a freak accident, whispering some incomprehensible words before she died. Having lost his authority and his symbolic importance as a priest, Hess has now become a pragmatic realist. He rationalizes all and any event refusing to transfer any authority onto himself. To restore his faith God, a "little piece of the Real" (Žižek 1991, 29–32) is required. At the film's end one last remaining Alien, whom Hess had previously wounded, holds his asthmatic son hostage, and begins to poison him with lethal gas. Hess recalls his wife's dying words and encrypts them as providing an answer as to how to defeat the Alien—which he does. In the end his son has also been "miraculously" saved. Having had an asthmatic attack he did not breathe in the deadly gas. Hess's faith in God has now been restored. He had correctly read the signs from the big Other who had at last "answered" him. This New Age ideology where the message from the symbolic Other can be decoded seems to substantiate capitalism' s postemotional consumerism. Rather than living with the "lack" of non-knowledge about ourselves, New Ageism provides an "answer" as to how to be a self-sufficient subject.

13

Looping Back to Video Games: The Question of Technological Interpassivity

Interpassive Agents of Cyberspace

Cyberspace "agents" such as a wand, mouse, data glove, and various on-screen avatars are extensions of the console-user's ego; they enable the software program to stand in as an alter ego. In cyberspace this decenterment of the self comes at a price as these cyber-agents begin to mediate our lives more and more. As Baudrillard remarks, the videotape (as well as cable TV) in a way, "watches" the movie for us. We need not trouble ourselves to drive to the movie center to see the film. In a similar way, the avatar in a chat community is e-moting for us, externalizing and embodying our very emotions. Through our disavowal of these agents—this is mere simulation, this is only a game, this is not "real"—we slowly let them take over our lives having to face the question of "impassivity" (Pfaller 2002; Žižek 1999b, 2002a), which is the other side of media interactivity that is disavowed.

When it comes to violent computer games, it is not the concern of becoming *desensitized* to the other person that is at issue. Buckingham and Allerton's (1996) review of the research literature found no proof to the claim that children watching violent videos become desensitized to RL violence, *mutatis mutandis* for violent video games. The question of desensitization, we believe is directed more to the *quality* of the experience than to any direct transference effects that such experience provides. By quality, we mean that the experience of affects is reduced to effects through the decontextualization and impoverishment of any social relationship to the Symbolic Order. Video games offer plenty of sensualized affects, but they are of the postemotional kind. They are interpassive; the machine "enjoys" our affective emotions through the avatar(s) who represent us. We invest our emotions in these cyber-agents. Action video games bombard the console-player with their hyperaesthetic effects of over-presence.

Although not nearly reaching the level of immersion VR environments such as the CAVE, these games evacuate the spectral presence of Symbolic Order, so that the console-player can be immersed in the fantasy space of

VR. Consider the proliferation of war and sports video games. Why are so many video games preoccupied precisely with these two areas, which obviously appeal to boyz and young men? One answer is that these two areas happen to be the remaining visages where the authority of discipline still supports a fraternal brotherhood; where community and teamwork are still forwarded through individual heroic effort. As Jones (2002) notes, the shift in video games in the last decade has generally shifted from killing monsters, vampires with a wand to killing avatars with a gun. In video games of war, the ethereal presence of the Real, an "indivisible remainder" as Žižek (1996a) theorizes it, remains vacant. Confrontation with the Real may never take place. Why? In RL war situation the unconscious haunt of the Real is very much present. The mourning and loss that results when someone that you know dies; the horrible devastation of the landscape, the social antagonisms and close friendships that develop between soldiers; the fantasies as to what the enemy looks like up-close; the question whether one could actually "kill" someone when finally faced with the decision; the displaced lives that happen back home and abroad during the war; the smell of decaying flesh, the cries and images that haunt soldiers long after the war is over; these are all "impossible" aspects of war, which do not come into "play" in a game situation.[1] This is precisely what makes playing it "safe" in the space of fantasy. The Real is screened out.

All games are abstracted from RL experiences and help sublimate the life's uncertainties, but video games intensify this retreat from the social world through their hyped effects. By reducing war to an object of representation a certain anesthetization (Welsch 1990, 9–12) or postemotionalism eventually sets in (Meštrović 1997). This is not unlike Bennetton's "reality advertisement" developed by Oliviero Toscani where social disasters and race relations have been spectacularized by decontextualizing the racial and social historical dynamics of the conflict to present images that categorize and essentialize race, ethnicity, and ecological disaster into stereotypical icons. The spectator can only nod in agreement or be shocked by the blatant simplicity of what is being presented.

This exteriorization of emotions so that they appear staged, packaged, specularized simulacra, devoid of embodiment, of affect or feeling, is part of a larger social shift to what Meštrović calls an "other-directedness." It is the loss of personal space and the ideal of a private life, an invasion by "an electronic order" (Birkerts 1998). This condition is brought about, we may add, by the constant proliferation of voyeuristic and panoptic media forms where we constantly see ourselves on screens. We are conditioned by the "normativeness" of a surveillance society as reflected on "reality television," spy camera, surveillance cameras in stores, schools, streets, home videos of our everyday life, digital photographs that seem to proliferate endlessly, then stored conveniently on CDs to become a future database for our "experiences." Such a thesis can help explain why there is so much screen-life violence to sublimate the increasing aggressivity that comes with the expectation of being politically correct and avoid the accusation of sexual harassment and sexual victimization. We are expected to wear a "happy face" when working in the service sectors because the customer is always right, and to "love your neighbor" who has come "too" close and invasive (as the proliferation of reality television court shows in almost all postindustrial countries shows). If that not enough we are expected to tolerate the constant flood of advertising that is telling us how we should live, what to wear, eat, drive, and so on. Postemotionalism is characterized by living one's emotions vicariously; that is, interpassively. Public figures must manage their image. Youth cultures are no different. There is peer pressure to have the right look. "Cool" is defined by a certain emotional stance and attitude. Opinion makers tell the public what to think and feel as an event unfolds. Meštrović argues that the "sacred" (what we have identified as the spectral throughout this book) has been eroded to where rites simply become packaged consumer events (Thanksgiving, Christmas). Death, in particular, has been shed of its mystery, as funeral rites are commercially packaged. As their name indicates, professional undertakers "undertake" the grief and burden from the family that used to help the healing processes of physically burying their loved ones. Now a symbolic scoop of dirt over the grave is enough.

These are examples of postemotional effects that are mistakenly identified as forms of "media desensitization," which elicit forms of passive inactivity and depression where there seems to be no need to engage with the political RL of the outside world to change it. Yet, the appearance is that we are frenetically engaged with RL through the aesthetic overkill, which comes with video games, telebanking, video gambling machines, participation in reality television shows, Internet shopping, and so on. More and more of our daily activity is given over to the telematic capabilities of "smart" machines. I can escape into my fantasy world where I do not need to engage the Other. Action games can become boring if they are not continually challenged and updated, the saga must change, new figures must be added, and new skills and challenges required. The question of computer games addiction illustrates perfectly the profile of obsessional behavior. It is the complete abandonment by the player to the demands of the game—exploring the complex environments, becoming better and better at selecting and using weaponry, obtaining more credit and power to last longer in the game, finding secret talisman and portals to discover new routes—which enables an escape of having to face the desire that is pressing on the teen by parents, school, peers (what we have designated as the Symbolic Order). Isn't that precisely the dilemma of youth today—the anxiety of not knowing where they exactly belong in the Symbolic Order because of the over-choice and uncertainty that exists? There are no assurances that a university degree will provide a well-paying position. Bill Gates, for example, is touted as a college dropout to show that all one needs its entrepreneurial savvy to "sell" one's talents. Add to this part-time work to make ends meet, employment uncertainty, and the possibility of losing the job one has, with the additional pressure to continually upgrade job skills, the increase of youth depression in postindustrialized countries should not be surprising. According to a report in Statistics

Canada (Allen et al. 2003), it takes approximately between seven to nine years after a teen graduates from high school to settle into his/her first position. Only 13–15 percent of youth finish university degrees.

The shadow side of intersubjectivity is interpassivity, the giving over of ourselves to the computerized programs to do our biding (Pfaller 2000, 2002). This is a subjective *decenterment* that purges us of our innermost emotions. For example, each time a book (or article) is Xeroxed the machine has interpassively "read" it for you. A bibliomane is now pacified for having acquired it. Now, it needn't be read. (The same applies to a videomanic's need to tape movies and shows.) Data banks of the information age are the largest interpassive reservoirs of all—the computer has already "thought" for you. Technology, in this view, begins to paradoxically take over our emotional and intellectual life for us through our own willing investment in a machine's capacity to act as a prosthetic *substitute* for our body and our emotions. A spaceship and the spacesuit would be the apotheosis of such interpassive logic when it comes to the body. As environments that are technically controlled actively from within, they externalize and maintain the astronaut's body. Other examples would include electronic massage units that are supposed to make us more fit by passively lying around while electric currents twitch the muscles; expensive limousines where the road is no longer felt, the car now becomes an enclosed insular environment, climatically controlled with a complete entertainment system; the increasing sophistication of wheel chairs and complete computerized mobilized environments for sufferes of Lou Gehrig's Disease (ALS) like Steven Hawkings and, no doubt, "smart" machinery for the disabled that will enable paraplegics to walk again, the dream of Christopher Reeve.

More mundanely, the "emotional prosthetic" is now carried out by the telematic revolution in television, especially "reality television" and video games. Television can continue to laugh for us (canned laughter on TV), work out our stresses as we watch an event (televised wrestling and boxing), help us deal with our intimate sorrow and suffering (televised soap operas and melodramas), get our kicks from seeing criminals and junkies arrested (reality cop shows), live out our athletic hopes (televised sport), our sexual desires, and frustrations (pornography), vote off or on our favorite or most despite character on a reality talent or game show, and on it goes. Interactivity carries this double meaning: on the one hand it means being actively engaged through an interface with a computer program, and on the other hand there is a certain passivity that comes about as an avatar (agent) does the act for you. Interactivity harbors within it a paradox—the immobilization of the body. The body, on one level, is reduced to a machine giving signals to another machine to do the work. In action video games, in particular, frenetic activity is involved. Yet, there is a certain giving oneself over to the computerized program.

Interpassivity is strikingly illustrated by the Japanese Tamagotchi toy. Which means "cute little egg," a mechanized virtual pet, a small round object with a screen that continually imposes demands on its owner, usually a child (Žižek 1999a, 106–110). When it beeps, the child must look on its screen to see what it wants. Must it be fed? Does it want to go to sleep? Does it need a "hug"? Pressing the right buttons satisfies its demands. A Godzilla version of the Tamagotchi had to be "fed" so that it would grow and mature. If its owner pressed the right buttons it "grew." Over the years its demand sequence would change. The Tamagotchi as Žižek explains, bred a number of virtual murders as children became frustrated having to cater to it incessant beeps. The earlier models possessed only one life; if neglected it died causing children to be heartbroken and mourning for its loss. Apparently, even Tamagotchi cemeteries appeared. The latter models installed a reset button to avoid the painful experience. Žižek makes the point that these toys did not resemble a "pet" as such; rather it was a symbolic object that worked on an exchange of signals. It was always in "control," beeping when it seemed to please. Like the big Other of the *Majestic* game, it had become the authority that regulated the lines of many children by its arbitrariness.

Action video games function on the interpassive level like Westernized Tamagotchis. They stage the game for an obsessional neurotic through addictive replaying so as not to confront the "real" (RL) world with all its contingencies. No need to have a "real" pet, a mechanical substitute will do; no need to confront "real" violence, simulated violence is just as well. Like the Tamagotchi, *Counter Strike, Doom,* or any other Ego game becomes a way to immerse and bathe the ego into its imaginary world so that the Other's desire is not faced. Parental authority is mitigated. At what point then does the sublimation of violence, which we have argued is a positive development, turn into its ugly opposite of addictive jouissance? Console-players become very upset when parents or figures of authority such as teachers unplug their game. Their narcissistic satisfaction is cut off, the repetitive action that assures jouissance is no longer available; the drives are not satisfied. These are games of interpassivity, games of addiction in the sense that they are the console-subject's *objet a*. The obsessional neurotic as addicted game player reduces the world to the function of *objet a* with which s/he can play games and have a passionate encounter. The game itself, like a Tamagotchi toy, has no desire, it only issues demands. Desire manifests itself only when a community of game players comes together, like *Counter Strike* tournaments where clans compete with one another. The desire to win the tournament, however, is not confirmed by the Symbolic Order; it is not done for parent's gaze (mostly moms) who bring the players (almost exclusively boyz) to these games, rather winning is for the community of peers, the boyz who have come to play. The prize money, a sign of purchasing power in RL, is minimal. To win as a clan is to declare a sense of perverse self-authorization, like establishing a clan in the virtual city of Neocron.

In 2001, Peter Molyneux came out with a new game called *Black & White*, which simply pales the original Tamagotchi in its implications for the interpassive subject. The interactivity of the game consists in a unique never-before available mouse interface. The game is completely mouse driven with no on-screen menus; the entire game can be controlled by the way the player scrolls the landscape by moving an on-screen "Hand" (which looks like an actual hand). A "spell" can be cast by creating a specific pattern on-screen with this Hand (a rectangular box painted with the mouse, e.g., summons up the fire spell). Different designs produce different spells. To begin with, the player is given a utopian world in complete harmony, a mythical Eden-like place where everything is in balance. The player receives power from Smurf-like citizens who inhabit this world at various citadels (environments). The way the console-player "Handles" them (excuse our pun) is entirely left open. There are no right and wrong rules to follow. We are back to the mythical staging of free and open choice. The Tamagotchi element is introduced early in the game where the player must go into the forests of the world and chose a crea-ture to bring back to the village (a cow, an ape, and a tiger) which is then let loose in the perfect world. This creature, in effect, becomes the player's alter ego—a sophisticated Tamagotchi. The Hand has to control the creature's actions on the villagers. There are no right or wrong answers as to what this creature does; an ape may eat a villager, but then the player's Hand has to decide what to do about it: to let the villager go, or let the ape eat the Smurf. The roving Hand, in effect, enables a player to play "god"; to become respon-sible for the acts of creation in the sense that this utopian world changes its fantasy space to become either darker—more Evil, or lighter, and brighter—more Good. The villagers even bow to the Hand thanking it for the "mercy" (the Good) it has done (performed a rescue or grown crops, for instance), bringing together a complicated confusion of moral and ethical choices. When the environment morphs by growing darker because evil has been chosen, the alter ego creature dynamically changes its size and shape as well.

The implications for "acting out" rather than "acting through" ego impulses are staggering. The game externalizes ethics as a dichotomous choice between good and evil, rather than the complicated dialectics between them. This fundamental tension is overlaid by a moral choice of either good or bad reinforced by the homage the Smurf-like creatures give to the player's magical Hand making its title *Black & White* a rather sardonic and ironic statement on RL. The game may have been inspired by Vincent Ward's film *What Dreams May Come* (1998), a magical realist film starring Robin Williams as Chris Nielson. After dying with his two children in a car accident, Nielson finds himself in "heaven" trying to reach his wife Annie (Annabella Sciorra), who lies in a state of purgatory (comma) after an attempted suicide, unable to bare the loss of her family. This impossible sce-nario is staged in the unconscious represented by Heaven and Hell, each of which are appropriately created through an artwork that Annie paints as she falls into a depression and eventual suicide. It is a journey by Nielson into the unconscious to release the "signifier" that holds her in bondage to this depression, raising the question of traumatic loss in a profound way. The landscape changes from dark to light as Nielson sojourns through the imag-inary words of the unconscious struggling to "reach" his wife.

Of course no direct comparison can be made between this game and the film, which we suspect are related in Molyneux's unconscious in some way, apart from the uncanny similarity in their magical realist overtones. However, they dramatically illustrate the distance between an "acting out" in the video game world, and an "acting through" in this particular film narrative, which tries to come to terms with an ethics of the Real. The linearity of time has been warped to provide the audience with the complications of loss and memory that an aesthetic of magical realism can effectively explore. What we have in *Black & White* instead is the reduction of the power of magical realism to explore the haunts of the unconscious to the surface effects of the ego in its interpassive states. In this case the "creature-like" forms it takes on as a dumb ape, a crouching tiger, and languid cow by a Hand that really does not "know" what it is doing, and will continue not to "know" when the screen turns all-Black, or all-White canceling out their difference. Only then can knowing (as *savoir*) begin, and an ethics of the Real confronted.

Are Video Games Perverse Acts?

Another way of answering why the proliferation of violent video games is to see this as a direct link to the loss of authority, of faith in the Symbolic Order. Playing violent games has become a way of staging a perversion to set limits on jouissance, for boyz to stage their own castration. This is the positive aspect Jones (2002) found when defending violent video games discussed earlier. Perversion belongs between psychosis and neurosis; the first is a foreclosure of the Law, the second is an integration into the Law. The pervert's response to the loss of Law (authority) is to establish the Law inversely. The desire is for the Law itself, for its castrating effects. Being "killed" in a VR computer game stages such a perversion, a form of jouissance. This is a masochistic form of play in its obsession. A masochist locates enjoyment in the very agency of the Law that prohibits the access to enjoyment. Since the Law for the teen player has not been fully established (the Law is his lost object) the teenage boy supplements this lack with an intricate set of regulations. Action computer games are the perfect ersatz Law. *They operate on precise rules of possibility.* The internal rules that do not guarantee an easy outcome are what make it so "punishingly" enjoyable. In a perverse way, these games establish a castrating Law that a neoliberal society and the parenting that goes with it have abandoned. The jouissance of constantly "losing" until one becomes better at a game should not go underestimated in establishing an ersatz Law: a respect for the game.

Violent action games seem transgressive, but the irony is that this transgression establishes the missing Law, it calls it back into play. In a time of ultimate and oppressive freedom where sons compete with their fathers for job and space, where mothers compete with their daughters to stay forever young, there is a strong disavowal by parents that the kids require directionality that doesn't simply recall tradition or religious orthodoxy. The most profound danger in this evasion can hold dire consequences as a regression into the pre-symbolic psychosis where paternal authority (Name-of-the-Father) is "foreclosed." Psychosis is characterized by the paradox of overproximity and externality. The externality occurs by the subject not engaging in the Symbolic Order. Words become things as opposed to "normal" speech where a gap between word and things enables sense making to occur. Language is thus devoid of a performative engagement with authority. There is no trust in the Other, no need to be obliged to another subject. This externalization of language now becomes overproximate in the sense that language takes a life of its own. Voices are heard inside the head telling the subject what to do. We have tried to make the point that there is no definitive link between violent video games and psychotic breakdowns, in fact, playing such games may have simply delayed rather than abetted the killing sprees at Columbine High School. But this doesn't mitigate that eventually a psychotic break did occur: VR and RL collapsed into one another.[2]

Thinking an Unpleasant Thought

The hypothesis that has haunted the last chapters of this section of the book goes something like this: we live in a postmodern culture, of which America is the paradigm case, where increasingly ambiguity and ambivalence are celebrated as social virtues. Demystifying, debunking, decentering, deconstructing, and questioning reality are the order of the day. The trust and faith in the grand narratives of modernity, as Lyotard (1984) had signaled, has waned as the promises of modernity have failed to emerge. This has resulted in a mistrust in authority of the Symbolic Order in general. The dangers of terrorism, totalitarianism, and right-wing nationalism threaten to play into this public fear of an acephalic state of affairs where conspiracy theories and paranoia have found a new breeding ground. The emergence of telematic technologies have enabled a way to creatively explore the anxieties that have emerged in the consumer societies of late global capitalism. At the same time these same technologies have enabled a poststructuralist subject to emerge, which treats identity as if it were a construct. The old nationalist identity no longer serves the purposes of capitalism, rather a global capitalism requires an identity that is flexible and multifaceted, able to consume more. Such a poststructuralist identity is characterized by a disavowal of emotional involvement in the Symbolic Order itself. In the United States the percentage of young people who vote is considerably low, and there is a prevailing cynicism that clouds the political landscape (Bewes 1997).

Such a disavowal is directly manifested through the simulacra created in cyberspace made possible by computerized digitalization. We decenter, exteriorize, and transfer our emotional life over to the "screen" as a package of *both* spectacular surface effects and as banal anaesthetized effects: video games and "reality TV" being the exemplary genres. More and more of our emotional life is given over to the screen willingly, enabling the machine to "enjoy" for us as we actively interact with it. In turn, we are supposed to feel relieved and satisfied. In Lacanian terms, the bodily *affects* of the unconscious core self—which constitutes the *depth* of the Self as *Je*—identified as the psychic Real, are displaced by the virtual reality of *effects*, as the *surface* of the ego (*Moi*). This is where "scientific" research takes pride in its search, focusing on the me-*moi*-ego rather than the Self-*Je*-psyche, on conscious recognition rather than the ego's unconscious desire and misrecogniton. Emotions are not felt "on the body," rather they become exteriorized virtual representations (simulacra). To "truly" feel youth, in particular, resort to acts of pain: self-mutilation (tattooing, piercing), sadomasochistic practices, and other extreme sublime experiences often related to sport where the death drive is near at hand. The extremes of anorexia and obesity seem to be the other bodily reactions to this "postemotional" state as Meštrović theorizes it, homologous to the "weightlessness" of the astronaut lost in (cyber)space and the fecundity of the Earth as the Goddess Gaia, a holistic system of checks and balances where nondegradable energy seems to be increasing to chaotic proportions. Will the system "explode" like the bad joke of the fat man eating too much, or will negentropy stave off its collapse and transform the system? This is the ecological anxiety of the age.

Because of the easy access to "enjoy" narcissistic consumption through VR imaginary play, it seems that the only way to "feel"—to gain access to the pain of existence—is to cut the body, mutilate it through tattooing, piercing, and razor slashing. The neoliberalization of consumerism to stylize your own individual narcissistic self, together with the possibility of being whoever you want to be in VR communities and chat lines, has resulted in the reduction of jouissance to the level of the body Real (Žižek 1999b, 372), while the externalization of excessive jouissance as a way to purge the ego of its aggressivity has been sublimated through the playing of violent video games.

The shock of a social realist film like Fernando Meirelles's *Cidade de Deus* (City of God) (2002), starkly shows RL violence of the children surviving in the slum housing project built on the outskirts of Rio de Janeiro in the 1960s. By the 1980s, nihilism and the cheapness of life have become standard fare, hope virtually nonexistent, with sadism the only way to fortify the ego. The redemption of "Rocket," a poor black youth too frail and scared to become an outlaw, is staged by substituting a camera for a gun to eventually become a journalist. The sublimation of violence through the camera lens is what gives him enough distance to find his way out of such hopelessness. The irony is that Rocket's redemption is achieved on the voyeurism of violent pictures that he sells to the newspaper because their own journalists are unable to enter the housing project. While he is an eyewitness to police corruption, extortion, and the brutality of gang warfare, the pictures he takes become simulacra once they are reproduced in the newspapers, little more than a way for the well-off to shake their heads at the tragedy that is taking place. Li'l Zé, the gang's sadistic and psychopathic leader is only interested that he gets his 15 minutes of fame by appearing on the front page of the newspapers.[3] The conversion of RL violence to VR violence through the camera lens in this context differs only in degree and not in kind from the "authenticity" of gangsta rap or a Bennetton advertisement. VR violent videos take this a step further by simulating "authenticity" to turn it into an ironic game. Rocket's photos become the basis for a violent video game called "The City of God" where the console-player becomes Li'l Zé who has to kill his gangster competitors in order to control all of the city's drug trades. Points are given for each gang member killed so that more powerful guns can be bought. If the console-player is able to conquer this environment, he can proceed onto the next level. Violence has been sublimated but also perverted. It has become once removed from tourist slumming where guides take the well-off to "visit" these housing units in protective buses to "talk" to the inhabitants.

The paradoxes that emerge in this mind–body split repeat themselves in the strange interstitial and fractal spaces of the in-between, as the boundary between inside and outside is constantly slipping or transgressing. Public/private is one such obvious site of this slippage; the colonization of private space by a continual invasion of surveillance to an Orwellian point where it has been suggested that we all can be traced through an electronic implant no matter where we are in the world. This is supposed to make the world "safer." The paradox of the individual/group seems to be another. The post-structuralist subject is supposed to be flexible, willing to adapt to job conditions rather than develop a lifetime career. Neoliberalism, informed by a capitalist economy, stresses individual rights, excellence, and competition within the pretense of group solidarity and democratic liberalism. (The reality television series *Survivor* illustrates this admirably.) The conflict results in divided loyalties, in a "culture of complaint" or indignation (Huges 1993) where victimization is foregrounded, litigation and suing the order of the day, political correctness (PC) and self-acclaimed guardians of morality abound, all in the name of "civilization" and the elimination of poverty, violence, and racism.

The ugly shadow underbelly of such a civilized society exemplified by "good Christian family values" continues to thrive, as so perceptively shown in the hit television series *Sopranos*. The family's name and its upper middle-class existence suggest harmony and happiness, a high note with associations to the ethereal-sublime voice of a church choir and the Catholic Church, which Carmela Soprano so deeply respects. But their sounds are much more grotesque and ugly, interrupted throughout by Tony's rage and racism, and clandestine Mafia dealings that Carmela continuously disavows. His seemingly mellow voice and dopey loveable style, especially around Carmela and his two children, Meadow and Anthony, Jr., are a frail cover-up for what he refuses to face—his own aggressive violence. When the two worlds collide, his home life and his crime life, Tony suffers from dizzy spells and faints, unable to psychically "work through" with his analyst, Dr. Melfi. The scheming vengeance of his elderly (now-deceased) mother and Uncle Toni and the haunt of the brutal ugliness of his own Mafioso dead father whom he has now become haunts Tony's unconscious. Family abuse, and the emergence of unrestrained jouissance are the disavowed side of American life. Nowhere are such anxieties expressed better than through the fantasies on primetime television which we explore in a forthcoming book on television.[4]

?

CONCLUSION

?

"ARE THE KIDS ALRIGHT?"

14

"ARE THE KIDS ALRIGHT?"

FEEDING ON THE TRANSCENDENCE OF YOUTH

The Romantic cult of youth and childhood that we discussed in the opening chapters is loaded with a vitalist rhetoric where children are the unique embodiment of the life force of Nature (*zoë*) upon which the human imagination is believed to depend upon. Metaphorically, they are the phantasmatic and fecund energy that potentially animates all persons regardless of their chronological age. Youth, from this perspective, mediate lived experience and transcendence. The capitalist construction of "youth" since its inception in the eighteenth century has become a fetishized substance—an ephemeral disembodied principle of resiliency and renewal. Postmodern forms of neo-Romanticism now displace the child with postadolescent youth, and place them in a similar position as an objet (*objet a*)—either too far away (remote and transcendent) or too close (too proximate and monstrous) to attain. Youthfulness is charged with a numinosity that is denied its authority, which usually comes with such quasi-religious objects of transcendence. More often, youth fall within the ambiguous constructions of adult desire like the case of JonBenet, or Calvin Klein's homoerotic exploitations of youthful eroticism—the teen porn underworld of underwear for the market. They are even characterized as screenagers, "a species in mutation," which is equated with the progress of technology that keeps adults young. As youthful cyborgs, screenagers exhibit the psychic prosthesis of openness, creativity, flexibility, and curiosity. Without this adults would fall into stagnation, decline, decay, and death—or, so it argued by Rushkoff (1996).[1]

This transcendence of youthful desire since its inception in the eighteenth century, has been best exemplified in our study by the machinery of designer capitalism. It extracts talent (*zoë*) for itself and presents it as packaged virginity or packaged spiritualism (*bios*): the boys groups ("new Castrati") and "chaste naughty virgins" of the pop charts, with the King of Pop, Michael Jackson as Peter Pan playing with his (artificially fathered) children in Neverland.[2] There is now a "Michael Jackson Baby Drop" on-line free software game to commemorate Jackson's baby waving incident in Berlin where he dangerously held his nine-month-old son Prince Michael II over the railing from the third floor of his apartment hotel. In the game, Jackson's avatar holds a baby from the roof of a building and drops it. The player has to place a basket under the baby before it hits the ground to score points. Jackson is suing for defamation MadBlast.com, which specializes in ironic spoofs on stars.

Romantic transcendent talent has eventually produced its own inverted monsters like Jackson, who try to exemplify its eternal youthful ideals as permanent childlike vitality unencumbered by biological destiny. Such a search can only end up tragically like the figure of Nick Nolte. His obsession to remain youthful included vampire-like blood transfusions, injections, and drugs; eventually he was arrested for driving under the influence of drugs, and placed on a three-year probation with counseling. Youthful talent also seems to be sucked up by Sunrise Industries in Silicon Valley. Small start-up firms become commodities to be bought and sold by venture-capital economy (Harrison 1994). "In Silicon Valley youth are not served so much as served on a platter, its energy and vitality consumed by vested interests" (Latham 2002, 165). For every Internet entrepreneur who strikes it rich in Silicon Valley there is a host of young people who act as the support staff. As programmers, telemarketers, website designers, and chat-room monitors, their outlook is far less rosy. The creative exploitation of engineers and programmers is conducted through flexible time, which actually exhausts and drains youthful energy, rather than making life more humane. It is not uncommon for youthful employees to pull off all-nighters in labs, or at computer centers to meet consumer deadlines (Lessard and Baldwin 2000). The third generation of hackers has been appropriated by the computer game industries as designers and programmers, once again transforming youthful play into alienated labor (Latham 2002, 191–192).

The height of Romantic paranoia was reached on December 26, 2002 with the announcement by CLONAID that the world's first clone baby has been born under the directorship of 46-year-old Dr. Brigitte Boisselier, a bishop in the movement. Many scientists remain skeptical and the proof has yet to be established. With cloning, death can be eliminated. Appropriately called Eve, the baby was born to an infertile couple in an undisclosed location. CLONAID scientists are now working on the next generation of clone babies for people carrying the HIV virus. People with AIDS will be able to have their own genetic offspring without any risk of passing the disease onto their children. The company was founded in 1997 by Raël, the leader of the Raelian Movement, an international religious organization, which claims that life on Earth was created scientifically through DNA and genetic engineering by human extraterrestrial race whose name Elohim, is found in the Hebrew Bible. According to the website, this was mistranslated by the word "God." The Raelian Movement claims that Jesus was resurrected through an advanced cloning technique performed by the Elohim. When compared to this, the television narratives of *The X-Files* and *Buffy* don't seem to be that far removed! Raël believes that the Elohim are 25,000 years ahead of us.

CLONAID eventually will be able to clone an adult person without having to go through the growth process, and then transfer memory and personality into this cloned being, the promise of eternal life will be had. This sounds like it came right out of Geoff Murphy's sci-fi thriller *Freejack* (1992). In the future, healthy virile bodies are needed to "jack-in" the memory and personality of aging, rich corporate executives who are ill or dying. Victor Vasendak's (played by Mike Jagger—now there's an irony) crack science team is able to snatch young bodies from the past just before they fatally die, and then bring them into the future for the transplant. Seems like Raël believes that he will have already solved the body problem!

Monstrous Child

In the early 1990s the two Disney films, Joe Johnson's *Honey, I Shrank the Kids* (1989) and its sequel, Randel Kleiser's *Honey, I Blew up the Kid* (1992) were symptomatic manifestations of a general societal guilt felt from the breakdown of the modern family structure. These were warning fantasies to parents everywhere (most often from a moral Right) not to neglect or abandon their children. Rick Moranis played Wayne Szalinski, the somewhat *ex*-centric nerdy inventor, whose technology does the dastardly deed—at first a laser-like machine shrinks his kids to a point of invisibility, and then blows one of them up to gigantic proportions. These two films illustrate the postmodern anxiety that youth has wrought. As strange as this may seem, parents no longer desire their children as they once did. In Hong Kong, the first house to shelter *men* from domestic violence has been founded in the New Millennium. When the object-cause of desire is no longer lacking, but has come too close, we lose the lack itself when desire inverts into its monstrous opposite. Isn't this what has happened? We fail to "see" our children, and when we finally do, they are the monsters we never expected. The invisibility of youth in the home is well illustrated by Buffy's mother Janet who simply has no clue what her daughter is up to, for two entire seasons of the series, apart from always getting into trouble. When she finally discovers that Buffy is a "slayer," she becomes hysterical. Her daughter has become a monster she never knew. The two movies illustrate that parents are unable to "attain" their children; that their children can only be approximated, but always missed as *objet a*. To do otherwise is to pervert their growth—prevent their success in finding their own way. But what if we unconsciously desire that they disappear? When they don't leave home, they become the monsters in it?

When youth become too close and proximate as an object of anxiety, they begin to threaten adult sensibilities, especially their identity. The post-Oedipal landscape of boys/boyz/bois and girls/gurlz/grrrls is such a threat. This has happened in the workplace and in the entertainment industry as a competition for jobs intensifies, and their monstrosity begins to appear. The traffic between reality and the transcendence promised to them by a Romantic vision begins to flourish in quite unexpected ways, especially through fairy tales and folklore to the horror of parents (and the Church). A Gothic side emerges. *Harry Potter* has now become an uncontrollable and unexplainable phenomenon. Wicca witchcraft and rituals by teenage girls appear "everywhere" it seems in literature and television: The three Helliwell sisters in *Charmed*, movies like

The Craft, the girlish *Sabrina, the Teenage Witch*. Books on witchery and witchcraft have become best-sellers. Like the *Potter* series, these all seem to be ways to contain the post-Oedipal fallout by taking the more threatening edge off by clearly drawing boundaries separating good and evil where morality is easily defined—unlike *Buffy*.[3]

The underbelly of Romanticism was its Gothic dark side that tried to ruin the transcendental myth of youth, and now this ruination has returned in its "post" forms. *Buffy*, for instance, presents the very deconstruction of Romantic notion of youth. As a neo-Gothic tale it inverts the usual Gothic narrative. It is adults who are the vampires. They are the ones who attempt to keep their youth and never die. In the very second episode ("Witch" 1002),[4] Mrs. Madison is a witch who switches bodies with her inept daughter in order to relive her glory days as a cheerleader. She steals her daughter's youth, and is in competition with her. The heroines in Gothic fictions were presented as virtuous, their goodness illuminated the "forces of darkness." They were hostages held by villains in the guise of father figures, relying on protection from paternal figures like brothers and suitors, trapped in castles and dungeons, and in their own bodies, unable to escape nor resist. Buffy, on the contrary, is presented as Dracula's equal ("Buffy vs. Dracula" 5001). In a single swoop, she is no longer the helpless heroine ready to be sexually "bitten."

BEATING THE CHILD—HARDER

The Romantic myth of transcendental youth is in ruins as children and youth become sources of fear, whether this is in the adult imagination or within the communities in which they dwell. Adults seem to be in a permanent state of moral panic and worry. Teenage sex in particular is their target (Levine 2002). A crisis has been reached as separate spheres between adult and youth have emerged—with an accompanying source of resentment. Youth have become the objects of adult anxieties and their rivals as is so evident today in the institutions of schooling, and in the media where the gulf between what is youthful and fresh and what is adult and outdated has grown as an in-between space of postadolescence, which remains confused. Youth are more likely to protest against free-trade agreements, globalization, ecological issues, and war than their Boomer parents (Klein 2000). Medieval witchcraft and magic through Goth music, television shows, and video games have become ways youth protect themselves from the vagaries of the adult world. A figure like Marilyn Manson has emerged an astute critic of the cynical attitude which persists amongst those adults who play the system for their own ends. As a grotesque antiheroic figure, Manson is the very antithesis of Michael Jackson: The King of Goth, perhaps.[5] Again we turn to *Buffy* in an episode called "Gingerbred" (3011) where Mothers Opposed to the Occult (MOO), headed by the chief witch persecutor Janet Summers are shown to be delusional, a product of a demonization that initiates moral panic. The

Goth world has become a way for a segment of youth to deal with their own psychic demons of depression and ennui when facing the Symbolic Order.

The tension between the transcendental and monstrous child has come to a collision course in post-Oedipalization, resulting in a schizophrenic policy toward youth. It teeters between the high anxiety of child protection advocates who panic that teens have gone to the devil; they must be saved from their corrupt music and culture. The fear and anger over losing control over their teenagers because they appear to be lazy or not doing well in school, especially by middle-class parents, leads to inordinate measures of punishment. Nowhere is this more apparent than the despicable practice of well-intentioned parents who send their teens to state-run or private boot camps to take part in "wilderness therapy" programs. The belief is that through tough love, fresh air, and strenuous exercise the rebellious child or teen will be straightened out. Instead the body count has risen to over 30 deaths since the 1990s when the popularity of these camps first began through suicide, accidental death, neglect of health, heart attacks, and in some cases starvation. The search is now to find a new euphemism to replace state-run military structured program as "boot camps," their reputation has been ruined despite their inevitable defenders. Hundreds of teens have been sent to such camps because they had experimented with drugs, committed petty thefts, were doing poorly in school, and defied their parents by not helping around the house with chores. The anxious monstrous object has, once more emerged and come too close; a death sentence had been pronounced upon "it." Even *The Sopranos* had an episode where Anthony Jr. was to go to a Military Academy. Fortunately he got very, very ill. We might call this particular strategy of conditioning teens "Reality Therapy" or "RL Therapy." It is surprising that some "young and bright" television executive hasn't suggested that a reality television series be made from an "actual" youth boot camp, rather producing the series *Boot Camp*. The philosophy that drives them is not any different than *Survivor*, except there is no monetary reward. The idea is to build self-esteem though physical prowess and survival skills, and to make the teenagers long to get back home to air-conditioning, ample food, and the other comforts of home.

A debate eventually emerged over the effectiveness of these camps. Despite the high recidivism rate among participants in boot camps, the belief still remains that they are effective *if* proper *aftercare* is given upon release, much like the enthusiastic advocates of reality television think as well. This forms a perfect economic circuit. Both the boot camp and the health-providing agency receive mutually beneficial advertising, the sort that has the public's sympathy. In the meantime, the kids are shuttled from one institution to the next to be doubly cured, so to speak. The concept of private boot camps and strict private schooling is unlikely to fade in the future given there is now even fewer life chances to be had for youth who have few life skills. The belief that discipline and responsibility could be achieved through rigid regimentation has had a long history, which Foucault's excellent study *Discipline and Punish* (1979) articulated. It is education as indoctrination that stresses basic training and skill acquisition, utilizing the same mechanisms as the army and the penitentiary system. The process deconstructs the individual's sense of self as undisciplined, illiterate, and out-of-control, while simultaneously reconstructing the individual in accordance with the values of efficiency and obedience to authority. The removal of inaptitude, disobedience, and inefficiency are the values to be instituted. Inspections, obeying orders (rules), punctual movement of students to save time, ceremony (to establish loyalty to the school institution), and a clear hierarchical chain of command are the classical behavioral modification tactics found in boot camps. There is a growing educational movement by conservative America to go back to these "traditional" methods that were instituted in schools by adopting a Taylorist principle of efficiency at the turn of the twentieth century.[6]

Skin-Ego Protection: The Enfolded Spaces of Youth

Designer capitalism has territorialized almost everything in sight as the only game in town. Its consumerist offerings present the bald and exposed aesthetics of addiction. There is no need any longer to pretend otherwise as Dior's new perfume fragrance, Dior Addict illustrates. We need to "Admit it," says the caption next to the bottle. There are a number of ways in which such territorialized capitalist space has been be invaded and evaded by youth.[7] These strategies require a different way of looking; such a perception only emerges when the viewer learns to perceive differently—for most adults this is not worth the effort. In an advertisement for the fragrance ISAbella [encrypted: It's beautiful], Isabella Rossalini lies on a red carpeted floor wearing a black dress with her back exposed. Behind her is a mirror and we see her bare back reflected in it. Written on her skin is "Seek the invisible," which appears written backward in the mirror. It is this "invisible" injunction of the fragrance's *objet a* that the youth have encrypted for themselves. Like Rembrandt whose notebooks were written in mirror writing so that the Church's gaze could be evaded as he explored questions of nature that were heretical to its doctrine, so have the most critical element of youth done the same. Or, at least we think so. The following points adumbrate positions that can be found in the next two books on music and television.

The first way has been to be lost in cyberspace. These take a number of forms. We have mentioned the Internet where civic-minded and activist websites remain anonymous, not advertising their whereabouts loudly through flashy home pages. Although they get found out, it is more by private e-mailings and e-e contacts. To avoid being Goooooogled, youth will take the skewed spelling of words to avoid being found easily. The grrrl revolution used this one. On the Net one will find many ways of spelling the standard /girl/ and /boy/. Equally successful has been the obsessional escape through computer games where parental supervision is wanting. We have mentioned the two sides to this: the positive benefits of sublimating violence and the fall into obsessive addictive behaviors.

A second way has been to develop a narrative form that is an open text, almost meaningless when viewed by single episodes. Any one episode appears fluffy, somewhat empty of content and substance. Some, of course, are more gripping than others. *Buffy, The Vampire Slayer* is a primary example here. An effort must be made to enter into its text, but with its pun(k) style[8] it requires some work to stay with it before the Buffyverse emerges. Perhaps it will remain unique in its presentment as an empty form—a unique *psychotic structure* in our view. The *X-Files* on the other hand, provides an enclave space of *resistant paranoia*.[9] It provides such a startling juxtaposition between "weird" and legitimated science that its fantasy structures offer a unique way to distrust expert authority, yet opens the door to entertaining the uniqueness of the unexplainable Real, which is always with us.

In our cyberspace section we mentioned the unique development of grrrl figures that appear in video game narratives, which provide cross-identifications for male and females alike. To preview our second companion book, *Musical Fantasies of Youth Cultures*, these grrrl cultures form one discourse of several other postfeminist developments. In the musical fantasies book we develop the "girl" and "gurl" discourses that complement and problematize post-feminism in other more complex ways, especially in the music scene. In a nutshell, another way of youth protection has been the various ways the signifier of "virginity" and being a "slut" have been played with on the post-Oedipal landscape. From using virginity as a pretense to "enjoying" one's body as do the "dirty virgins" in the pop music industry, to an attempt at stealing virginity "back" from patriarchy and claim ownership over by playing the "abstinence card." The whore, ho, and slut have also been used to turn the signifier around as a grrrl and "fly girl" complaint that specifically addresses the continued degradation of women.

A fourth way, undoubtedly has been the music video revolution. Again to preview our companion book, the best music videos are so cleverly encrypted that they generally pass undetected by the adult gaze. They also seem like a form of non-sense, which requires time to grasp. Lyrics need to be downloaded, the super-narrative of the band's message has to be understood, and the intertextual quotes that refer to previous songs, CDs, and groups caught. This is a daunting task. The video is the new postmodern hieroglyph that can only be "read" by knowing that keys can open up its meanings. The very best are dense corticalizations, compressed associations, and imploded meanings that fan(addicts) can play again and again for full satisfaction.

A fifth way that we have lightly mentioned now and again throughout the video game revolution is the way youth have begun to explore their identities through a "schizophrenic mirrored self," alter-ego projection exteriorized in the mirror. This is a form of self-protection as well. This practice is much more prevalent in the music industry, again developed more fully in the exploration of musical fantasies. The alter egos created by rap musicians like Eminem and the split screen of the mirror by artists like Pink are ways youth are talking to themselves and others. In this development, actual masks are not worn but dealt with on the Imaginary mirror. They are able to directly address the struggles within their psyches by reworking and replacing the signifiers that define their inner cathected Other, so as to be able to deal with authority figures in their own terms, especially the institutional authorities like school, family, and the state.

A sixth way complements the range of postfeminism that has developed in postmasculinity—boys/boyz/bois. To once more preview what has been developed in the music scene, we develop the way Punk Rock and Nü Metal attempt to address the destructive dystopian and apocalyptic anxieties of the Symbolic Order through Goth themes: the clever social commentary of KoRn videos, for instance, with their direct address to familial struggles, homophobia, and the abandonment of fathers and the suffocation of their mothers. The dream of Techno music as a universal rebirth is a more ambitious strategy that we explore. It is an escape into the primal *Klang* of an *in utero* experience, a protectionist fantasy of draping the Earth with a blanket of peace and harmony that is quite at odds with global capitalism. Finally, even the transcendence of the new Castrati, the Boys Bands have given preadolescent teens a way to approach sexuality in somewhat of a protectionist manner.

With the decentralization of modernist "grand narratives," the idealized moral and existential frameworks that spiritually inspired people and helped organize their identities are being decentered. Capitalism remains the only game in town and neoliberalism the only philosophy that supports it (see Sennett 1998). Youth are faced with searching for social ties, a sense of identity and recognition. In the beginning of the Third Millennium *Star Wars*, *Lord of the Rings*, and *Harry Potter* have all become megahits; yet these are male narratives in desperate search for the fantasy of a new Master Narrative that can globally unite differences. In a time where Christian and Islamic ideologies seems to be dividing the globe recentering authority once again, let us keep the hope alive that other scenarios, more ecological and peaceful will present themselves. Our youth are trying, and so should we.

NOTES

INTRODUCTION: A ROAD MAP
OF WHAT'S TO COME

1. For a rather insightful and clever critical review of Žižek's major books see Terry Eagleton (2003) who remains steadfast in his wit and arm's distance stance to Žižek's brand of Lacanese, but very fair in his assessment only made possible by a critic with a very broad reading background in philosophy and literature.

2. A third book on television is now in progress, which includes chapters on reality television, *Buffy, the Vampire Slayer* and the *X-Files*. See jagodzinski (2003c) for a reading of reality television along with *The Truman Show*.

3. On the "ethics of the Real" see Zupančič (2000) and Jaanus (1997).

4. Music videos are given closer treatment in our accompanying book *Musical Fantasies of Youth Cultures* because of their short length, and their exemplary status as to the changes of perception that are taking place through digitalization and video.

5. For an attempt to grasp the idea of the Real in relation to pedagogy see jagodzinski (2002a).

6. This is our term for an array of emic research strategies: ethnography, endomethodology, thick description, participant observation, phenomenology, action research, and so on. The world is composed of two parts: "endo," which means "within," and "thegm," which is the Greek suffix for "speaking." Hence, endothegmatic research examines what is spoken from within.

7. We have decided to use this expression "s/he" as a way of getting around the she/he problematic.

8. The agalma in the Greek context referred to various types of objects, always precious, which were invested with magical powers that transferred over to whomever possessed them. The social significance of such power through possession is obvious. In transference what we "love" is what is "agalmic" because it gives us what we lack, but think the other has. An agalmic object is invested with "surplus value," like a fetishistic object. As discussed by Antonio Quinet, "The Agalma of Lacan," The Clinic on Transference: Jacques Lacan's Seminar VIII, Formations of the Clinic in the Lacanian Field, English-Language Seminar in Paris, June 26, 2003 as directed by Colette Soler.

9. The notion of the *sinthome* is developed more fully in relation to the fan(addict). See chapter 14 in *Musical Fantasies of Youth Cultures*. *Sinthome*, in a nutshell, refers to the singularity of the symptom of a person's fundamental fantasy. Should it become unraveled, the subject loses all firm ground of his or her Being.

10. This designation will be used throughout the body of the text. S stands for the Seminar, followed by the number and a shortened reference as to the seminar's

name. We shall also do this with Freud's work by referencing SE (Standard Edition) followed by the volume and the year of Freud's writing.

11. In *Musical Fantasies of Youth Cultures* we concentrate on the journals of Kurt Cobain, e.g., and Marilyn Manson's interviews, KoRn's media statements, Gangsta Rap lyrics, and so on.

12. See the interesting essay by Roberto Harari (2002) and the musings of Dragan Milovanivic (1997) for bringing together chaos theory with Lacanian topology.

13. For a full explication of fan(addiction) see *Musical Fantasies of Youth Cultures*, chapter 14.

14. The question of postfeminism finds its most important expression in the contemporary music scene where virginity becomes the contested signifier. See part III in *Musical Fantasies of Youth Cultures* where the concept of the "dirty virgin" and grrrl cultures are elaborated.

1 A HISTORICAL ANDENKEN: YOUTHFUL APPROPRIATIONS

1. Similarly, the cruel initiation rituals of clitoridectomy are to be understood in the same way. It's not that these traditional practices are attributable strictly to patriarchy; in some cultures that perform clitoridectomies the men are perceived as powerless with considerable authority invested in the hands of older women who perform these rituals. It is again being recognized by the culture's Symbolic Order so as to embrace tribal traditions. Women who forego this procedure refuse to recognize the way this big Other is said to be protecting their honor and showing its respect for them. By cutting away the clitoris and sewing up the vaginal lips the belief is that virginity is being preserved. The young girl's body is exoticized since men are now denied this special part of her body until marriage (Salecl 1998, 141–168).

2. This argument adumbrates our contention that libidinal "life" as identified by the Greek term *zoë*, distinguished from *bios* as Agamben (1998) maintains, refers to the forbidden surplus jouissance that must be forfeited as we enter the social order of language. We refer to *zoë* as "musical noise" in *Musical Fantasies of Youth Cultures* where we develop its transgressive implications.

2 OUR HYPOTHESIS: YOUTH FANTASIES LACANIAN STYLE

1. In chapter 11 of *Musical Fantasies of Youth Cultures* we argue that Michael Jackson and Avril Lavigne are simply two sides of the Peter Pan fantasy.

2. This concept shall be explained as we continue. For a complete account of the Real as applied to education see jagodzinski, 2002a. See also Edmond Wright (2001) and the very accessible read by Sara Kay on Žižek (2003) for grasping this allusive concept.

3. We ask that the reader be patient given that *das Ding* (The Thing) is yet another concept in Lacan's lexicon that appears strange when first encountered. We hope that by the end of the study its meaning will be grasped. Evans (1996) has written a useful dictionary cross-referencing Lacan's terms.

4. Luce Irigaray's criticisms of Lacan's phallocentrism are to be found throughout her oeuvre. See especially, 1985. Lacan's theorizations are descriptive and not

prescriptive, and hence we continue to find them fruitful in understanding the post-Oedipalized condition of postmodernity.

5. This superbaby fantasy of an immortal child is explored in Spielberg's film, *Artificial Intelligence* (2001), where 11-year-old David is sufficiently human enough not to be identified as yet another "mecha" to be sadistically tortured. He has an ever-ending love for his "mother," Monica, the woman who adopted him as a substitute for her real son, who remains in cryo-stasis, stricken by an incurable disease.

6. We have introduced this homology here only as a short-handed way to eventually show how these three homonyms refer to Lacan's three psychic registers: site for the Real; sight for the Imaginary, and cite for the Symbolic Order. We will italic the word in the homonym that is appropriate to the context, otherwise it will not appear italicized.

7. Winnicott's object relations theory (1971) is the best known, being especially strong in Great Britain where his theories and their derivatives have begun to infiltrate cultural studies as the text-reader theoretical venues explored by the Center for Contemporary Cultural Studies in Birmingham became exhausted and limited. Harrinton and Biebly (1995) have applied Winnicott's theories to soap fans. Silverstone (1994) has made use of Winnicott in his studies of television culture, and Hills (2002) has gone the furthest in an attempt to provide a general theory of fan culture by modifying Winnicott's core theory of play.

8. We have decided to leave it in its French spelling because of its nondefinable status and untranslatability. See Nobus (1998) for various authors who explore its development throughout Lacan's oeuvre.

9. The question of the self-esteem of young women is examined in chapter 11 Dilemma of Gurlz, *Musical Fantasies of Youth Cultures.*

3   A LACANIAN APPROACH TO MEDIA

1. On the phenomenon of piercing and tattooing in youth cultures written from a Lacanian perspective see, jagodzinski 2002c and 2003b.

2. On the difference between Judith Butler's poststructuralist position and Lacan's spit-subject, see Žižek (1999b, "Passionate (Dis)Attachments, or, Judith Butler as a Reader of Freud"), Tim Dean (2000), and Kay (2003, 92–100).

3. In brief, *sinthome* refers to the fundamental symptomatic fantasy that anchors us in "reality." Unraveling that fundamental fantasy leads to a pathology. Woman is the *sinthome* of man and vice versa. See Thruston (2002).

4. The Mark Chapman testimony can be found on-line: http://www.geocities.com/ SouthBeach/Keys/6624/chappy.html.

5. Lacan's earlier 1950s approach to language had this structuralist dimension about it. This analogy of the unconscious with language must be always interpreted as an open-system structuralism, and unique to each individual (see Dor 1997). Our speculations concerning linguistic traumatizations of the voice here rely on Boothby's own innovation. Lacan's rereading of Freud's grandson's fort/da game as a phonetic differentiation between "absence" as represented by the nonsense signifier "o-o-o" (in fort) when the reel is thrown out of the crib and out of sight, and "presence" as represented in the return of the reel as "a-a-a" (in da) identifies signification at the unconscious level with the play of the differential phonemes that now provide a linguistic mastery of the drives with a "string attached to them."

The closed circuit of meaning of the holophrastic a-o (absence-presence) would not have been possible without the string that was attached to the reel which provided the necessary means and agency to bring it back into sight.

6. The human vocal tract is capable of producing an amazing number of different speech sounds. The UCLA Phonological Segment Inventory Database (UPSID) recognizes 921 different speech sounds, 652 consonants, and 269 vowels found in 451 languages. Still, the number of speech sounds (phonemes) used by any individual language is quite limited. According to Maddieson (1984) the average lies between 20 and 37.

7. The example Žižek (1996a) uses is "the painfully low and uninterrupted trumpeting of the 'shofar,' a horn used in the Yom Kippur evening ritual which marks the end of the day of meditations" (149–150). Salecl (1998) argues in the *Odyssey* adventure the Sirens did *not* sing. They remained silent, meaning they refused to accept their symbolic castration.

4   IS KRONOS EATING OUR CHILDREN?
HISTORICAL FATHERS

1. The word "cult"—referring to secretive and "mysterious" religious beliefs and rituals—is a derivative of the "cultivation" of land, of cereals, and also "culture," which refers to spiritual and intellectual cultivation. Without the intervention of a "third term" between mother and child there would be no Culture.

2. U.S. Department of Health and Human Services in 1993 reported that more than half, and some say almost all of sexual abuse is visited upon children by their own family members or parental substitutes (Levine 2002, 28).

3. This was illustrated when the state of Oregon tried to pass Measure 9 in 2000, which would have targeted the gay and lesbian community of students as a threat to "normal" kids, not in need of the same protection. The measure was defeated.

4. Copjec (1999) raises Agamben within the context of her essay, but does so to dispute his thesis and reinstate Foucault and Walter Benjamin's analysis of biopower as establishing itself in the eighteenth century (esp. 248).

5. These questions are raised in response to Copjec's essay. On Aquarian New Ageism see Grasse (2002) as a representative.

6. Schiller (1996) provides the definitive statement of Romantic ideal of the child in 1795. "They are what we were; they are what we should once again become. We were nature just as they, and our culture, by means of reason and freedom, should lead us back to nature. They are, therefore, not only the representation of our lost childhood,...but they are also representations of our highest fulfillment in the ideal (85)."

7. See chapter 9, "The New Castrati: Men II Boys" in *Musical Fantasies of Youth Cultures*.

8. Copjec (1999, 245–248) criticizes Agamben for failing to inquire further into the biological definition of life. Contra to his thesis she restates Foucault and Walter Benjamin linking sovereign power with death over life with the medical gaze of the nineteenth century. This discrepancy does not directly dismiss our thesis.

9. The figure of Freud's *Nebenmensch* (neighbor) (see *Outline*, SE XXIII) as represented on "reality TV" is directly pertinent here. The neighbor is someone who we are suspicious of if s/he gets too close—becoming an anxious object and a threat. See jagodzinski (2003c).

5 THE CONTRADICTORY DEMANDS OF THE SUPEREGO: CONTEMPORARY FATHERS

1. The spirit of early capitalism meant that any idle time lead to disgrace of the subject. All forms of imaginary satisfaction like idle talk, having too much sleep, indulging in luxury were subject to moral condemnation. The shift from this productive mode of capitalism to a consumptive one now demands imaginary satisfaction.
2. In "Love Thy Neighbour? No, Thanks!" Žižek (1997a, 45–85) offers a number of political examples of the anxiety invoked by a neighbor's proximity that is manifested through racist acts of ethnic cleansing.
3. Meadow reminds her father when the two of then are looking at colleges and universities she might potentially attend that it's the 1990s. Tony retorts that at home it's still 1954, the days of *Father Knows Best*. HBO's original title for the series was to be "Family Man" (Gabbard 2002, 144).
4. In a bazaar situation where art imitates life and vice versa, Robert Iler who plays A.J. was arrested in 2001 along with three other youths in Manhattan's Upper East Side and charged with two counts of second-degree robbery and one count of marijuana possession.
5. According to George Pitcher (2002), spin-culture has heard its "death cry" as a new advocacy is setting in. In our opinion, this thesis sounds more like a time of recovery after too much image "bingeing."

6 THE LOSS OF SYMBOLIC AUTHORITY IN POSTMODERNITY

1. Lacan describes the drives as "montage" and "collage" (S XI, *Four Fundamentals*, 169) rather than machinic. They are more eclectic than mechanical or hydraulic. The difference is in the way Lacan treats the drives as registering negatively, aiming for both lack and signification. Even when they fail in their aim to find the object of satisfaction, the process itself is satisfying.
2. The Chief Justice was William Rehnquist, a staunch Republican appointed by Reagan. Sandra Day O'Connor was also a Reagan appointee looking to retire and wanting a Republican president to choose a conservative successor. Anthony Kennedy was also a Reagan appointee. Antonin Scalia, Clarence Thomas, and David Hackett Souter were all appointed by Bush. Republican Gerald Ford appointed John Paul Stevens. That left two democratic judges: Stephen Breyer and Ruth Bader Ginsburg.
3. Robbie Davis-Floyd and Joseph Dumit (1998) have edited a book, which explores the "cyborgification" of the child, and the way technology has now mechanized all aspects of the birthing process.
4. Jean François Lyotard (1988) made a distinction between litigation and a *différend*. In litigation the dispute could be judged and solved because both victim and perpetrator were on the "same page." They use the same language game when it came to the Law. In the case of a *différend* two incommensurate language games confront one another; e.g., an oil company wants to extract oil from land, which an indigenous tribe claims to be sacred. There is no way of negotiating these two idiolects. Justice Berger, e.g., in 1977 declared a ten-year moratorium on the McKenzie Valley Pipeline because the Metis and Alaskan Natives felt that the "carrying capacity" of the land would change, resulting in a major disruption in their way of life of hunting and trapping.

5. These statistics come from the U.S. based institute, Center for Mental Health Services (CMHS) reported in 1998. On-line: http://www.nmha.org/infoctr/factsheets/15.cfm.
6. Jackson's changing face is charted on-line: http://anomalies-unlimited.com/Jackson.html.
7. See chapter 13, "The New Virginity: The Nostalgic Return of the Veil,," in *Musical Fantasies of Youth Cultures* where we explore the way chastity and virginity have been approached by Catholic and Islamic young women who wear the *hejab* to create a space of their own by propping up the missing Oedipal Father. We discuss the writings of Wendy Shalit (1999) and Mary Pipher (1994).

7 MEDIA VIOLENCE AND YOUTH (YET AGAIN!?)

1. In response to a newspaper ad, 116 male students were paid $5.00 or 1-hour extra credit slip; the Milgram participants were paid $4.50 for an hour's work.
2. Doom II, it should be added, has two secret levels whose access is quite tricky. The episodes recreate the first and last levels of the first episode of *Wolfenstein 3D*. The id Software company makes both products. The setting is Nazi headquarters and the idea is to maximize the death of Nazi soldiers. The German version of Doom II lacked these two levels due to the ban on Nazi material. The graphics contained swastikas and giant portraits of Hitler.
3. As examples: *The Book of Virtues: A Treasury of Great Morals, The Moral Compass, Why We Fight: Moral Clarity and the War on Terrorism, The Children's Book of Heroes* (ed.), *The Educated Child: A Parent's Guide from Preschool Through Eighth Grade, The Children's Book of America, The Broken Hearth: Reversing the Moral Collapse of the American Family, The Death of Outrage: Bill Clinton and the Assault on American Ideals, Why We Flight: Moral Clarity and the War on Terrorism.*
4. See chapter 3, "The Perversions of Gangsta Rap: Death Drive and Violence," in *Musical Fantasies of Youth Cultures.*
5. Examples include: *Atlantic*'s cover, "Growing Up Scared" (Karl Zinsmeister, June, 1990); *Time*'s cover, "The Deadly Love Affair Between America's Youth and Firearms" (Jon D. Hull, "A Boy and His Gun," 1993); *Newsweek*'s cover, "Teen Violence: Wild in the Streets" (Barbara Kantrowitz, "Wild in the Streets," 1993); *Time*'s cover "Our Violent Kids" (Anastasia Toufexis, June, 1989); David Ansen's "The Kid's Aren't Alright: A Powerful Portrait of Deadly, Disaffected Teens" (*Newsweek*, June 1, 1994). The German equivalent, *Der Spiegel* and the Austrian equivalent, *Profil* have been reporting on the same "youth crisis" with equally vivid front cover designs.

8 BETWEEN POPULAR BELIEF AND FACT

1. "Video Game Culture: Leisure and Play Preferences of B.C. Teen" is available on-line: http://www.media-awareness.ca/eng/issues/ violence/resource/reports/ vgames.htm.
2. Moore's documentary has been discredited for its misrepresentation of "facts" and for its deceptiveness. Thomas Hardy's (2001) "Bowling for Columbine: Documentary or Fiction?" carefully deconstructs Moore's representation especially of NRA's president, actor Charlton Heston, saving him from accusations of being a racist. Hardy's analysis shows that all documentary films are constructions

and makes a case as to why the NRA are not the "bad guys" Moore makes them appear to be. For our own argument, Hardy's attempt to discredit the number of homicides in the United States due to firearm use as compared with other countries that Moore makes an issue is especially damaging to his own argument. No matter how one plays with the numbers, homicides due to firearms in the United States far outstrip any other country by *thousands of deaths*, a "fact" that can, of course, can be disavowed. Available on-line: http://www.hardylaw.net/Truth_About_Bowling.html.

9   GIRL/GURL/GRRRL VIDEO GAMES AND CYBERSPACE

1. This chapter complements the development of girl/gurl/grrrl music cultures as discussed in part three, "The Hystererization of the Music Scene: The Gurlz/Girls/Grrrls," in *Musical Fantasies of Youth Cultures*.
2. Grrrl Video Culture, URL: http://dmoz.org/Society/People/Women/Arts_and_Entertainment/ Gamerss/.
3. In New York City the Guerrilla Girls who wore gorilla masks attempted to subvert the visual art world through their pranks and performances to the hegemony of men in the museums and art galleries (see Isaak 1996).
4. Grrrls in Comic Books: Gallery. URL: http://www.gnofn.org/~jbourg/grrls/comix/gallery.htm.

11   FANTASY STRUCTURES IN VIRTUAL COMMUNITIES: THE PERVERTED GAZE

1. We would like to thank Andrea Loibnegger for making us aware of this site and Karin Lenzhofer for her insights into *Ally McBeal* and Fisher-isms.
2. To distinguish a perverted gaZe from a normative neurotic gaze of the big Other we have capitalized the Z as a quotation to Cronenberg's *eXistenZ* (1999).

12   THE DREAM OF TOTAL KNOWLEDGE: HYPERTEXTUAL FANTASIES

1. The hyperreal/banal binary is especially evident in "reality television" where the consumerism of goods is continually hyped as desirable and then deflated as being worthless. *Survivor* series always offers some form of "junk" food as a reward for winning an immunity challenge; *Fear Factor* has contestants eating vile substances to win commodity prizes and cash; celebrities attempt to become "ordinary" players in such series as *The Simple Life, The Osbournes, Celebrity Boot Camp, Newly Weds: Nick & Jessica*, and so on. The ordinary transformed into the extraordinary and vice verse, forms a vicious circle to maintain the entertainment factor.

13   LOOPING BACK TO VIDEO GAMES: THE QUESTION OF TECHNOLOGICAL INTERPASSIVITY

1. The War on Iraq has become the first "reality" televised war in distinction from the Gulf War, which was the first virtual war with no casualties shown. Journalists were "embedded" with soldiers reported back the "real" (RL) war to those at home.

The term "embedding" the military used was a perfect signifier for the way in which journalists laid in "bed" with soldiers so that bonding and alliances would grow, enabling more "human" emotion to be portrayed. This was a new form of postemotionalism for the viewing audience, confusing once more VR and RL.

2. See chapter 8, "Beyond the Law: The Anti-Slacker as Mass Murderer" in *Musical Fantasies of Youth Cultures.*

3. Fernando Meirelles visited Li'l Zé's family in the "city" expecting to meet a completely dysfunctional family. He was surprised to meet his mother who was polite, kept a clean house, sent her boys to school, and claimed that she had raised him like the rest of her children. She had no explanation for his cruelty.

4. Throughtout our journey over the mediascape of youth fantasies, reality television has often been mentioned in many contexts as one such way these fantasies have found expression. Our forthcoming book examines the genre of "reality television" and two exemplary television series that capture the paranoia and the psychosis of the perverted media landscape: *X-Files* and *Buffy, The Vampire Slayer.* We argue that both are reactions to the loss of trust in Symbolic authority and explore that loss of faith in exemplary ways.

14 "ARE THE KIDS ALRIGHT?"

1. This idea is prevalent when it comes to Techno music with its attempt to find an Ur-sound. See chapter 15, "Let's Rave not Rage! New Age Techno Hippies & Digital Electronica," in *Musical Fantasies of Youth Cultures.*

2. These themes are more explored in *Musical Fantasies of Youth Cultures.* For an analysis of postmodern female bodies theorized through a Greimasian semiotic square see jagodzinski (2003a).

3. The soteriology of the Buffyverse is explored in an upcoming book on television.

4. These designations refer to the season (integers of 10) and episode (beginning with 01) in that season; e.g., 1002 indicates the first season, episode two.

5. On Marilyn Manson see chapter 7, "Serial Connections: The MM Show," in *Musical Fantasies of Youth Cultures.* MM refers to Marilyn Manson.

6. For the examination of a specific case of such efficiency by Joe Clark, the principal of Eastside High School, an inner-city school in Paterson, New Jersey from 1983 to 1991, see jagodzinski (2003d.) John G. Avilden's film *Lean on Me* (1989), tells Clark's story.

7. We see these strategies differently than is commonly argued from Michel de Certeau's (1984) standpoint where he differentiates between "tactics" and "strategies." Youth are said to use tactics, the subversive practices for their own resistance and pleasure, as opposed to strategies that refer to policies by those in power to remain in control. Hence popular art for de Certeau is these tactical practices (struggles over the sign) performed on texts or text-like structures.

8. The play is on pun and punk. Joss Whedon presents a punning style and "punkish" in the way it "spikes" at you through its humor. I have used a similar style. See jagodzinski (1997).

9. See Hipfl and jagodzinski (2001).

BIBLIOGRAPHY: YOUTH FANTASIES

Acland, Charles. R. 1995. *Youth, Murder, Spectacle: The Cultural Politics of "Youth Crisis."* Boulder, San Francisco, Oxford: Westview Press.

Agamben, Giorgio. 1998. *Homo Sacer: Sovereign Power and Bare Life.* Trans. Daniel Heller-Roazen. Stanford, CA Stanford University Press.

Ahmed, Akbar S. 1992. *Postmodernism and Islam.* New York: Routledge.

Alcorn, Marshall W. Jr. 2002. *Changing the Subject in English Class: Discourse and the Constructions of Desire.* Carbondale and Edwardville: Southern Illinois University Press.

Allen, Mary K., Shelley, Harris, and George Butlin. 2003. "Finding Their Way: A Profile Of Young Canadian Graduates" (February 24, 2003), *Statistics Canada,* http://www.statcan.ca/english/IPS/Data/81-595-MIE2003003.htm.

Anderson, Craig. A. and Karen E. Dill. 2000. "Video Games and Aggressive Thoughts, Feelings, and Behavior in the Laboratory and in Life," *Journal of Personality and Social Psychology* 78 (4): 772–790.

Anzieu, Didier. 1989. *The Skin Ego.* Trans. Chris Turner. New Haven, Ct: Yale University Press.

Aoki, Doug. 1996. "Sex and Muscle: The Female Bodybuilder meets Lacan," *Body & Society* 2 (4): 59–74.

Ariès, Phillipe. 1962. *Centuries of Childhood.* London: Cape.

Althusser, Louis. 1977. *For Marx.* Trans. Ben Brewster. London: Verso.

Ayers, William, Bernardine Dohrn, and Rick Ayers (eds.). 2001. *Zero Tolerance: Resisting the Drive for Punishment in Our Schools: A Handbook for Parents, Students, Educators, and Citizens.* Foreword by Reverend Jesse L. Jackson. New York: New Press.

Balibar, Etienne. 1991. "Is There a 'Neo-Racism'?" In *Race, Nation, Class: Ambiguous Identities.* Etienne Balibar and Immanual Wallerstein (eds.), Trans. Chris Turner, pp. 17–28. London and New York: Verso.

Ballard, Mary E. 1999. "Video Game Violence and Confederate Gender: Effects on Reward and Punishment Given by College Males," *Sex Roles: A Journal of Research* (October). On Line URL www.findarticles.com/cf_0/m2294/1999_Oct/59426457/p1/article.jhtml.

Balsamo, Anne. 1995. *Technologies of the Gendered Body: Reading Cyborg Women.* Durham: Duke University Press.

Barker, M. and J. Petley (eds.). 1997. *Ill Effects: The Media/Violence Debate.* New York: Routledge.

Bataille, Georges. 1962. *Erotism: Death & Sensuality.* Trans. Mary Dalwood. San Francisco: City Lights Books.

Baudrillard, Jean. 1981. *For a Critique of the Political Economy of the Sign.* Trans. Charles Levine. St. Louis: Telos Press.

Baudrillard, Jean. 1990. *Seduction.* Montreal: New World Perspectives.

Bauman, Zygmunt. 2001. "Excess: An Obituary," *Parallax* (18): 85–91.

Beder, Sharon. 2000. *Selling the Work Ethic: From Puritan Pulpit to Corporate PR.* London: Zed Books.

Benger, Robin. 2002. "First Person Shooter." Directed and written by Robin Benger. *Canadian Broadcasting Corporation,* aired September 3, 2002.

Bettelheim, Bruno. 1976. *The Uses of Enchantment: The Meaning and Importance of Fairy Tales.* Harmondsworth: Penguin.

Bewes, Timothy. 1997. *Cynicism and Postmodernity.* New York: Verso.

Biehl, Janet. 1991. *Finding Our Way: Rethinking Ecofeminist Politics.* New York and Montreal: Black Rose Books.

Birkerts, Sve. 1998. "Into the Electronic Millennium." In Richard Holeton (ed.), *Composing Cyberspace: Identity, Community, and Knowledge in the Electronic Age,* pp. 311–322. New York: McGraw-Hill.

Bleibtreu-Ehrenberg, G. 1990. "Pederasty Among Primitives: Institutionalized Initiation and Cultic Prostitution," *Journal of Homosexuality* 20 (1/2): 13–30.

Boothby Richard. 1991. *Death and Desire.* New York and London: Routledge.

Boothby Richard. 2001. *Freud as Philosopher: Metapsychology After Lacan.* New York and London: Routledge.

Boym, Svetlana. 2001. *The Future of Nostalgia.* New York: Basic Books.

Braidotti, Rosi. 2002. *Metamorphosis: Towards a Materialist Theory of Becoming.* Cambridge, UK: Polity Press.

Brennan, Teresa and Martin Jay (eds.). 1996. *Vision in Context: Historical and Contemporary Perspectives on Sight.* New York: Routledge.

Bryson, Norman. 1984. *Tradition and Desire: From David to Delacroix.* Cambridge [Cambridgeshire]; New York: Cambridge University Press.

Buckingham, David. 1993. *Children Talking Television: The Making of Television Literacy.* London: Falmer Press.

Buckingham, David. 1996. *Moving Images: Understanding Children's Emotional Responses to Television.* Manchester: Manchester University Press.

Buckingham, David. 2000. *After the Death of Childhood: Growing Up in the Age of Electronic Media.* Malden, MA and Cambridge: Polity Press.

Buckingham, David and M. Allerton. 1996. *Fear, Fright and Distress: A Review of Research on Children's Emotional Responses to Television.* London: Broadcasting Standards Council.

Buck-Morss, Susan. 1975. "Socio-economic Bias in Piaget's Theory and Its Implications for Cross-Cultural Studies," *Human Development* 18: 35–45.

Burman, Erica. 1994. *Deconstructing Developmental Psychology.* London and New York: Routledge.

Butler, Judith. 1990. *Gender Trouble: Feminism and the Subversion of Identity.* New York: Routledge.

Butler, Judith. 2000. *Antigone's Claim. Kinship: Between Life and Death.* New York: Columbia University Press.

Cassell, Justine and Henry Jenkins (eds.). 1999. *From Barbie to Mortal Kombat: Gender and Computer Games.* Cambridge, MA: MIT Press.

Chandler, Alfred. 1997. *The Visible Hand. The Managerial Revolution in American Business.* Cambridge, MA: Harvard University Press.

Chandler, Daniel. 1999. "Personal Home Pages and the Construction of Identities on the Web." URL: http://www.aber.ac.uk/media/Documents/short/webident.html#F.

Children Now. 2001. *Fair Play? Violence, Gender and Race in Video Games.* URL: www.childrennow.org/media/video-games/2001/fair-play-2001.pdf.

Clifford, James. 1988. *The Predicament of Culture: Twentieth-Century Ethnography, Literature, and Art.* Cambridge, MA: Harvard University Press.

Clover, Carol. 1992. *Men, Women and Chainsaws: Gender in the Modern Horror Film.* Princeton, NJ: Princeton University Press.

Coontz, Stephanie. 1992. *The Way We Never Were: American Families and the Nostalgia Trap.* New York: Basic Books.

Cooper, Alvin and Sportolari. 1997. "Romance in Cyberspace: Understanding Online Attraction," *Journal of Sex Education and Therapy* 22 (1): 7–14.

Copjec, Joan. 1999. "The Tomp of Perseverance: On *Antigone*." In Joan Copjec and Michael Sorkin (eds.), *Giving Ground: The Politics of Propinquity*, pp. 233–266. London and New York: Verso.

Croissant, Jennifer L. 1998. "Growing Up Cyborg: Development Stories for Postmodern Children." In Robbie Davis-Floyd and Joseph Dumit (eds.), *Cyborg Babies: From Techno-Sex to Techno-Tots*, pp. 285–300. New York and London: Routledge.

Cumberbatch, G. and D. Howitt. 1989. *A Measure of Uncertainty: The Effects of the Mass Media.* London: John Libbey.

Davis-Floyd, Robbie and Joseph Dumit (eds.). 1998. *Cyborg Babies: From Techno-Sex to Techno-Tots.* New York and London: Routledge.

Dean, Tim. 2000. *Beyond Sexuality.* Chicago: University of Chicago Press.

Debord, Guy. 1994, *The Society of the Spectacle.* New York: Zone Books.

De Castell, S. and M. Bryson. 1999. "Retooling Play: Dystopia, Dysphoria and Difference." In Justine Cassell and Henry Jenkins (eds.), *From Barbie to Mortal Kombat: Gender and Computer Games.* Cambridge, MA: MIT Press.

De Certeau, Michel. 1984. *The Practice of Everyday Life.* Trans. Stephen F. Rendall. Berkeley: University of California Press.

Deleuze, Gilles. 1983. "Plato and the Simulacrum," *October* 27: 45–56.

Deleuze, Gilles and Félix Guattari. 1983. *Anti-Oedipus: Capitalism and Schizophrenia.* Trans. Robert Hurley, Mark Seem, and Helen R. Lane. Minneapolis: University of Minnesota.

Deleuze, Gilles and Félix Guattari. 1987. *A Thousand Plateaus: Capitalism and Schizophrenia.* Trans. and Foreword, Brian Massumi. Minneapolis: University of Minnesota Press.

DeMause, Lloyd. 1974. *The History of Childhood.* New York: Psychohistory Press.

Derrida, Jacques. 1982. *Margins of Philosophy.* Trans. Alan Bass. Chicago: University of Chicago Press.

Dibbell, Julian. 1998. "A Rape in Cyberspace, or How an Evil Clown, A Haitian Trickster Spirit, Two Wizards, and a Cast of Dozens Turned a Database into a Society." In Richard Holeton (ed.), *Composing Cyberspace: Identity, Community, and Knowledge in the Electronic Age*, pp. 83–98. New York: McGraw-Hill.

Dietz, T.L. 1998. "An Examination of Violence and Gender Portrayals in Video Games: Implications for Gender Socialization and Aggressive Behavior," *Sex Roles* 38 (5–6): 425–442.

Dolar, Mladen. 1996. "The Object Voice." In Renata Salecl and Slavoj Žižek (eds.), *Sic 1: Gaze and Voice as Love Objects*. Durham and London: Duke University Press.

Dole, Marcus, A. 1999. *Poststructuralist Geographies: The Diabolical Art of Spatial Science*. Lanham, Boulder, and New York: Rowan & Littlefield Publishers Ltd.

Doel, Marcus A. and David B. Clarke. 1999. "Virtual Worlds: Simulation, Suppletion, S(ed)uction and Simulacra." In Mike Crang, Phil Crang, and Jon May (eds.), *Virtual Geographies: Bodies, Space and Relations*, pp. 261–283. New York: Routledge.

Donohue, Elizabeth, Vincent Schiraldi, and Jason Ziedenberg. 1998. *School House Hype: School Shootings and the Real Risks Kids Face in America*. Justice Policy Institute. URL: http://www.cjcj.org.

Donziger, M. 1996. *The Real War on Crime: The Report of the National Criminal Justice Commission*. New York: HarperCollins.

Dor, Joël. 1997. *Introduction to the Reading of Lacan: The Unconscious Structured Like a Language*. Northvale, NJ and London: Jason Aronson, Inc.

Dreyfus, Hubert L. 1972. *What Computers Can't Do: A Critique of Artificial Reason*. New York: Harper & Row.

Driscoll, Catherline. 2002. *Girls: Feminine Adolescence in Popular Culture and Cultural Theory*. New York: Columbia University Press.

Eagleton, Terry. 2003. "Slavoy Zizek (Enjoy!)." In Terry Eagleton, *Figures of Dissent: Critical Essays on Fish, Spivak, Zizek and Others*, pp. 196–206. London: Verso.

Edwards, Lynee. 2002. "Slaying in Black and White: Kendra as Tragic Mullata in Buffy." In Rhonda V. Wilcox and David Lavery (eds.), *Fighting the Forces: What's at Stake in Buffy the Vampire Slayer*, pp. 85–97. Lanham, MD: Rowan and Littlefield.

Ehrenreich, Barbara. 1998. "Put Your Pants On, Demonboy." In Richard Holeton (ed.), *Composing Cyberspace: Identity, Community, and Knowledge in the Electronic Age*, pp. 80–82. New York: McGraw-Hill.

Elliott, Anthony. 2000. "The Ambivalence of Identity: Psychoanalytic Theory in the Space Between Modernity and Postmodernity." In Anthony Elliott and Charles Spezzano (eds.), *Psychoanalysis at Its Limits: Navigating the Postmodern Turn*, pp. 110–144. London: Free Association Books Ltd.

Evans, Dylan. 1996. *An Introductory Dictionary of Lacanian Psychoanalysis*. London and New York: Routledge.

Evard, Michele. 1996. " 'So Please Stop, Thank You': Girls Online." In Lynn Cherny and Elizabeth Reba Weise (eds.), *Wired Women: Gender and New Realities in Cyberspace*, pp. 188–204. Seattle: Seal Press.

Export, Valie. 2001. *Export Ob/De+Con(Struction)*. Philadelphia, PA: Moore College of Art and Design.

Fairclough, Norman. 1989. *Language and Power*. London; New York: Longman.

Fairclough, Norman. 1992. *Discourse and Social Change*. Cambridge, MA: Polity Press.

Ferganchick-Neufang, Julia. K. "Virtual Harassment: Women and Online Education," *First Monday*, on-line journal. http://www.firstmonday.dk/issues/issue3_2/fergan/#references.

Fink, Bruce. 1995. *The Lacanian Subject: Between Language and Jouissance*. Princeton, NJ: Princeton University Press.

Fink, Bruce. 1997. *A Clinical Introduction to Lacanian Psychoanalysis: Theory and Technique*. Cambridge, MA: Harvard University Press.

Fiske, John. 1993. *Power Plays, Power Works*. New York: Verso.

Flieger, Jerry Aline. 1997a. "Overdetermined Oedipus: Mommy, Daddy, and Me as Desiring-Machine," *South Atlantic Quarterly* 96: 599–620.

Flieger, Jerry Aline. 1997b. "Is Oedipus On—Line?" *Pretexts: Studies and Writing in Culture* 6 (1): 81–94. URL: http://www.telefonica.es/fat/eflieger.html.

Flieger, Jerry Aline. 2001. "Has Oedipus Signed Off (or Struck Out)?: Žižek, Lacan and the Field of Cyberspace," *Paragraph: A Journal of Modern Critical Theory* 24 (1): 53–77.

Foucault, Michel. 1979. *Discipline and Punish: The Birth of the Prison.* Trans. Alan Sheridan. New York: Vintage Books.

Foucault, Michel. 1980. *The History of Sexuality.* Trans. Robert Hurley. New York: Vintage Books.

Freedman, Jonathan L. 2002. *Media Violence and Its Effect on Aggression: Assessing the Scientific Evidence.* Toronto: University of Toronto Press.

Freud, Sigmund. July, 1895. "Irmas Injection." In *The Standard Edition of the Complete Psychological Works of Sigmund Freud*, ed. and trans. James Strachey, vol. IV. pp. 107–121. London: Hogarth, 1953–1974. Cited as SE IV.

Freud, Sigmund. March, 1898. "The Psychical Mechanism for Forgetfulness ('Botanical Monograph')." In *The Standard Edition of the Complete Psychological Works of Sigmund Freud*, ed. and trans. James Strachey, vol. III, pp. 291–295. London: Hogarth, 1953–1974. Cited as SE III.

Freud, Sigmund. 1900. *The Interpretation of Dreams, "The Butcher's Wife Dream."* In *The Standard Edition of the Complete Psychological Works of Sigmund Freud*, ed. and trans. James Strachey, vol. IV. pp. 146–151. London: Hogarth, 1953–1974. Cited as SE IV.

Freud, Sigmund. 1919. " 'A Child is Being Beaten': A Contribution to the Study of the Origins of Sexual Perversions." In *The Standard Edition of the Complete Psychological Works of Sigmund Freud*, ed. and trans. James Strachey, vol. XVII, pp. 175–204. London: Hogarth, 1953–1974. Cited as SE XVII.

Freud, Sigmund. 1939. "Moses and Monotheism." In *The Standard Edition of the Complete Psychological Works of Sigmund Freud*, ed. and trans. James Strachey, vol. XXIII. pp. 7–140. London: Hogarth, 1953–1974. Cited as SE XXIII, *Moses.*

Freud, Sigmund. 1940. "An Outline of Psycho-analysis." In *The Standard Edition of the Complete Psychological Works of Sigmund Freud*, ed. and trans. James Strachey, vol. XXIII, pp. 139–143. London: Hogarth, 1953–1974. Cited as SE XXIII.

Friedberg, Anne. 1993. *Window Shopping: Cinema and the Postmodern Body.* Los Angeles: University of California Press.

Friedenberg, Edgar Zodiag. 1959. *The Vanishing Adolescent.* New York: Dell Publishers.

Fromm, Eric. 1951. *The Forgotten Language: An Introduction to the Understanding of Dreams, Fairly Tales and Myths.* New York: Grove Press.

Fromm, Eric. 1952. *The Forgotten Language: An Introduction to the Understanding of Dreams, Fairy Tales and Myth.* London: Victor Gollancz.

Fukuyama, Francis. 1989. "The End of History?" *The National Interest* 16 (Summer): 3–19.

Furger, Roberta. 1998. *Does Jane Compute? Preserving Our Daughter's Place in the Cyber Revolution.* New York: Warner Books.

Fruss, Diana. 1992. "Fashion and the Homospectatorial Look," *Critical Inquiry* 18 (Summer): 713–737.

Gabbard, Glen O. 2002. *The Psychology of The Sopranos: Love, Death, Desire, and Betrayal in America's Favorite Gangster Family.* New York: Basic Books.

Gaily, Christine Ward. 1996. "Mediated Messages: Gender, Class, and Cosmos in Home Video Games." In P.M. Greenfield and R.R. Cocking (eds.), *Interacting with Video*. New Jersey: Ablex Publishing Co.

Gasché, Rudolphe. 1986. *Tain of the Mirror: Derrida and the Philosophy of Reflection*. Cambridge, MA.: Harvard University Press.

Gauntlett, D. 1995. *Moving Experiences: Understanding Television's Influences and Effects*. Luton: John Libbey.

Gergen, Kenneth. 1991. *The Saturated Self: Dilemmas of Identity in Contemporary Life*. New York: Basic Books.

Gillespie, Marie. 1995. *Television, Ethnicity and Cultural Change*. New York: Routledge.

Gilligan, Carol. 1982. *In a Different Voice: Psychological Theory and Women's Development*. Cambridge, MA: Harvard University Press.

Gilmour, Heather. 1999. "What Girls Want: The Intersections of Leisure and Power in Female Computer Game Play." In Marsha Kinder (ed.), *Kid's Media Culture*, pp. 263–292. Duke and London: Duke University Press.

Giroux, Henry A. 1996. *Fugitive Culture: Race, Violence, and Youth*. New York: Routledge.

Glass, Loren. 2001. "After the Phallus," *American Imago* 58 (2): 545–566.

Goldmann, Lucien. 1964. *The Hidden God: A Study of Tragic Vision in the Pensées of Pascal and the tragedies of Racine*. Trans. Philip Thody. London: Routledge & K. Paul.

Goux, Jean-Joseph. 1990. *Symbolic Economies: After Marx and Freud*. Trans. Jennifer Curtiss Gage. Ithaca, NY: Cornell University Press.

Goux, Jean-Joseph. 1992. "The Phallus: Masculine Identity and the 'Exchange of Women,'" *di f f e r e n c e s: A Journal of Feminist Cultural Studies* 4 (1): 40–75.

Grasse. Ray. 2002. *Signs of the Times: Unlocking the Symbolic Language of World Events*. Charlottesville, VA: Hampton Roads Publishing Company.

Greenfield, Patricia M. and Rodney R. Cocking. 1994. "Effects of Interactive Entertainment Technology on Development," *Journal of Applied Developmental Psychology* 15 (1): 1–2.

Groppe, Laura. 2000. "*Childrennow. Girls and Gaming: Gender and Video* Game Marketing." URL: www.childrennow.org/media/medianow/mnwinter2001. html.

Grrls in Comic Books: Gallery. URL: http://www.gnofn.org/~jbourg/grrls/comix/ gallery.htm.

Grrrl Video Culture, URL: http://dmoz.org/Society/People/Women/Arts and Entertainment/Gamers/.

Grossman, Dave. 1995. *On Killing*. Boston: Little Brown Ltd.

Gudmundsson, Gester. *European Commission White Paper on Youth Consultation Process: Report of the Research Consultation Pillar*. URL: http://europa.eu.int/ comm/education/youth/ywp/research.pdf.

Gutwill, Susan and Nancy Caro Hollander. 2002. "Zero Tolerance or Media Literacy: A Critical Psychoanalytic Perspective on Combating Violence Among Children," *JPCS: Journal for the Psychoanalysis of Culture & Society* 7 (2): 263–273.

Hall, Stuart. 1981. "Cultural Studies: Two Paradigms." In Tony Bennett, S. Boyd-Bowman, C. Mercer, and J. Woolacott (eds.), *Culture, Ideology and the Social, Process*, pp. 19–37. London: Open University Press.

Hallward, Peter. 2003. *Badiou: A Subject of Truth*. Minnesota and London: University of Minnesota Press.

Harari, Roberto. 2002. "The Sinthome: Turbulence and Dissipation." In Luke Thurston (ed.), *Essays on the Final Lacan: Re-inventing the Symptom*, pp. 45–58. New York: Other Press.

Haraway, Donna. 1991. "A Cyborg Manifesto: Science, Technology, and Socialist-Feminism in the Late Twentieth Century." In Donna Haraway, *Simians, Cyborgs and Women: The Reinvention of Nature*, pp. 149–181. New York: Routledge.

Hardt, Michael and Antonio Negri. 2000. *Empire*. Cambridge, MA: Harvard University Press.

Hardy, Thomas. 2001. *Bowling for Columbine: Documentary or Fiction?* URL: http://www.hardylaw.net/Truth_About_Bowling.html.

Harrington, C. Lee and Denise D. Bielby. 1995. *Soap Fans: Pursuing Pleasure and Making Meaning in Everyday life*. Philadelphia: Temple University Press.

Harrison, Bennett. 1994. *Lean and Mean: The Changing Landscape of Corporate Power in the Age of Flexibility*. New York: Basic Books.

Hayles, Katherine N. 1999. *How We Became Posthuman: Virtual Bodies in Cybernetics, Literature, and Informatics*. Chicago: University of Chicago Press.

Heard, Gerald. 1963. *Five Ages of Man*. New York: Julian Press.

Hennessy, Rosemary. 1993. *Materialist Feminism and the Politics of Discourse*. New York: Routledge.

Hennessy, Rosemary. 2000. *Profit and Pleasure: Sexualities in Late Capitalism*. New York: Routledge.

Herman, Judith Lewis. 1981. *Father-Daughter Incest*. Cambridge, MA: Harvard University Press.

Hersh, Seymour. 1997. *The Dark Side of Camelot*. Boston: Little, Brown.

Hertz, Neil (1983). "Medusa's Head: Male Hysteria under Political Pressure," *Representations* 4 (Fall): 27–54.

Hills, Mat. 2002. *Fan Cultures*. New York: Routledge.

Hipfl, Brigitte and jan jagodzinski. 2001. "The Paranoiac Space of the X-Files," *SIMILE (Studies in Media & Information Literacy Education)* 1 (2). Available on-line: http://www.utpjournals.com/jour.ihtml?lp=simile/issue2/issue2toc.html.

Hodge, Bob and David Tripp. 1986. *Children and Television: A Semiotic Approach*. Cambridge: Polity Press.

Holeton, Richard (ed.). 1998. *Composing Cyberspace: Identity, Community, and Knowledge in the Electronic Age*. New York: McGraw-Hill.

hooks, Bell. 1994. *Teaching to Transgress: Education as the Practice of Freedom*. New York: Routledge.

Hughes, Robert. 1993. *Culture of Complaint: The Fraying of America*. New York: Oxford University Press.

Hunter, Ian. 1988. *Culture and Government: The Emergence of Literary* Education. London: Macmillan.

Hutchins, Edwin. 1995. *Cognition in the Wild*. Cambridge: MIT Press.

Huyssen, Andreas. 1986. "Mass Culture as Woman: Modernism's Other." In Tania Modleski (ed.), *Studies in Entertainment: Critical Approaches to Mass Culture*, pp. 188–208. Bloomington and Indianapolis: Indiana University Press.

Ian, Marcia. 2000. "The Unholy Family: From Satanism to the Chronos Komplex," *Journal For The Psychoanalysis of Culture & Society* 5 (2): 285–289.

Ian, Marcia. 2001. "The Primitive Subject of Female Bodybuilding: Transgression and Other Postmodern Myths," *di f f e r e n c e s: A Journal of Feminist Cultural Studies* 12(3): 69–100.

Inness, Sherrie A. 1999. *Tough Girls: Women Warriors and Wonder Women in Popular Culture*. Philadelphia: University of Pennsylvania Press.

Irigaray, Luce. 1985. *Speculum of the Other Woman*. Trans. Gillian C. Gill. Ithaca, New York: Cornell University Press.

Irwin, William. 2002. *The Matrix and Philosophy: Welcome to the Desert of the Real*. Chicago, Illinois: Open Court Publishing Company.

Issak Jo Anna. 1996. *Feminism & Contemporary ArtL: The Revolutionary Power of Women's Laughter*. New York and London: Routledge.

Jaanus, Marie. 1997. "The Ethics of the Real in Lacan's Seminar VII," *Literature and Psychology* 43 (1–2, Spring): 1–18.

jagodzinski, jan. 1996. *The Anamorphic I/i*. Edmonton: Duval Press.

jagodzinski, jan. 1997. *Pun(k) Deconstruction: Experifigural Writing in Art & Art Education*. Mahwah, NJ: Lawrence Erlbaum Associates, Ltd.

jagodzinski, jan. 2001. "Recuperating the Flaccid Phallus: The Hysteria of Post-Oedipal Masculine representation and the Return of the Anal Father," *Journal For The Psychoanalysis of Culture & Society* 6 (1): 29–39.

jagodzinski, jan. 2002a. "A Strange Introduction: My Apple Thing." In jan jagodzinski (ed.), *Pedagogical Desire: Authority, Seduction, Transference, and the Question of Ethics*, pp. xiii–lx. Westport, CT: Bergin & Garvey.

jagodzinski, j. 2002b Winter. "The Ethics of the 'Real'." In "Levinas, Lacan, and Buddhism: Pedagogical Implications," *Educational Theory* 52 (1): 81–96.

jagodzinski, j. 2002c. "The Drive Toward Piercing & Tattooing: Postmodern Bodies of Performative Excess," *JPCS: Journal for the Psychoanalysis of Culture & Society* 7 (2): 251–262.

jagodzinski, jan. 2003a. "Women's Bodies of Performative Excess: Miming, Feigning, Refusing and Rejecting the Phallus," *Journal for the Psychoanalysis of Culture & Society* 8 (1): 23–41.

jagodzinski, jan. 2003b. "The Pierced and Tattooed Body: The Branded Skin-ego of Post-Oedipalization." In Heinz Tschachler, Maureen Devine, and Michael Draxlbauer (eds.), *The Embodyment of American Culture*, pp. 73–86. Münster: Lit Verlag.

jagodzinski, jan. 2003c. "The Perversity of Reality Television," *Journal for the Psychoanalysis of Culture & Society* 8 (2): 320–329.

jagodzinski, jan. 2003d. "The *Jouissance* of Authority: The Emotional Turmoil in 'Laying Down the Law' in *Lean on Me*," *Journal of Curriculum Theorizing* 19 (1): 65–86.

Jameson, Fredric. 1972. *The Prison-house of Language; A Critical Account of Structuralism and Russian Formalism*. Princeton, NJ: Princeton University Press.

Jaspers, Karl. 1953. *The Origin and Goal of History*. Trans. Michael Bullock. London: Routledge & K. Paul.

Jenkins, Henry. 2000. "Lessons from Littelton: What Congress Doesn't Want to Hear About Youth and the Media. Part I–IV," *Independent School Magazine*. Winter. URL: http://www.nais.org/pubs/ismag.cfm?file_id=537&ismag_id=14.

Jones, Gerard. 2002. *Killing Monsters: Why Children Need Fantasy, Super Heroes, and Make-Believe Violence*. New York: Basic Books.

Kafai, Yasmin B. 1996. "Gender Differences in Children's Construction of Video Games." In Patricia M. Greenfield and Rodney R. Cocking (eds.), *Interacting with Video*. Norwood, NJ: Ablex Publishing.

Kafai, Yasmin B. 1999. "Video Game Designs by Girls and Boys: Variability and Consistency of Gender Differences." In Marsha Kinder (ed.), *Kid's Media Culture*, pp. 293–315. Duke and London: Duke University Press.

Katz, Jon. 1997. *Virtuous Reality: How America Surrendered Discussion of Moral Values to Opportunists, Nitwits & Blockheads like William Bennett*. New York: Random House.

Kay, Sarah. 2003. *Žižek: A Critical Introduction*. Cambridge: Polity Press.

Kellner, Douglas. 2001. *Grand Theft 2000: Media Spectacle and a Stolen Election*. Lanham, Boulder, New York, Oxford: Rowland & Littlefield Publisher, Inc.

Kent, Steven L. 2001. *The Ultimate History of Video Games*. Roseville, CA: Prima Publishing.

Klein, Naomi. 2000. *No Logo: Taking Aim at the Brand Bullies*. Toronto: Alfred A. Knopf.

Kohlberg, Lawrence. 1963. *The Development of Children's Orientations Toward a Moral Order*. Basel: S. Karger.

Krauss, Rosalind. 1987. "Video: The Aesthetics of Narcissism." In John Hanhardt (ed.), *Video Culture*. Rochester: Visual Studies Workshop.

Krisberg, B. 1994. "Distorted by Fear: The Make Believe War on Crime," *Social Justice* 21 (3): 38–49.

Kristeva, Julia. 1991. *Strangers to Ourselves*. Trans. Leon Roudiez. New York: Columbia University Press.

Kristeva, Julia. 2000. *The Sense and Non-sense of Revolt: The Powers and Limits of Psychoanalysis*. Trans. Jeanine Herman. New York: Columbia University Press.

Kristeva, Julia. 2002. *Intimate Revolt: The Powers and Limits of Psychoanalysis*. Trans: Jeanine Herman. New York: Columbia University Press.

Kroker, Arthur. 1992. *The Possessed Individual: Technology and the French Postmodern*. New York: St. Martin's Press.

Lacan, Jacques. 1960–1961. *The Transference, Seminar VIII*. Unofficial Translation.

Lacan, Jacques. 1977a. *Écrits: A Selection*. Trans. Alan Sheridan. New York and London: W.W. Norton & Co.

Lacan, Jacques. 1977b. "Desire and the Interpretation of Desire in *Hamlet*," *Yale French Studies* 55/56: 11–52.

Lacan, Jacques. 1979. *The Four Fundamental Concepts of Psycho-Analysis, Seminar XI*, ed. Jacques-Alain Miller, trans. Alan Sheridan. Harmondsworth: Penguin Books. Cited as Cited as S XI, *Four Fundamentals*.

Lacan, Jacques. 1991. *Le Séminaire. Livre XVII. L'envers de la psychanalyse, 1969–1970*, ed. Jacques-Alain Miller. Paris: Seuil. Cited as S XVII, *Envers*.

Lacan, Jacques. 1992. *The Ethics of Psychoanalysis. Seminar VII*, ed. Jacques-Alain Miller, trans. Dennis Porter. New York: W.W. Norton. Cited as S VII, *Ethics*.

Lacan, Jacques. 1993. *The Psychoses. Seminar III*, ed. Jacques-Alain Miller, trans. Russell Grigg. New York: W.W. Norton. Cited as S III, *Psychoses*.

Lacan, Jacques. 1995. "Position of the Unconscious (1964)." Trans. Bruce Fink. In Richard Feldstein, Bruce Fink, and Marie Jaanus (eds.) *Reading Seminar XI: Lacan's Four Fundamental Concepts of Psychoanalysis*, pp. 259–282. Albany: SUNY Press.

Lacan, Jacques. 1998. *On Feminine Sexuality, the Limits of Love and Knowledge, 1972–1973. The Seminar of Jacques Lacan XX, Encore*. Translated with notes, Bruce Fink, ed. Jacques-Alain Miller. New York: W.W. Norton. Cited as S XX, *Encore*.

Lanham, Richard. 1993. *The Electronic Word: Democracy, Technology, and the Arts*. Chicago: University of Chicago Press.

Lankshear, Colin, Michael, Peters, and Michele Knobel. 1996. "Critical Pedagogy and Cyberspace." In Henry Giroux, Colin Lankshear, Peter McLaren and Michael Peters (eds.), *Counternarratives: Cultural Studies and Critical Pedagogies in Postmodern Spaces*, pp. 149–188. New York: Routledge.

Latham, Robert. 2002. *Consuming Youth: Vampires, Cyborgs, and the Culture of Consumption.* Chicago: University of Chicago Press.

Laplanche, Jean. 1998. *Essays on Otherness.* Trans. John Fletcher. New York: Routledge.

Lenham, Richard. 1994. *The Electronic Word: Democracy, Technology, and the Arts.* Chicago: University of Chicago Press.

Lenhart, Amanda, Lee Rainie, and Oliver Lewis. 2000. *Teenage Life Online: The Rose of Instant-Message Generation and the Internet's Impact on Friendships and Family Relationships.* Washington, DC: Pew Internet and American Life Project. On-line URL: http://www.pewinternet.org/reports/pdfs/PIP_Teens_Report.pdf.

Lessard, Bill and Steve Baldwin. 2000. *NetSlaves: True Tales of Working the Web.* New York: McGraw-Hill.

Levine, Judith. 2002. *Harmful to Minors: The Perils of Protecting Children from Sex.* Minneapolis: University of Minnesota Press.

Lucas, Tim. 1998. "Youth Gangs and Moral Panics in Santa Cruz, California." In Tracey Skelton and Gill Valentine (eds.), *Cool Places: Geographies of Youth Cultures,* pp. 145–160. New York: Routledge.

Lyotard, Jean François. 1984. *The Postmodern Condition: A Report on Knowledge.* Trans. Geoff Bennington and Brian Massumi. Minneapolis: University of Minneapolis Press.

Lyotard, Jean François. 1988. *The Différend: Phrases in Dispute.* Trans. Georges Van Den Abbeele. Minneapolis: University of Minnesota Press.

Lyotard, Jean François. 1991. "Representation, Presentation, Unrepresentable. In Jean Lyotard." *The Inhuman: Reflections on Time.* Trans. Geoffrey Bennington and Rachel Bowlby, pp. 119–143. Stanford, CA: Stanford University Press.

Lyotard, Jean François and G. Larochelle. 1992a. "That Which Resists, After All," *Philosophy Today* 36 (4): 402–417.

Lyotard, Jean François. 1992b. "Mainmise," *Philosophy Today* 36 (4): 419–427.

Lyotard, Jean François. 1992c. *The Postmodern Explained to Children: Correspondence 1982–5.* London: Turnaround.

MacCannell, Juliet Flower. 1991. *The Regime of the Brother: After the Patriarchy.* New York and London: Routledge.

MacCannell, Juliet Flower. 2000. *The Hysteric's Guide to the Future Female Subject.* Minneapolis and London: University of Minnesota Press.

Macpherson, C.B. 1962. *The Political Theory of Possessive Individualism: Hobbes to Locke.* Oxford: Clarendon Press.

Maddieson I. 1984. *Patterns of Sounds.* Cambridge: Cambridge University Press.

Males, Mike. 1999. *Framing Youth: Ten Myths About the Next Generation.* Monroe, ME: Common Courage Press.

Manoff, Robert Karl. 1998. "Telling the Truth to Peoples at Risk: Some Introductory Thoughts on Media & Conflict." URL: http://www.nyu.edu/globalbeat/pubs/manoff0798.html.

Manovich, Lev. 2001. *The Language of the New Media.* Cambridge, MA: The MIT Press.

Maslow, Abraham H. 1965. *Eupsychian Management; A Journal.* Homewood, IL: R.D. Irwin.

Massey, Doreen. B. 1994. *Space, Place, and Gender.* Cambridge: Polity Press.

Mayne, Judith. 1993. *Cinema and Spectatorship.* New York: Routledge.

McClintock, Anne. 1993. "Sex Workers and Sex Work," *Social Text* 37: 1–10.

McLaren, Peter and Morris, Janet. 1998. "Mighty Morphin Rangers: The Aesthetics of Phallo-Millaristic Justice." In Shirley R. Steinberg and Joe Kincheloe (eds.), *Kinder-Culture: The Corporate Construction of Childhood*, pp. 115–128. Boulder, CO: Westview Press.

McNamee, Sue. 1998. "The Home: Youth, Gender and Video Games: Power and Control in the Home." In Tracy Skelton and Gill Valentime (eds.), *Cool Places: Geographies of Youth Cultures*, pp. 196–206. London and New York: Routledge.

McGavran, James Holt (ed.). 1999. *Literature and the Child: Romantic Continuations, Postmodern Contestations.* Iowa City, IO: University of Iowa Press.

McGowan, Todd. 1998. "From Enjoyment to Aggressivity: The Emergence of the New Father in Contemporary Society," *Journal for the Psychoanalysis of Culture & Society* 3 (1): 53–60.

McGowan, Todd. 1999. "The Master Amid Rumors of His Demise: Politics in a Time of 'Satisfaction,' " *Journal for the Psychoanalysis of Culture & Society* 4 (1): 72–80.

McIntosh, Alastair. 1996. *From Eros to Thanatos: Cigarette Advertising's Imagery of Violation as an Icon into British Cultural Psychopathology.* URL: http://www.alastairmcintosh.com/articles/1996_eros_thanatos.htm#.

Media Analysis Lab. 1998. "Video Game Culture: Leisure and Play Preferences of B.C. Teens," *October.* Simon Fraser University, Burnaby, British Columbia, Canada. URL: http://www.mediaawareness.ca/eng/issues/violence/resource/reports/vgames. htm.

Merleau-Ponty, Maurice. 1968. *The Visible and the Invisible*, Claude Lefort (ed.), trans. Alphonso Lingis. Evanston, IL: Northwestern University Press.

Meštrović, Stjepan. 1997. *Postemotional Society.* London, Thousand Oak; New Delhi: Sage Publishers.

Meyrowitz, Joshua. 1985. *No Sense of Place: The Impact of Electronic Media on Social Behavior.* Oxford: Oxford University Press.

Milgram, Stanley. 1965. "Some Conditions of Obedience and Disobedience to Authority," *Human Relations* 18: 51–75.

Miller, Jacques-Alain. 1994. "Extimité." In Mark Bracher, Marshall W. Alcorn, Jr., Ronald J. Corthell, and François Massardier-Kenney (eds.), *Lacanian Theory of Discourse: Subject, Structure, and Society*, pp. 74–86. New York: New York University Press.

Miller, James. 1993. *The Passion of Michel Foucault.* New York: Simon and Schuster.

Milovanovic, Dragan. 1997. *Postmodern Criminology.* New York: Garland.

Montgomery, Kathy C. 2001. *Teen Sites.com: A Field Guide to the New Digital Landscape.* New York: Center for Media Education (CME). URL: www.cme.org.

Moravec, Hans. 1988. *Mind Children: The Future of Robot and Human Intelligence.* Cambridge: Harvard University Press.

Morgan, Jay Scott. 2001. "The Mystery of Goya's Saturn," *New England Review* (Spring) URL: http://www.middlebury.edu/~nereview/morgan.html.

Morrison, Toni. 1987. *Beloved: A Novel.* New York: New American Library.

Morton, Andrew. 1999. *Monica's Story.* New York: St. Martin's Press.

Mulvey, Laura. 1975. "Visual Pleasure and Narrative Cinema," *Screen* 16 (3): 6–18.

Nobus, Dany. (ed.). 1998. *Key Concepts of Lacanian Psychoanalysis.* London: Rebus Press.

Noel-Smith, Kelly. 2001. "Harry Potter's Oedipal Issues," *Psychoanalytic Studies* 3: 199–207.

Paglia, Camille. 1998. "Animal House," *Salon* January 22. URL: http://www.salon.com/news/1998/01/22news_pagl.html.

Papert, Seymour. 1980. *Mindstorms: Children, Computers, and Powerful Ideas.* New York: Basic Books.

Pfaller, Robert Hrsg. 2000. *Interpassivität: Studien über Delegiertes Genießen.* Wien: Springer Verlag.

Pfaller, Robert. 2002. *Die Illusionen der Anderen: Über das Lustprinzip in der Kultur.* Frankfurt am Main: Suhrkamp Verla.

Phillips, Kevin. 2002. *Wealth and Democracy: A Political History of the American Rich.* New York: Broadway Books.

Pipher, Mary. 1994. *Reviving Ophelia: Saving the Selves of Adolescent Girls.* New York: Ballantine Books.

Pinar, Bill, William M. Reynolds, Patrick Slattery, and Peter M. Taubman. 1995. *Understanding Curriculum: An Introduction to the Study of Historical and Contemporary Curriculum Discourses.* New York: Peter Lang.

Pitcher, George. 2002. *The Death of Spin.* John Wiley and Sons Ltd.

Plant, Sadie. 1997. *Zeros + Ones: Digital Women + the New Technoculture.* New York: Doubleday.

Plotz, Judith. 2001. *Romanticism and the Vocation of Childhood.* New York: Palgrave.

Postman, Neil. 1983. *The Disappearance of Childhood.* London: W.H. Allen.

Prigogine, Ilya. 1997. *The End of Certainty: Time, Chaos, and the New Laws of Nature.* New York: Free Press.

Prosser J. 1998. *Second Skins: The Body Narratives of Transexuality.* New York: Columbia University Press.

Provenzo Jr., Eugene F. 1991. *Video Kids: Making Sense of Nintendo.* Cambridge, MA: Harvard University Press.

Provenzo Jr., Eugene F. 1998. "Video Games and the Emergence of Interactive Media for Children." In Shirley R. Steinberg and Joe L. Kincheloe (eds.), *Kinder-Culture: The Corporate Construction of Childhood*, pp. 103–114. Boulder, CO: Westview Press.

Provenzo Jr., Eugene F. 2000. *Children and Hyperreality: The Loss of Real in Contemporary Childhood and Adolescence.* Testimony before the Senate Commerce Committee Hearing on "The Impact of Interactive Violence on Children," chaired by Senator Sam Brownback, March 21, 2000. URL: http://commerce.senate.gov/hearings/0321pro.pdf.

Putman, Robert. 2000. *Bowling Alone: The Collapse and Revival of American Community.* NewYork: Simon & Schuster.

Rand, E. 1995. *Barbie's Queer Accessories.* Durham and London: Duke University Press.

Rand, Ayn. 1966. *Capitalism, the Unknown Ideal.* New York: New American Library.

Reed, Evelyn. 1975. *Woman's Evolution from Matriarchal Clan to Patriarchal Family.* New York: Pathfinder Press.

Roberts, Martin. 1991. "Mutations of the Spectacle: Vitrines, Arcades, Mannequines," *FCS*, ii: 211–249.

Rose, N. 1985. *The Psychological Complex: Psychology, Politics and Society in England 1869–1939.* London: Routledge Kegan & Paul.

Rushkoff, Douglas. 1996. *Playing the Future: How Kid's Culture Can Teach Us to Thrive in an Age of Chaos.* New York: HarperCollins.

Salecl, Renata. 1998. *(Per)versions of Love and Hate.* London and New York: Verso.

Sanders Barry. 1995. *A is for Ox: The Collapse of Literacy and the Rise of Violence in an Electronic Age.* New York: Vintage.

Schiller, Friedrich von. 1966. *Naive and Sentimental Poetry and on the Sublime*. New York: Frederick Unger.

Schowalter, John E. 1983. "Some Meanings of Being a Horsewoman," *Psychoanalytic Study of the Child* 38: 501–518.

Schulweis, Harold. 1994. *For Those Who Can't Believe: Overcoming the Obstacles to Faith*. New York: HarperCollins.

Sennett, Richard. 1998. *The Corrosion of Character: The Personal Consequences of Work in the New Capitalism*. New York: W.W. Norton & Company.

Shalit, Wendy. 1999. *A Return to Modesty: Discovering the Lost Virtue*. Toronto HarperPerennialCanada.

Shalit, Wendy. 2000. *A Return to Modesty*. Touchstone, New York.

Silberman, Steve. 1998. "We're Teen, We're Queer, and We've Got E-mail." In R. Holeton (ed.), *Composing Cyberspace: Identity, Community and Knowledge in the Electronic Age*, pp. 116–120. Boston: McGraw Hill.

Silverman Kaja. 1983. *The Subject of Semiotics*. New York and Oxford: Oxford University Press.

Silverman, Kaja. 1992. *Male Subjectivity at The Margins*. New York and London: Routledge.

Silverman, Kaja. 1996. *The Threshold of the Visible World*. New York: Routledge.

Silverstone, Roger. 1994. *Television and Everyday Life*. New York: Routledge.

Simmons, Rachel. 2002. *Odd Girl Out: The Hidden Culture of Aggression in Girls*. New York: Harcourt.

Slack, Jennifer Daryl. 1996. "The Theory and Method of Articulation in Cultural Studies." In David Morely and Kuan-Hsing Chen (eds.), *Stuart Hall: Critical Dialogues in Cultural Studies*. New York and London: Routledge.

Sloterdijk, Peter. 1987. *Critique of Cynical Reason*. Trans. Michael Eldred. Foreword by Andreas Huyssen. Minneapolis: University of Minnesota Press.

Smith, Helen. 2000. *The Scarred Heart: Understanding and Identifying Kids Who Kill*. Knoxville, TN: Callisto. URL: http://www.violentkids.com/.

Snyder, Jon R. 1988. "Introduction to Gianni Vattimo." In Gianni Vattimo, *The End of Modernity: Nihilism and Hermeneutics in Post-Modern Culture*. Trans. Jon R. Snyder. Cambridge: Polity Press.

Sobchack, Vivian. 1992. *The Address of the Eye: A Phenomenology of Film Experience*. Princeton, NJ: Princeton University Press.

Sofia (Sofoulis), Zoë. 1999. "Virtual Corporeality: A Feminist View." In Jenny Wolmark (ed.), *Cybersexualities: A Reader on Feminist Theory, Cyborgs and Cyberspace*, pp. 55–68. Edinburgh: Edinburgh University Press. [Reprint of "Virtual Corporeality: A Feminist Perspective]," *Australian Feminist Studies* 15 (1992): 11–24.

Soong, Roland. 2001. "Telenova Fantasies." http://www.zonalatina.com/Zldata211.htm.

Springer, Claudia. 1996. *Electronic Eros: Bodies and Desire in the Postindustrial Age*. London: Athlone.

Steffensen, Jyanni. 1998. "Slimy Metaphors for Technology: The Clitoris is a Direct Line to the Matrix." Paper presented at a conference titled "Discipline and Deviance: Technology, Gender, Machines." Duke University, Durham, North Carolina (October 2–4), URL: http://ensemble.va.com.au/array/steff.html.

Steinberg, Shirley and Joe Kinchloe. (eds.). 1997. *Kinderculture: The Corporate Construction of Childhood*. Boulder: Westview.

Stern, Susannah R. 1999. "Adolescent Girls' Expression on Web Home Pages: Spirited, Somber, and Self-Conscious Sites," *Convergencies* 5 (4) (Winter): 22–41.

Stone, Allucquère Rosanne. 1996. *The War of Desire and Technology at the Close of the Mechanical Age*. Cambridge, MA: MIT Press.

Stone, Merlin. 1976. *The Paradise Papers: The Suppression of Women's Rites*. London, Virago: Quartet Books.

Strauss, William and Neil Howe. 1991. *Generations: History of America's Future, 1584–2029*. New York: William Morrow and Company, Inc.

Strauss, William and Neil Howe. 1993. *13th Gen: Abort, Retry, Ignore, Fail?* New York: Vintage Books.

Strauss, William and Neil Howe. 1997. *The Fourth Turning: An American Prophecy*. New York: Broadway Books.

Strauss, William and Neil Howe. 2000. *Millennials Rising: The Next Great Generation*. New York: Vintage Books.

Sucharitkul, Somtow. 2000. *The Ultimate Mallworld*. Atlanta: Meisha Merlin.

Suler, John. 1996–2003. *Life at the Palace: A Cyberpsychology Case Study*. http://www.rider.edu/~suler/psycyber/palacestudy.html.

Sullivan, Edward. 1977. "A Study of the Kohlberg's Structural Theory of Moral Development: A Critique of Liberal Social Science Ideology," *Human Development*, 20: 352–375.

Tanner, Nancy. 1981. *On Becoming Human*. Cambridge: Cambridge University Press.

Taylor, Mark and Esa Saarinen. 1994. *Imagologies: Media Philosophy*. London: Routledge.

The Economist, "The New Demographics, November 1, 2001." URL: http://www.economist.com/displayStory.cfm?story_id=770839.

Thurston, Luke. (ed.). 2002. *Essays on the Final Lacan: Re-Inventing the Symptom*. New York: Other Press.

Turkle, Sherry. 1995. *Life on the Screen: Identity in the Age of the Internet*. New York: Simon & Schuster.

Turkle, Sherry. 1996. "Virtuality and Its Discontents," *The American Prospect* 7 (24) (December 1) URL: http://www.prospect.org/print/V7/24/turkle-s.html.

Turkle, Sherry. 1997. "Seeing Through Computers," *The American Prospect* 8 (31) (March 1–April 1). On-line URL: http://www.prospect.org/print/V8/31/turkle-s.html.

Turkle, Sherry. 1998. "Identity in the Age of the Internet: Living in the MUD." In R. Holeton (ed.), *Composing Cyberspace: Identity, Community and Knowledge in the Electronic Age*, pp. 5–11. Boston: McGraw Hill.

Ullman, Ellen. 1998. "Come In, CQ: The Body on the Wire." In Richard Holeton (ed.), *Composing Cyberspace: Identity, Community, and Knowledge in the Electronic Age*, pp. 32–47. New York: McGraw-Hill.

Van Orden, Bob. 1999. "Top Five Interactive Digital-TV Applications," *Multichannel* 21 (June): 142–145. URL: http://www.findarticles.com/cf_dls/m3535/mag.jhtml.

Vattimo, Gianni. 1988. *The End of Modernity: Nihilism and Hermeneutics in Post-Modern Culture*. Trans. and Introduction by Jon R. Snyder. Cambridge: Polity Press.

Verhaeghe, Paul. 1999. *Love in a Time of Loneliness. Three Essays on Drive and Desire*. Trans. Plym Peters and Tony Langham. New York: Other Press.

Virilio, Paul. 1999. *Politics of the Very Worst: An Interview by Philippe Petit*. Trans. Michael Cavaliere, ed. Sylvère Lotringer. New York: Semiotext(e).

Walkerdine, Valerie. 1986. "Video Replay: Families and Fantasy." In Victor Burgin, James Donald, and Cora Kaplan (eds.), *Formations of Fantasy*, pp. 167–199. London and New York Metheun & Co. Ltd.

Walkerdine, Valerie and June Melody. 1993. "Daddy's Gonna Buy You a Dream to Cling to (and Mummy's Gonna Love You as Much as She Can): Young Girls and Populr Television." In David Buckingham (ed.), *Reading Audiences: Young People and the Media*, pp. 74–88. Manchester: Manchester University Press.

Warren, Elizabeth and Tyagi Amelia Warren. 2003. The *Two-Income Trap: Why Middle-Class Mothers and Fathers Are Gong Broke*. New York: Basic Books.

Walkerdine, Valerie. 1990. *Schoolgirl Fictions*. London: Verso.

Weizenbaum, Joseph. 1976. *Computer Power and Human Reason: From Judgment to Calculation*. San Francisco: W.H. Freeman.

Welsch, Wolfgang. 1990. *Ästhetisches Denken*. Stuttgart: Phillip Reclam.

White, Emily. 2002. *Fast Girls: Teenage Tribes and the Myth of the Slut*. New York: Simon and Shuster.

White, Hayden. 1978. *Tropics of Discourse: Essays in Cultural Criticism*. Baltimore: Johns Hopkins University Press.

Wilcox, Dorothy. 1996. "Computers and the Internet: Listening to Girls' Voices. Unpublished Master of Arts. Fairbanks, University of Alaska." URL: http://www.northstar.k12.ak.us/home/dwilcox/thesis/contents.html.

Williams, Linda. 1991. "Film Bodies: Gender, Genre, and Excess," *Film Quarterly* 44: 2–13.

Williams, Linda. 1994. *Viewing Positions: Ways of Seeing Film*. New York: Rutgers University Press.

Wilson, Louise. 1994. "Cyberwar, God, and Television: Interview with Paul Virilio," *CTHEORY* (e-edition), Article 20. http://horsdal.uradio.ku.dk/~enterprz/virilio.html.

Wink, Walter. 2001 (October 1). "Babylon Revisited: How Our Violent Origins Resurface in Today's Mainstream." URL: http://www.medailit.org/Violence/articles/babylon.html.

Winnicott, D.W. 1971. *Playing and Reality*. New York; London: Routledge.

Winn, Marie. 1984. *Children without Childhood*. Harmondsworth: Penguin.

Wright, Edmond. 2001. "Introduction: Faith and the Real," *Paragraph* 24 (2): 5–22.

Young-Bruehl, Elisabeth. 1996. *The Anatomy of Prejudices*. Cambridge, MA: Harvard University Press.

Žižek, Slavoj. 1989. *The Sublime Object of Ideology*. London: Verso.

Žižek, Slavoj. 1991. *Looking Awry: An Introduction to Jacques Lacan Through Popular Culture*. Cambridge, MA: The MIT Press.

Žižek, Slavoj. 1992. *Enjoy Your Symptom: Jacques Lacan in Hollywood and Out*. New York and London: Routledge.

Žižek, Slavoj. 1993. *Tarrying with the Negative: Kant, Hegel, and the Critique of Ideology*. Durham: Duke University Press.

Žižek, Slavoj. 1994a. *For They Know Not What They Do: Enjoyment as a Political Factor*. New York and London: Verso.

Žižek, Slavoj. 1994b. *The Metastases of Enjoyment: Six Essays on Women and Causality*. New York and London: Verso.

Žižek, Slavoj. 1994c. "The Spectre of Ideology." In Slavoj Žižek (ed.), *Mapping Ideology*, pp. 1–33. London: Verso.

Žižek, Slavoj. 1996a. *The Indivisible Remainder: An Essay on Schelling and Related Matters*. New York and London: Verso.

Žižek, Slavoj. 1996b. "'I Hear You with My Eyes': or, The Invisible Master." In Renata Salecl and Slavoj Žižek (eds.), *Sic 1: Gaze and Voice as Love Objects*, pp. 90–126. Durham and London: Duke University Press.

Žižek, Slavoj. 1997a. *The Plague of Fantasies*. London: Verso.

Žižek, Slavoj. 1997b. *The Abyss of Freedom/Ages of the World by F.W.J. von Schelling*. Ann Arbor: University of Michigan Press.
Žižek, Slavoj. 1999a. "Is it Possible to Transverse the Fantasy in Cyberspace?" In *The Žižek Reader* (ed.) Elizabeth Writę and Edmond Wright, pp. 102–124. Oxford: Blackwell Publishers.
Žižek, Slavoj. 1999b. *The Ticklish Subject: The Absent Centre of Political Ontology*. London: Verso.
Žižek, Slavoj. 2000a. *The Art of the Ridiculous Sublime: On David's Lynch's Lost Highway*. Seattle: The Walter Chapin Simpson Center for the Humanities.
Žižek, Slavoj. 2000b. "Class Struggle or Postmodernism? Yes, Please!" In Judith Bulter, Ernesto Laclau, and Slavoj Žižek (eds.), *Contingency, Hegemony, Universality*. London and New York: Verso.
Žižek, Slavoj. 2001a. *The Fragile Absolute*. London and New York: Verso.
Žižek, Slavoj. 2001b. *On Belief*. New York and London: Routledge.
Žižek, Slavoj. 2001c. *Did Somebody Say Totalitarianism; Five Interventions in the (Mis)use of a Notion*. London and New York: Verso.
Žižek, Slavoj. 2002a. "The Interpassive Subject," *Symptom* 3 (Fall/Winter 2002). URL: http://www.lacan.com/newspaper3.htm.
Zupančič, Alenka. 2000. *The Ethics of the Real*. London and New York: Verso.
Zylinska, Joanna. 2001. *On Spiders, Cyborgs and Being Scared: The Feminine and the Sublime*. Manchester and New York: Manchester University Press.

FILMOGRAPHY (BY YEAR)

TELEVISION SERIES

280 Index